NICK TOWNSEND has be[...]
than 25 years. He is [...]
Independent on Sunda[...]
Tottenham Weekly He[...]
the *Daily Mail*. Nick no[...]
is a trusted friend and [...]

All the author's proceeds from this book will go directly to DAFA, a charity aimed at improving the lives of the poor and sick in Zambia. Any contributions will be gratefully received and should be sent to: DAFA, c/o Market Street, Omagh, Co. Tyrone, Northern Ireland.
Alternatively, they can be sent to Barney Curley, c/o The Mirage, William Street, Windsor, Berks.

GIVING A LITTLE BACK

BARNEY CURLEY

BARNEY CURLEY
with Nick Townsend

CollinsWillow
An Imprint of HarperCollinsPublishers

First published in hardback in 1998
by CollinsWillow
an imprint of HarperCollins*Publishers*
London

First published in paperback in 1999

1 3 5 7 9 8 6 4 2

A CIP catalogue record for this book is
available from the British Library

ISBN 0 00 218828 7

Printed and bound in Great Britain by
Clays Ltd, St Ives plc

PICTURE ACKNOWLEDGEMENTS
Gerry Cranham pic no 2, 4, 7, 8, 9, 19, 21, 22, 52;
Daily Mail 53; Liam Healy 44; Trevor Jones 5, 20;
Mirror Syndication International 39; Laurie Morton 51;
George Selwyn 6, 50; Stephen Markeson/Times Newspapers Limited 48.
All other photographs supplied by Barney Curley.

Contents

ONE

'Your game is backing winners'

It was a sultry September's day in 1987 and I was sitting on a bale of hay enjoying the sunshine at my home in Stetchworth, a village just outside Newmarket. I was trying to make some sense of the most gruelling episodes of my life, when I got the call from one of my oldest and most valued friends. I'd known Tommy Stack – the man who partnered Red Rum to a historic third Grand National victory in 1977 and who had just started out on a training career – since we had been students together at Mungret College in Limerick way back in the late fifties. He had just heard, as had all the racing world and beyond, that, faced with High Court action, the all-powerful Jockey Club had climbed down over its decision to disqualify me for two years after what became known as the 'Robin Goodfellow affair'. I had been the first man to force the Jockey Club to quash such a verdict and punishment.

If they had carried through their threat I would have been a pariah, unable to set foot for two years on any racecourse or stables licensed by the Jockey Club. That meant I would have been unable to carry out my business as surely as if you had withdrawn a licence to drive from a lorry driver or struck off a doctor from the medical register. Yet coupled with Tommy's congratulations was a pointed addendum.

'Now, Barney, please do us all a favour. Here is what you

should do,' he said. 'You sit down and write a nice little letter to the Jockey Club, thanking them for giving your licence back. Then you put the letter with your licence in an envelope and send both off to them and go your merry way.' He added: 'Pack in training racehorses now and concentrate on what you're good at. Your game is backing winners.'

Whether he intended it or not, his words had the effect of a verbal slap on the cheek – and it smarted. Although if I'm honest with myself, I have to admit that his advice was right. You don't have to own or train horses to back them. He has always enjoyed winding me up, but this, though diplomatically expressed, was serious advice and its meaning was brutally apparent. Tommy found training all too time-consuming as it was. He couldn't believe there was a man alive who could concentrate on training and betting, successfully. As I put the phone down, I said to myself, 'The cheeky little b******. I'll let him know who can train horses and who can't.'

Yes, I was good at backing winners; I'd been winning serious money consistently for around twenty-five years, and nobody else had ever been able to claim that, and probably won't ever again, given the state of 'safety-first' bookmaking in this country. But I had never been just a gambler; I firmly believed that I was better at training racehorses. Tommy might have intended it as well-meaning advice, but to me he had cast down the gauntlet. This was a challenge and I relish nothing more than to be confronted with one, and had done ever since I started out, against everyone's advice, as a self-confident young man in his twenties. Barry Brogan, another friend of mine and Tommy's from our college days, whose riding career had ended in ignominy after he admitted to throwing races, once described me as 'meticulous, methodical and arrogant. Nothing flustered him.' He wasn't too far out with that analysis. Certainly a piece of insolent questioning of my ability from one of my closest confidants was not going to deter me.

Admittedly, the whole business with the Jockey Club had left me exhausted. Yet, I drove straight away over to my yard at Exning, on the other side of Newmarket, and surveyed the remnants of my horses. All the best ones had been sold when I thought I might lose my licence. What was left was an uninspiring bunch, but they would do. I immediately rang round and got bookmakers to lay me prices on a special bet. They bit my hand off. If you considered the facts, you couldn't blame them. I didn't have that many horses, perhaps fourteen, and I hadn't had a winner for ages. Even with decent horses, I'd trained only nine winners in the previous jump season. I'd never been a pot-hunter like those stables which regularly turned out consistently large quantities of winners. I wasn't, let's be candid, a conventional racehorse trainer by any stretch of the imagination. I was, and still am, unique, because absolutely everything revolves around the betting.

With a few notable exceptions I've always operated a system where there would be no great targets or plans for my horses; a scheme would suddenly evolve as I watched them work on the gallops. Yet, despite what Tommy and others may have thought, there was a method in my mayhem. I'd wander about the yard and people would think I was taking no part, but I'd be watching, and waiting. There would always be someone else in charge of the day-to-day running of the yard. It would be boring for me watching them hacking around, but once they were on the gallops and working I'd use my eyes.

To prove myself to Tommy, it would take more than one big gamble, or 'touch', on a horse. I'd already shown I could do that on numerous occasions over the years. I wanted to demonstrate that I could do the job consistently. So, I challenged several bookmakers to lay me a bet that I couldn't send out ten winners before the end of the year. I remember in particular Colin Webster, whom I have known for years, laying me £3,000 to win £7,500 and the expression on his face told

9

me that he thought Christmas had come early. Colin, who is originally from Leeds, though he now bets in the south of England, is as game as they come and puts the so-called Big Three high street bookmakers to shame. He is probably one of the biggest private bookmakers in England and, to my knowledge, has never closed a winning account. His view has always been exceedingly simple: 'Some backers give you useful clues, and if you don't want to hold on to a bet, you can lay it off.' He is a wonderful judge of odds, although on this occasion he was caught napping. In all, I laid out £126,000-to-win-£275,000. They must have thought I was the biggest mug since Terry Ramsden, who reputedly lost £57 million to the bookies. After all, B.J. Curley was a fellow who had only just regained his licence after several months, had never trained that many winners in his life anyway, and had only three months to do it, with the possibility of abandonments, come the onset of winter. An expression containing the words 'slaughter' and 'lamb' came to mind. Anybody who laid me that bet probably thought they were stealing money and were probably surprised they weren't accused of theft. Bookmakers fell over themselves to take my money.

It was a thoroughly reckless wager on my part. Prior to that I'd only trained nine winners in two years. My strike rate of winners to runners had been diabolical since I got my licence in England in November 1985, and I'd had to sell most of my best horses when it looked as though I'd be off the course for a considerable period. Organising horses to win to order is a most difficult objective – at any level.

It was more of a junkyard than a racing yard. They were mostly broken down bits and pieces of horses. The 'shrewdies' who laid me the bet were only too aware of that, but everyone assumed I was on an ego trip. Friends told me I had got no chance. I had no real idea whether I could do it. My policy has always been to just drift along until I find the kind of challenge on which I have perennially thrived. But I knew there would have to be no hanging around. I really had to get stuck into the job quickly and to be totally committed to it. I lived in a room above the yard for those three months. But whatever else I lacked I've never suffered from any deficiency of self-assurance. Back in 1975 I'd pulled off one of the biggest racehorse betting coups the world has ever known, and nine years later I'd successfully raffled my mansion in Ireland. I've no real idea how I've prospered financially over the years, but I must have won millions. I keep diaries, and I know I come out well on top every year. There was no reason why I shouldn't achieve this, too. It was to prove damn hard work and I'd challenge any of today's trainers, given my ammunition, to succeed.

I had one winner early on – 30 September – and then it all went quiet. My pals used to rag me, 'So, when does this bet actually finish, Barney? In 1999 or the turn of the century?' Another rang and said, 'You've definitely gone this time, Barney. This is it.' That's really why I had the bet. I said to myself, 'I'll show all these fellas that they're talking rubbish.' It gave me great pleasure to produce winners first time out that hadn't run for two or three years. It proved I could do the job.

Finally, after three months of controversy – a word that has hounded me ever since I came into racing – winner number ten obliged at the humble outpost of Folkestone. I don't remember many races from the distant past, but this one, the 1.45 – the Sellindge Handicap Hurdle – with prize-money of less than £750 to the winner, was special. I had bought Experimenting as a yearling and had waited eight years for him to do a 'job' for me. He had been another of my 'invalids' whom I had been unable to sell when my licence was taken away. He had already broken down twice. It was at moments like that when you appreciated having a jockey like Declan Murphy, whom I had brought over from Ireland with me three years earlier, on your side in the heat of the battle. The horse needed holding together and he gave it a typically restrained, patient ride. They were travelling easily in the lead at the fifth, were relegated to second two out, but, finding better ground up the stand side, took it up again before the last and quickened to beat Albert Davison's Matelot Royale by six lengths.

I couldn't believe the goodwill and interest. It suddenly dawned on me. To me, travelling down to Folkestone from my Newmarket base that afternoon was just another day's work. I'd had some great days racing all over the world, but the reaction of the crowd that day was something the likes of which I'd never encountered before. You wouldn't have got it in any other country, and I include Ireland in that. They started to cheer when that horse hit the front, and it spread from the public through to the bookmakers. And don't forget, it was the favourite and would have been a bad result for them. I could hardly get into the winners' enclosure to welcome Experimenting and Declan. One of the racing correspondents had to help me through the throng. I couldn't believe the commotion that followed. Folkestone is normally associated with a gentle ripple of applause, but I still retain that image of all the crowd surging around the parade ring cheering. There were shouts of 'Well done, Barney – that's shown 'em.' I thought it was just me and the bookmakers in our own private war, until that tumult erupted.

In Ireland you expect such a reaction. Anyone who has ever been to the Cheltenham Festival will comprehend the emotion which accompanies an Irish winner. But I never realised that such generosity of spirit existed in England too. That day, the racegoers saw me as one of them and that was as important to me as winning the bet. If you're a gambler, you must always have your eye on the next scheme. I said I would leave all the money – my stake and winnings, which added up to £401,000 – in the pot and see if anyone would lay me 2–1 against me training another ten in the first three months of the following year. After all, the bookies had the weather in their favour. There would probably be abandonments. The phone never rang.

The only call I received was an intriguing one from a middle-man representing some Arab interests, who asked me whether I'd like to become their private trainer. We never got beyond the preliminaries, so I never even discovered the source of the offer. Quite simply, money can't buy me and never will. Not even silly money, which always comes with strings attached. In any case, if I need it I go out and win it. I captain my own ship and I've never been anyone's first lieutenant. The buzz to me has always been getting a horse ready and backing it successfully. Yet, strangely, as I reflected on it all later, and tried to put everything into perspective, I felt no real joy, or exhilaration, other than the satisfaction of overcoming a challenge. The winning bet was an after-thought, just another entry in my diaries which contain not snippets of family news but a figure, followed by + or −, a daily account of my winning, and losing, bets. After thirty years there has never been one when I've failed to finish on top. I've made millions over the years, but I stress out of necessity rather than avarice. I've always set out to achieve something that nobody else has done; not as a means to an end. I wouldn't have a clue how many winners I've had. I have always just wanted to beat the system.

Those three months encapsulated everything I'd experienced in horse-racing: the brushes with authority, the gratification when everything goes to plan and the bitter sense of frustration when it doesn't. Yet, I felt the realisation ever more strongly that I could do something better with my life. I wanted to counter the impression people have of me as an obsessive gambler, without another thought in my head other than whether a horse has a chance in the 2.30 at Leicester.

I've been betting big – by which I mean usually £5,000

minimum at today's values – for thirty years and I've always won at it. I'm in my sixties now and I've no intention of getting to seventy and still be gambling. I'd like to spend the rest of my life trying to help the poorest of the poor. I don't have that much interest in money. I think I'm capable of doing something better. If I'm honest, I feel I have wasted my life. I've never felt comfortable in racing, or have achieved anything that really mattered. I think it was Phil Bull, the founder of Timeform, who talked of horseracing being 'the great triviality of life' – and he was right.

Now, in my remaining years, I want to do something worthwhile. I had to ponder long and hard before agreeing to write this book. I am a private man, and though I have always been one to speak my mind on issues – indeed, it has got me in trouble often enough – I have not, until now, been prepared to reveal my own story. I have agreed to on condition that all proceeds from this book will go towards a charity I have set up in conjunction with jockey Frankie Dettori and many other good people in Northern Ireland. It is called DAFA – Direct Aid for Africa – and is aimed at improving the lives of the desperately poor and sick in Zambia. I have it in my mind to raise £1 million. There are many reasons for wanting to help, but I suppose it all goes back to an old adage of my late father which I believe in firmly: 'Wise men don't forget to give a little back.'

TWO

'But for me, you wouldn't be here'

It is the small hours of the morning in the early 1930s in the small County Fermanagh town of Irvinestown. All is peaceful, with most of the town's inhabitants sleeping off their day's labours or the effects of a decent night's drinking, until, like something reminiscent of that famous scene from *Toad of Toad Hall*, a motor car comes roaring erratically into the main street. The demon at the wheel is Charlie Curley, then in his mid-twenties, something of a playboy and one of the first men in the county to own a motor car, a Model T Ford no less. His aunts, Minnie and Annie, who loved nothing better than to indulge their nephew, have bought him the snarling beast.

The trouble is that tonight, by no means for the first time in his carefree twenties, Charlie Curley is drunk-in-charge as he shatters the peace of that otherwise tranquil community. And there is a bend ahead which leads into Pound Street and a bridge over the river. In a nearby house young Tommy Maguire is awoken by the commotion; aroused from his slumbers, he hears a car career along the road, smash through a bridge and then the splash of it plunging into the river. He dashes out, leaps into the water as it laps around the car and wrenches open the door to pull the driver free. The police arrive at the scene soon after, but not before Tommy and his family have carried Charlie out and hidden him in their house.

Many years later, big Tommy achieved renown as a fine Gaelic footballer who played for Fermanagh – and my esteem as a fearless gambler. He also ran an ice-cream shop in the town, where my friends and I would call in for a penny cone coming home from school. Sometimes he'd be standing at the door, gesture me in and whisper to me, 'Come over here, Doc.' He used to call my father that and then bestowed the nickname on me, too. He'd hand me an ice-cream and, being the kind man that he was, no money would ever change hands. As he did so, he'd smile and say, 'Only for me, you wouldn't be here.' I never understood what he meant until I was a lot older. My father preferred to keep me in ignorance. Understandably, it was not a memory Charlie Curley liked to dwell on. No doubt, one or two of those with whom I've clashed sabres over the years would have preferred that young Tommy had arrived a little later on the scene. Without his presence of mind my father would almost certainly have drowned.

A dry throat and a taste for liquor has run in my family, at least the male side. Both my uncles, Tommy and John, had a liking for alcohol, and the latter drank himself to death. That's one of the reasons why I don't indulge. I've seen what it can do to you. Anyway, in the business I pursued, a befuddled brain only serves to tilt the balance in the bookmakers' favour more than it is already. You always need a clear head. I've seen too many people who combine their drinking and gambling and end up losers.

I can't claim to have been totally abstemious. I've had the occasional glass of wine, or maybe a shandy on a hot day, but it's always in the back of my mind that if I'm going to be good at what I'm doing, I don't drink. There was a religious explanation for my temperance, too. I was brought up in a staunch Catholic household and when we were young you had to make a sort of pledge, an offering to God. Mine was to say I wouldn't drink. It was a kind of sacrifice in reparation for the sins of those who had offended God by their intemperance. I've kept to that, by and large, which is not the easiest thing to do in Ireland, where nearly everybody enjoys a drink. But it's been a big help in life. Some people drink to instil themselves with confidence, or maybe because they're unhappy, but I have never needed that crutch.

No doubt more than a little chastened by the incident, my father's brush with death at least brought a little more sobriety to his indulgent life-style, though by no means completely. Charlie Curley was a rather more sober character, in both senses, when he married my mother Kathleen on 24 November 1938 at Whitehill Parish Church. I inherited two traits from my father. One was a compulsion to beat the bookmakers; the other was a complete inability to administer finances.

It was typical of Charlie Curley that he had just £1 and ten shillings in his pocket on that most important day in his life. He gave the pound to the priest, his great friend Father Bernard Lappin, who conducted the service, and promptly lost the rest. My mother and father had met at a *ceilidh*, or dance, in Dromore and were devoted to each other from that day until my father's death in 1988. Yet the union didn't have an auspicious beginning. For one thing, there was no question of a honeymoon. And their wedding table might have been bare, too, had they not been friendly with the Gallaher family, who owned a shop down the road and allowed them to buy food on credit for the next month. Every other penny he could beg or borrow had been required to pay the £25-a-year rent on a small farm and cottage, named 'Coladergan', perched above the Irvinestown to Dromore road, in an area of bleak farmland, with the Brougher Mountains dominating the horizon towards the southeast.

The following year on 5 October, a month after the onset of World War Two, my mother gave birth to Bernard Joseph Curley – Bernard was soon shortened to Barney – and the first of two sons and four daughters. I'm told that I was an enormous baby at 12 ¾ lb. My mother, who had me at home, with just a midwife present, was in labour for three days. They said she'd been so internally damaged by the birth that she was unlikely to be able to bear any more children, but she proved medical opinion wrong by having another five!

My early childhood, coinciding with the deprivations of the War years, was tough but happy enough. One of my first recollections was, as a child of four, walking to Tummery School, which was over two miles away, in my bare feet. I did possess a pair of shoes, but they were kept for best – like church on Sundays. It was exceedingly sore on the feet, because the roads are nothing like they are today. It was like walking on a dirt-track and you'd be wincing constantly as you pierced yourself on sharp stones.

Another early memory brought home to me graphically the full enormity and horror of the conflict being waged hundreds of miles away. English and American airmen were stationed just a few miles away at Castle Archdale, on the eastern shore of Lower Lough Erne. The castle had been constructed by John Archdale, an English settler, or planter as they were known, who came to Ireland from Norfolk in 1615. It was destroyed during the Williamite Wars but had been rebuilt, and during World War Two it was used by the RAF from 1941 as a base for seaplanes, mostly Sunderlands and Catalinas, and other aircraft. We were familiar with the drone of aircraft of all types returning from missions as I sat and played at home while my mother did her housework. But this sound was ominously different. I'll never forget the sound of a spluttering engine, then dashing out with my mother and watching a bomber pass over us, with flames pouring out of its engines. It was a couple of miles away when it crashed into a bog but we still heard the explosion. It was so loud it could have been in the next field. The crew of four were killed and the airmen were buried at the graveyard in Irvinestown. I say a prayer for them when I go there to visit my relatives' graves.

Irvinestown was very much embroiled in the War. When they got leave the pilots and ground crews drove their jeeps into town and packed the bars and dance halls. Some married Northern Ireland girls and took them back to England or America. Those men were regarded as heroes and were very much the town's adopted sons. It's ironic, and sad, to think that in recent years members of the British armed forces became a target for some members of that same community who perceive them as an oppressive occupying force. Irvinestown is only a ten-mile drive from Omagh, a town I know very well and where our DAFA office is located. Those of us with many good friends and relations living and working there will never forget that dreadful day, 15 August 1998, when 28 people were killed and many others injured by a car bomb in the city centre. Twenty minutes in the other direction is Enniskillen, where, in 1987, eleven civilians attending a Remembrance Day parade were killed by an IRA bomb.

I spent my formative years, from ten to my early twenties, at various colleges in the South. When the fires of sectarian conflict were being kindled I was studying for the priesthood and almost oblivious, and certainly impervious, to the explosion of hatred that was to ensue. By the time the Troubles broke out in the late sixties I was nearing 30 and living in the south of Ireland. Despite being a Catholic, I like to think I can take a broader perspective than many on the subject of the Troubles.

Through the centuries, Lower Lough Erne, a spectacular fifty miles of waterway which has an abundance of history and mystery about it, has had a great influence on the life of the community. My great regret is that the Troubles have deterred visitors, although there is always an angler or two to be found at the local hostelries who cannot resist the prospect of a gleaming trout or salmon to be reeled in.

There is a chain of islands down the lake, which in the Middle Ages became stopping-off points for pilgrims on their way to St Patrick's Purgatory, an important shrine on Lough Derg in County Donegal. The town itself is named after the Irvine family, originally of Scottish origin, who were Royalists and supporters of Charles I and his men. They settled in County Fermanagh and married into local planter families and lived in a grand house on the site of what is now Necarne Castle on the outskirts of the town, until they were forced to flee to Enniskillen Castle during the Irish rebellion of 1641. The house, originally built in 1611, was burnt down in their absence but when they returned they built Castle Irvine, as it was then called. Since then it has been rebuilt and refurbished over the centuries and descendants of the Irvines were in residence until 1922. For a time it was occupied by the South Staffordshire Regiment, who patrolled the border between Northern Ireland and the Irish Free State.

Since World War Two it has fallen into disrepair; at one stage it was used for keeping hens and today little more than a shell exists, although a splendid Ulster lakeland equestrian park has been constructed in the magnificent grounds. Several years ago I was approached about the possibility of buying the castle for £250,000. But caution got the better of me. It would cost a fortune to restore it to its former glory.

Our three-bedroom cottage and farm was one of several smallholdings of about twenty acres outside Irvinestown, just across the county border in Tyrone. We grazed about thirty cattle and there was some arable land, generally of poor quality, where corn was grown. We also cut peat, an essential part of winter life in Ireland then, years before central heating became commonplace. I'd go down to the bog with my father and help him cut it out with a spade, after which it was left on the edge of the bank to dry. We'd then carry the turf home by horse and cart.

The farmhouse was always damp. There was very little heating, except in the kitchen, and I was frequently laid up with chest ailments. At four years old I had a bout of rheumatic fever. My mother insisted on plying me with numerous home remedies to inhale which effectively cleared my system. My health improved when the family moved into the town and, later, when I went to boarding school in the South.

We also reared pigs, which meant that when the pregnant sows were ready to give birth they were brought into the kitchen so that the warmth would give the piglets a better chance of survival, particularly in the winter. There they'd stay for about a fortnight. As we owned ten sows there was a good chance that at any one time the kitchen would echo to the sound of squealing. Occasionally, we had a sow of a nasty disposition who could wreak havoc. Some were sent to market, but a few were home-slaughtered – knocked on the head with a mallet – and my mother would then cure the bacon by salting the meat and hanging it up for a fortnight. The Curley family's staple diet involved bacon and 'poundies', a tasty concoction of potatoes pounded together with spring onions and butter.

In the summer the kitchen was also used for ripening corn, and over the year got into a bit of a state. It didn't please my mother who has always been very houseproud and wouldn't have a spot of dirt in the house. But her dilemma was that every pig was crucial to our livelihood in those days and she realised that the alternative was her family starving. She was, and still is, a tough woman who hailed from a farming background; her uncle, Francie Farry, had been a farmer and she concentrated on raising livestock, which my father took to market. My mother was prepared to work eighteen hours a day in order to keep a decent home for her family. She celebrated her 91st birthday on 5 February 1999 and still lives in Irvinestown, where I visit her regularly.

My father, a small, wiry man, was a very promising footballer in his youth. He was what you'd now call a striker and was considered gifted enough to be offered a trial with Glasgow Celtic, but his mother wouldn't allow him to travel. At that time Glasgow was a world away. You may as well have said you were emigrating to Australia as saying you were journeying from our village to Scotland. He played Gaelic football too – for the county.

He always prided himself on his fitness. One night, when he was around fifty and I was a teenager in the pink of health, we were walking together up a street in Irvinestown called Back Street. My grandmother lived about 150yds away and I challenged my father, 'I bet I can beat you up to the house.' We set off and after seventy-five yards he was in the lead and would definitely have beaten me, except that his ankle suddenly cracked. He should have been doubled up in agony, but he shrugged it off and refused to have it seen by a doctor. My father was one of those people who would never go to a hospital. After that, he always walked with a limp. Yet, he was always very active until the day he died on 18 December 1988.

The Irvinestown of my youth was a quiet, anonymous sort of place, but it did have a Derby. There aren't too many towns that can claim that distinction. On the wall of Mahon's Hotel there remains to this day a lot of memorabilia, including the conditions for the 1945 Irvinestown Derby. Prize-money was £50 for the 1m 6f (one mile, six furlongs) event, an open handicap Flat race. My father would take me to Irvinestown Races as a child. The rules sounded pretty draconian – 'Any suspicious riding by a jockey will be dealt with severely' was one – but I am reliably informed there were a few strokes pulled there over the years with horses being 'stopped'.

My father could be a difficult man to get on with, but as I got older I had a tremendous amount of respect for him. If I frequently paint him in a critical light, that does not detract from the tremendous admiration and affection I felt for him and how I appreciated the sacrifices he made for his family. It would be unfair to infer that he was anything but a good family man. On that theme, I wouldn't want to overstate his consumption, either. My father was a real character in the area. He was known to enjoy a laugh, and, in common with most of his countrymen, he loved a drink; but he was not an alcoholic. It was just the occasional binge which was liable to get him into trouble. Mind you, that could last days, maybe a week, which wasn't so bad if he remained in the neighbourhood. If he was in another village it would induce my mother into a state of panic, because he'd also be driving a car. At that time the roads weren't very good and the combination of excess alcohol and poor driving conditions could be desperately dangerous, as I've already described. Like many drinkers my father would always set out with the best of intentions. He'd say to my mother, 'I'm away for two hours' – and that's all he had in mind. But when it got to four and more she would be ringing the pubs in the neighbouring villages to determine his whereabouts so that someone could be dispatched to pick him up, take his car keys off him and drive him home.

I knew my mother was unhappy about my father's drinking and the embarrassment of having to go out looking for him. And it upset us as children because we didn't know where he was. My mother must have had the patience of Job to live with his vices, both drinking and gambling. Yet, in my hearing, there was rarely a cross word between them. I always vowed not to impose such misery on my own family. Mind you, I do have one vice: I've smoked since the age of twelve and to this day my mother scolds me about it. 'Barney, are you still smoking?' she will say as I walk in the house. It is, I admit, a dreadful habit and very anti-social.

When my father got married, he settled down; at least,

comparatively so. He still had a taste for the drink, but there would be no more recklessness. My parents had a very happy life together. My mother was one of these women who'd have the philosophy, 'Harp on and it'll only get worse.' She used to let things run their course.

There was always a very religious atmosphere in our house. Those values were imbued from childhood and have remained strong right until the present day. Family prayer was an important part of our daily lives and we were taught to have respect for people like clergymen, and for people worse off than ourselves. Not an evening would pass when we didn't all kneel before a picture of Mary, mother of God, and say the rosary. From one generation to another, I do the same. Example is a great thing. First thing in the morning I kneel before a photograph of the Sacred Heart and say a prayer, 'Lord, lay your hand on my head and see me through the day.' It doesn't take ten seconds.

It was through my parents' example that later in life I went to study for the priesthood. My father used to say to me, 'Life's very short. It's over in a flash. It'll go like that for you too. Try to live your life giving a thought to other people.' I try to adhere to that, although I'm not very successful. I would never claim to be a saint. If the just man falls ten times a day, I fall thirty times. And I do not like to be portrayed as some kind of 'Holy Joe', trying to convert people to my way of thinking.

For close on fifty years of his life my father never missed going to mass in the morning. Even if he'd had a rough night the previous evening and had arrived home seriously the worse for drink, he'd still be at church bright and early the following morning. He instilled in us to put our trust in God. It permeated through to me. I've had good days and bad days on the racecourse but nothing's ever worried me. I have faith in Him and self-confidence in myself.

Our parents sacrificed everything for us. They gave very

little thought to themselves. We always looked forward to Christmas because if our parents had a fiver left they would spend it on us children. Sunday was my favourite day, one I awaited with eager anticipation. One of our neighbours, James O'Neill, owned a pony and trap and it was a great thrill to clamber in and be driven the three or four miles to church at St Dympthna's in Dromore. As a child I wasn't that bothered about actually going to church; it was the getting there that entranced me ... as exciting for me then as it is for youngsters setting out for a pop concert today. My father couldn't take us. He had bought an early Austin which he used as a taxi and would be driving Father Bernard, who couldn't drive, to Whitehill Parish Church about three or four miles out in the country where he was curate. During the week, too, he'd drive Father Bernard around the parish to visit the sick and elderly in what was a closely knit, but remote, farming community.

I recall Father Bernard, who died in 1964, with great affection. He was a small man but great in stature. After the birth of my brother Cahal (Irish for Charles), who is two years my junior, and my two eldest sisters, Anne and Mary, his visits to our home grew more frequent. He took a great interest in our family and my father was always in his debt. Father Bernard knew the car was on hire-purchase and that if he paid my father by the day he would immediately gamble or drink it away instead of paying off his instalments. So, he insisted on paying him at the end of each month so that he could pay all his bills.

I don't remember rationing, but recall my parents talking about it. Where there's a loss, there's always a profit. And the gain here was smuggling. During the War, my father took advantage of food scarcity to 'import' sugar and butter from the South, where it was then much cheaper, and 'export' tea back across the border which was only about eleven miles away. It was easy money. By day he would ply his taxi for legitimate hire and ferry Father Lappin round and at night he would use it for his clandestine activities. My father was by no means alone. Smuggling was part of the local black economy. If you got caught, Customs would probably seize your car, but it didn't happen often. As the British Army found later, it was impossible to check all the roads across the border. My father's reasoning was that he was only cheating the system; not an individual. That was thought acceptable in Ireland at that time.

Another treat we all used to look forward to was Sundays at the seaside in summer. After church the family would pack into my father's little Ford van and drive the thirty-two miles to the west coast and the resort of Bundoran, with its views over Donegal Bay. It took a couple of hours because there were always long queues to cross the border at Belleek, where the world-famous china is produced. We were ravenous by the time we arrived, but my mother would have brought some beautiful ham from Harry Lennon's shop and make sandwiches as we brewed the tea.

Towards the end of the War my father bought a Ford truck and began a highly profitable business, driving round the country to the farmers each day and buying six chickens here and ten rabbits there, maybe a few dozen eggs. These he would sell on to the wholesalers who would then export them to the English and Scottish markets. He doesn't sound like a mogul of the markets, but he had a flair for business. Together with the proceeds of smuggling, he made at least £1,500 when he sold up all his stock and, in 1946, moved the family into town and our new rented home in Blakley Terrace, for which he paid five shillings rent a week. It made him one of the wealthiest men in the area and he could concentrate on his first loves: owning and training greyhounds, and betting in earnest. Just under ten years later he had made an excellent job of losing everything.

THREE

A first foray into betting

My father had a profound affection for greyhounds. He was not alone. The whole town had a weakness for gambling and everything would halt between two and five o'clock when the menfolk were betting on the horses. At night they'd all head off for the dog stadiums. Sometimes my father made the seven-hour return journey to Celtic Park, Belfast, but he bet more regularly at the local tracks, at Lifford, Dungannon and Clones. The latter was just over the border in County Monaghan which had the added attraction of allowing him to smuggle back a few pounds of butter.

He was never that interested in racehorses. Dogs were his passion and he had a kennel full of them in the late forties and early fifties when we moved into town. Even his betting couldn't compare with the Maguire family, of whom my father's saviour Tommy was but one of the brood. They were probably the biggest gamblers in Irvinestown and accordingly enjoyed a certain mystique among us youngsters. They also bought and sold poultry and farm produce, though on a larger scale than my father. But it was the magnitude of their betting that made them such glamorous figures to an impressionable schoolboy.

One brother, Jim Maguire, used to place bets for the playboy Prince Ali Khan. The father of the Aga Khan, he had horses in England and in Ireland with Hubert Hartigan, then one of the biggest trainers in Ireland. Prince Ali had 'putters-on' of money, just as I have today, to avoid attention. When I was very young, Jim, who lived only about fifty yards from us, would show me his diary of bets he'd put on for Prince Ali, often recording £1,000 here and there. I never knew whether he'd won, but it certainly impressed an innocent like me. So much so that by my teens, Jim was my absolute idol. Apart from anything else the man had so much style. He would sit there like Al Capone outside his house with his twenties-style hat, waistcoat and double-breasted suits and would reminisce about his racing exploits. He was like a god to me and a significant influence on my future.

As the years passed, I became equally fascinated by my father's gambling. He was betting £100 here, or £200 there. It would have classed him a major player just after the War. In truth, few could have provided a more potent argument against the hazards of the game. To observe him, in later years, squander a small fortune should have been a salutary lesson to a schoolboy growing up in Northern Ireland.

I was six when we had moved into town and a couple of years later I exhibited my first piece of business initiative. I went out and bought two piglets to fatten up at five shillings each and kept them in a hut in the backyard. Immediately I got home from school, I'd go round the neighbours, collecting their slops or leftovers of food, which we'd call 'brock', in a bucket. By the time it was full it was pretty heavy for a boy of my age, but I always had the incentive of a profit at the end of it because it was costing nothing to keep them.

As they grew I kept asking my father when we could take them to the market. I was expecting £5 or £6 apiece for them each. He just kept putting me off. Then, one day, the pigs disappeared. I asked him about my money for these pigs, but I never got a penny. Not unusually at that time, he must have been short of a few bob. For me, it was six months wasted and a grave disappointment for the young entrepreneur. I suppose, even at that age, I was displaying a desire for a challenge, that I was prepared to take a risk, and not just sit around and depend on the efforts of others. My father, like most Irishmen, loved his sayings. I will always remember him telling me about a fellow, now long dead, called Charlie Keenan, who took a decidedly cynical view of his fellow man. 'Oh, they'll promise you the moon,' he would say, 'but you'll have to go up and get it yourself.'

About the same time that I dabbled in pigs I placed my first bet. I acted as a 'runner' for my grandmother, Annie, who would send me up to Dan McBride's, the local bookie, to place her daily flutter. (Betting shops were still illegal at that time.) She'd have three sixpenny doubles and a sixpenny treble, which added up to two shillings – ten pence in today's money – and always followed a jockey called Bill Rickerby, 'Doublew Rickerby' she used to call him, whose cousin was Lester Piggott. She'd give you a little piece of paper with two shillings wrapped in it and you'd always find someone outside to put the bets on for you. It wasn't a bad strategy. Bill was Jack Jarvis's stable jockey and partnered 1,324 winners over a career spanning thirty-seven years – remember, there were considerably fewer meetings then. He was the 'Royal' jockey for many years, and also rode for Lord Rosebery.

In the nicest possible way, my grandmother had much to answer for, because the whole atmosphere of that seedy betting office fascinated me and was responsible for me setting out on that perilous road from which so many stumble and fall. If she had a 'touch' and won a pound, she'd give a me a shilling commission, which was enough for a drink and three pastries.

It was just a tiny room with a newspaper pinned to the wall showing the fields of runners, mostly of English racing. There was no commentary, not even 'the blower' from the course, and the results came through by phone, so it was all rather anti-climactic, not to say fraught with malpractice. Nobody exactly knew when races were 'off' and there was an inevitable delay before results were known. There were always rows about punters learning the result before the bookie and trying to back the horse before he realised what was going on. The bookie could hardly call in the police, so disputes frequently ended in fights.

The legalisation of betting shops in 1961 did much to reduce the dubious practices that went on; although it is doubtful whether the punters' interests were truly served when the government of the day effectively handed bookmakers a blank, signed cheque book and obligingly refrained from setting up any form of regulatory body.

After a couple of years I summoned up the courage one day to have a bet myself and won £4, which was a tidy sum then in the late forties. All I remember was that Martin Malony, the great Irish jockey, won on all three of my selections. I collected the money, and to celebrate went straight into a nearby shop and bought a bottle of lemonade and about twelve cream cakes. I scoffed them all and was immediately sick as a dog.

My interest in horseracing gathered pace and I discovered a new means of financing it. My next money-making venture was to set myself up as an agent for Littlewoods – because of my age, I had to pretend I was an adult – and run a shopping club. It involved delivering home shopping catalogues to our neighbours, Mrs Keenan, Mrs Maguire, Mrs Gormley, Mrs Sweeney and my Aunt Greta among them, and collect their money, normally two shillings a week, for items they'd ordered. The important thing was to have the money in by half past twelve on a Saturday, so that I could go down to Kitty Spratt's with the proceeds of around £2. She was the wife of the local barber, Johnny, but, more significantly, she lived next door to the bookie's. She was one of the town's great punters and was reputed to have ten or twelve bets every day.

A group of us fearless punters would congregate in her kitchen, where she had all the newspapers ready, and we'd talk about what we fancied. Johnny would be out front cutting the hair while she spent the proceeds of it in the kitchen. It was like a mini betting shop, and a home-from-home where you never went hungry. She'd do a fry-up to see you through the afternoon. It was a right den of iniquity!

I had all kinds of weird and wonderful bets. Doubles and trebles, accumulators – you name it. I wouldn't think of doing that now but such is the blissful ignorance of youth. And I wouldn't think of backing all Saturday afternoon as I did then, either. That's where I learnt all my bad habits about the horses. There were always adults around to put on my bets.

Of course, if I lost I'd be in trouble, as I often was. If my catalogue customers had £2 in the kitty and wanted a pair of shoes, they expected to see them. If my bets went down I'd have had nothing to send to Littlewoods on the Monday. Fortunately my grandmother would always come to my assistance with a hand-out. I must confess that I lost more than I won at that time, which was hardly surprising for a lad of ten or eleven, but it all taught me a valuable lesson: I quickly learnt that it was a very hard game; I saw a lot of people going skint.

My parents were strict in that they made sure we went to school and church. They gave us the stick when needed, and a good thing too. A whack never did anyone any harm. I would never claim to be the best-behaved child, although my pranks weren't exactly deserving of a term in a young offenders' institution. When I got to ten and eleven we'd knock on doors and run away and block people's keyholes, that kind of thing. There was a family on the street called the Sweeneys, with whom there was always a little bit of aggravation. I'd be playing together with Seamus and Patsy and someone would break a window. We'd always blame it on each other.

Just along from our house there was a creamery where the vans were parked which brought milk in from the country. My brother Cahal was mad about trucks and he and a lad named Joe Oliver, who would later become Lester Piggott's head lad, would be climbing in continually, letting the handbrake off and driving them around. Cahal was always mad about driving and later ran a garage. He won the Circuit of Ireland in Easter 1974 – when he was sponsored by our mother! He also won the Donegal International Rally and the Manx Rally in the same year.

There was a great camaraderie about the place. I grew up with a lad called Barney Maguire, who also lived in Blakley Terrace. We played marbles and football together, that sort of thing. He started an electrician's business and in thirty-five years he never sent a bill to our family. My mother liked to pay her way, and always asked for an invoice. He would say, 'I'll send it next week' – but never did. He died a few years ago and is one of the people I say a prayer for every night.

As I approached eleven my life, and almost certainly my outlook on life, was to change drastically when my parents told me that I was to go away to a boarding school, just over the border in Monaghan town.

CHAPTER FOUR

College days

I protested vehemently that I didn't want to go, but it was to no avail. 'It will be good for you in the long run' was the general tone of my parents. I sobbed my eyes out. When they drove me down there it did nothing to mollify my unhappiness. Though I was less than forty miles from Irvinestown, St McCartan's College, a gaunt, grey stone institution, built in 1840 on top of a hill overlooking Monaghan town, was a daunting new home for a boy who had not yet celebrated his eleventh birthday. But there I was to stay – until I was expelled at fourteen.

I couldn't blame my parents' aspirations for me as St McCartan's lacked nothing in prestige. Seamus McKenna, who became Chairman of the Bar Council, was an ex-pupil, and others went on to become eminent barristers and surgeons. I have no doubt it was the professions that they had in mind for their first-born son. It was a great thing in Northern Ireland at the time to be well educated and my parents believed they were doing their best for me. The college was subsidised by the Catholic Church and run by priests, who would have taken very little salary. That used to go towards the running of the place. It cost my parents about £100 a year to send me there.

Although it was in the South, albeit just over the border, I was sent there because it was a Diocesan College and

Irvinestown belonged to that particular diocese. The one major disadvantage to the dozen of us from the North who joined that year was that Irish Language was a compulsory subject in the South. Considering most of us didn't understand a word of Irish, it made life somewhat difficult. In contrast, boys from the South had spent five years at primary school learning the language and were already fluent. My antipathy towards the subject soon became too evident. I was thrown out of Irish classes and never learnt a word. We thought it was unfair being up against such disadvantages and got off on the wrong foot. We just didn't try a lot of the time.

It took me several months before I got used to being away from my parents. I was very homesick. After leading a relatively pampered home life, I didn't enjoy being herded into a dormitory with twenty other boys. Apart from anything else there were rats. I woke up one morning to find one chap's ear had been chewed!

The regime was very strict, with a 'fagging' system like an English public school. We first-year boys had to clean the older boys' shoes or go and fetch the ball for them when they were playing handball, which is a game like squash but where a hand is used instead of a racquet. There was a roughness and toughness about the place, which reflected an austere era. The 150 boarders – there were also day boys – were woken at seven o'clock by a bell out in the yard. Just to make sure, the dean, Jonjo McKenna, would do his rounds to see that everyone was out of bed smartly. We had to wash in cold water and have cold showers. Obviously the religious element was very strong and it first sowed the seed that I might continue theological studies at some point. We had mass every morning at 7.30 am and were taught by priests from the local diocese.

The food was very basic, which was not surprising in Ireland in the immediate post-war years. Potatoes were the staple diet and sometimes you got so hungry you'd stuff an extra helping in your pocket. If we had meat at all, it was more fat than flesh. The highlight of the week was being served one sausage on Sunday morning. I had to make up for it during holidays, when I went home. If my parents visited me in mid-term, they'd bring me, maybe, a pound of butter, a bottle of HP Sauce and a jar of jam. It was hardly manna from Heaven but you had to guard it zealously and put your name on it because everything was in such short supply and somebody would whip it, given half a chance. After six weeks of the first term my mother sent me ten shillings, which I was supposed to eke out until Christmas. Later, I found another way to boost my income.

There was a tradition of inscribing your name with a knife in the refectory table. One day I was putting the finishing touches to my memorial: 'Remember Barney Curley, 7th Feb, 1954'. Everybody used to claim that somebody else had done it to get you into trouble. But I was caught red-handed. The priest nearly took my head off with a swat of his hand. 'Don't you worry,' he scolded me. 'We'll remember you alright and you'll be remembered wherever you go, too.' It proved to be a portentous statement.

I got up to my fair share of devilment. I was in the chemistry laboratory one day when the teacher, Father Byrne, had me filling some interconnected glass apparatus with water to demonstrate an experiment.

'Curley, turn on the water,' he instructed me. 'And switch it off when I say stop. Turn it off immediately.'

Of course, I didn't. I let it flow and the whole thing exploded with the pressure, much to the amusement of my classmates. Not surprisingly, I was sent out of class and made to stand outside the door. A little nun, Sister Mary-Anne, walked past.

'Are you alright?' she inquired kindly.

'Oh, I'm not well, sister,' I said.

'Oh, you poor boy, you should have the day in bed.'

To my delight, I was sent off to the dormitory, spent the day in bed and the good sister fed me of the best. I was more than happy to idle my time away.

I got away with it then; more often than not I got the cane – three stripes across each hand which was enough to make them swell – and I wouldn't be against such punishment. It teaches you something. I've never been for a soft regime and it didn't do us any harm. You got it for smoking, for not being in for studying, for ducking into town down the side roads to buy sweets, and other minor felonies – and not trying hard enough in class. I pleaded guilty to all those, and more, over my years there.

The problem with segregating the sexes is that as soon as boys reach adolescence the temptation of girls rears its head. The only chance of meeting any of these mysterious creatures was when we walked up to Monaghan Cathedral, up Dublin Street. Everybody tried to time it so our procession coincided with the girls from the convent across town and we'd chat them up in our gauche teenage way. The priests, meanwhile, tried desperately to organise it so there was as little contact as possible.

There was a lot of homesickness and many tried the 'Great Escape', particularly us boys from the North. It became a regular occurrence for boys to hang around by a wall at the bottom of one of the fields and then slide out when they thought no one was looking, down to the, now disused, railway cutting for the Armagh-Enniskillen line and walk to Monaghan town station. If you tried to abscond by road there'd always be a nosy neighbour reporting you to the college. It was the rail line or nothing.

The favourite destination was Enniskillen, where many of the boys came from. It wasn't a terribly bright idea. When they got to Enniskillen, who would be waiting there but the dean or his assistant? It was obvious which area you'd be heading for.

I tried it once myself during my first year, which was the hardest. I got on the train, and, having this ominous feeling they'd be waiting at Enniskillen, I got off at the stop before. It worked and I made it home. My mother was quite pleased to see me, but I was brought straight back again. There was so much flack when I got back, I didn't fancy doing it again. Anyway, they'd be keeping a close eye on you. It was like a prisoner-of-war camp. The only difference was the college didn't have a siren, searchlights and guards with machine-guns. If they thought there'd been a break-out there would be a roll-call, and once they discovered someone had gone missing all hell would break out.

Once you'd done that there was no chance to get into town for spurious visits to the dentist, which was my usual method of taking an afternoon off. For the next term you were confined to your cell, as it were. There were a few legitimate means of temporary escape. One was to play for one of the college's Gaelic football teams. That was enough incentive for me to try hard and I became one of the captains. If you played a team from, say, Armagh, which was twenty miles up the road, you'd have a good meal out afterwards and it would be eight o'clock before you came back into college again. You'd have a steak or something – great, compared with the mush you used to get.

We had played Gaelic football at school, and although I wasn't that good I was what you'd call a trier. John McElholm, who was a major figure in the Gaelic Football Association, had taught me at my junior school, St Molaise in Irvinestown. Unfortunately, that connection never seemed to enhance my game, although it improved as the years passed.

I remember players like Roundy Landers and Jimmy Kahan, who played for Kerry, which always boasted a strong football team; and Pat O'Neill and Kevin Armstrong who played for Antrim. Fermanagh weren't much good so we'd support Antrim, but Northerners always aligned themselves to the six Northern counties in the All-Ireland finals. I'd have my ear to the radio to listen to my hero Michael O'Hehir doing the commentary. He had such an unmistakable voice. We'd all try and impersonate him. I went to many games, at Croke Park in Dublin and the Ulster final at Clones. Later on in the sixties County Down from the North came along with a new, fast, slick brand of football, with a lot of passing; I suppose today they'd call it 'total football'. They won the All-Ireland final, which was unheard of because the Northern teams hadn't a tradition of winning matches – it would be like Southampton winning the Premier League championship. I usually went with my father and I remember Down had a player called Jim McCartan, a real bull of a man. I used to feel so proud when he knocked down someone from Cork or Kerry or Galway. There was an explosion of partisanship when the crowd got behind their teams, but there was no violence at those games – at least, only on the pitch. There were great celebrations the year County Down won in Dublin. I was lucky enough to be there. It was a big day in Northern Ireland and, strangely enough, it did much to unite the province, despite the religious divide. Although it was a Catholic game and the Protestants would give the impression that they weren't really interested, they'd be quietly listening to the radio. The Protestants wouldn't let on, but they'd be just as proud.

I was always keen on sports and on the field I always wanted to win. The priests who picked the teams were very strict about selection. You had to give 100 per cent. If they didn't consider that you were giving your all you'd be dropped without warning. That happened to me. But what really upset me was missing my day out. Being dispatched to college had put a stop to my Saturday betting sprees, but not my fascination for the horses. If I could get hold of a newspaper I'd still keep abreast of races and results. On days of big races, like one of the classics, I used to spend it in the betting shop in town. The usual ploy was to arrange a dentist appointment. You'd make an appointment for a check-up, then tell the priests that you had to return later in the afternoon for some treatment and it wasn't worth coming back to college in between.

One day I was strolling through Monaghan and caught sight of a priest, our Greek teacher, Monsieur Flanagan. I didn't give it a second thought. He rarely asked me any questions in lessons because I was hopeless at the subject. The following day I was sitting as usual at the back of the class. He had given us sentences to learn the night before and he was walking up and down as we translated them.

'The soldiers went up to the Acropolis to fight,' he recited. I looked towards the front at the boys who were good at Greek, expecting them to be asked. Instead, he looked at me. 'Mr Curley?'

I had never previously been asked a question in my three years in his class. I hadn't done the homework so I had no idea. I hummed and hawed. He came over and swatted me across the back of the head. 'So, you wouldn't know anything about Acropolis, would you?'

I never answered, but I knew what he was alluding to. Acropolis had been favourite for the Derby and was the big 'talking' horse at the time. He had obviously seen me go into the bookie's, but being a decent fellow he hadn't reported me and just wanted to let me know that he knew precisely what I'd been up to.

These betting expeditions were pointless without money to invest. Times were hard, and although my mother used to send me ten shillings it didn't go far. That used to have to last me the term, so there were all sorts of money-making rackets. Once I'd begun to develop my confidence in my last year I started all sorts of schemes. One was to organise 'horse races' round the sports fields. The bigger boys were the 'jockeys', and they would hang on to the jackets of the smaller pupils, the first years and a few second years, who were the 'horses'. It sounds bizarre, but it was very popular.

There were always two bookmakers, of whom I was usually one, with our blackboards on which we chalked prices. Sometimes I was a 'jockey', in which case I made sure that one of my pals was a bookie. Stakes were normally a shilling or two, with betting maybe 3–1 or 4–1 the field. Over an afternoon there would be three or four races with six or seven runners each. To win a pound on a race was an absolute fortune. You could go into town and dine out several times on steak for that. Of course, it would all have to be very clandestine. We'd whisper, 'Racing Wednesday, three o'clock.' When all was quiet and the priests were otherwise occupied, at the predestined time all the 'horses' and 'jockeys' would congregate.

We were always encouraged to use our own ingenuity in our free time. The priests appeared to be pleased that we'd devised our own 'sport', which was clearly good for our health. I fared well because I soon spotted this little fellow from my neighbouring village who was a right flying machine, a real Nijinsky. A sign of things to come, maybe? His name was Josie Slevin, who now has a grocery shop in Dromore, Co Tyrone. I used to be his 'jockey'.

Inevitably, there were all sorts of shenanigans, especially with me involved as bookmaker. It was important to get a good break, but if he wasn't 'off' that day, I'd hold on to his jacket or contrive to get him boxed in and go for a non-existent gap on the second to last bend and lose. I'd have my cronies there to back another 'runner' for me with the other bookmaker and, of course, my bookie would 'lay' Josie Slevin, who'd come through with a strong, late run and just fail to win. Of course, when Josie was 'off' and fancied and the money was down, I'd allow him to break in front and run as he liked. My bookie never knew what was going on and no one else seemed to catch on, either. Just to make sure it looked authentic, and appear as though we were 'triers', I sometimes gave him a thump on the back, but all the time I'd be holding him back. If a priest arrived on the scene we'd quickly get rid of the bookies' board and pretend that we were playing football. But we made a healthy profit on that for twelve months.

It was during my time at college that I had one of my most disastrous punting trips ever. It was the summer holidays and four of us, my cousin John Carney, two of my friends, Eugene O'Reilly and James O'Kane, both of whom later became priests, and myself, decided to go to the six-day Galway Festival. We lost virtually all our money the first day, and the remainder we lost at the dogs that night. We ended up sleeping in the car, a Volkswagen Beetle, at Salthill, beside the sea. I'm told that I spent the night lying on the floor, with my feet hanging out of the window, periodically breaking into a Tommy Steele song, 'When My Steam Boat Sank in the Ocean'.

In my early teens a favourite haunt was the St Molaise Club, named after the patron saint of Irvinestown. There was nothing very holy about it. From the age of twelve, on holiday from college, I'd be out playing football, then in the evening head for the hall. My friends and I would sit there for hours waiting for our turn to play billiards, but it was *the* place to be. We learnt to be streetwise. I used to watch the old men playing poker and pontoon, and learned how to play. I was pretty good at billiards then and it was very popular at the time. Top players like Joe Davis came to play exhibition games. By the time I was sixteen I was in the senior team which competed against local towns. There was quite a bit of needle in those games, too, and the lack of sportsmanship was more redolent of a modern professional football manager than an amateur pastime. I remember playing our staunch rivals, Enniskillen, and being paired with a real cocky character called Pa' Adams. When I beat him he just slung the cue on the table and stalked out. Mind you, I was probably pretty flash myself then.

My worst sin was that I didn't study very hard. At that age I thought it wasn't for me. But I was found out when the exams came up when I was fourteen – the intermediates, they called them, which I suppose were the equivalent of 'O'-Levels. I did enough to pass English and Maths. I also did very well in Irish, which was rather surprising given that I spent the lessons standing outside the door and, of course, never learnt a word. I had persuaded a classmate, Eugene O'Reilly, who was absolutely brilliant in the subject to do the exam for me. He passed with honours himself and, fortunately, was bright enough to ensure that B. Curley's paper was not up to the same standard, otherwise there'd have been the equivalent of a stewards' inquiry.

That collaborator remains one of my best friends. He went on to enter the priesthood and joined an organisation called the Kiltegan Fathers who do missionary work in Africa. He has spent the last thirty years there. He's a wonderful man and the happiest fellow in the world, although he doesn't have a dollar to his name. On the day that I go up to meet my Maker, I'd happily travel under Father O'Reilly's passport number.

I tried to pull a similar stunt in Greek, but I made one serious mistake. We had an 'unseen' as they called it, where you had to translate Greek into English, having not seen the passage before. I said to the fellow next to me, 'pull over your paper', and I did a terribly rash thing: I just copied it, word for word. It was a stupid error, two pupils handing in the same translation, word for word. That simply didn't add up. I had an inkling something was wrong when my father rang up and said, 'The president of the college wants to see you and me tomorrow.' He added, 'Have you any idea what it's about?' I feigned ignorance, although I had a fair idea. What had happened was the examiner in Dublin had rung up the college and said, 'Listen, I've been marking two of these papers and it's clear one boy has copied it off the other.' The president of the college, Canon Connelly, didn't have to think very hard before coming to the conclusion that it was me who was the culprit. The other fellow had a reputation as a very scholarly young man.

Canon Connelly told me in front of my father, 'This is a disgrace to the college. Your classmate has been barred from the exam, too, so you've ruined him and we're expelling you.' He told me to stay away from the college. I still don't know why I did it. Fortunately my father was not greatly into education and I was a pretty smooth talker, so I wormed my way out of it somehow. I had already convinced him that students from the North didn't stand a chance in the South. As far as my father was concerned the dice were loaded against me, so at least I escaped his wrath. I had a good brain but I don't regret not studying harder. I'd have been nurtured into a particular occupation, like a solicitor, and I know now that it wouldn't have suited me.

After I was expelled, Canon Connelly, appreciating that I was contemplating entering the priesthood, found me a place with the Christian Brothers at St Michael's in Enniskillen and I spent two years there. Back in the North, I didn't have to concern myself with learning Irish there, and in addition it was a day school. I can't say I ever enjoyed attending either establishment. I don't think I really learned anything and I always dreamt of going home. If I had a boy of eleven now, I don't think I'd send him to boarding school. During my time at St Michael's I must confess to spending most of the time in Larry McKeown's betting office, idling my time away listening to 'blower' commentaries. I had the odd bet, but fortunately did not have enough cash to finance any significant wagers. Back at home, my father had got himself into enough problems with his own gambling ... enough to threaten the livelihood of the entire family.

FIVE

A dog's life for the family

Even with the innocence of youth, it didn't take me long to discover how crooked greyhound racing was in those immediate post-War years. My father was one of the worst offenders, although that wasn't how he viewed it. It never occurred to him that 'stopping' dogs was morally wrong. As far as my father was concerned, he fed, watered and trained the dogs and he was entitled to run them how he wanted. He used to 'stop' them regularly at that time. There were no dope tests then and he gave them tablets which didn't appear to do any permanent harm, but slowed them by a second – which was worth about ten lengths, and that was enough to get them beaten.

Belfast had two tracks, Dunmore Park, where you could run your dog on a Saturday night, and Celtic Park, which staged dog racing on a Monday night. The latter also doubled as a home for Belfast Celtic Football Club. One Saturday night he headed off to Dunmore to have a gamble on a dog of his called The Fag. He backed it to win a substantial amount of money and, opening at 10–1, it started 6–4 favourite. The dog won with consummate ease and could have virtually performed acrobatics down the straight and still got up to be first. He was around a second faster than his rivals.

On the following Monday night The Fag was due to

compete in a confined sweepstake at Celtic Park. This race was for moderate dogs and if The Fag had done his fast time before entries closed a week or ten days beforehand he wouldn't have been allowed anywhere near the race by the Celtic Park management. But the rules allowed him to take part and there was nothing they could do. We arrived at the track to find, not surprisingly, that our dog was something like 7–2 on, and even at that price all the professionals were backing it. There were gamblers piling on their money with bets of £200-to-win-£700 and £100-to-win-£350 being offered and taken. That night the chances of our dog's number coming up was, seemingly, as big a certainty as the sun doing likewise the following morning. I had my doubts.

It should be understood that my father was like me in later years. Not a word would pass his lips about his betting intentions, even to his family. He'd explain, 'It's not that I don't trust you; it's that you could pass on the information in some other way. There's a lot of smart people about, and just by talking to you they could get it out of you. They could tell by your expression or by a gesture if the dog was fancied.' He'd never, ever, tell us when the dogs were 'off'. The only time you'd know something was going down was when he produced the money, just like myself at the horses.

The Fag ran deplorably and finished fourth, beaten by about seven or eight lengths. His time was considerably slower than two days earlier. The big players knew immediately what had happened. My father might just as well have ambushed them at gunpoint. He had 'stopped' the dog. With a second in hand, he could just about have fallen at the first bend and still got up and won. But 7–2 on simply wasn't my father's kind of price.

There was pandemonium. The place was packed out with a couple of thousand people, and what followed was a sound that has remained with me … a rhythmic stamping of feet on the floor of the wooden stand. It's the reaction you get at soccer games when the home team is 5–0 down, but only rarely at the dogs.

The punters were disgusted, understandably so, and the cry went up: 'Out. Out. Out.' If they'd got their hands on my father they'd probably have strung him up from the nearest Belfast shipyard crane.

Meanwhile the management had taken the dog up to their offices. My father was understandably reluctant to collect him. 'You go up and get the dog,' he urged me. 'Tell them you're taking him home.' I did as I was bidden and the manager asked who I was. When I uttered the name 'Curley', he snorted and declared, 'Send your father up.' I pretended that I did not know his whereabouts.

The fellow glowered at me and said, 'You want to find him.' There was no alternative. I went down and said to my father, 'Now, Boss (that's what we children used to call him), they won't give him to me. You'll have to go.'

Grudgingly, he went up to face the management's wrath. The message was clear. 'As long as your name is what it is,' he was told, 'you'll never run a dog here again.' That was it and we made a very quick exit.

The McAlindens, a big Belfast bookmaking family who ran the stadium, were as good as their word. My father never took a dog to Celtic Park again and they never took an entry from him. Celtic Park was the prestige track and it was a disgrace to get warned off it.

Indeed, it was many years before a Curley of any name went there with a dog again. In 1970 I was offered a greyhound by a couple of brothers, Mick and Tony Fahey, bought it for £300 and put it in training with Ireland's top trainer Ger McKenna. It was named Portumna Wonder and it won the Ulster Sprint at Celtic Park. The prize-money can't have been more than £500, but I backed it heavily ante-post and won something like

£5,000. The event was sponsored by the legendary bookmaker Sean Graham, with whom I was to develop a long, if not always harmonious, relationship. He presented me with the trophy.

Ironically, as I will describe later, I did have a bookmaker's pitch at the stadium for a time in the mid-sixties, by which time my father's activities were consigned to legend. That infamous night, as always, there was never any intention by my father to conspire with the bookmakers to 'lay' the dog. That would have meant him imparting secrets to third parties, which he would never do. It was all just part of an orchestrated, long-term plan to fool the bookies – which unfortunately, of course, also deceived some of the punters.

As I grew older he began to embroil me in his chicanery. Once, when I was about fourteen and on holiday from college, he sent me with one of his greyhounds to the Lifford greyhound track, a mile or two the other side of the River Foyle from Strabane. I was driven by Ernest McCaffrey, a taxi driver, who regularly took his dogs and knew the score. Just before we set off, my father, who was off to Belfast with another dog, handed me a little ball of mincemeat. 'Now,' he instructed me firmly, 'when you get to Strabane, give this to the dog.' I didn't need telling that the tablet was in the meat.

Irvinestown to Lifford is a fair ride and on the way I got thinking to myself. My analysis of the situation was this: 'If I don't give the dog the meat, he'll almost definitely win – and probably at a good price.' I was already calculating my winnings. The taxi-driver was keeping a close eye on me in his rear-view mirror. He knew the instructions, too. When we got to Strabane, I just motioned with my hand and pretended to give my canine travelling companion the meat. If Ernest had been looking, my sleight of hand was enough to deceive him.

I had £2 on the dog at 6–1 and he duly won by five or six lengths and I won £12. Both my father and I arrived back about midnight and he demanded to know how we'd got on.

'We won,' I said. He looked flabbergasted. 'He couldn't have won,' my father declared defiantly, obviously having a big betting scheme planned for the dog. 'Oh, yes. Five or six lengths,' I shrugged, trying to conceal my guilt. So he thought about it for a moment. Now, these tablets had been supplied, perhaps unwittingly, by Gerry Magee, the local chemist. He was used to people taking their problems to him. But not the one he was confronted with that night. And not at that hour. Suddenly my father sprang up from his chair and exclaimed, 'The fool's given me the wrong pills.' He was inclined to be very hot-tempered at times. He strode down the street and I followed at a discreet distance. Despite the late hour, he started to rap on the chemist's door. Eventually someone stuck their head out of the window and there was a right commotion, with my father accusing him of being stupid. All I could do was just watch and keep out of it and feel slightly ashamed. Eventually it blew over. I never let on to him either, even when I got older.

I felt pretty pleased with myself. Going back to school £12 the richer was like having hundreds in your back pocket today. That incident was a typical illustration of my father's quick temper, and he was always a very bad loser. Much though he was devoted to them, he made sure his dogs felt it when he believed they had not done their best. I remember one of them running poorly one night at Clones and when we got home out of the car, and he thought there was nobody looking, he gave this poor animal a right few kicks up the backside. Fortunately, his anger would subside equally quickly. I was never really frightened of him, because you knew if you could keep out of his way for a minute or so he'd quieten down and be reasonable again.

My father always had a touch of recklessness about him. He'd rush into projects without really thinking about the consequences. When we moved into Blakley Terrace, he already had it in his mind to build a new house for the family.

He had the money initially, too. He'd prospered from smuggling and had sold all the stock in the farm; he could have gone out and bought five houses. There was a plot in Fairgreen Street, left to him by his aunts Minnie and Annie, and he started the work in 1955.

He also launched a new business, buying chickens and rabbits from farms and selling them to wholesalers who shipped them over to Glasgow and London. His family had been involved in the same trade. My father's only outlay was a truck and all the transactions were in cash, of course. I don't think he believed in paying tax. He used to try and dupe my mother into believing that there wasn't much profit in it – and would have got away with it if I hadn't 'grassed' on him.

Being at college then, I considered myself a really bright young spark. During the holidays I used to tag along with my father on his rounds and I soon got suspicious about what he was up to. We'd stop at all the farmyards, maybe thirty a day, and when he got out and bought his goods I always listened in to what he gave the farmer and quietly kept details in a little book. Later, I added up what he'd paid out. Towards the end of the day we'd head across to the wholesalers, who paid him out. I had a little squint and subtracted one from the other and it didn't take a degree in maths to realise that he had made about £30 from his day's work. It was, as we say in racing, 'a right touch'. As we arrived home, my mother would say, 'How did you get on today, Charlie?' He'd shrug, 'Ah, no good. Waste of time.' But, as children do, I spilt the beans. I blurted out, 'He's got £30.' which started a right old row. It came as a complete surprise to him that I'd been checking up on him, and he gave me the kind of look that parents do when they suddenly realise that their children are growing up. He wasn't really angry but said I was becoming a bit too smart for my own good – and his. After that he was always a bit cagey about what he told me. You couldn't blame him.

My father had been attempting to conceal from my mother precisely how much of his income was going on greyhound betting. All he was interested in was doing his rounds as quickly as possible and heading off to the dogs. Where we differed was that my father was completely obsessed with gambling. When I became involved with betting I could walk away from it at any time.

He had a dozen dogs, mostly kennelled at the rear of the house. He'd work them in fields around the town. A few hundred yards round the corner from our house there was one particular field in the Lack Road which had the benefit of a steep gradient . He'd wave his handkerchief at the top and I'd slip the dogs to him.

You'd start off puppies by walking them four or five miles a day. He'd do that in the morning and my brother and I would help out later when we came home from school. He was constantly stressing to us how important it was to keep them on the go. We shouldn't stop and chat to people and allow the dogs to rest. He would even sneak out down the road after us to check that we were doing it properly. One day we let him down. There was a small stream where my brother and I would take our jam-pots to catch small fish and collect tadpoles. We'd taken a couple of dogs with us and tied them to a tree. We were concentrating so hard on our fishing, he caught us unawares – you've never seen me move so fast, because if he'd have got hold of us he would have thrown us in the water for allowing his beloved dogs to be idle. Luckily he didn't catch us and we kept well away from him for a few hours. Despite his explanations, as children we didn't really appreciate that tying up these dogs, that were bred for speed, and letting them lie in the sun, wasn't doing much for their racing futures.

Nothing would ever persuade my father that his dogs should not take priority in life and they soon started taking a toll on his business. It would get to 2.30 pm maybe, when he'd seen twenty of his thirty customers, and he'd take out his fob watch and realise he'd have to get back to town to go off to the dogs at 3.30 pm. He'd conveniently forget about the rest of his customers, who wouldn't have been very happy when he actually turned up the following day. It was perishable produce he was dealing in and it wouldn't keep that well. But he had a gift of sweet-talking them and he'd give them some cock-and-bull story about the truck breaking down.

At the track, he had some very good nights, but, increasingly, too many bad ones. Simultaneously, he had started to build the new house for the family in Fairgreen Street, Irvinestown, having always believed in the principle of owning your own property. When it was about three-quarters completed, he ran out of money to finish it, and there was nothing in the pot to pay for the work that had already been done. The house had the roof on, but no doors or windows. The builders and decorators were demanding payment and he even owed the local petrol station. The builder, Stanley Potter, realising that his chances of getting paid were diminishing as every night's greyhound racing passed, came and took the keys and seized my father's car in lieu of part of the debt. My father had a big Austin A70, considered a very flashy motor car at the time, and he was immensely proud of it. I can't say I blamed Stanley, although he probably found it was on hire-purchase anyway! That was the final blow. He was down to what we Irish call 'Shanks's pony'. He was walking on his feet.

It takes some doing to lose a veritable fortune and to fail to profit from running and betting on your own greyhounds, but my father managed to achieve it. It got to the stage where he was in dire straits, and to get out of trouble he 'stopped' one particular dog for about six months to get him in the worst grade imaginable, before plunging all he had left on it. The bet was £300-to-win-£2,100 and it would have solved all his problems at a stroke. And it was some stroke that he intended to pull that night. It was a sprint, and despite the dog getting left several lengths behind he was in front again by the first bend, only to stumble, roll over and break his back. In horseracing, steeplechasers and hurdlers all too often suffer that fate, but it rarely occurs on the greyhound track. It was wretched luck. I still have a vivid picture of him trudging down the track, picking up his dog and carrying it back through the middle of the stadium. There were tears in his eyes. 'The party's over, Barney,' he declared. 'I've played my joker and lost.'

He knew it was the end of the line – it was his 'nap' gone west. My mother didn't have to inquire what had happened when we arrived home. His demeanour said it all.

That was his last serious bet. He couldn't even borrow money to try and recoup his losses and things went from bad to worse over the next six months. Fortunately, my mother always had a pound or two hidden away to ensure we wouldn't starve. Her mother, Annie Farry, lived with us, and she was a great help to the family, too. But it was a terrible blow to the family's pride to have people coming to the door looking for money. I knew that drastic measures were required if we were to settle those debts. We'd have to go to England and earn the money we owed.

The fourteenth of August 1956 is a date stamped indelibly on my mind. It was a miserable day for all of us and many tears were shed when we left. We didn't have the price of a berth on the ship from Belfast to Liverpool, so we slept underneath the lifeboats. At that moment it must have brought home to my father how far he had fallen. What did Oscar Wilde say? 'We are all in the gutter but some of us are looking at the stars.' We were staring at a black hole.

It must have been very tough on my father because he had been used to all the comforts of life, just as it was a cultural shock for me coming out of boarding school and the realisation that I had several months of hard work in front of me. He was dedicated to my mother and their six children. Worst of all, it meant him leaving my two youngest sisters at home, Amelia who was only about two years and four months, and Sheila who was fourteen months. By then, Mary and Anne were nine and ten, and Cahal was fourteen. Irish parents can be very undemonstrative; at times they don't show much affection to their children. But they still love them very much. It must have broken his heart to leave his babies for so long. Having had a family myself I know what that must have meant to him. It must have been a dreadful experience for a man of his background who, at that time, was about fifty.

There had really been no alternative. When you're betting it's easy to get yourself into trouble without really realising it. He probably owed around £2,000, mostly to the local garage for petrol and to the builder and decorator, but, knowing him, he would never have admitted that he didn't have it. For as long as possible he'd have tried to bluff his way out of trouble. In truth, a lesser man than him would have lain low for a few months. When people realise you have nothing they don't really press you. But we had always been brought up to pay our way. Uppermost in my mind was that the people who had done the building work were entitled to their money and we had to get it somehow.

Families can offer their support at moments of such crises; but instead of rallying round, my uncles just gave me a lot of aggravation. 'Your father's letting down the family. He should be ashamed of himself. He owes half the district, while we hardly owed a penny in our lives,' my Uncle Tommy would chide me when I was home from boarding school. 'It's a wonder he doesn't do something about it. And it's a wonder you don't either, you big loaf, instead of going about studying. A big, strapping lad like you should go to England and try to earn some money, get this debt paid. You're disgracing the family name, both of you.' And so it went on.

I had no real argument with them, though, and I knew what had to be done. Fortunately, I always had a bit of go about me. My father and I got talking one night and I said to him, 'You don't have any chance here, Boss. I'm at school, but I'm old enough now to pull my weight. We should go to England.' He thought about it for a week and we decided to go. He may have been up to all kinds of trickery with his greyhounds, but the way he brought us up, it was wrong to owe people money if you could avoid it. His only reservation was that it would break into my education. It hurt me, because I knew it wasn't what my parents had in mind for me. They had a vision of a decent education followed by a profession or the priesthood; not toiling in some English factory. But at least I was young and it was an adventure, of sorts. If I accompanied him it would take only half the time to raise the money we owed. Reluctantly he agreed.

The relative states of employment meant that there was much emigration from Northern Ireland to England at that time and we travelled with a pair called Jim Valentine and Jim Cassidy, who were working in England and had been back on their holidays. We could earn four times in England what we could at home and, in addition, there was plenty of work across the Irish Sea. It was my first time in England and, although there were many Irish emigrants on the train to Manchester, I never detected any anti-Irish feeling. That has remained true to today.

The place we headed for was Urmston, an industrial area dissected by the River Mersey and which is about three miles west of Old Trafford, home of Manchester United. It was a bleak landscape, dominated by factory chimneys expelling their foul wastes, but we could not afford to be choosy. The first night we spent at a lovely boarding house in Flixton Road, which was where Jim Valentine was staying. The landlady,

Mrs Deaney, served us up a hearty meal, but we couldn't stay on there and the next night we had to fend for ourselves.

Looking for work and digs simultaneously can be a soul-destroying business. The following night it was getting late by the time we found a house run by a Mrs O'Brien, who took us in. It was a wonderfully charitable thing to do, because she didn't have any vacancies. It meant us sleeping in a room with twenty others. They were mostly middle-aged to elderly, a real league of nations it was, too, and half were drunk. The rest of them appeared to be suffering from some form of sickness and coughed all night. Mrs O'Brien had a big heart, but she had no understanding of how to run a boarding house; she took in any waif or stray that came to the door. At least in the morning we got a good Irish breakfast.

The next place only lasted a couple of nights. My father wasn't happy with this particular landlady's cooking and told her so. He was used to home comforts, my mother being an excellent cook, and advised her in undiplomatic terms that real food was not dispensed out of tins. He also wanted everything done for him. We arrived back at 11.30 pm one night to find our suitcases standing outside the front door. She said he was too pernickety. We spent the night on the street, not that we slept for long anyway.

By then we had both got jobs in a factory which made plastic moulds on the Petrochemicals Industrial Estate in Urmston. My father mixed dyes, while, as a sixteen-year-old schoolboy, I was initially entrusted only with sweeping the factory floor. I'll never, ever forget it. We used to work double shifts, which meant us getting up at 4.30 am to get the five o'clock bus, and we wouldn't return to our digs until 11.30 pm at night. We only got about four hours sleep at nights. It was thoroughly arduous, but it was the only way we were going to escape from our financial crisis.

Eventually, we got a room, if you call it that, in Princes

Road. We were there for about a year. It had a hearth and just enough space for a double bed, and somewhere for us to keep a few clothes. As autumn turned to winter we'd come in at 11.30 pm and it was unbelievably cold and damp. There was no heating, apart from the fire we'd light in the small hearth in an attempt to keep us warm. We did all our cooking on a little stove, although my father's fussiness didn't make it easy. But there we stayed for nearly twelve months, until we'd saved enough money to pay off our debts and return home to the family.

After those double shifts I could hardly make it back to our digs, such was my fatigue. But there was no way we would go back until we could walk through Irvinestown with our heads held high and debts paid off. We sent home £35 a week to my mother, which was virtually everything we earned. That enabled her to pay off my father's debts within the year. I got £1 pocket money. Very occasionally we'd go to the White City greyhound track in Manchester – not to bet, just to watch. My father retained a love for greyhounds aside from betting.

Meanwhile, my brother Cahal had left school to join the big local contractors, Scallon's, who gave him work labouring on the roads. He got £3 a week and kept ten shillings for himself. His contribution kept the house going. My mother could live on very little. She was a great trier, often against impossible odds. She was a proud woman who would never have owed anyone in her life. Her maxim was, if you owe, you have to pay – no matter how long it takes. Her brother had a farm out in the country at that time and he would have brought her in potatoes. She was a great one for making her own bread and still is.

After a couple of months, one of the directors, Mr Tosh, came to see me. He'd been looking through my details I'd given when we'd applied for work, and was intrigued by the fact that I'd been to a prestigious boarding school. Because I'd studied science he wanted to switch me to a different part of the factory where I'd be working in the laboratory. Sweeping floors, he said, was not a suitable job for me. I told him I was quite happy and didn't want to leave my father and my friends to go into the white-collar side of the works with a lot of science graduates. Eventually, though, I agreed. I had to dress better and turn up with a shirt and tie. My father was very proud of my 'promotion' to a job which involved testing plastic for strength. I found the work relatively easy because I'd had a fair science grounding at college.

I didn't see my father so much then but, every so often, he'd get a break and come down for a smoke. Each time he was a different colour, depending on the dye he'd been working with. If he was covered in black or yellow, they'd all laugh and call him the black Irishman or the Chinese Irishman. But there was nothing malicious about it; he always got on well with everyone. In the longer term, that work caused his death. I would say there was no doubt about that. He was mixing dyes for the moulds and there was dust everywhere – nobody thought about such equipment as masks then – which damaged his lungs and, although he lived to the grand age of eighty-one, he had been poorly with a chest ailment for fifteen years before that.

Until that time, I'd never really thought about religion. But then I realised how deep his faith was and how he coped with those tough times. It was his faith in God that helped him through that episode in his life. He must have said 'Our Father' and ten 'Hail Marys' five times. He'd recite it when we were coming home on the bus at night and I'd join in. He always insisted on going to mass, even if it affected his work. He had a litany of sayings, which I still use today: 'Don't lose your faith', 'Look after everybody else's pound as though it is your own' and 'Imagine you are on a ship that is sinking. Never get involved with the kind of man who would be hiding in the lifeboats with the women and children.' For a man without much formal education, it made a lot of sense.

To get coal for our little fire we had to walk over the railway bridge to the depot. For half a crown you could get it delivered but my father would heave the sack on his back and hump it home to save the charge. It probably weighed over a hundredweight and it was all of half a mile. We'd buy a bag of coal and a bag of slack, which is what they call coal dust. It smouldered away and meant the coal lasted longer. You had to fill the sacks yourself, which I helped him with, but he wouldn't let me help carry them. In many ways, he still treated me as a child. We'd have to make two trips and it was a filthy job. To my eternal discredit, although I put it down to the immaturity of my years, I felt humiliated and was terribly ashamed of my father. I'd walk well behind him in case anybody associated me with this dirty little man heaving coal.

It was a humdrum, tedious existence. There was no drinking for my father; no betting for either of us, although we visited Manchester racecourse and, about a fortnight before we left, had a trip to Haydock Park, where Pat Taffe rode two or three winners. I had a ten-shilling double on two of his winning mounts, which allowed me to go home in rather more style than I departed. That win allowed me a visit to a store in the city called Weaver to Wearer where I bought my first ever suit to come home in. It cost a couple of pounds.

We allowed ourselves just one indulgence to break up the monotony of our labours. Every other Saturday, we'd catch the bus to Old Trafford. As a child I had been an Arsenal fan, albeit from a great distance. A neighbour of ours, Jack Murphy, who had spent twenty years in England, was responsible for that. He had been a great Arsenal supporter and used to get as drunk as forty cats every Saturday night. It was a hilarious combination. On his way home, to the delight and amusement of my brother and me, he used to re-enact, in his own dishevelled, uncoordinated style, great Arsenal goals as he passed our home. If only Cliff Bastin could have witnessed what his goals inspired!

That was the extent of my knowledge of English football until I went to Manchester, because we had always been encouraged to play and follow the Gaelic code. To be there, actually standing on the terraces at Old Trafford, was an experience a teenager from a small town in Northern Ireland could only have dreamt of. The excitement was unbelievable – we were really vocal supporters, standing behind one goal.

United had a magnificent team, too, back in 1956, only two years before the Munich air disaster. They had last won the championship in 1952 and manager Matt Busby had rebuilt a team of youngsters into one of the finest the English game had seen. We were fortunate enough to watch the so-called Busby Babes take their first faltering steps, and by the end of the season be on their feet and up and running, securing the league championship from Blackpool by a then record margin of eleven points. And that was when there were only two points for a win.

In particular, I'll always remember a big, strong, strapping fellow, who was so deceptively agile. His name was Duncan Edwards and he was quite brilliant. Their team was virtually unchanged all season. It was Ray Wood in goal, Bill Foulkes, Mark Jones, Roger Byrne, Eddie Colman, Bill Whelan (or Jackie Blanchflower), Duncan Edwards, Johnny Berry, Tommy Taylor (who was top scorer with twenty goals), Dennis Viollet and David Pegg. There was an Irish connection, too, which made 'our' team all the more attractive: Jackie Blanchflower, brother of Tottenham's Danny, played twelve times for Northern Ireland and Bill Whelan wore the green shirt of the Republic on four occasions. Two years later all of that team were playing for United and all were on the Munich flight that went down on take-off in February 1958. Ray

Wood, Bill Foulkes, Jackie Blanchflower, Johnny Berry and Dennis Viollet were the only survivors of that twelve.

The day approached, with mounting excitement, when we could board the train bound for Liverpool and a ferry to Belfast. We should have arrived at Irvinestown proud men, our debts paid off and our reputations repaired. But my father was too embarrassed to walk up the high street and in the end I had to ring Gerry Magee and ask him to pick us up from the station.

In many ways it had been a miserable eighteen months; yet, if I lived my life over again, I would want to experience that period in my life once more. It was strangely fulfilling and gave me an appreciation of life outside my own community. It made me realise how much I'd been pampered until then. It also brought me a lot closer to my father. You develop a special relationship when it's just him and you, day in, day out, for more than a year.

When he returned from England, my father's 'betting tank' was inevitably empty, and although he continued with his dogs in a small way the experience had taken the edge off him. He always had a greyhound about, even when he was in his seventies, but just for a bit of fun. He had been seriously chastened by the whole sorry episode and had been taught a brutal lesson that it was not an easy game in which to be a winner. It should have been a salutary warning to me, too, of the devil that inveigles the uninitiated into gambling. But I never let it deter me.

Our house in Fairgreen Street could now be seen to and it was finished, complete with a small grocery store, a year later. My mother still lives there, although the shop has been converted into a hallway. There was a great community spirit and local families and businesses all joined in to get it going. Don Charlton, who had a shop in the same street, sent some chocolates, a wholesellers called Reihills gave us fizzy drinks and Hudsons, a wholesale grocery firm, supplied us with items like tea. The shop was a popular local amenity and should have done quite well, had we not all been pilfering cigarettes – all the family smoked – as we passed by. The counter was not very large and it was no great problem, if you had long arms, to lean over and lift forty cigarettes. My other target was Quality Street – I was particularly partial to purple-wrapped ones and I removed them from their packets, which upset some of our customers. All in all, I'd say we smoked and ate our way through a fair amount of the profits. Somehow, despite our best efforts, our mother made it pay. She served the customers and my father helped out occasionally, although he was not very popular because of his hot temper. If customers asked for, say, Heinz baked beans and we didn't have any, he'd give them an alternative without an apology or explanation. Woe betide them if they started objecting, he'd merely insult them and give them the benefit of his expertise on beans. He was not what you'd call customer-friendly. Fortunately for the image of the shop, he wasn't around too much because he had set up another business, buying and selling pigs.

Even during the construction of the house, the family business initiative was already to the forefront. One of the most important dates in Irish history – at least for those with a Protestant perspective – is 12 July, the day in 1690 when 'King Billy' (William III) defeated the former king, James II, at the Battle of the Boyne. Our half-built house was directly on the main route of an Orange march. Thousands of people used to line the route as the procession of marchers and bands passed. My brother and I set up a little stall selling bottles of mineral water, together with sandwiches and cakes my mother had made. Then, such marches were just part of the local calendar and there was no hint of violence. I was enthralled by the bands marching past. It was a highlight of the year for me. The fact that ours was a Catholic house would not deter us from making a profit from the day, but you got the occasional bigoted attitude: 'That Barney Curley,' muttered one voice. 'He's some b******, giving refreshments to the Orange Men.' There was about 200 per cent mark-up, but we sold out. Typically for the Curleys, we paid for them after we sold them.

The work bug had bitten me and that summer I worked for Ulster Creameries in Belfast for ten weeks. It was an ice-cream factory, and my job was to load it on the vans. I got £6 or £7 a week, which included lots of overtime; it wasn't bad for the times, but you'd hardly have known I'd earned a penny. I had gambled it all away on the greyhounds at Celtic Park and Dunmore Park and on horseracing. I was the original mug punter, backing tips in the newspapers. When I departed to return home my soles were worn through and I'd had to stuff my shoes with thick paper in order to fill in the holes. I didn't even have the money to get them repaired, let alone buy new ones. I could barely pay for my digs and I didn't even have the price of a bus or train fare home from Belfast. Fortunately, at Dunmore Park I met one of the Scallon family, Seamus, who used to race greyhounds then, and he brought me home.

I returned with about five shillings and took all my pals to the cinema in Dromore with it. That was it, the result of three months' work, all gone. I must have looked like Charlie Chaplin walking up our street to the house. My mother's face was a vision of annoyance and shame. But her mood brightened considerably when I told her how I saw my future. I intended to study for the priesthood.

SIX

Taking up arms with the stormtroopers

Shortly after I came back from England I had made my mind up that I wanted to become a priest. It was a combination of factors that influenced my thinking, but most important were my parents' faith and my experience of deprivation, working all those hours in Manchester. It had all made me think about priorities in life and the value of sacrifice.

Normally, if you join a religious order you become a noviciate for twelve months. During that period you work, pray and study very hard, and are isolated from the outside world, apart from the occasional walk. Then you make up your mind if you want to proceed. There are no home comforts and you go there with the ideal of giving your life to God.

I was only sixteen, and too young to immediately become a noviciate, for which you had to be eighteen, so I went to Ballinafad College in County Mayo – which is best described as a finishing school for teenage boys planning on joining the priesthood. My eventual aim then was to join a religious order called the Society of African Missions, or the SAM as it was more commonly called.

We all got chores, and the favourite one, particularly for us smokers, was cleaning the college car. We all volunteered for that, or working on the tractors from the college farm – which was self-sufficient, the college grew its own vegetables – because they'd have to give us the keys. The priests would always be on the prowl, sniffing the air to see if anyone was smoking, but if you started the vehicle and revved it, it was very hard to detect the cigarette smoke. The other jobs we all enjoyed, strangely enough, were pulling out beet or picking potatoes. It was exceptionally hard work and by the end of a day your back was racked with pain but we were out in the fresh air. It was also good for hassle-free smoking.

Somehow, and this time I must protest my total innocence, I got my marching orders from that institution too. I think in the workplace today they'd call it 'constructive dismissal'. It was all because of a big craze at the time for stamp collecting. Many of the boys used to send away for packets of postage stamps from all nations. One of the boys, Prontias McDermott, overran his credit limit and sent his next order off in my name. It was the sort of thing kids did at the time. He didn't pay for the stamps and the superior, Father Grace, blamed me for not only running up this bill, but also selling them on to the rest of the boys.

There was a fearful row because I didn't even have an album to collect them in. I had as much interest in stamps as I had in knitting jumpers. As a not altogether untainted reputation preceded me, nobody was inclined to take my word for it and, after two years there, I decided to move again.

I just left and applied to a Jesuit College in Limerick. By even contemplating this step, you can be assured that I was taking the priesthood seriously. The Society of Jesus is an order founded by Ignatius Loyola, Francis Xavier and others, in Paris in 1534, to defend and propagate the Roman Catholic faith. Its members are bound to poverty, chastity and obedience, as they carry out their duties of preaching, educating and hearing confession. It had a very rigorous training process. Whereas the normal period to study for the priesthood was six years, it took thirteen years to become ordained as a Jesuit priest. As they say, 'send me the boy and I'll give you the man'.

Despite leaving Ballinafad under a cloud, I was welcomed by the priests at Mungret College. Admission demanded a basic standard of education, and they also sought a reference from your parish priest at home. In my case that was Father Lappin, who fully supported my application.

I always had a great regard for Jesuit priests, the 'stormtroopers of the Catholic Church' as they are often referred to. They have had their critics and have been regarded as too revolutionary by some, but there's no compromise with the Jesuits, which explains why they have been in the forefront of so many religious controversies. I am thankful that it gave me the opportunity to study philosophy. It greatly aided my thinking, and helped me distinguish between right and wrong.

I was very much influenced by some of the great Jesuits and their life stories. My mother prays to a great Irish Jesuit, Father John Sullivan. He gave everything for other people, just like Mother Theresa did. My parents never tried to sway me, but as their elder son I'm sure they were pleased with my decision. My fellow students came from a wide range of backgrounds; some had very wealthy parents, but it was of no consequence – they had to forsake all worldly goods.

The Jesuits adopted a system, of which I thoroughly approved, where the fellow in charge, the Father Rector, would do the job for three years, then move down the ladder to the very bottom rung and become an ordinary priest. It's a great system because it gives you humility. People get to a certain position of power or accrue some wealth and begin to think they're God Almighty. This system helps give them a perspective on life. There's a danger for all of us that we can become detached from reality.

Mungret was an old building, and though not enormous – there were probably only about seventy to eighty of us there at any one time – it had its own farm and practised self-sufficiency. We studied academic subjects, including philosophy, history, English, Greek and Latin, but the fundamental idea was to train you to do your best and toughen you up.

It was excellent training because you were under a strict timetable. There is much mystique and misunderstanding about the Jesuits, so I will recall something of my time at the college. It was a harsh regime, but that is all part of the training – to put you through the mill and really test out your commitment to the faith; in that way it's like the Army. I would recommend any young man who wants to be properly equipped for life to go to a Jesuit school, regardless of religion. I tried to get my son, Charlie, into Stonyhurst, one of the top Jesuit colleges in England, because I had been so impressed, but he didn't have sufficient academic qualifications.

The routine was very authoritarian from the moment the college bell tolled every morning at six o'clock to wake us in our dormitories. The whole philosophy of the place was different from an ordinary boarding school. Here, the accent was more on chastisement for failure in class or misbehaving rather than approval of success and good conduct.

After washing and dressing there was an hour's meditation in chapel, a time when you thought about your life and God, and how you could make yourself better. We prayed in silence. Then it was on to mass for another thirty minutes, followed by a simple breakfast. None of our meal portions were very substantial and it wouldn't have been much, some porridge and toast maybe. We ate nothing fried, except on Sunday mornings when, as a treat, we might get a sausage and one slice of bacon. During breakfast one of the priests would perhaps read out part of the life of one of the saints, but otherwise we would eat in silence.

As may have become evident by now, I have always been keen on my food and it was a major sacrifice. But I accepted that because sacrifice was a significant part of the Jesuit philosophy. You offered that up to God as part of your efforts to try and be a Premier League player in His league of sinners. Making sacrifices was part of getting you to that station. We were allowed some indulgences. Being eighteen and upwards, we could smoke, but only in a small hut well away from the main buildings, after breakfast, after lunch and after supper.

After breakfast we attended classes all day through to three o'clock, except for a break for lunch. English involved reading Shakespeare, Milton and the classics, which I have to admit I enjoyed. I had matured since my days at St McCartan's and was now at an age that I could appreciate such great writers. Unlike St McCartan's, where I had put in very little effort, here I wanted to do well. There was a point to it all, which was entering the priesthood. The priests were pleased with my progress. I had pretty good marks in my exams and, at that time, I had made up my mind to dedicate my life to God.

When I was at college and really putting in the work it was a great feeling of satisfaction, despite the exacting regime. To say every night, going to bed, 'Well, I did my best.' They were among the happiest years of my life.

The end of the afternoon was games time. They were very keen on sport. There followed more study from 5.30 to 7.30 pm in study hall. Again it was conducted in silence. Then, after supper, there was more study until nine o'clock. Before lights out in the dormitories we went down to the chapel again, where we said our rosary. Once a fortnight you went to confession.

It was lights out at ten o'clock. Sunday was mostly free and given over to games. There were no classes, although we were still expected to study at night. We got home for a couple of weeks at Christmas and could have a visit in the first term, and at Easter, but that was it. There was little free time and certainly no time for pranks or distractions, except for racing which still cast a powerful spell over me.

The college was divided into two institutions, one strictly theological, for the scholastics like me; the other, much larger, for lay pupils who would, primarily, be going on to university. One of those was a boy called Bobby Barry, whose father Jim trained horses in County Limerick. Occasionally, Jim collected Bobby at the back entrance because the priests allowed him out to ride for his father. I used to join them, although my absence was unofficial. I never asked for permission. They just picked me up at the bottom of the lane and I was always back in for evening study. I just loved the racing, even though I had very little money to bet with.

We would drive to Limerick Junction racecourse, which was only about three miles away on the road into the city. I recall Bobby winning a couple of 'bumpers', one on a horse called Chenille War. Later on in life I used to reflect on those afternoons out after I'd had a winner myself at Limerick, but at the time the experience simply enthralled me. Betting shops were one thing; that was one of the first race meetings I remember going to. The sheer exhilaration of actually being on the racetrack, with the brilliance of the jockeys' colours, the thud of the horses' hooves and the baying of the bookies, was something I'd never experienced before. The direction I took in later years was undoubtedly heavily influenced by those days out with Jim and Bobby Barry.

Two other 'lay' pupils were also to figure largely in my life. One was Barry Brogan, whose father Jimmy, a fine jockey in his day, had trained Gold Legend to win the 1958 Irish Grand National. And there was a character who was an excellent rugby player and runner by the name of Tommy Stack. Bobby went on to train briefly, but after marrying Lady Sarah Stanhope they became owners of Mellon Stud, just outside Limerick, where Secreto was broken, among others. (The college had something of a racing tradition. Another famous Mungret old boy was Vincent O'Brien.)

During each term you would go on 'retreat', where you were silent for four days, a period which you devoted to God. In a strange kind of way it was very satisfying and cleansing. You just listened to lectures and prayed. It wasn't easy for the first couple of hours not to talk to someone, but you got used to it. You meditated on many things, like your commitment to the priesthood.

One man who had a great influence on me and gave us a number of retreats was Father Robert Nash SJ, who had a presence of being so very close to God. If he couldn't move you with his words, nobody could. He taught me a prayer which I still say today:

> *I must die, I know not the day, the hour or the place;*
> *God, grant me the grace to lead a good life;*
> *And to die a Holy and happy death.*

There were, of course, no luxuries. We were all training to go on to places where there would be none of the pleasures of the secular world. You were completely in – or you were out. With this place there were no half-measures.

Despite the hardships, it was amazing how happy a place it was. They were halcyon days. There was a great spirit of comradeship. Some boys were much more gifted, but everyone was anxious to help one another. It gave me an outlook that, yes, you need money to get by, but it's not really that important. I say that despite having spent much of my life winning and losing thousands a year. The happiest people I have ever met are some of those Jesuit priests. They lived a very strict lifestyle, but they were wonderfully content. They seemed to have the secret of life. It taught me that it is wrong that the wealth of the world is in so few people's hands, the rest possessing next to nothing. The happiest people I've met in life are the ones whose belongings fit in a suitcase, like Father

Eugene O'Reilly, one of my closest friends, who has spent most of his adult life in Africa helping other people. I can talk to him for hours. Most people I just about manage to say 'hello' and 'goodbye' to. That training taught me never to be afraid to speak up if I thought there was something wrong. Those priests gave me the strength to stand up and be counted.

Rugby, which was not really my game, was the college sport, followed by soccer; there was not much Gaelic football or hurling. We had four soccer teams, A to D, and I was in the A team. I wasn't bad at the game, but over a period of five or six months I slipped down teams until I was among those who could hardly kick the ball. The priest in charge thought I wasn't trying my best, but there was more to it than that. I felt myself getting weaker and weaker. The first couple of months I was good until half-time. The last month I only lasted the pace for about ten minutes. My energy was ebbing away and I was suffering from sweats. The trouble is when you're young, you never think you're ill. My classwork was suffering as well, but I tried to ignore it.

We went out to play one day and the next minute I felt this massive pain across my chest. I was twenty and taken to hospital in Limerick with the assumption that it was a heart attack. An X-ray quickly established the real cause: I had tuberculosis, or TB as it is more commonly known. It is not a virus but a bacteria, and highly contagious; you've never seen a hospital so quick to get rid of anyone in your life.

I was taken to a sanatorium at Killadeas, which stands at the end of a track that winds round high above Lough Erne. By good fortune, it was not far from my home. The empty shell of the sanatorium still stands today, looking out over those islands, which have an almost mystical quality about them. I still return there occasionally. If it were turned into a plush country club or hotel, people would pay big money for a view like that. Then, in the early sixties, some would have paid millions to get out of the place still breathing.

In those days 'the great white plague', as it was known, was still a killer disease. Even with youth on my side – I had then turned twenty-one – my family and friends knew that the chances were that I'd come out cold and feet up because it was in its advanced stages. The disease, which used to be known as 'consumption' because victims were seemingly consumed before their relative's eyes, has afflicted mankind for centuries. Even Egyptian mummies have been found with the characteristic lesions, and at one time it became known as 'leprosy of the lung'.

Recently, a new, virulent form of the disease has been discovered, and there are still about 6,000 cases a year, though these days it is cured entirely by medication. It was particularly common in the nineteenth century, until its decline after 1882 when, at the height of the tubercular epidemic, the Prussian bacteriologist Robert Koch isolated and identified the tubercle bacillus, thereby establishing the contagious nature of the disease. The development of X-rays in 1895 also helped in its diagnosis.

The cure, if there were to be one, was crude but effective for the fortunate ones. You just lay on your back for twelve months, or even longer. You didn't move or speak. Not that you could, because you were so fatigued. It saps away your strength. The object is complete rest. You just lay still and rested with the 'benefit' of the fresh air that blew in straight off the Lough. Your cure was aided by a nutritious diet and scrupulous hygiene. That treatment did not so much cure tuberculosis as help the body's immune system confront the disease and helped damaged tissue to scar and seal and hence contain the bacilli.

Switzerland was a favourite destination for the more well-heeled who contracted tuberculosis, but this particular location wasn't a bad second-best. On some days the winds would cut through you like a frozen lance. The windows were up all the time, and you dare not close them, no matter how cold it was – the nurses would be straight back to open them.

Generally, the disease is characterised by fever, night sweats and a delicate, pale complexion, although in my case it was quite advanced before the discovery was made. But you knew your possible fate from the day you were taken in. They were dying like flies around me. When you arrived you were just laid on your back and injected in the backside at five every morning, It sounds like something Hattie Jacques would perform on a luckless patient in *Carry On, Doctor*, but there was nothing in the least amusing about this treatment. The first few jabs were relatively painless, but then the skin got tough and it turned sore, and you knew this unpleasant routine would go on for another six months.

The seven or eight of us in our ward dreaded every morning, because if someone sticks a needle in the same place for days on end they run out of areas to put them. And some nurses were not as accurate as they might have been. Fortunately for me, streptomycin had been developed for about ten years by then. You had to take two or three of these massive tablets a day. They were these foul-tasting things which upset your stomach. A lot of patients just couldn't get them down, but I knew I had to if I were going to survive. It was considered a wonder medicine, healing diseases that penicillin could not, but in some cases it proved futile – the TB bacillus was nothing if not tenacious.

Streptomycin was the only hope you had. The bad cases, and the older people, died, but I pulled through. My constitution was a bit better than the older patients. You were so weak, you didn't want to eat. You just lay there and waited to recover – or waited to meet your Maker. If you didn't start improving after two or three months, that was the end. At that stage the doctors would start giving you regular X-rays and the most wonderful moment was to have them come round and say: 'I think you're improving.' That gave you encouragement you'd pull through.

It was a very frightening experience. It was the first time I had confronted death, and it was always on your mind. There were some very wealthy people there and they could do nothing. You couldn't buy your way out of a place like that. It gave me a realisation of the foolishness of life. People try to accumulate wealth, and the day before they die are still trying to make the next million. It is such folly.

Even in a place like that you were segregated by religious beliefs. It was nothing said, just a subconscious thing that everybody was aware whether you were a Catholic or a Protestant. It was like going back to early schooldays. Rightly or wrongly, such information was, and is, important to people. Yet, if there was ever an argument against the evils of sectarianism it was embodied in the man who looked after me. Doctor Warmington, a Protestant from Enniskillen, was utterly dedicated; outside religious orders I've never seen devotion like it. He seemingly lived in that hospital day and night, caring for us. His name is engraved in my memory. In the early hours of the morning if you were having trouble sleeping he'd be there, and then bright and early the next morning. Under his care, many patients recovered who had no right to. Much of it was just his words; he encouraged them to get better. Even when it was obvious that they were destined for the next world he'd still give them optimistic words right to the end. If there's a place called Heaven, he's there in a prime seat in Row A.

It was also when I first realised how dedicated nurses are. There were two in particular, nurses Guy and McCrory, both from Irvinestown, whom I liked. Nurse Guy was always very jolly, always had a joke, however miserable you were feeling. It gave you a lift.

I remember the day when I first started to walk again. I made it a few yards around the grounds to a seat overlooking the lough, but I was still so weak I couldn't get back. I had to have the sanatorium van driven round to collect me.

There was always a big welcome from the hospital care workers. Most of them were Protestants too. There was Joe Shackleton, who later became bank manager in the town. I opened an account with him and never changed. Being the type of person I am, I always gave him a fair deal of trouble, but he always had great confidence in me and helped me a lot. And there was Douglas Hudson, who ran the wholesalers which stocked our shop. People like that never leave your memory. They always revived your flagging spirits when they came round with a laugh and a joke. It needed it. The atmosphere was very sombre. It didn't matter how fit you were, when that disease embraced you it could crush you to death, whatever your age. It was a democratic disease, being no respecter of age, wealth, position or talent. John Keats, the Brontë sisters, D.H. Lawrence and Franz Kafka all perished from tuberculosis.

I became quite friendly with one chap Peter Cox, a Gaelic footballer, who was a great strapping fellow. He deteriorated at one time, but he got better. Every six weeks they wheeled us down for an X-ray to check how our lungs were progressing. After about nine months, Doctor Warmington said, 'I think you're showing improvement. There's no guarantees but I think you're going to make it.' Can you imagine how I felt? It was a wonderful feeling, after being there nine months in no man's land, when it could have gone either way. Even then, I had to stay for another three or four months just to be sure. My parents, who had been most worried all this time, came for me. Their faith must have been important to them then.

I promised myself then that if ever I got better I would never panic about anything in life again. That has stayed true to today. It was a tough experience in one way, but it made me appreciate and savour whatever life I had left.

I stayed at home for twelve months recuperating. It had drained me and I was still very weak. I was just going for short walks and slowly building up my strength, returning for check-ups and X-rays. The doctors advised me not to smoke. I obeyed them initially, but it didn't last of course. Still, I made a good recovery. Until recently I used to swim regularly. Well into my fifties I would turn out for the Newmarket trainers' football team who played the jockeys. Mind you, I wouldn't be able to sleep for the week afterwards and I had pains all over.

In only one way did TB take a physical toll: to this day, I can't pull up the girth and tighten them on the horses and I'm not that strong in my right hand. It was also around that period that my hair fell out. Whether there's any connection with the TB, I don't know. I just ignored it. If it happened now you'd probably be getting advice from doctors, and counselled for some kind of trauma, but then it didn't create much of a stir. It's not the worst thing in the world, and, judging by the state of some footballers and actors, a bald pate is in vogue rather than undesirable these days.

During these years, I drifted apart from many of my contemporaries. I lived a different life from other young people in the area. I never went dancing and had no time or inclination for socialising; it just didn't occur to me. In my teens, it was always in my mind to give my life to God. Priests didn't get married, so I never thought about girlfriends. In later life it must have been embarrassing for the girls I knew to find that I had so little knowledge about the opposite sex! But they were wonderful happy years. People don't realise how, if you try and give to Man Above, how much he'll give back. It's the safest bet there is. Give Him one good work, and he'll always give you back ten. I've never glimpsed so much pleasure, in the purest sense of the word, when working in the fields or on retreat. There were little fleeting glimpses of pleasure at doing something for others. I'm not being pious, but I would get nothing like that sensation out of racing. You couldn't compare ten Derby winners or ten Gold Cup winners with that.

I had fully intended to go back to the seminary and pick up where I had left off. Racing didn't particularly interest me at that stage of my life. But when I returned I just could not get back into the swing of things. There were so many years to get through before I became ordained, and my health wouldn't have stood it.

I got a lot of headaches. Whether I was trying to drive myself too hard to catch up, because the studying there was extremely demanding, or maybe I went back too quickly, I don't know, but I couldn't get going as I had done previously. Possibly, the illness took more out of me than I thought it had. It was a long time to be lying on your back. I just couldn't concentrate. The priests were very sympathetic and fully understood what I'd been through. But after a couple of months, and having given it a long, hard thought, I decided to leave. It wasn't for me.

I was twenty-two. My parents didn't try and dissuade me, neither did the priests. They said to think about it, pray about it and leave it in God's hands. I left and said there might be something else in life for me. I always thought the Fellow Above would give me a nod in some way – although He probably had second thoughts before nodding me towards what I'm doing at the moment! As I was leaving, the head priest said, 'Barney, anything you want to do, you can do it.' Somehow, I don't think he had in mind what I ended up doing.

I didn't regret my decision, but I will always look back on that as a crucial part of my life. It was wonderful training for life. It gave me something that you can't buy: the ability to think clearly. It also gave me the ability to assess people very quickly. I reckon I can weigh most people up in two minutes. It gave me confidence to stand up against anyone, head to head. It taught me values that were really important in life. To think of your fellow man; to be charitable to people; that we're all the same, whatever our colour or creed. That has stayed with me. Even the lads in the yard and other people who have worked for me, I take an interest in what they're doing, if they've got any problems – they're not just numbers or commodities.

It's nice to have winners, but it doesn't really make any difference to me. I have a competitive edge, I like to give of my best, but not for any worldly glory or financial gain. If I lived my life again I'd volunteer to go to Manchester, which was a very tough existence and transformed me from a boy into a man, and study for the priesthood. Both those experiences shaped my life for the better. Since then, I have never regarded myself as a religious man, although I do go to church regularly on Sundays. It's only half an hour in the week to give to your Maker. That's nothing. But I do believe in God, and I do believe we have to give an account of our stewardship in life and we will be judged on how we treat our fellow man. But He's every man's God and very merciful.

SEVEN

Victim on 'Murder Mile'

I had made a fleeting acquaintance with death, but escaped the full welcoming handshake from our Maker. It changed my whole attitude to life.

During my holidays from college I had worked for a large Irvinestown-based firm named J.J. Scallon, selling lime to farmers in Fermanagh and Tyrone. There was no basic wage, but I made half a crown commission for every ton I sold. It was a great job because I had use of the van out of work hours, and, more importantly, I learnt a lot from Eugene Scallon, who ran that side of the operation.

As it turned out, I didn't make a bad salesmen. It sharpened me up, because, until then, I never knew much about business. J.J. Scallon had risen to prominence as road contractors and had then branched out. Eugene, one of the sons, who was a little older than me, had started his own business in Omagh. When I left Mungret College I worked for him again for around six months, this time selling oil to farmers. It is the only time in my adult life that I've had a full-time occupation and been an employee.

I had a great regard for Eugene. He was a thoroughly upright character and never encouraged you to cheat customers, which wouldn't have been the case everywhere in the area at the time. He emphasised that if you delivered fifteen tons of lime to someone you charged them for fifteen tons, not for twenty.

There was always a close association between the Curleys and the Scallons. My brother had worked for them as a labourer on the roads, and my eldest sister, Mary, went to work in the office at Scallon's before she married Dolan McBride from Omagh, who now runs a pub and nightclub in the town.

Anyone who has survived TB will testify as to what a debilitating illness it is. I needed a year's convalescence. It was during this period that I bumped into an acquaintance of my father named John James McManus, a second-hand car dealer, among other trades, in Enniskillen. He brought cars over from England and Scotland and sold them in Northern Ireland. 'I've got a nice car, would suit you,' he said in that familiar manner of his ilk. He had assessed his potential customer expertly. The car was a big red Zephyr, one of the top motors at the time and very luxurious. I was determined to buy it. You always remember your first car, and the number plate was CXS 279. It was about £200 and there was no way I could afford it. I was virtually penniless. 'Money's not a problem,' he shrugged with a knowing laugh. I asked him what he meant. 'Oh, I'll do a little doctoring of the books,' he explained. 'I'll put you down for a deposit which you don't have to pay, and the remainder I'll get on hire-purchase for you.' I also got insurance on credit from a friend in the town called Billy Charlton who was later to figure prominently in my life. Billy had a finger in so many pies that it would have needed a master pastry-maker to keep up with his wheeling and dealing. If only all business transactions were that easy. I was on the road without having to cough up a penny.

A few months went past and there had been no payments to the HP company forthcoming. John James made it clear that I'd have to start paying my instalments somehow. The only business with quick, easy money in it was smuggling – taking goods into the South where they were either scarce or of poorer quality. I hit on the scheme of 'exporting' Gillette razor blades into the Republic. The blades just weren't as good quality down South and they were far more expensive. Most importantly, a large quantity could be secreted in a relatively small space.

I bought them from a big supermarket in Enniskillen, where they'd sell you goods wholesale if the orders were big enough. There were no questions asked if you paid cash. I was forced to borrow the money to buy the blades from John James with the promise of repaying him once I sold them in the South. Those Zephyrs had big doors and I'd remove the inside covers of all four before packing in an enormous amount of blades. I'd be carrying, say, 120 packets and getting £2 a packet profit from them – which was not to be sniffed at then.

Whatever scheme I've devised in life, trust in my lieutenants and foot-soldiers has been crucial. This was no exception. I'd take along a fellow named Francie Maguire, who was much older than myself and on whom I knew I could depend. We'd pull up at the Customs post and the Customs officers would just have a perfunctory squint inside and maybe open up the boot. To all outward appearances we were just young fellows out for a drink in the South, or maybe off to a dance. Nothing was ever said. The worst thing that could happen to you was that they'd seize your car and your goods, plus you'd get a fine, which would effectively put you out of business.

We'd cross the border at different points. Obviously, the patrols would get suspicious if you crossed at the same place every few days. So, we inter-changed between Swanlinbar, Belleek, Clones and Aughnacloy, none of which were a long run from home. We'd choose appropriate times to avoid detection. If there was, say, a football match in Clones on a Sunday, we'd cross there and it would be assumed we were football fans. The road through Belleek led into Bundoran which was a big seaside resort, and if you went on a Sunday with the hundreds of other cars it would be assumed you were holidaymakers. If there was a dance at Swanlinbar we'd go then. Like my betting later on, it was a question of doing your homework.

We went through the proper channels, whereas when my father was doing it he'd go through all the back roads. We didn't attract much attention. We hardly had the look of hardened gun-runners or drugs-traffickers. Once across the border it would take three or four days to dispose of the blades, mostly direct to shops in towns down the west coast and Limerick.

We probably made approaching 100 trips over a period of a year or so. On the return journeys I'd try and look in at a race meeting to multiply up the profits. By this time I was twenty-three and still only betting small amounts. I was learning the hard way about horses and gambling. When I first started in earnest, I was betting anything up to £50 but ending up leaving most of it in the bookies' satchels. I was still an innocent when it came to gambling and getting value, and was no great judge of horses, either. I went round with John James McManus, the fellow who sold me my first car, and he helped me open a betting account with a bookmaker called Davy Meehan. Davy inquired, 'How much is he worth?' My pal replied, 'Oh, give him £300 credit.'

Now, at that time £300 would have bought you two decent motor cars. Of course, being the impulsive young man that I was, I ran up that amount in a few days and I had no money to settle the debt. It was fortunate he didn't give me £3,000, because I'd have probably got through that just as easily. I decided it was prudent to avoid Davy, who was a prominent bookmaker in the South, but at least I knew I could attend Northern meetings because he didn't bet at those. One day I turned up at Downpatrick, where, to my dismay, I walked straight into Davy.

'I'm sorry,' I blustered. 'I haven't a sausage.'

'I can believe that,' he said wryly, but added, to my relief, 'Pay me back when you can.'

I did eventually honour my debt to him, although about three years too late. I will never forget his kindness. He was what we call in Ireland a 'decent man'. Some years later, when I was living in England, I got a phone call from my friend Joe 'Big Bucks' Donnelly to say that Davy wouldn't last the week. I flew over to Dublin to say my goodbyes. I say a prayer for him every day.

I have always attributed my initial fascination with the racecourse to those days out from college with Bobby Barry and his father Jim, but another venture in my mid-twenties was to give a sharper edge to my latent gambling reflexes and greatly enhance my education. I joined 'the enemy' and set myself up as a bookmaker, ironically enough at the scene of my father's greatest disgrace, Celtic Park. I thought it would be easy money. Nothing could have been further from the truth.

I applied to the McAlindens for a betting pitch, and was allocated one which allowed me to bet in a notorious area of the track known as 'Murder Mile'. The reputable, long-standing, big-money bookies operated as normal by the side of the track, but a group of us, perhaps a dozen, were up on the hill, which got its epithet because it was reckoned every hoodlum in the county was there making a book and any unsuspecting punter would get murdered – metaphorically, of course.

My companions there were like me – pot-less and chancers. I never had any money and I had to borrow it to make a book. The sources were varied, but all possessed a common degree of doubt whether they'd ever get it repaid by the following morning. My principal source was one of my cousins, Angela McElholm, now Angela Maguire, who used to run a hairdressing salon. I'd drop in at four o'clock and 'borrow' the takings out of the till and promise to pay her back the next day.

Another ruse involved Cathal McDonald, who ran a pub called the U-Cum-Inn in Dromore and was always a ready source of cash. If Angela was running short of money, Cathal was always my next port of call. He'd cash a cheque for me without any question. I'd go to the dogs, hoping to win enough to have the money in the bank over the next couple of days, so that the cheque would clear. Many's the time it didn't.

The final possibility was another cousin, John Carney, who was then the local breadman. People living in isolated communities out in the country depended on his service, and at the allotted time they'd stand outside at the end of their lane, where it joined the main road, and wait for him. John had much in common with my father. He was a fanatical greyhound man, frequently to the detriment of all his responsibilities. As likely as not, come three o'clock, just like my father, he'd glance at his watch and finish work, and he'd roar past them to get to the track and place his bets, pretending he hadn't noticed his customers, who were left standing empty-handed.

Not that I was too concerned about his customers. My only interest was the cash he had in his satchel. As a rule, John was a good businessman and always had a few spare pounds. He didn't bank his money until Saturday morning and often used to lend me a few notes as a float on the race-evenings, Mondays, Wednesdays and Thursdays. The only problem was that it was the firm's money and he'd want it back the next morning, which could prove difficult if it had been a bad night. There would be a right old panic and he would come hammering on my bedroom door at my mother's, which I'd carefully locked before retiring. I'd pretend to be asleep and if he didn't take the hint I would just bellow, 'Leave me alone.' Usually, he gave up until later.

John also owned greyhounds, one of which he called Green Sash, although there was nothing deliberately provocative about it. He used to run the dog at Dunmore Park, which was a fiercely Protestant area. He may as well have shouted: 'Up the IRA!' That dog was nothing but trouble. One night he was inadvertently responsible for starting a riot in Dunmore Park. There was a scheme going on where a heavily backed dog was expected to win; unfortunately it got left several lengths in the traps. The hare-driver was in collusion with the people behind the scheme and slowed the hare. In all the confusion, John's greyhound, who was nothing like the same class, and a long price, came through and won. It didn't go down well and there was such a disturbance that the place was closed down for a fortnight.

If you are making a book the theory is that, with a certain caution, you should end up with some percentage of profit, however small; however, I approached it with the attitude of a greenhorn gambler. I'd turn up with maybe £30 or £40 and set out with the intention of making £100 on the first race. I'd stand there bold as brass and lay the favourite at any price and invariably got knocked out. That would be the finish of me. It was exciting to be part of it all, but really I had no idea what I was doing. To make it all the more embarrassing, the fellow on the next pitch was Jimmy Nelson, a gambler at heart and one of the best I've ever seen. He was only up there with us because he enjoyed the company – and so that he could look down at the serious bookmakers and see the prices they were chalking. If there was a dog he liked he'd send one of his three or four runners down with the instruction to 'leave no prices on the board'. I loved to hear that phrase and yearned for the day when I could do likewise. He'd bet £1,000 at a time, even then.

That would be a long time coming for me. At the time I was ending up with an empty satchel 90 per cent of the time. The first race of the night was normally a trial event, where some dog would suddenly find a lot of time on his previous best. The punters always appeared to be clued up, but I wasn't. As often as not I'd be wiped out. Undeterred, and after watching Jimmy in action, I decided one night that a more profitable ploy to set me up for the rest of the night was to have a bet on the hot favourite in the first race. I had no cash, but there was a chap down below among the serious bookmakers called Danny McGarry – 'Little Danny' as we called him, because of his diminutive frame, although in terms of laying a bet he was one of the biggest bookmakers around at the time – and I'd often had to send down and borrow £30 or £40 to keep me going during the rest of the meeting. Without a pound to my name, I strolled down to him and shouted out, as cocky as you like, 'An even hundred on the favourite, Danny.' Belfast people have a wonderful sense of humour and, as quick as a flash, he turned to me with a grin all over his face and just said, 'Stick it in the net, Barney. You'll get twice as much back if he wins.' Which was as polite a put-down as he could muster of declaring that where a certain B. Curley was concerned, it was cash bets only. He knew all about my reputation.

The put-down was for my own good. In hindsight, I appreciated it. The next race night we were walking in together and he took me for a cup of tea. A highly religious man who went to mass every day, Danny became like a father figure to me. He told me firmly, 'This is the end. You're on the way to disaster. You are not a bookmaker. All you want to do is gamble.' He persuaded me that I was on the road to ruination. I took his advice and a couple of months later I packed it in. Before I did so, Danny, always sartorially elegant himself, had taken me to his tailor and got me fitted out for a suit which raised my reputation and my self-esteem. I will always thank him for giving me a very important education.

I only lasted as a bookmaker at Celtic Park for around six months. But one legacy was that I first met Sean Graham there, although I should stress he was one of the respected 'layers', not up with us on 'Murder Mile'. Meanwhile, I was having great fun, driving my Zephyr up and down the country. It was a wonderful car and petrol was not expensive. You could drive all day and all night for next to nothing. I made a lot of contacts in the South who were to become important to me in the next stage of my life. Completely out of the blue a fellow named 'Pio' McCann, who lived in one of the neighbouring villages, knocked at my door and asked me if I would manage his pop band.

EIGHT

Getting the show on the road

To this day, I still have no idea why 'Pio' – his nickname was derived from his initials, P.O. – picked on me. We knew of each other by name but that was about it. I can only conclude that someone had told him that, working for Scallons, I must be fairly shrewd and businesslike. Anyway, whatever his rationale, he just turned up on my doorstep one evening and told me he was a guitarist and singer in a showband called The Claxton. If they had a proper manager, they could hit the big-time.

Showbands were a uniquely Irish phenomenon and the equivalent of English pop groups, although in my opinion they were better. They had a fuller sound, consisting of a drummer, lead singer, two guitarists, and maybe a tenor saxophone, trombone, trumpet player or piano player. There were usually seven or eight of them compared with their counterparts across the Irish Sea whose normal line-up consisted of three guitarists, who also sang, and a drummer.

It was a daunting schedule. They'd play six nights a week, and they were long sessions, too, into the early hours of the morning, with only Monday off. Most of them were working during the day as barbers or postmen – all manner of jobs. They all had long hair, or so it was considered at the time, just like the Beatles. Inevitably they played a lot of the Liverpool lads' material, as well as all the other big pop hits of the day. It was a wonderful sound and the youngsters loved it. Even I could appreciate it. More pertinently, from my point of view, there was plenty of money in it, a ready source of 'Mister Greens' to use the colloquialism of the day.

Most of the boys couldn't read music, but that didn't detract from performances. In fact, it probably enhanced it. Their enthusiasm, sense of rhythm and the variety of instruments made it more enjoyable than the English pop bands being spawned at the same time, talented though some of them were. Looking back, I should have seized the opportunity eagerly. But I had lived something of a sheltered life, the last few years particularly so, and I wasn't convinced.

I looked at 'Pio' and thought to myself, 'Is this man a penny short of the full shilling?' I said to him, 'What did I do to deserve an evening like this? I know nothing about pop music. You've been misinformed; I know nothing about it.' Apart from learning a little about classical composers at college, I had absolutely no interest in music. If they'd asked me what a quaver was, I'd probably have thought it was a member of a religious sect. I didn't even know what was No. 1 in the charts. 'Pio' was a real loquacious character, and would not take 'no' for an answer. He just kept reiterating that they thought I'd be good at it. He spent three or four hours trying to convince me. Eventually, I got rid of him, but 'Pio' just kept returning, perhaps four or five times. He approached it from all different angles. When the lure of money didn't attract me, he'd come back with another move. Eventually, I succumbed and said I'd give it a try. That was unusual for me, because normally I stick to my guns.

It was ridiculous. I'd never been in a dance hall or attended a disco in my life and there I was, with nothing more than an empty diary, a telephone and maybe an adequate degree of salesmanship, starting from scratch to make a group of lads that nobody had really heard of into pop stars.

As I pondered the prospect it brought back memories of my family's last venture into the music business. When I was a child, my grandfather, Tommy Curley, had been leader of a twenty-strong brass band, consisting mostly of Curleys and Carneys, who toured pubs in outlying villages, collecting donations on the way. It was a popular attraction. I was roped in myself as a ten-year-old, although, having absolutely no talent and having proved that I was never going to master the trumpet or trombone, I was given the not particularly onerous task of playing the triangle.

Whatever else you could say about Tommy, he was undoubtedly the best-dressed man in the county. He always set out with a smart suit, starched shirt and gold watch on a fob. His problem, one that he obviously passed on through his genes, was that he was inclined to take a drink at every hostelry in which the band performed. By the end of the night, he had to be thrown on the back seat of the bus and taken home, oblivious to what was going on around him. The other band members enjoyed winding him up by sticking a knife into the slot of the collecting tin and removing the cash while he was snoring away. By the time he got back home he was in such a dishevelled state that you wouldn't have recognised the man who set out and my grandmother, 'Ma' Curley as she was known, gave him a real tongue-lashing.

Like my father, Tommy was a dealer during the day, visiting farms in his pony and trap and buying up fowl and eggs, selling them on to wholesalers who shipped them to the mainland. He would regularly go to the market in Pettigo, about eleven miles away on the Fermanagh-Donegal border. Again alcohol took its toll by the end of the day and legend had it that the pony knew its way home and would deliver my grandfather to his front door while, the worse for wear, he slept it off in the back. So, encouraged by such tenuous family links with showbusiness, I began my new life as an impresario. My job was simple enough: to get dates for the boys and negotiate payments. It was selling by any other name, knocking on doors and telephoning people. The Claxton was a small-time band with big ideas. They had been playing in a very confined area, within a radius of about twenty to thirty miles of Irvinestown and Omagh, mostly just in village halls, and were determined to get into the major venues in the towns and cities.

No matter what I threw myself into, I could always catch on quickly and was soon into the swing of things. I was fortunate in that I knew someone in virtually every big place in Ireland through my horseracing contacts. I got what I could for them, but initially the money was of secondary importance. They were virtual unknowns outside their own community and it was important that they just got out and established a reputation. In those early days, they would only make, say, £30 a night split between them – and I got 20 per cent of the take.

But I had my eye on bigger things. They wanted to be stars and I was reaching for them. During this period, a lot of big halls in the South had opened up. One, in particular, was in a village called Dromkeen, just outside Limerick City. It was a vast place, attracting 3,000 people there to dances on a Sunday night, and that's where I wanted my boys to perform. In the winter of 1963 I got it – my first big-time booking. To wheedle my way in I got rather carried away, hyping up The Claxton to a ridiculous extent. I called the owner, Packy Hayes, having been introduced to him by one of my racing associates, and gave him the full spiel about this absolutely fantastic band. There was no question, as far as I was concerned, that we should be given a date and made top of the bill for the Sunday night dance. That's how, with much economy with the truth and a liberal quantity of deceit, I got my boys in as the top act at one of Ireland's prime venues, supported, if you will, by another group of 'unknowns'. The Claxton were billed as 'The latest sensation from Northern Ireland' and they were, so the publicity went, 'Going right to the top'. I was feeling mighty pleased with myself.

There were a lot of top acts from the North at the time, particularly from Derry City, where the number one band was called Clipper Carlton. So this was a considerable achievement. This was the big-time already, and I'd only just begun. In addition, we were to be paid a fortune for those early days, about £50, so I couldn't have felt more chuffed with myself if they'd made me president of Ireland. I was strutting around like the most prized peacock.

The boys had never experienced anything like this before. As we approached the venue, the route was lined with posters emblazoned with photographs of the lead singer, Jimmy Magee, who, it must be said, had a superb voice. We all felt very proud, and the fellows in the band were of the heartfelt opinion that I must be the best manager of all time.

The boys made their entrance and started singing, and, from where I was standing near the stage, it all seemed to go fine. At least, nothing was said until after the show. Then the owner called me over, looked me in the eye, and muttered grimly, 'Barney, never, ever, do anything like that again.' Well, that brought me down from Cloud Nine; yet for the life of me I couldn't understand what he meant. What we'd apparently failed to take into account was that our band only carried amplification equipment to fill small halls and audiences of 150. This gigantic hall needed an extremely powerful system to fill it and the result was that the whole performance was just tinny and insignificant if you were any distance from the stage. The audience, apparently, couldn't hear a single word and the music had no substance to it. The management had been, by all account, besieged with complaints all night. It had been like playing a transistor radio in the middle of a football pitch. I had no idea about such electrical engineering logistics. As long as they were making a noise, it was fine by me. Well, somehow we got paid and we made our way home chastened by the whole experience. There was plenty of time to think about what had happened and to take stock. The roads were so bad then that we didn't arrive home until nine or ten the next morning, me in my car, the boys in the van.

Not long after, I made the long haul back to the dance hall and apologised. It was no laughing matter. I realised what mayhem I could have caused; there could have been a riot. Packy appreciated me for doing that and, in time, we actually became quite good friends. But I knew it was time to take stock; it was one thing selling a band to unsuspecting dance hall owners; our reputation would dwindle to nothing if the band didn't have the professionalism to go with it. I had deluded myself, or perhaps just been deluded. I thought these were the greatest musicians in the world; I'd been going along with what they'd said to me. It brought all of us down to earth and the conclusion was that we disband the act and start afresh.

I had got to know quite a few people in the business and I was receiving some good advice. I recognised that what was wanted was good amplification, no matter what it cost, and to weed out the weaker members. In all honesty, it hadn't been just the amplifiers; there were also too many passengers holding back the good musicians. So we got a new, professional band on the road, with new equipment and they all got new suits. We also changed the lead singer, not because he wasn't any good, but because Jimmy Magee wanted to concentrate on the family business, a coachworks, and didn't want to turn professional.

We amalgamated two local bands, The Claxton and the Polka Dots. We kept the latter's name and I selected the best out of the two for the new line-up. I was beginning to develop an ear for pop music and what people enjoyed dancing to. I may have been a relative novice but I was unstinting in my desire to get things right. I'd do a lot of my own market research, just strolling around and chatting to the punters. In the halls at the time their favourite was Fats Domino. It had a good beat for dancing.

The Polka Dots thus came into being, culminating with the lead singer recording a solo single and becoming the first Irish artist to enter the English Top Twenty. His name was Frankie McBride, from Omagh – always a talented town for musicians – and the song was 'Five Little Fingers'. I was there in the recording studio when he made the record. The engineer, who was known to be a good judge, told me it was going to be a winner.

Of course, if someone like Frankie suddenly made it into the charts, it created new problems. Like the fact that future dates had been sold too cheaply. The solution was that I conveniently lost the booking book, where dates and fees were recorded. Instead of £40 a night, I'd say it was £300, feigning ignorance about the originally agreed sum – with an artiste in the charts we could ask for virtually what we liked. He was a wonderful singer and it was a mystery to me how he didn't really make the big time. In my view he was Sinatra-class. But he was a sanguine, easy-going sort of fellow and I think it was because he wanted to stay in Ireland and not go to England or America. When I last heard, Frankie was still crooning over in London.

The Polka Dots became popular and made records in their own right. Their songs were played on all the Irish radio stations and they performed around the country, and in England and Scotland, for twelve months. We did a lot of rock 'n' roll, and Chuck Berry and Elvis Presley numbers were particular popular with the band and their audiences. They were very exciting times. But it was an arduous routine. We would leave maybe at 10 am, drive down to Clonakilty in south Cork, get there at 7 pm, get on stage at ten, play to one or two – they'd often play for two and a half to three hours, non-stop – then drive back, not returning home before eleven or twelve the next day. But that was the price of stardom. They had become household names in the Republic.

I normally went along because it was important to know how your band had gone down with the audience. I was a great one for feedback and you needed to keep your wits about you. It was not just a matter of booking dates any place, any time; you wanted your venues to be packed, so you had to think carefully about where to place the band and keep them away from their rivals, of which there were about five or six big acts at the time.

Inevitably, the success of the Polka Dots and my rising reputation in the music world brought me offers from other bands. Some splendidly exotic names were brought within the Curley stable of stars. I had Brian Call and The Buckaroos and Hugo Duncan and the Tall Men. Members of those bands are all still singing and playing in Ireland.

Some were a phenomenal success. It was Easter Sunday 1971 when Hugo and the boys first took to the road. By October of that year, Hugo's rendition of 'Dear God' had stormed to No. 1 in the Irish charts, and stayed there for no fewer than twenty-two weeks. I had numerous offers to buy the contract of the young 'superstar', but I told them all: 'I wouldn't accept £50,000.'

A lot of these guys were stable, family men who wanted a regular income, rather than £50 one week and £200 the next; so I did a deal with them in which I took all the money and paid them a wage. I did that for the next four or five years, during which time I was also beginning to bet seriously. You could always sell a second-class act on the back of a top one. It worked fine if you had a good band, but I ended up with three, of which one carried the other two – although the popularity of them all fluctuated. I never had the heart to tell the other two, 'You're no good, go and do something else', so I'd carry on paying them.

There were some wild nights and, despite developing a taste for the music – I quite enjoy traditional Irish and some pop music – it was still something of a culture shock for a young man who, only three years before, had been immersed in philosophy and the classics in the tranquillity of the seminary at Mungret.

It goes without saying that most of the boys enjoyed a drink and, before going on stage, would naturally down a few beers. During the session, which could last three hours, they'd have to discreetly go off to relieve themselves. At the time the venues did not possess the same safety precautions as now, with signs indicating exits, toilets and fire escapes. One night down in Kilkenny where the boys were playing at a beer festival, much to their delight, 'Pio' McCann decided he had to go to the toilet before the performance started. He dashed off the stage, strode through a door and stepped straight into space. It was twelve feet to the ground.

The band started up without him, but there were, maybe, a couple of thousand people there and soon the realisation dawned that we had no bass guitarist. The sound wasn't right. It was like the Rolling Stones playing without Keith Richards. After ten minutes we began to get concerned. Someone went out to look for Pio and he was discovered lying there in agony, hollering for help.

So badly had he injured his knee that he couldn't come back on to play. We took him off to hospital, where his knee was beginning to swell, but they just gave him some pain-killing tablets and he came back and returned, limping, to the stage. He got a rousing reception. He was no Jumping Jack Flash that night. But, as they say, the show must go on.

Some of the fellows who staged those dances were real

scoundrels. Any excuse at all they'd dock you 20 per cent, which was the usual penalty for turning up late or with a band a member short. If you promoted your band as having eight members when they booked you, that's how many there had to be on stage on the night.

One night at a gig, we were missing a man. We could only muster seven. Fortunately a student named Pat Fahey, at Queen's, Belfast, now a solicitor in Omagh, was mad about the bands and sometimes travelled with us. The trouble was he couldn't play a guitar, indeed any instrument, and he couldn't sing. We got him dressed up in a suit and put him up on the stage with a guitar, not plugged in, and he just pretended to strum away all night, looking for all the world a brilliant musician.

That kind of thing happened regularly. I suppose at a push I could have filled in myself, but I didn't exactly look the part. In the eighties and nineties a bald or shaven pate has become commonplace amongst celebrities – today it is practically compulsory – but then it just wasn't fashionable in the least.

We got smart. Ultimately, it was to prove too smart for our own good. We could see that the halls were packed with 2,000 people and yet we were taking home maybe £70 a night at best. I soon realised that the owners were getting all the money and the bands, not to mention their managers, were getting next to nothing by the time it was split up. I was one of the first to demand a percentage of the night's takings rather than a fee. It started at 50–50.

We were made under that system. Say there were 2,000 paying ten shillings. That made a £1,000 take, of which we got half. For a time we were like Arab princes, all driving about in new cars. So what if you damaged one? You simply took it to the garage and bought another. During that period it was easy come, easy go, all cash in the back pocket, and nothing so irritating as tax.

To make sure you weren't done, it was normally the road manager's job to stand at the door and count the people going in. But I was soon to gain my own personal assistant who carried out that task – my wife.

I met Maureen when I was twenty-eight. I'd known one or two girls before then but nothing very serious. I was down in Killarney with one of the bands and took time off to go to the racecourse to back a horse named Herring Gull, trained by Georgie Wells and ridden by Tommy Carberry, in a maiden hurdle. I had looked closely at the form and thought he was a good thing, although the price was nothing special; I had something like £100-to-win-£110. He duly won, although not by much. It wasn't a great feat of analysis. Herring Gull turned out to be a very decent horse and later won the Irish Grand National. Fate took a hand because if he'd got beaten I'd have departed straight away as I would have had no money, other than for petrol. But I decided to hang around and watch the other races and I got talking to Maureen.

It turned out she was from St Helen's, Lancashire, though of Irish extraction. She was nursing at the time and over on holiday with a couple of friends. I gave her one of our showband promotional cards, which would give Maureen and her friends free admission to the dance hall where the boys were performing.

She took one look at it and burst out laughing. I asked her why. 'My name's Curley, too,' she explained. It was a 50-million-to-one chance. There are very few Curleys about.

We made arrangements to meet that night at a dance and our relationship took off from there. We weren't courting for long. Although Maureen was about ten years my junior we got on immediately and I was very impressed with her outlook on life. She was so intelligent for someone so young. We got married in St Helens and I don't remember too much about it except that I had to sleep in the same room as my brother-in-law John McGrirr on the night before the wedding. He got extremely drunk and, as I had an aversion to alcohol, it was not the most pleasant night I've ever spent.

We came straight back to Irvinestown that night, together with my mother, whose house we stayed in temporarily. In the showband business back then, there was no time for such pleasures as a honeymoon. Actually, we did manage a break a few weeks later when I got a few pounds together and we went to a hotel amid the beauty and splendour of Donegal. The first day we were playing table-tennis and we were both so determined to win that Maureen knocked the table and it fell on my ankle. I was incapacitated for the rest of our time there. I had to hobble about on a stick for three or four days.

Maureen was always very well organised and practical. Before the wedding she started to question me about where we were going to live. When we first met, Maureen had the opinion that all gamblers ended up skint some time. She thought any money I had would all go again unless it was tied up in bricks and mortar. She liked everything to be paid for. To keep her off my back, I told her that I'd bought a house for us. I talked about it in glowing terms, too. Was there a drawing room? I said there was. And what was the colour scheme? I said I'd get it painted whatever colour she wanted. Which was all very unfortunate. It was all in my imagination. She rang me from England, and was talking about the colour scheme.

'Will you get the living room papered?'

'Of course,' I agreed.

It was ten days before the wedding and I was starting to panic, because there was still no house on the horizon. Fortunately, I bumped into my old pal Billy Charlton outside my solicitor's office in Irvinestown.

He said, 'I hear you're getting married? Where are you going to live?'

I said, 'I don't have any place.'

'I've got the house for you,' he said. 'It'll be ideal.'

It turned out that he owned one in Omagh. It had been rented out to an Army major and had everything: furniture, fittings, cutlery and crockery. It would cost £2,000.

I said, 'Billy, there's only one snag. I don't have enough money.'

He was always a streetwise fellow and said, 'Never you mind, we can work something here.'

There was an obliging Allied Irish Bank manager in Omagh and he was our best chance of a loan. He was always a good man to approach after lunch, when he'd had a few drinks. The first problem was that I had no job, but Billy said, 'You spin him this line, that you're big in business, that you're exporting tyres.' Well, I was in a sense, although, to be more accurate, I was smuggling them at that time. But at least I was able to support that application for a mortgage with all the receipts I had from ATS in Omagh who had supplied my tyres. The second problem was that I had no money to put down. We used the same scam as we had for my first car. I'd pretended to give Billy a £1,000 deposit for the house, and he'd organised the documentation to confirm it. I told the bank manager that the house was costing £3,000, that I was putting up one-third and I was looking for the outstanding two-thirds, or £2,000, from the bank. The banker fell for it and I got the money for the house which was £2,000.

Billy Charlton was also responsible for getting me involved in a distinctly dubious business venture in England, where we started the Cosmopolitan Insurance Company with offices based in Barnet. He was a genius, but could never stick with anything, which was probably fortunate in this case.

We'd fly over to London every Monday morning and return to Irvinestown on Friday nights. In between we'd spend the week travelling around London in a chauffeur-driven black

Rover spending money as though it was going out of fashion. We were the original high-flyers. The locals in Irvinestown must have thought we were robbing banks.

I was still an innocent in many ways and I genuinely had no real idea what was going on. I didn't set out to cheat anyone, but it was a scam. We placed adverts for car insurance, our clients duly paid their money for their policies and the cheques were flowing in, but we never considered the possibility of having to pay out for claims. Doctor Emil Savundra tried a similar scheme and was jailed. He was arrested for fraud in February 1967 after his extraordinary TV inquisition by David Frost. Savundra was Chairman of the Fire, Auto and Marine Insurance Company which had collapsed the previous year with losses of £1.4 million. Many people did not get paid out on claims, and during the Frost interview, when many of his victims were present, Savundra said, 'I do not want to cross swords with the peasants.' We were at the same scheme, though on a lesser scale, and they couldn't cope with an investigation into us as well. Fortunately, my solicitor in London told me, 'You'll have to resign or you'll go to jail.'

The week after Savundra was arrested, the Board of Trade Directors came to see Billy. I don't think they wanted two cases on their hands, and compared to Savundra we were probably small fry. The essence of their message to him was, 'You have a choice. You either close up or we'll arrest you.' Billy closed up.

Billy died not long ago and he is one of the people I pray for every day. Another is my solicitor from those days, Turlough Montague. I still do business with his son, Andrew, who is involved with DAFA and was out in Zambia with me early in 1998.

At one stage I became a bit of a jack-the-lad. I was running around, writing out cheques here, there and everywhere as if there were no tomorrow. Turlough called me in one morning and asked me how things were going.

'Oh, fine,' I said.

He surveyed me with a concerned countenance and said, 'Have you a cheque book?'

I said, 'I do.'

'Can I see it?'

When I handed it over he just opened his drawer and laid it inside. 'There,' he said. 'I don't hear very good reports about you.'

I started to bluster my innocence. But he said, 'Stop the messing. I'm setting you up with a good bank in Irvinestown and when you write cheques you have money in the bank to meet them. That's the way banking works.'

It was a lesson well learnt and I never looked back.

So the house in Cannon Hill, Omagh, was mine. And I had gained domestic peace. It was a bungalow, had three bedrooms, and was a splendid property. We lived there for about three years, although initially, just like my purchase of the motor car, there was no money to make the loan repayments. Fortunately, it was not a big problem because the showbands were fast becoming a lucrative source of income by then.

We had been in the bungalow two or three years when 'Pio' McCann announced he was getting married. He came from the Catholic town of Dromore and his wife-to-be, Rae, came from Ardstraw in Tyrone, a very Protestant area, and that was frowned upon to say the least. Both families were disgusted with them. In fact, it would be true to say that both their lives were very much in danger at that time. Patsy was getting really wound up and complaining to me. They were having trouble buying a house, because neither of their families would help out. I said they could have ours. We moved out virtually on the spot, went to my mother's for a couple of weeks and then we moved to a flat in a Georgian house, a really nice place, on the

Dublin Road. We lived there for two years before taking the decision to move to the South.

Pio was one of the mainstays in the band, so I had to get him fixed up somehow. I also got him a loan from the bank. (He's still living in that house today – it's what I call 'a lucky house' – and they've had five children.) He downed that brown ale like it was water and had one fiery bad temper; he was highly strung and always fighting with everyone, but Rae kept him on the straight and narrow.

He thought I was God Almighty. No matter what he wanted, he thought that I could fix it. Now a disc-jockey and radio presenter in Omagh – I went there recently to find that, to my amusement, Pio was the local 'celebrity' who was to switch on the Christmas lights – he always had grandiose ideas; and they didn't just end with acquiring my expertise. Pio, who sang and played bass guitar and was a great aficionado of Fats Domino, acted as my lieutenant and was always trying to sign up new singers for our band. Running a band was like managing a professional football team nowadays, with big money involved in transfers. Pio always wanted to prise the big stars away from other bands for his band. He'd say to some fellow he thought was a star in the making, 'Come to us and we'll pay you £200 a week,' and the band might only be earning £200 a week in total.

He attempted to persuade a girl singer, called Margot, sister of Daniel O'Donnell, who is a big star in Ireland now, to perform with us. God only knows what he offered her. And he'd say, 'Oh, Barney'll give it to you.' Suffice to say I didn't. However, one singer he did persuade me to hire was Mary McGonigle. She was a really top-class performer whose beautiful voice was more usually found filling Carnegie Hall than the village hall. It cost us big bucks to hire her, rather like persuading Eric Cantona to go to Manchester United, but we considered it worthwhile because it drew in people to listen to the band. Her first date with us was at the Town Hall, Killarney, and the place was jam-packed. There was a grand introduction: 'And now, straight from Carnegie Hall ... ' At that moment our lead guitarist was supposed to play her in, but he was in the wrong key and it was far too high for her. It threw her completely, there was no way she could reach the note and she just broke down on stage. She had to be taken off and never returned that night. Mary 'not quite straight from Carnegie Hall' McGonigle was distraught. Probably nothing like that had happened to someone of her calibre before. I was standing at the back and you can imagine my embarrassment. Fortunately, she didn't take it too badly and sang with us on later nights.

The smuggling was always in the back of my mind because it was such easy money. I hit on another ruse. It was well known that the tyres manufactured in the South weren't up to much. The ones they made in Cork at the time would maybe last only 10,000 miles. Yet, they weren't allowed to import Michelins, which were, of course, a very good brand, and available in the North. The bands worked Wednesday to Sunday nights, so, apart from making bookings, I had Monday and Tuesday free. I was aided and abetted by another cousin of mine, Herbie McElholm, brother of Angela who ran the hairdressing salon. He was the 'roadie' and driver for one of the bands.

It's surprising how small a size a deflated tyre can be compressed into if it's tied up with string. We'd load them into one of the Ford Transit vans used by the bands and would hide them with their equipment: the drum kit, the guitars and the trumpets and so on. Those tyres were like gold-dust because they would last five times as many miles. We'd take up to thirty tyres, and an excellent money-making racket it was, too. They cost maybe £3 or £4 each, from a big depot in Omagh with no questions asked. We sold them to garages and individuals for about £10. It was so easy. Everybody wanted them. We did a trip nearly every Monday.

Again, we didn't normally create any suspicion. There was a continuous stream of showbands travelling down to the South. We had the name of the bands on the side of the vans so it was a great facade for what we were really up to. One Monday morning was different. We had a full load of tyres and had crossed the border at Butler's Bridge and had gone through Cavan Town when we turned a corner and ran straight into a Garda checkpoint. (I think we found out later there'd been a robbery and they were on the lookout for suspects.)

Herbie was driving and I was 'riding shotgun', as they used to call it. I remember Herbie screaming, 'Jesus Christ, I'll never see Breda and the children again. We'll get twenty years for this!' I was always very cool and I said, 'Herbie, now just settle down. Be yourself. Be calm.'

Now, we couldn't turn back, as that would have aroused suspicion anyway, so we pulled up when the Garda stopped us. By chance, on the way down I'd been reading all about Cavan football team in the newspaper, about how unlucky they had been in defeat the previous day. So, I said to the fellow who stopped us, 'Were you at the football yesterday?'

'Oh, indeed I was.'

And I got into a conversation with him about the match, about how some player had missed an easy 'free'. I said, 'Did you ever see anything like it?'

I had struck lucky because he was a big fan. Meanwhile the traffic was building up behind us and people were getting impatient. Eventually, he just asked, 'What have you on board, boys?'

I said casually, 'Oh, showband equipment.'

'Where are you going?'

'Wexford.' It was a long way down South. I said we were going to some hotel or other.

He glanced quickly at all the equipment. 'Alright, boys,' he said. 'You've got a long journey.' And off we set.

That was the nearest we ever came to being caught. I don't think Herbie ever came on any more trips and I packed it in myself after a couple more. The bands were getting busier and you had to think to yourself, 'if we're caught the group is ruined' – it would have been terribly bad publicity.

The band members had no idea what I was up to. At that time in Northern Ireland there wasn't much work and it needed enterprise to make money, unless you went to England. I was one of many smugglers at the time.

Any free time I had was spent at race meetings and I tried to time it so that I could look in on the way back from a smuggling trip. All the time I was learning about racing, although it still hadn't crossed my mind to go into it seriously. Until then I was as big a mug punter as everyone else. I didn't bet big, but in London taxi drivers' terminology I was doing 'the knowledge'. I'd see how the horses looked and watch the races very closely until it got to the stage where I thought I was a fair race-reader. I'd be looking for a horse that I thought was unlucky, or one that needed a different trip.

I was increasingly dividing my time between the bands and betting. I would have been punting in multiples of a hundred occasionally, but not regularly.

By now Maureen had given birth to our first daughter, Catherine, who was born in 1969. She often accompanied us to the dances as well. She must have been the best-travelled child in the world. There were all kinds of fiddles perpetrated by the dance hall owners and Maureen would count the money on the door while I was sorting out the band members' welfare.

The boys tended to get a bit hyperactive after gigs and needed winding down, like footballers after a match. I kept an eye on the chaos, otherwise there could be trouble, with their drinking and their desire to impress the girls, but I never had a problem, personally, on either count. It was so embarrassing as the boys charmed the girls with their dancing technique during songs whereas the manager couldn't put one foot in front of the other. They'd all be gesturing from the stage, taking the mickey.

Drinking and performing were virtually inseparable activities, but I soon discovered there was drug-taking going on, too. I turned a blind eye because hard drugs weren't involved; it was mostly what were then called 'purple hearts'. But on one occasion it was all too evident. I went down to the newsagents in Omagh to collect the papers at about 9.30 am one morning and found one of our guitarists all dressed up with his band suit on. He was so spaced out that his timing had gone. He thought it was evening. I asked him how he was.

'Oh,' he said, in an annoyed tone. 'These fellows are always late. They're already half an hour late.'

I didn't know a lot about drugs but I knew that with him in his condition there was no point lecturing him on the folly of his ways. But it was, at the very least, potentially embarrassing, so I hauled him into my car and I brought him up to the house. We got him into an armchair, but then the chair fell apart. It was like a Whitehall farce. Eventually we settled him down and Maureen had him rambling on for hours until he eventually came down from whatever he was on.

I can't say I was always a model of restraint myself. There was one night in Omagh about which I still feel shame to this day, although I do have an excuse. We all went along to an all-night concert, at which Luke Kelly of The Dubliners was performing. There must have been 7–8,000 of us there. Maureen had earache and went home, but I stayed on. I can only think that someone spiked my drink, because I landed up on the stage, reeling about and behaving like an absolute idiot. And there I was, supposedly a pillar of the local community. I also parked my car in the middle of the street and blocked all the traffic. Maureen was not at all pleased when she heard about it. It was a fierce let-down to do that in front of all your friends.

In our heyday I'd organise three-week tours on the mainland, taking in The Ardee in Manchester, The Harp in Birmingham, before moving on to London where there were, and still are, big Irish communities. We'd play The Gresham at the top end of Holloway Road, and The Galtymore in Cricklewood and The Buffalo in Camden Town. It was all a complete contrast to my Jesuit College days, and I often thought about the incongruity of that; but I just felt that was what God wanted for me. I have always been a fatalist. Whatever I've got in life, or lost, that was my destiny. I believe there is a programme mapped out for us all the way through to the end. If the Lord had wanted me to be a priest, that's what I would have been. I don't think He wanted that. I have always looked at things that way, no matter what I've done.

Eventually the bands self-destructed. The more money they made, the more they wanted to earn. I had no worries; up until I got married I was still living at home so my expenses were minimal. 'Once your cap was on, your house was thatched' as we used to say in Ireland. Some musicians became overnight superstars and their managers became very popular with venues, which were then mostly individually owned, not as these days part of a conglomerate.

The showbands went on for about three years and we enjoyed quite a bit of success. It was a boom-time for them, corresponding to that exciting era of 'the swinging sixties' when The Beatles hit the scene. My bands were as big as anyone around. I had three very good acts and programmes like 'The Late, Late Show', presented by Gay Byrne, would be ringing up constantly and asking my bands to go on. We'd get our friends to buy up as many singles as possible to help get their records high in the charts. You got 'greens' every night, all cash in hand, so we didn't pay any tax – there was no such thing as VAT then – and we were all driving round in the best cars and enjoying a glamorous lifestyle.

I squandered a lot of my money on cars. I bought a Caravelle, the first Renault sports car, which came on the market in the mid-sixties. It was a flashy two-seater. I wrote it off on a bend one night driving into Dromore, after only a couple of months. It was one of three write-offs in as many months. It caused a few insurance problems and cost me a lot of money. About a month later, I got a Peugeot 404, a very nice car. I was going to the greyhounds one night, then on to a dance. We were late and I drove straight into what I thought was a mass of black. It turned out to be a herd of cows. There were two or three of us in the car and we were lucky to get out unscathed.

For all the money we earned, I didn't end up with anything out of the business. Part of the reason was that I had a simple philosophy of rewarding the people who had helped me on the way up when I was struggling; those who had given me a date for a lower league band. To them, rather than demand a high percentage, I'd agree a booking with my top band and then say afterwards, 'Give me whatever you think.'

There were some people – though not many – I could ring up and they'd do anything for me. One such fellow was T.P. O'Connell, who ran the Astoria at Bundoran. He was always very good to me when I had bands which no one wanted. When I got into the big-time I gave him top dates.

In the end, our avarice destroyed the game. It was a classic case of slaying the golden goose that had laid the golden egg. We started looking for 60 per cent, then 70 per cent of the take; but it was all so short-sighted. It was ruining the people who had to bear all the expenses of building the places and running them, with all their overheads. They couldn't put enough back into their business and the dance halls started becoming run-down. Looking back, we took too much money out and the bubble burst. It was a silly, serious mistake and a valuable lesson learnt. That's how I've been able to see so clearly that the bookmakers are doing the same with racing, as I'll discuss later. The money in racing is not going back to the people who finance the show, the owners.

One morning I woke up and knew it was time to pack it in. I decided this was the moment to finish with the bands, although many of us still keep in touch. The boys tried to persuade me to stay on, but I told them they'd have to get along without me. I had started off a total greenhorn, but had struck lucky; it was the business to be in at the time. And I wasn't a bad operator.

I decided now was the time to go gambling seriously.

NINE

Pubs, betting shops and the stench of a scam

In 1971 I set off to the Cheltenham Festival with no more than £700 in my pocket and came away with £50,000. Crisp was one of my 'banker' bets, and there was also a strong supporting cast of other winners. For anyone who loves jump racing, and I've been enamoured with the game for nearly forty years, Cheltenham is the Mecca. I've been every year since then, with the exception of 1997 and 1998 when I was in Zambia on charity business.

I have always held the opinion that when you're winning you should crack on and get as much money down as you can; when you're out of form you should ease back. At the Festival that year I was so red hot that I was in danger of spontaneous combustion. That's when the bookmakers fear you; not when someone backs a winner, thrusts his winnings in his pocket and plays safe, saying, 'I'll be back tomorrow.' He'll only back a loser tomorrow and then go and chase it.

I don't have instant-recall of many races. Lester's win on Roberto in the 1972 Derby was an outstanding feat; so was that day when Michael Dickinson watched his five runners come home in a procession, led by the winner Bregawn, in the 1983 Gold Cup. They were great achievements, but as a betting man it didn't mean a lot to me. They have no relevance for me when I back a horse the next day. It is knowledge that is of no use to you. It's the same when people say, 'How many winners have you had?' I wouldn't have a clue. If they said, 'How much did you win?', I'd know. It's always in my mind. Not that I'd tell them.

There are, however, a handful of victories that do remain in my memory and Crisp's Cheltenham Festival win in the National Hunt Two Mile Champion Chase, now known as the Queen Mother Champion Chase, was one of them. Apart from anything else, it was my first major successful gamble. The Australian-bred Crisp had defied 12st 7lb to win easily under Richard Pitman in his preparatory race, a handicap chase at Wincanton five days earlier. His victory in the Two Mile Champion Chase was, if anything, even more facile. Paul Kelleway sent him into the lead at the tenth and he won by twenty-five lengths from New Romney, with the 13–8 favourite Royal Relief another ten lengths away in third. At 3–1 and over, I regarded his price as exceptionally good value.

That was the start for me as a big-time gambler. I'd proved to myself it could be done and I was supremely confident that it could continue. I've seen gamblers over the years who've put thousands on, yet there's had to be a whip-round to bury them. Betting is all about knowing 'when to hold them and when to fold them' – and on those three days the former stood me in good stead. Even today, more than a quarter of a century on, I still love that challenge and it gives me a great buzz to have the 'layers' clucking like a barn of turkeys as Christmas approaches. I have a very active mind and I take a certain pride that no one has ever achieved what I've done before, certainly not on such a scale.

I returned to Omagh, where Maureen and I were living at the time, and it had quickly swept around the town that I had won a substantial amount. Today, it would be like a lottery winner being in their midst.

The town has always been a haven for people with schemes up their sleeves and I was inundated with advice on how to invest my winnings. A fellow I knew in one of the banks, the assistant manager called Brian McInerney, said, 'D'you know, Barney, you're going to lose that money if you don't put it into something.' You might have imagined he would try and get me to open a deposit account at his bank; but not a chance of it. He had something far riskier in mind. Just by chance, of course, he had a customer who had some financial problems and Brian had suggested to him that he should dispose of the large pub he had for sale in Castle Street. I knew nothing about pubs, and the pair of them saw me coming from as far away as Dublin Airport. I bought the pub for around £30,000 and decided to rename the place in celebration of my good fortune. And so, the good people of Omagh witnessed the opening of … the Cheltenham Arms.

The advice came thick and fast. Friends told me that the real money was not in pubs or bars, but in venues for singing and dancing. This place had a very large rear space to it, so I was persuaded to build a cabaret lounge, with carvery, at a cost of £70,000. It was sheer madness. We got planning permission, despite the fact that it was adjacent to the Catholic Church and the graveyard. The next thing, as soon as we started developing it, the graveyard started to fall in on top of us. It was sacred ground and we had no end of trouble with the parish priest.

We also had some trouble from an infestation of rats which came scurrying out of the graveyard. We tried an ages-old remedy to rid ourselves of the scourge. My mother used to send down relics, which are holy pictures, with a tiny bit of cloth on the back from a saint's holy robes. St Francis of Assissi was the man to pray to, being the patron saint of animals. We placed all these relics between the floorboards, and any place we could get them, to try and get rid of the rats. I don't remember whether it did the trick or not, but we managed to eradicate them somehow.

If that wasn't bad enough, a chap came in one day brandishing a Garnishee Order, which sounds like a request for something to spread on your food, but is actually something far more serious. It said that my firm of contractors, run by a chap named Paddy Corey, was in debt to a supplier and any money I was due to pay the contractors should go to them instead. I put the document in my pocket, forgot all about it, and the next thing I was in court being told I was liable for the supplier's money. The builder's supplier, Keown's, had taken me to court for paying the contractor instead of paying him. The order was now against me and I ended up paying double. I had to pay the contractor and his supplier for materials that were nothing to do with me. With all my legal costs for that, sorting out the graveyard problem and the building costs, the whole thing ended up costing me about £120,000. The contractor didn't have the money, so I couldn't even get it back from him. I wasn't too happy, but I always had a lot of time for Paddy and his family, so I was pleased to help him in a roundabout kind of way. Despite everything, he never went down in my estimation.

When I owned the pub I was going racing as much as possible, probably three or four days a week, which was about maximum anyway in Ireland. It was hard work. The roads were not good then, and you'd be driving all day and all night. I always worked on my own. I made up my mind early on that there was one way to the poorhouse and that was to listen to people in racing. That was the best way to go skint.

My parents never said much about how I'd turned out, but I knew by the expressions on their faces that they weren't that pleased. I'm sure they were saying to themselves, 'Where is this man going to end up?' I'd had a decent education, despite my clashes with authority, and they thought I could have got a good job, a profession, rather than driving around betting and running a pub. Maybe my father's decline at the game still haunted their thinking. My father didn't have great confidence in me making money out of horses. He was always quoting this relation or that friend who had gone skint. I not only succeeded, but made far more than he could ever have dreamed of.

I had always liked Omagh, with its twin-towered church and a lively ambience, which many people liken to a French town. Many of the band members came from the area so it was inevitable that we had based ourselves there. At the time I had the pub, I bought my first betting shop in the town, too, at Kevlin Road in 1970. It was small, reasonably cheap, and had a very short lease on it. I didn't fancy it much, but somebody said I should buy it.

The next one was a reasonably big premises in Market Street, Enniskillen. I bought it from John James McManus, who had sold me my first car. Billy Charlton, who was, as usual, knee-deep in deals, said to me one day, 'You know that John James is fed up with that betting shop, you should buy it and have a go.' Well, again, 'fools rush in where angels fear to tread' and I bought it. Actually, that's not strictly true, because I didn't have a penny in my pocket. We had agreed a price of £3,000 and when I arrived at the office of my solicitor, Turlough Montague – who also acted for John James – knew my financial position precisely and I could see him looking at me, wondering how I would pay for it. I bluffed my way through the meeting and a sign went up in the shop, saying 'Under New Management from March 31st'.

It wasn't long before John James found out that I was financially embarrassed, and went dashing round to say, 'Take that notice down. That man has no money.' Fortunately, I did what I was best at – I went out and backed a winner to obtain the money and harmony was restored. I bought another one in Forthill Street, Enniskillen, and one in Lisnaskea, as my empire expanded. By the following year I had bought another office in Lisnaskea and one in Castle Street, Omagh. In those days betting shops tended to be privately owned rather than major chains. I ended up with five or six at one time under the name of The Barney Curley Organisation.

It will have become apparent by now that I was somewhat suggestible; but that didn't mean I wouldn't look at any proposal carefully. If I thought the odds were in my favour, I'd take a chance, when others would perhaps be more cautious. By the time I appeared in court in 1978 to defend myself against claims of 'welching' I was apparently worth £1.2 million, so I must have done something right during those years. I had also learned a lot about the betting business, so there was no way we were going to be caught napping when someone tried to take us for £90,000.

I was down in the South when one of my managers, Gerry Donnelly, rang me up and said that a fellow had had a £60 five-horse accumulator and all five had won. It worked out at about £360,000, but we had a pay-out limit of £90,000. 'He's looking to be paid out a couple of thousand on account to celebrate tonight with a few drinks,' said Gerry. 'I don't have it. Will you come and sort it out.'

My replay was short, but not so sweet. 'Give him nothing,' I barked. 'I'll be up in the morning.'

Even as I drove up the vibes were suspicious and as soon as I looked at the bet I knew it was a scam. You smell these things. And this stank more than a batch of two-week-old Dublin Bay prawns left out in the sun.

There was no such thing as a machine to time the bets in those days. You operated on trust. This slip had appeared from nowhere and it was clear a young lad, whom we'd just taken on, was in collusion with the punter. He had apparently taken the bet during a time when Gerry had been out of the shop, had put the slip at the bottom of the pile and conveniently failed to tell Gerry that there could be a substantial liability, which, had it been genuine, would have allowed us to lay it off. Indeed, the clerk concerned, Niall Devlin, who was dismissed immediately, had not even mentioned the winning bet until an hour after the last race.

The 'off' times of the selected races were also all within a half-hour period, which added to my suspicion. But the most significant pointer was the scale of the stake – remember, we're talking about twenty years ago. Even today, you wouldn't find too many punters who'd have such a large amount of money on a five-horse accumulator. It just didn't ring true. I told Gerry, 'We're paying nothing.'

Of course, bookmakers became legal nearly 40 years ago, but what Parliament has never done is to make betting debts enforceable under law. By and large it is probably the best system, with payment of debts being left as purely a matter of honour and trust between 'layer' and punter. Those who feel wronged can still create serious problems for the bookmaker concerned. This particular fellow, by the name of Lawrence McSwiggan, soon made it clear he was not prepared to accept defeat, and his exposure as a cheat, with good grace.

He complained and on the basis of that the rural magistrate, or RM as they are more commonly known, at Omagh Court, one Basil McIvor, rejected our evidence and refused a Certificate of Character and Suitability to enable me to renew my licence at shops in Kevlin Road and Castle Street in the town. Clearly McSwiggan hoped that I might be persuaded to make him some ex-gratia payment to get him to drop his objection. He didn't know how stubborn I can be. That's why we both ended up giving evidence at a two-day hearing in July 1978. It produced many column inches in the *Ulster Herald* as the case became a *cause célèbre* locally and further afield.

McSwiggan, described as 'a 33-year-old cafe owner' of Killybrack, Omagh, said he had been betting for eighteen years, mostly doing quads (four-timers) and five-horse accumulators, and used my shops regularly. He claimed that I had 'welched' on a huge winning bet. Niall Devlin tried to make out that he had no understanding of 'dangerous', or potentially large bets, and said he considered the wager to be a mug's bet. For my part, the issue was quite simple: I told the court the bet was placed in my Kevlin Road office an hour after the horses had won on 4 July that year and that there had been collusion between McSwiggan and Devlin, who didn't bring to light the 'winning' bet until 4.50 pm, despite the last horse having come in at 3.30 pm; there was no ticket issued for the bet, which was supposedly placed at 1 pm; and I also added that this dubious pair just happened to have been seen together at Cheltenham and then stayed together at an exclusive hotel at Galway races.

I could scarcely believe the pronouncement of Mr McIvor: 'The applicant [my good self] did not strike me as an honest man in the witness box,' the magistrate declared, adding he had been satisfied it was a properly laid bet. 'If this bet was put on after 3.30 pm with the knowledge that the net result would be a claim for £90,000, this would be a simply spectacular piece of fraud.' He also claimed that our system of monitoring was ignored.

His words told you that whatever his knowledge of the law, his experience of betting was minimal. On the one hand he said that it was chance-in-a-million that anyone would put £60 on five winning horses; on the other he said that my suspicions were unfounded and that I was trying to avoid paying winnings on a properly laid bet.

The case against me was aided by the fact that there was also a little problem over a £1,300 tax debt, which, he said, indicated that I had doubtful financial standing. There was also an objection to the fact that I did not live in Northern Ireland, but that, at least, was rejected. The conclusion to all this was that Mr McIvor refused the certificate in order 'to protect the public'.

Now, I am not one who would normally speak ill of the judiciary; it exists to protect us all, without favour, and sometimes decisions go against you, but even to this day the words and actions of Basil McIvor still irritate me. As far as I was concerned, he was as mad as a hatter. I couldn't understand how he had become a magistrate in the first place.

But that didn't help me as I sat and pondered how the law, like the Lord, can move in mysterious ways. After the ruling, the licences on some of my other offices expired, but fortunately we were allowed to keep all the offices open until the appeal, which took place two months later. Even if I'd lost I did have the option of transferring the licences to my Enniskillen manager, Eamon Bradley, who was a licensed bookmaker himself. There was no need. This time, in a mere two hours, a judge found in my favour. I won the appeal at Tyrone County Court, despite the police also lodging an objection and adding to the list of those opposed to my licence. Even my father had to appear to testify that I spent two or three days of every week in Irvinestown. I also confirmed that the tax debt was now paid. I was unequivocal about the bet that had caused the whole commotion. I told the judge the supposed winning bet was 'the greatest take-on of all time'. Fortunately, Judge Frank Russell showed rather more common sense than Mr McIvor. The whole affair was a good illustration of the fact that Omagh was the sort of town where you had to be wide awake or there would always be someone who'd catch you napping. There were all kinds of devious schemes perpetrated. You had to be wise to everything and everyone.

In my second shop in Omagh, in Castle Street, a punter had

a yankee – a four-horse accumulator where you collect if two, three or all four of your selections win – on some night racing. In those days shops were not open in the evening and the results were checked the following morning. This fellow had had the audacity to come in at night through the skylight, after the results were known, and alter his betting slip. He claimed the next day that he was owed £4,000 but again we refused to pay out. In that business you have to have a nose to smell deceit and dishonesty. Gerry was not long in the business and a very trusting fellow. I eventually sold that shop to Micky Donnelly. Gerry still works there for him. Micky has done well, which gives me great pleasure, and he is now on our DAFA committee.

During this time I had developed into that rare creature, a gambler-cum-bookmaker. As I will explain later, the two generally mix like oil and water. Soon, I realised that I would have to make a choice and it didn't take me long to decide that the shops would have to go.

I've had my rows and feuds over the years, and inevitably there're a few things I regret. When I sold up, one of my betting shops, in Armagh, was bought by Billy Charlton. He didn't get round to paying me, or not immediately. So, with the impetuosity of those early years, I picketed the shop! I stood outside and berated customers as they entered, 'This man has not paid me for this betting office.'

Billy was very friendly with my mother, who thought the world of him. Of course, the first person he told the story to was her and I got some serious abuse. It was a mistake. He wasn't a bad guy at all. He had helped organise my first house for me. In hindsight I was far too quick to do it. He paid eventually, but it didn't do the business much good. It was a serious mistake to take it upon myself to try and ruin a good friend. In different circumstances, I'd do the same again, though. If someone owed me and I thought he had no intention of paying, I'd picket his home and picket his business if necessary.

TEN

Roberto to the rescue

During the days before we married, Maureen got chatting to my eldest sister, Anne. She warned my young bride-to-be to be very careful. 'Barney has only one interest in life – and that's gambling,' she said. Nowadays, a successful gambler has a bit of prestige; he would be admired as a risk-taker and an adventurer, a kind of Indiana Jones of the racing world. But then it had rather more sordid connotations. The public associated professional gambling with organised crime and razor gangs at racecourses, despite the fact that the last such battle, I am reliably informed, was waged at Lewes in 1937! Even if you weren't a hoodlum, you were likely to be an incorrigible lounge lizard that women were made to be wary of falling for.

Maureen was always intelligent enough to recognise the reality. From our first days together she knew I was a business gambler, not a gambler for the fun of it. Also, I was connected with no one. She questioned me about it, of course, and I just tried to reassure her. 'Look, I'll always keep you once I really get going.' I don't think she's ever really worried since those early days. When I go to the racecourse she just thinks of me as going off to work like any other professional man. Except I don't wear a bowler and a pin-stripe and carry a copy of *The Times*; just binoculars and a note of the horses' form.

You'd never know if I'd won or lost. I can walk into a room and you'd have absolutely no idea whether I'd won £100,000 or lost £50,000. If I lose today, no matter; my philosophy is that I'll win tomorrow.

I would never try to stifle free will, but from the moment they understood such things, I did my best to put my children off, particularly my son Charlie who would have been most inclined to try and emulate me. I would simply tell them that winning at this game was virtually impossible. I was only doing what Gerry Magee had done to me all those years before, that day when I told him I was going gambling.

Back in Irvinestown, Gerry had been the the local chemist – he was the fellow who had supplied my father with those tablets which 'slowed' his greyhounds – and was the best-educated man around. He was like an unofficial mayor, who signed forms for you as a responsible adult and was someone we all respected. He loved racing, too. 'Gerry,' I said. 'I'm packing it all in and going betting.' It was like he'd been told a close relation had died, the expression on his face was so pained.

'Barney, please,' he said. 'Don't be mad. Don't be a fool.'

I said, 'I think I can do it.'

He shook his head. 'You're crazy. No one has ever done it and you're not going to be the first. Forget about it.'

He sat me down in his sitting room, and gave me a stern lecture on the folly of my ways. He gave me examples of those he had known who had ended up on skid row and said that I would end up there with them. I said I was going to have a shot at it anyway. I had made up my own mind and I wasn't in any mood to take anyone's advice, even his, and off I went. Gerry's long dead now, but I think he eventually felt very proud of me. He never said it, but I think he used to admire me. He didn't want to encourage me in case I was a disaster, but I think he felt I hadn't done a bad job. He was right to do so, and I respected him for it; but I thought I had a talent. I was winning, and fairly consistently. I had no doubt I could make it pay, even though those images of my father's failures – and of many men he knew, too – would always ensure that I didn't get carried away.

To be a success you had to be out of the ordinary, and I knew I was. By the early seventies my betting was becoming serious. I would be having bets of £1,000 to £2,000, that kind of scale, at Leopardstown, The Curragh, Naas, all the big tracks. I was intent on building up reserves, my 'tank' as I call it, for the future.

Yes, there have been times when I have my doubts. Like all gamblers I've gone through horrendously bad patches; times when I just couldn't pay, barring a miracle. I thank God that I've usually been blessed with one when I've needed it.

The 1972 Epsom Derby, when Roberto prevailed only because of an inspired piece of riding by Lester Piggott, is an excellent case in point. Without the maestro, Vincent O'Brien's colt, who barely stayed the twelve-furlong trip, wouldn't have got his head in front on the line – and mine would have been on the block. I'd go as far as to say that I wouldn't be here today, at least not in racing. I'd gone through an exceptionally bad week or two in Ireland and couldn't pay my debts. I owed it to the big boys – Richard Powers, Sean Graham, the Mulligan Brothers. I needed to settle, and quickly. Once you say you can't pay, you get a bad name and there's no more efficient bush telegraph than the betting fraternity. Your credit might be curtailed for good. I owed £30,000, which was not an enormous sum to win even then, but it was a considerable sum of money when you couldn't get your hands on it. I was getting desperate, but I had a strong fancy for Roberto in the Derby and I realised he could be my salvation. I scraped together £10,000 in cash and headed off to Epsom.

Maureen knew nothing about it and would have had no idea of my parlous state. I thought Roberto would be about a 7–2 chance, but the snag was that I wasn't familiar with English racing so I didn't know how to go about the business of obtaining the best value. I have always looked for value; that's always been my way. But I didn't think I'd get that in the betting ring with cash. I feared being taken for a ride if I just wandered around with £10,000 trying to back a fancied Derby runner with Piggott riding. I could envisage them offering me only 3–1, which was the eventual starting-price (SP), and I was determined to get at least 7–2.

Fortunately, I met up with Cecil Hobson, Ladbroke's representative and a Northern Ireland man. I threw myself on his mercy and told him, 'Cecil, I want to back Roberto to win the Derby. I have no account, but I have the cash. Can you help me?' Cecil was a fair man, and he in turn introduced me to Leslie Spencer, William Hill's representative, who laid me £3,000-to-win-£10,500. That was my first bet on an English racecourse. With Cecil's help, I got the rest on at similar odds with other bookmakers. Eventually I got all my money on – £10,000-to-win-£35,000 – and Lester played his part by riding a sublime race on Roberto and, with the aid of that famous staccato employment of the whip near the line, getting up to win by a short head from Rheingold. It was one of his finest performances in a glittering career. It was very close, although I was certain he had got up.

It took an age before the photo-finish was announced. Simultaneously, and to my abject horror, a stewards' inquiry was announced. It was agony as I sat and waited. If there had been the slow toll of a single bell, there couldn't have been a more funereal tone to proceedings. The sun beat down on me as I just slumped there on the steps oblivious to the crowd around me, all enjoying their Derby day out. It was probably only twenty minutes but the whole process seemed to last the duration of the afternoon. Normally, I keep very cool under such circumstances, but that was one of the few occasions when I sweated up worse than the horses. You can imagine my relief when the announcement boomed over the Public Address, containing those three wonderful words: 'The result stands.'

It was make or break day for me. If Lester had got beaten there would have been no way back after that. I would have been totally cleaned out. I would have been left with a huge debt and nothing more to bet with. Yet, even then I was exceedingly philosophical about it. If you get in a state about the outcome of a race you're only giving your mind aggravation. Since those days, I've always judged success or failure over a period. It's like a City speculator playing the market.

That was a quarter of a century ago, but my attitude towards gambling and money hasn't changed. Inside, I'm a contented fellow. If I win a race, fine; if I lose, it's not important. There's more to life than winning big races or landing major gambles. It sometimes annoys me that it's the only way some people perceive me.

It may be hard to believe, but I have absolutely no interest in money, no interest in building up monuments to my life's work, or wealth for its own sake. You can't take it with you. There's no pocket in the dead man's shroud. In fact I'm a desperate nuisance to the bank because I'm just not switched on to money. The only man who would know that is my bank manager, John McCann. There have been enough times when he has called me down to London to say: 'Barney, now this is serious. If you don't buck yourself up you're going to be skint.' I don't want to depart this world, leave ten million to my family and have people saying, 'He did well, didn't he?' He was the man who pulled off a bit of a coup at Ascot or the fellow who skinned the Irish bookies alive with an audacious plot at

Bellewstown. I want to leave this world thinking I'd done a bit of good. Wealth, and how it's accrued, can be very misleading. If you rob a man of £4 million and give half to charity, that doesn't clear your conscience. In Ireland we call it 'buying fire insurance'. They cheat people all their lives, then, when they're about sixty they open a home for the disabled, or something similar, in a belated attempt at salvation before they meet their Maker.

I've owned betting shops and I've had a bookmaker's pitch at the greyhound track, yet the truth is that I wasn't born to be a 'layer' – at heart, I'm not a 'layer', I'm a punter. It's a different mentality and you can't do both. Those who try to combine them tend to end up broke. If I needed a reminder of that essential rule of betting law I received it on Derby Day in 1982.

Vincent O'Brien's Golden Fleece was well-fancied for the Epsom classic, particularly by the Irish, and I made the error of thinking there was easy money to be had … by laying it to lose. I got people to 'stand' him for me at over the odds, acting in a bookmaker's role if you like. That was probably my worst week's gambling, and I got it wrong in a major way. I ended up with liabilities of £150,000 on Golden Fleece and exacerbated my plight by losing another £100,000 on other bets.

There were no excuses. My judgement just misfired completely. As a Derby favourite, I considered him to be a bad horse and still believe I was right. What I hadn't really taken into sufficient account was that he was competing in a less than average year. Golden Fleece never ran again, so we never knew how good – or moderate, as I believed – he was, although, significantly, he didn't turn out to be much of a sire. I simply hadn't liked the horse in his races before the Derby, although, in fairness, he had defeated Assert in his immediate 'prep' race and that horse did turn out a decent type. Nothing much became of his Derby rivals. Touching Wood, the runner-up, at

40–1, for instance, was basically a stayer and went on to win the St Leger. Golden Fleece had also drifted from 9–4 favourite to 3–1 before the 'off', which is not a good sign in such a strong market.

A lesser man might have been persuaded to pack it in immediately. I remember walking back to the train at Tattenham Corner and reflecting on what had gone wrong. But I never panicked and I didn't allow it to get to me. I wasn't particularly upset. I didn't go racing the next day, because I never believe in chasing money. I feared I might do just that. As I've said previously, I've always taken the view that if you're hot you should strike, but if you're cold you should back off and reassemble your forces. I effectively retired for three months. I thought if I stuck around I could do myself more damage.

The children were young, so, a day or two later, I took them and Maureen off to California where we rented a house on the beach at Del Mar, right next door to the doyen of American trainers, Charlie Whittingham, whom I'd met once before at Santa Anita racecourse. It was just the kind of haven we needed. I always think of the old Bing Crosby song, 'When the turf meets the surf in old Del Mar …'

We spent three months there and in a way it was a period of convalescence, every bit as important as my time recovering after TB. Yes, I brooded on what had happened at Epsom. I thought I'd lost my touch. But my good fortune was to be around Charlie. I learnt so much from him. He had an eye for detail and missed nothing about his horses. Many consider Charlie to be the greatest trainer in the world and, on and off, over three or four years I have picked up knowledge from him.

I got up every morning at twenty to five and just watched him work. He was a genius with those horses and had a knack of knowing when they were beginning to peak at the top of their form. It was a gift, which I like to think I also possess in my own way. For all the science involved – the blood tests, the weighing of horses, working on split times – it all comes down to watching the horses.

Charlie's a very unassuming man, and not a great communicator, but, if he liked you, he invariably passed on to you a nugget of his expertise every week. He was also very thoughtful. I went with him once to Hollywood Park, where he had a runner in a million dollar 'bonus' race. Yet, he was more concerned about the fact that I had got lost. I had taken the wrong escalator; so all I had was a succession of attendants saying, 'Charlie's looking for you' and 'Charlie's getting worried about you.' It was quite embarrassing, when he should have been concentrating on his runner.

I was fortunate in that Charlie took a shine to me. Because I don't put on any airs or graces I think I had his respect and trust. He was very similar to myself in that you didn't think he was watching you, but his eye was all-seeing. They called him 'the bald eagle', and that was not merely because of his gleaming pate, but also because he was like that magnificent bird which can see the minutest of detail from the sky. Charlie also had a great sense of loyalty to those around him.

He was responsible for one of the best responses I've heard, when asked on TV after Estrapade's victory in the Arlington Million at what point exactly he thought she'd win the race. 'When we entered her,' he had shrugged. That's how I operate, too.

Over the years I had three horses in training with Charlie. I had great hopes for one of them, a filly called Alianna. I normally buy horses towards the cheaper end of the market and train them myself. In 1984 I laid out £150,000 on a horse with classic form as an investment. Alianna, trained by Tony Redmond at Kildare, had finished second in the Irish 1,000 Guineas, just a neck behind Terry Ramsden's Katies, despite

129

being hampered. She had been unplaced in the Irish Oaks, but ran decent races in the Phoenix Champion Stakes at Phoenix Park and the Sun Chariot Stakes at Newmarket, and I thought she would be a nice mare to race in America and then sell or send her to the paddocks for breeding. I bought her from the syndicate that owned her, a group who included Joe 'Big Bucks' Donnelly, a bookmaker acquaintance of mine, and flew her over to Charlie Whittingham.

Alianna ran a good preparatory race, even though she was unplaced at Belmont Park, and Charlie, not given to exaggeration, said to me, 'That filly could win the Arlington Million.' Now that race, run at Arlington International, is a hot event. In 1983 it had been won by Luca Cumani's Tolemeo, ridden by Pat Eddery and was worth over £400,000 to the winner. I went off to Australia for a couple of months full of expectancy. When I returned I had a message to ring Charlie.

'Is that filly of yours insured?' he said without preamble.

My heart sank. 'No,' I replied.

'I'm afraid she's dead.'

Apparently Alianna had suffered a twisted gut and nothing could be done to save her. Prior to her death I had been offered half a million for her. The same day that I was told the news I went off racing at Sedgefield, where prize-money was a couple of thousand if you were lucky and reflected that Dame Fortune was a capricious mistress.

Alianna wasn't the only high-priced investment I got involved with. A couple of years earlier I had bought a three-year-old named Prince Echo from Liam Browne for around £100,000. He had been third, behind Kings Lake, in the 1981 Irish 2,000 Guineas and fourth in the July Cup. I thought Prince Echo might improve as a four-year-old, so I sent him to Henry Cecil. He ran in the July Cup and a few other races, but didn't really sparkle, and eventually I sold him to stud in New Zealand for £120,000.

Gambling is like many other things in life. Sometimes it never goes right for you. You get a bad run and you start thinking you'll never win again. But the secret is not to panic. Many men would have capitulated after that reverse at Epsom, but I gave myself time and thought it through; as Alan Byrne once wrote about me in the *Sunday Independent*, contrasting me with Terry Ramsden, 'Curley is different. He has lasted the pace. When it comes to serious gambling for big stakes, he is a stayer rather than a flashy sprinter ... he has won enough to stay in the race longer than virtually anybody else.' I mean nothing boastful in reproducing that. It is an accurate assessment of how I operate.

I certainly don't worry about losing a lot of money on any one day; like when I had a particularly bad afternoon at Galway Festival and lost £100,000 on I'm A Driver, beaten in a bumper, and others . I've always had it in my mind to go back there and win it back. I nearly did so in the summer of 1998 when Cohiba ran a good race, only to be beaten by a real pile-driver of a horse, a five-time hurdler winner, named Quince. Anyway, I'll be back. I may have even gone for four or five months without a winner and been down maybe £400,000. But what really counts is the balance sheet at the end of the year. I have never had a losing one yet. My advice to punters has always been to focus their resources on high-quality racing; it tends to be more profitable because every horse and jockey is trying its best and the form is more reliable. Yet, perversely, the English Derby, the so-called 'Blue Riband of the Turf', which should turn out the top three-year-olds, has brought me as much despair as it has success.

In 1986, my potential winnings of £250,000 went down when Dancing Brave just failed to overhaul Sharastani, but the following year Reference Point compensated to the tune of £200,000. I particularly remember 1988 when I was bullish about the chances of Unfuwain. I was as enamoured with Dick

Hern's charge as I had been dismissive of Golden Fleece. He had already won the Chester Vase by eight lengths and I thought he was the one horse in the field that year with the potential to become a great champion. I'd seen him win at Epsom and he reminded me so much of Dick Hern's 1979 winner Troy, on whom I won £150,000.

So confident-looking was he that I'd backed him ante-post at 10-1 to win £120,000, plus I topped him up on the day, when he started at 9-2, to make potential winnings of £200,000 in all, although Jimmy Fitzgerald had taken ten 'monkeys' (£5,000-to-£500) off me as we were coming back on the train from Sandown on Whitbread Gold Cup day!

What could go wrong? He even had one of my favourite jockeys on his back in Steve Cauthen, who seldom got into trouble, had a good clock in his head and kept his mounts well balanced. There was no explanation for the way Unfuwain ran. He was hugely disappointing, finishing only seventh behind Kahyasi after leading from four out to two out. Later he would atone, and exhibit his true form, by winning the Princess of Wales' Stakes at Newmarket and finishing runner-up to Mtoto in the King George VI and Queen Elizabeth Diamond Stakes at Ascot.

The 1997 Derby will go down as one I will always recall fondly, and not merely because Benny The Dip did the business for me. Before the race I had backed him at £10,000 each-way. He was 10–1, but I felt he was a decent, genuine horse. It was not normal for me to back each-way, but I considered that extraordinarily good value. I don't normally tell other people what I'm backing, but I mentioned to John Martin, 'Captain Keen' to his readers in the *Irish Independent*, who had given me some valuable publicity over my DAFA charity, that Benny The Dip was one to be on. I hope his readers benefited from the advice. Entrepreneur was all the rage. He had been the 'talking' horse all winter and Michael Tabor's colt had already won the 2,000 Guineas, though, significantly, he had enjoyed a far better run than some of his rivals, particularly the three-quarter-length runner-up Revoque.

On the Thursday night before the Derby I went round to see Benny The Dip's rider, Willie Ryan, who is retained by Henry Cecil. He is one of the three current Flat jockeys I rate most highly, along with Frankie Dettori and Jimmy Quinn. There had been suggestions that he lacked big-race experience; Willie was better known by most people for partnering Cecil's second-strings and work-riding, but I regarded him as one of the most underrated jockeys around, a fine rider with a very sharp brain. I didn't mix my words and told him straight out: 'Willie, I've got a big interest in Benny The Dip.' We chatted a little, and I explained to Willie, 'If this Entrepreneur is as brilliant a horse as he's made out to be, I'm a very bad judge. If he is, then Revoque is a champion. And he's not. You can figure out that just by looking at the video of the 2,000 Guineas.'

I had also laid Entrepreneur to lose about £10,000, just as I had with Golden Fleece fifteen years before, although this time not quite so rashly. Even if you fancied him, evens was no value. I know he won the 2,000 Guineas, but he had the run of the race and in the last 100yds Revoke, who didn't have, was going two strides for his one. So, if Entrepreneur was a good horse, it made Revoke a top-class champion. I didn't think so. Few other people, least of all the tipsters, took that line of thought. It's yet another example of hype and home reputation overcoming rational thought and why you should never listen to anybody. My only concern was that Willie hadn't won too many prestige races before, and had certainly gone nowhere near the Derby winner's circle. It doesn't take much to influence a rider's mind and have him believing that he can't win a race because of the opposition. I was confident that Willie wouldn't allow that to happen, but it didn't do any harm to tell him that night that he was going to win the Derby. I felt that what I said would be a positive influence. He knows me well enough to understand that I'm not a dreamer and not liable to platitudes. I knew he respected my judgement and I wouldn't just say he'd win for the sake of it. Most importantly, he'd know I wouldn't throw good money at a worthless cause. He really gave the horse a splendid ride and won by a short head. He told me later that the first thing he thought of after passing the post was me saying I had a big interest. So, maybe I made my small contribution. Yet, that was one of those days when I was more pleased for Willie and Benny The Dip trainer John Gosden than myself. Nobody deserved to ride a Derby winner more than Willie, or train one more than John. I must remember to put a few pounds in a Personal Equity Plan (PEP) for Willie.

ELEVEN

Caught in the crossfire

With the situation in the North deteriorating, we moved in 1972 to Ashford in County Wicklow, a forty-five-minute drive south of Dublin, and one of the most beautiful parts of Ireland. The BBC TV series *Ballykissangel* is filmed around there.

I had already had a couple of unpleasant first-hand experiences of what was to become all too familiar in Ulster. I had been to the races in the South and was approaching Aughnacloy on the Monaghan-Tyrone border as I travelled back to the North one night. When I drew up at the border post on the southern side, a Garda officer warned, 'You don't want to be going over there. If you go, it's at your own peril. They're expecting trouble.'

Of course, fools rush in, and I said, 'I have to go on, I'm in a hurry.'

His parting shot was, 'It's your own fix' – by which he meant it was my funeral. It nearly was, too.

I had got perhaps half a mile further down the road before an Army officer jumped out from the side of the road and waved me down. He shouted, 'Get down and keep your head down. Turn off the lights. We're expecting trouble. How the hell did you get up here, anyway …?' His words were cut short when all hell broke loose. IRA gunmen started firing from the hill and, with mounting horror, I realise I was trapped in the middle of an attempted ambush. As the Army on the ground responded, I was caught in the crossfire. Bullets were ricocheting all around me and it was too dangerous to move on. We were pinned down for about half an hour. I felt safe in the car, and it was probably fortunate that I only learned later that the bullets could have gone through the bodywork, and possibly ignited the fuel tank. The gunmen wouldn't have known, and probably wouldn't have cared, that I was an innocent abroad in that border territory, which was effectively a war zone. Eventually, it fell silent for a quarter of an hour, and my saviour said, 'Go on, it's safe enough. Just put on your sidelights and drive on.'

Whether there were any casualties I don't know. I was just happy to get out of there as fast as I could. But I'll always be indebted to that Army officer, who could have just looked after his own skin. He had been in the full glare of my headlights which were illuminating the whole area and he'd probably given away his men's position. I couldn't have created more of a target if I'd hoisted a beacon. He risked his life and showed great bravery. I often think about those soldiers. The sad thing is that they often didn't know what they were going into or why they were doing it when they put their lives at risk on patrol.

There was always a lot of activity involving the security forces in and around Omagh, where there was a large British Army base, but this was my first brush with it for real. On another occasion, a bomb went off as I was walking out of our house. It blew me up against a wall. When I'd dusted myself down, I'd decided that was it. I've always been lucky in life that I've made the right major decisions at the right time. It was time to move. I decided there and then that my generation might never see the end of it. If I hadn't left then, I might well have spent the rest of my life in Northern Ireland.

It was clear the Troubles were escalating, even before 1969. With all the grudges, it was building up by the day. I had a lot of time for Unionist leader Terence O'Neill, Prime Minister from 1963 until 1969, who was a great forward-thinker. His government had already been making some conciliatory gestures to the Catholic community, because he could see the country was heading for disaster. 'This country has to change,' he declared.

Nobody has ever tried to sign me up to support a particular cause. People realised early on that, although I am a committed Catholic, I can see both sides' point of view. I'm no bigot and I see everybody, be they Unionists or Nationalists, as equal. I want fair play for all. Today, if I have a winner, I hope and believe it's cheered as loudly in the Shankhill as it is in the Falls. I have as much in common with both communities.

I lived in Northern Ireland for thirty years and the people who helped me on the way, gave me a start in life, were mostly Protestants. I have always regarded them as fine, hard-working, honest people, and with men like Gordon Wilson there is always hope. Back in the sanatorium, Doctor Warmington was a Protestant; yet the way he dedicated his life to curing people of all creeds struck a chord with me. I also had a Protestant bank manager, Joe Shackleton, who did everything in his power to give me a start in life. When my parents opened up our grocery shop, the big local wholesalers, Hudson's, were Protestants; yet, Douglas Hudson gave us the goods to start the shop on credit. I'm very broad-minded about other people's religions. Some day they'll have to meet their God. And He's everybody's God. And on the day of reckoning, He'll know all our faults and what we've done for other people. Religious affiliation won't help them then.

My parents never tried to dissuade me from associating with Protestant boys. It was just that you were aware from an early age of the religious divide and you never had much contact. We played Gaelic football; they played soccer. It was frowned on for a Catholic boy to play soccer, although I was always quite keen. As I was growing up, we'd watch the civil rights demonstrations and Protestant marches, though as a community everybody was still at peace. I could see there was a lot of wrong-doing towards the Catholics and I knew from my own experiences that discrimination existed. The Protestant population didn't want Catholics in the best jobs; they wanted to keep the professions for themselves. That's why many of us from my part of the world, where there was a Catholic majority, ended up as club-owners, publicans, bookmakers, running or playing in showbands, or became tricksters of one sort or another. Despite being very well educated, I had to smuggle to get a living in the early days. Apart from working briefly for the Scallons, I didn't even bother seeking employment. I don't feel any bitterness about that, although I can understand people who would. On the other hand, I can also see that the Protestants might not get a fair shout in a united Ireland. They have their rights and traditions, including the Orange marches, and I can understand that they don't want those eroded in the name of unity.

It has been the politicians and the leaders of factions who have had no interest in anything but their own narrow cause, that have led our people to destruction. Too many of my countrymen just listened to all these madmen and would not utter a word. Northern Ireland has so many good people, but there have not been enough with sufficient backbone to stand up and be counted and say: 'this is wrong'. That's why there are children who've grown up never seeing anything but violence and who have so much anger and hatred in their hearts. It's a desperate situation. To some, it's probably about as relevant as supporting rival football teams, but their father and his father have passed the doctrine on down the line and that's it. There are young people in their twenties who have never known peace; they've never known a police station not set in concrete with barbed wire protecting it.

No one close to me has ever been deliberately shot at, or been involved in any way in terrorism. I have never condoned violence, even for political ends, but I can understand the motivation of those who have got caught up in it. As far as successive British governments were concerned, it was no man's land; nobody wanted to know about the Six Counties until the bombs started going off on the mainland. They must also take a large share of the blame.

I have nothing but respect for the people of England, Scotland and Wales, who have responded with great stoicism to their soldiers and civilians being killed for nearly thirty years. Certainly, in my years on the mainland I have never experienced any discrimination. Indeed, I sometimes wonder if England doesn't take enough pride in its own traditions, heritage and heroes. There's a picture hanging up at the nightclub I now own in Windsor. A young fellow came up to me one night and asked, 'Is that you up there?'

'That,' I said patiently, as I looked at him incredulously, 'is one of the most famous Englishmen of all time.'

The photograph is of Field Marshall Montgomery.

Who's to say I wouldn't have turned out the same as some of my countrymen, had it not been for my education and my move to the South? Although I went to Catholic colleges, there was none of the bigotry in the South that you get in the North. But I know that at least I would have stood up for what I believe in. There're too many who've sat there for fifty years and said nothing. That's why if someone stamps on my toes at the racetrack I'll speak out, no matter who it upsets.

I've never been approached to be a politician, but behind the scenes, I have had my opinion sought on political situations. I've always been friendly with former Irish Prime Minister, Albert Reynolds, who should be given some credit for how the situation has improved in Northern Ireland. But politics has never been for me. I've always believed that carve-ups between businessmen and politicians, where one buys the other, in however minor a way, was like fixing a race. It was cheating.

At the time of writing, there is optimism with the Mitchell Agreement in April 1998 that at last a peaceful end is in sight, but it will take some remarkable compromise from the hard men of both sides of the divide and equal rights for all.

In hindsight, I suppose I could have become a target, either because of my perceived wealth, my increasing notoriety and my religious background. After that experience in the sanatorium, death did not trouble me; I was only concerned about my family being caught up in the violence, particularly as I was away from home frequently with long journeys to the racecourses in the South.

The legacy of the terrorism is that one of the most beautiful areas of the country is ignored because tourists still regard it as 'bandit' territory. People on the mainland raise their eyebrows if you talk about going there; but it's not like that at all. It saddens me, because Northern Ireland is my home, and I'd love to see it prosper. Lester Piggott, who was to become a friend of mine when I moved to Newmarket, told me about ten years ago that he had been invited to Down Royal, a racetrack in the North, near the Maze prison. Understandably for a prominent Englishman, he asked me whether he should go. I appreciated his concern, with the newspapers and TV increasingly covering bombings and shootings. Without giving it a second thought, I told him he would be safe. I told him, 'It's the best country in the world, and the most wonderful people. I'll guarantee you 100 per cent, you'll be back safe and sound.' Apart from anything else he was a national sporting institution, and an attack on him would damage rather than enhance any cause. I also encouraged Frankie to go when he was invited to the Ulster Harp Derby at Down Royal.

I believe there is hope for Northern Ireland. For the first time in my life I'm optimistic. There is a new Assembly, and there appears to be people emerging from the Protestant side who are much more representative of their communities than those before them.

During the marching season, I was very impressed by the Rev. William Bingham, a new man on the block, who put his case clearly and fairly, and was quite unlike the hotheads we have seen over the years.

We also moved to County Wicklow because, increasingly, I was spending a lot of time going racing in the South. Business wasn't particularly good up there and I sold up everything and we departed. I was particularly relieved to get rid of the pub, which was a real albatross around my neck. But things had gone from bad to worse, mostly due to my own ignorance of the business. I was not what you'd call streetwise about the catering trade. What did begin to register, so to speak, was that the tills never tallied. It was getting out of hand.

When I make a decision there is generally no turning back. I said to my solicitor, 'I want this place sold by tomorrow.'

He said, 'You can't sell a place in a day. It has to be advertised.'

I said, 'You have to. Before your office closes this evening I want no further interest in it. I'm sick of it. I don't want to hear any more about the Cheltenham Arms.'

He sold it, for £40,000-£50,000. I probably made a loss of £100,000 on the whole escapade. It was a total fiasco. But I didn't really learn my lesson. Many years later I was to buy a nightclub, which I run to this day. I've become a bit more clued up since then.

Down in Ashford we bought a place called Boswell Stud, which was set in eighty lush acres. It consisted of the original, typical Irish country Georgian house, which the previous owner, Frank Fitzpatrick, a Northern Ireland lawyer based in Dublin, had found too small for family and friends and had built a modern Spanish-style villa, a replica of his holiday home in Spain.

We lived in the old house, considering the 'annexe' an extravagance, and used it mainly for putting up visitors. One such guest was Paddy Broderick, who had come over to ride Peter Easterby's all-conquering Night Nurse in the Irish Sweeps Hurdle at Leopardstown in December 1975. Night Nurse was hot favourite, starting at 6–4, and defeat was inconceivable. There was a theory going around at the time that, at thirty-six, Paddy was getting past it and shouldn't have been partnering such a supreme champion. On the day of the race he cut himself terribly shaving, which didn't exactly inspire confidence as to the state of his nerves. If he couldn't grasp his razor blade firmly, how would he fare with half a ton of horse in his hands? I spoke to him just before the race and his demeanour told me everything I wanted to know. He looked me in the eyes and said, 'There is no panic. He will win.' Night Nurse did so, by five lengths. Paddy didn't hang around to celebrate. He flew straight back to see his little daughter, Alison. Twenty-four years on, she is now married to my assistant trainer, Andrew Stringer, and also works in the yard. It's a small world.

I had bought Boswell Stud, lock, stock and barrel for about £120,000 and my purchase included a few show-jumpers, some of them unbroken, and mares. I kept my racehorses there, mostly 'stores' – horses that are put out to grass to strengthen up, with the eventual aim of sending them jumping at five or six.

Sue Sinclair, a keen English horsewoman in her early twenties, heard that I'd bought the place and that it would be a good place to train show-jumpers. She used to ride them at the Dublin Show, Ballsbridge, and won a few events, but there was no money in it. It was just the prestige. She was a very good rider, but there was always a conflict of interest and a lot of competition between the racehorse and show-jumping staff. I had no real interest in the show-jumpers. If there was a decision to be made between going to a show or a race meeting the latter took precedence and she wasn't very pleased when I didn't turn up, especially when, as often happened, she did quite well.

Eventually I decided that we should concentrate on racehorses and I sold all the show-jumpers. We had a team of about twenty, and sold them to the Italians and the Dutch. Some made £10,000 and Slaney Hill, one of our best horses, made around £20,000, which was a fair price at the time.

When we moved in, a piggery for 100 sows and 700 pigs had been half-completed by Frank. We'd been there a year and one of the locals said, 'You're very foolish, Barney. You should complete those stys because there's a lot of money in them.' The fellow seemed sensible and I allowed myself to be persuaded. We finished the building and went out and bought 100 sows.

As if I hadn't seen enough pigs in my childhood, I was to be surrounded by the things at Boswell Stud. We ended up with 300 or 400 pigs, with a couple of men running the operation. After a few months, I sensed something was wrong, because rather too many appeared to be dying, but it came to a head when, after about a year, my bank manager at the Northern Bank in Bray asked me to drop in.

'Is it important?' I asked him.

He said, 'I think it is.'

I knew it was nothing to do with my betting, because I was faring well in that respect.

'Now, Mr Curley, have you any idea how your pigs are going?' he asked me.

'Oh, fine,' I replied nonchalantly. 'We have the odd one dying, of course, but otherwise it's OK.'

He sat back in his chair and gave me a knowing look. 'Well, do you want to know how you're *really* doing?'

Well, in truth, I had absolutely no idea. All I'd seen were trucks pulling in and pulling out and taking the animals off to market. I thought there might be an overdraft of maybe £400 to £500. He leaned across and informed me quietly, 'I have to tell you that this operation has cost you £20,000 and if you carry on it's going to get worse. It will need thousands invested just to break even.'

I was flabbergasted. I went home and counted them and found there were about 400. I dealt with it as I do with many problems in my life. I didn't hesitate. I said to the men, 'Sell them, sows, piglets, the lot, send them all to the market. I want them out. In ten days I don't want there to be a pig anywhere near this place.' A week later not one remained. I've always had a strong view that you should get value for money, but it didn't take much to buy a pig off me at that time.

It wasn't the only failed enterprise I was involved with. I also launched a free newspaper called the *Northern Advertiser*. It was one of the first free publications around, certainly in Ireland. The headquarters were in Omagh, and it was delivered throughout Fermanagh. I drove up every week, five hours from Wicklow and five hours back, for a management meeting to discuss progress. We had six or seven staff and it was more or less breaking even. After twelve months, I was becoming concerned that we were getting nothing but trouble with distribution. There were too many complaints from readers and advertisers. One week I made up my mind. I drove up to the meeting and, before anything else was said, declared, 'As from now this newspaper is closed. There will be no printing next week.' That's the way I've operated all my life.

Left: Yes, I did have angelic features once! My younger brother Cahal (left) and me in our days as altar boys.

Below: My father Charlie, pictured as I remembered him best as a child – with his beloved motor-car and one of his greyhounds.

An unusually studious-looking B J Curley (that's me, fourth from the right, middle row) during my time at Mungret, Limerick.

My home town of Irvinestown, though it doesn't look much like this now. It was taken back in the forties when I was a young boy.

Above: My parents, Charlie and Kathleen, pose us up for a family group. That's me in the centre (in the days when I still had hair, and a lot of it, too!), my younger brother Cahal, and eldest sister Ann.

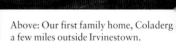

Above: Our first family home, Coladerg a few miles outside Irvinestown.

Left: Stop me and buy one ... A day out Bundoran with my cousin John Carney.

n the road with The
axton, the first showband I
as asked to manage. Who
id showbusiness was
amorous? The shades and
it are the give-away that I'm
e manager … and the fellow
th all the headaches.

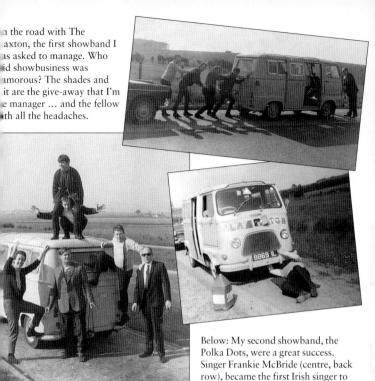

Below: My second showband, the
Polka Dots, were a great success.
Singer Frankie McBride (centre, back
row), became the first Irish singer to
break into the British Top Twenty.

Above: As this advert in the *Sun* newspaper said, 'It was the chance of a lifetime'. All you had to do was buy a ticket to win my mansion in County Westmeath. A total of 9,000 did.

Above: The winning ticket, number 41877, which made Tony Ray of Tewkesbury and his syndicate the proud new owners of Middleton House. They never moved in, and it was sold a few months later.

□ CURLEY (right) with Yellow Sam, who landed his first big coup.

Left: He was no Arkle, but Yellow Sam's jumping at the little course of Bellewstown was enough to cause mayhem among Ireland's bookmakers. That's me with 'Sam' and Liam Brennan (left), one of the best trainers I've been involved with.

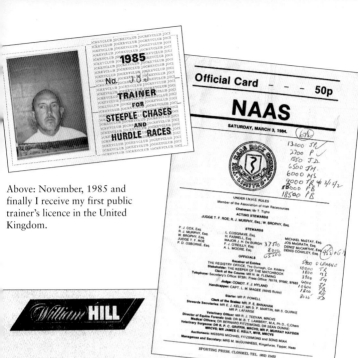

Above: November, 1985 and finally I receive my first public trainer's licence in the United Kingdom.

Above: A souvenir of my first win as a trainer in my own right and a list of some of the bookmakers who had to pay out. I'm Incommunicado wins at Naas in 1984.

Mr. B. Curley,
Harrathon Court Stables,
Exning,
Newmarket,
Suffolk.

CW 71567

5th July, 1988

Dear Mr. Curley,

I am sure that you will realise that from time to time we undertake a review of our credit clients' accounts in order to ascertain whether it is economic for the Company to maintain them.

We have just completed such a review and as a result I am obliged to tell you that your account comes into a category by virtue of which we are unable to continue to offer you credit betting facilities. I am therefore giving you notice by this letter that your account will be closed at the end of business on Wednesday the 6th July 1988, and with the exception of any outstanding ante-post commitments, no further commissions can be executed on your behalf after that date.

Yours sincerely,

A.C. Enright
Client Services Executive

Left: A letter of commendation? Well, virtually. A standard missive from bookmakers William Hill to those who win too much. They will not lay anyone with any knowledge – that's why my money is now bet underground.

Maureen and I celebrate a win at the dogs with my greyhound Portumna Wonder, who has just won the Ulster Sprint at Celtic Park in 1970. Also pictured are my old sparring partner, the late Sean Graham (centre), who presented the trophy, and trainer Ger McKenna (second right).

Maureen, Catherine and Charlie celebrate after I'm Incommunicado' win at Naas – my first as a trainer.

I have always been more of a menace than a maestro behind the wheel, but my brother Cahal has always been fascinated by cars. He won several competitions including the Donegal International Rally, the Manx International Rally, and the Circuit of Ireland.

Above: A note from bookmaker Pat Whelan after the light plane I was travelling in crashed near Chester. 'Next time you owe me, kindly travel by train,' was his sympathetic message.

bove: My cousin John Carney, ith his greyhound Green Sash. hat dog was nothing but trouble. e won a race at Dunmore Park nd it caused a riot.

Above: I take my hat off to British racing justice, after the Jockey Club reversed its decision to disqualify me for two years in 1987. It was a landmark in British racing history.

Left: Lester Piggott has the whip hand as usual, as he enjoys a morning's spin near Killarney, with me and my son, Charlie, the course secretary, Finbarr Slattery (rear) and Peter Winborne, Lester's pilot. Lester had travelled to ride at the course the previous evening.

Left: In happier days, a chat with Channel 4 betting pundit John McCririck at Kempton in 1991. We later fell out over an article he wrote and we haven't spoken since.

Right: Outside our house at Stetchworth. The personalised number plate was a rare indulgence, and I later sold it to a London casino for around £30,000.

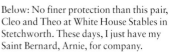

Below: No finer protection than this pair, Cleo and Theo at White House Stables in Stetchworth. These days, I just have my Saint Bernard, Arnie, for company.

Above: Pre-race advice for a youthful-looking Declan Murphy, the rider I had persuaded to come over from Ireland and ride for me. Along with Graham Bradley, he's probably the best horseman we've seen in recent years.

I certainly learnt the hard way about business and financial dealings. In 1974, a horse owner friend of Bunker Hunt, had recommended that I buy shares in silver. I bought £160,000 worth, thinking there was easy money to be had. The silver market collapsed and I was wiped out over one Whitsun weekend.

Down in Wicklow I also got to know a cattle-dealer named Peter Begley. I knew nothing about farming, but decided to buy calves and fatten them up. Too many of them went the same way as the pigs, succumbing to all manner of diseases. Initially, I blamed Peter for selling me poor animals, but there was nothing wrong with them. It was the conditions they lived in, with wind blowing in, and they were all catching pneumonia. He was as honest a man as you'd find and we became very friendly. Peter was soon to become an integral part of my gambling operation.

I also began buying yearlings as 'stores'. One of them was a horse I bought for around £1,000 and named Yellow Sam. Over the years I've owned hundreds of horses and he was among the worst I've ever had. Yet he was to change my life irrevocably.

I'd always been attracted by the idea of owning horses as mediums for gambling – though my first two ventures should have deterred me from the whole idea. It certainly didn't even cross my mind at that time that I might one day train them. I bought an interest in my first while I was still managing the bands. Charge Straight was trained by Christie Grassick, based at Phoenix Park. The mutual connection was John James McManus, who had horses with him. I bought a half-share for around £500 and John James kept half.

Barry Brogan was around at the time. He was riding as amateur jockey for Tom Dreaper, the man who trained Arkle, and I had known Barry at Mungret. Not knowing a lot about the business, I got him to work Charge Straight a couple of times. I was told the horse had been absolutely flying on the gallops.

We took him over to Ballinrobe, in the west of Ireland, full of expectation. He's the first horse I've ever seen, barring an accident, to pull up half-way in a 'bumper', which is the common name for a race on the Flat for National Hunt horses that have never hurdled or jumped fences. To say that I was a very disgruntled owner would have been putting it mildly. I didn't have another horse with Christie, who retired, although his son Michael now trains successfully and is a decent, honest man.

Around the time I got married in 1968, I bought my first horse from Liam Brennan, who was based near The Curragh, where he had about thirty horses, mostly jumpers. He had bought Tanzara, an ex-Flat horse, from one of his neighbours (John Oxx's yard) and it looked a bargain when Liam sold him to me for about £500. In fact, he was to prove considerably more costly than that.

Liam, who was married to a girl from Omagh, was also introduced to me by John James McManus, who, it will be realised by now, was a not inconsiderable go-between. It was to prove a lucrative relationship, although we didn't get off on the right foot. I wasn't familiar with ownership; I was slow in settling the training bill for that first horse and I soon discovered Liam had a ferocious temper. He was within an inch of walloping me at Mallow one evening because I had not paid him. Eventually we became very close. Indeed, I have to thank Liam for much of my early insight into racing. A former jockey, he had an excellent way with horses and, in a sense, was my mentor. He talked a lot of sense and taught me much about the game, including the importance of sealed lips. The first thing I learnt was the more people that knew your business, the less chance there was of a successful gamble. And Liam liked a 'touch', there was no doubt about that. He loved to line a horse up for a race, and more times than not they collected. If anyone had the temerity to ask if they were 'fancied', he just glared at them. That obviously suited me.

Pat Meaney, who was at one time work rider for Major Dick Hern, was Liam's stable jockey. He had served his time as apprentice with Paddy Slater, who was a master of racehorses and came to England and won many races. There were a couple of other characters who played a crucial part in my learning process: Michael Fitzgibbon, who ran a big furniture store, and vet Bill Dowling were both from Thurles and were pals of Liam and Paddy. I don't know how their respective businesses survived because they went racing virtually every day it took place. They knew a lot about horses, so I just used to listen in to all their conversations. It was a great education and an excellent grounding to listen to them talking about, evaluating and placing horses.

I was a late-starter at the game and I wasn't steeped in it, like some. I had to work harder than most to understand it. Even to this day I wouldn't be that great a judge of a horse standing in the yard. The only gift I had was a natural eye to watch a race and a horse in work.

Liam's main attribute was that he never rushed his horses, he brought them along quietly. He never got stuck into them early and never worked them very hard. He picked that up from Paddy Slater, who was an advocate of long canters rather than all-out gallops. Charlie Whittingham, the doyen of American trainers, who I was to encounter later on, was much the same. He gave them all the time they needed, too. Yet, Liam had the knack of having them fit first time out. If they were expected to win, he could produce them spot-on. The same thing applied to Charlie Whittingham. It might explain why Barney Curley can do the same. There's a gift to it.

Liam's excellence with the horses contrasted with his poor business acumen. He was useless with money and eventually he gave up training because of it. Not that he got it right with his opinion of Tanzara. The horse was a professional loser, a 'thief'. He never finished nearer than second. He would have finished second to Arkle if he could have. Suffice to say, Tanzara never won for me, although he enjoyed a new lease of life when we sold him and he went to England. It was not an auspicious start. But then, what did I know about it? Like many, I had plunged headlong into the mire of unpredictability that is ownership.

It didn't deter me for long, though, because an unlikely named character called Little Tim came along pretty quickly. He was my first winner when successful in a 'bumper' at Mallow in 1972. Bobby Barry rode him and we backed him from 20–1 down to 8–1. I always liked to repay a good turn and I picked Bobby because he and his father had been very good to me. Little Tim, named after Liam's nickname of Tim Frazer – although I've no idea where he got that epithet – was pretty good and went on to win more races. It was the first time I laid out and won serious money. Little Tim hadn't shown a great deal, but in typical Brennan style he was brought along patiently until the trainer was convinced he was spot-on.

The night before the race I had called a number of trusted collaborators to a meeting room at the Cheltenham Arms. That night it was more like a conspirators' den in a scene from a gangster movie, with the boss issuing the instructions and his ten men bidden to obey, on pain of death. Well, maybe that was a slight exaggeration; most of them worked for me and knew the score. They were honourable men and each had their own little group of 'putters-on' whom they had to trust implicitly. They departed into the night with instructions to travel round the country backing the horse. Just about anybody who was working for me was involved … showband members, people working in the betting shops and pubs – there were between thirty and forty in all.

I gave them a list of numbers of betting offices and £100 each in cash. Four of them travelled to Limerick; four would travel to Galway. In those days there weren't the bookmakers' chains there are now and information wasn't passed on to other shops, so our men could start out early, say 11.30 am. Each shop tended to work independently of the other and there had been no big schemes until then, so none of the shops suspected anything untoward was going on.

The country track of Mallow, about ten miles north of Cork, is a good galloping course with a long straight. If you get boxed in there is plenty of opportunity to extricate yourself. No excuses needed to be proffered that day. It was satisfying, indeed, as Little Tim stormed up that straight to win comfortably by a length or two.

We stayed at the Isle of Skye Hotel, near the track, and then drove back to Omagh where my 'putters-on' all 'weighed in', as we used to say, at the Cheltenham Arms the next day. Not surprisingly, that room became known as the weighing room. One of my 'putters-on' couldn't have been more incongruous; she was my wife. But undeterred, I had sent Maureen, who had come to the races with Catherine, then less than three years old, along to the Tote and told her to have a '£100-on'. It was number seventeen and she thought she'd add her own tenner to my stake. In her haste she hadn't realised that the Tote girl had given her £100 on seventeen and £10 on seven. Fortunately, she got paid, over £2,000, on my winning bet, but not on hers. Since that day she has never had another bet and left it all to me.

I had a right good 'touch' on Little Tim that day and won at least £40,000, a lot of money at that time. But remember we had put on no more than £4,000. I wasn't to know it at the time, but that exercise was a valuable rehearsal for a really big scheme in 1975.

Another of my early successes was Fair Rambler, a very good-looking, tall, black horse. I bought him as a yearling and he turned out be a multiple winner, the first time being at the big Punchestown meeting in 1973. I had already learnt by then that if you could pitch a runner, 'unfancied' by anyone but you, in against a good horse, you were laughing at the bookmakers' expense. This was an excellent case in point. One of his rivals was an ex-Vincent O'Brien Flat horse, Grand Lachine, who happened to be trained by an old sparring partner of mine, Mick O'Toole. His charge was a real 'talking' horse, and thought to be 'nailed' on that day. The course was buzzing about his chance, and he was a very hot favourite. It suited me fine. We decided to have a real go because we felt we had a good horse, too. The support for Grand Lachine helped to keep our horse out at 20–1. We duly beat him.

Having also won a big handicap hurdle at Naas, Fair Rambler was well exposed in Ireland and, in 1976, he became the first horse that I campaigned on the mainland, a strategy that was to prove hugely successful. We disguised our plans by running him twice that season in novice chases, finishing fifth at Limerick and fourth at Leopardstown, before we sent him to Hereford and the Landon Memorial Long Distance Hurdle. It was a three-mile conditions event, with only four runners, but effectively it was a match between ours and a horse of Stan Mellor's, named Cartwright. Again, that was also thought to be a good thing and again I used it to my advantage. But to ensure his price was worth backing I exploited the avarice of one of my 'putters-on'.

The rule with all my men has always been, 'If I ring you, back my horse as instructed; if I don't ring, you don't bet on it – and, just as significantly, you don't back anything else in that race. You take no part whatsoever, because it may betray my hand if bookmakers have a shrewd idea who the backer is working for.' This fellow – he is still alive and all I will say about him is that he was also a bookmaker – tried to be a bit too smart. If I didn't call him, he'd back the fancied horse in our race, on the assumption that mine wasn't 'off'. It didn't take me long to establish what he was up to. So, I deliberately didn't call him to back Fair Rambler, but rang all my other bet placers. The result was that he assumed, wrongly, that Cartwright was the one to be 'on'. He put his money on, others followed, and while Fair Rambler eventually started at 5–4, and Cartwright 11–8 on, I got on at prices up to 5–2. It proved a tougher duel than we might have envisaged, but Ben Hannon got mine home by one and a half lengths with a sustained run. It was no fluke.

TWELVE

'I'm pulling off a big coup today ...'

You'd visit the country track of Bellewstown in County Meath for the wonderful scenery alone. In the midst of golfing country, the views are spectacular. It's about twenty-three miles north of Dublin as you head towards Belfast, then turn off towards the coast down winding lanes. Perched high up on the Hill of Crockafotha beside the village, with the Mountains of Mourne in the distance, its more romantic visitors associate it with the smell of strawberries and cream and freshly mown hay. Its sharp, left-handed, nine-furlong track only had an outside running rail added in relatively recent times. For many years a makeshift barrier was provided by horse boxes and trailers – and that was to stop the horses colliding with picnic parties just out to enjoy a day's racing and take the bracing air.

But on Wednesday 25 June 1975 I wasn't there for the benefit of my health, only the health of my rocky finances. In those early years, after Lester and Roberto had been my saviours three years before, there were a couple of tricky moments but then I 'hit the wall' again in a serious way. I'd had a very bad run and had already sold the show-jumpers to try and make ends meet.

I had a chat with Liam Brennan and told him, 'I badly need to pull off a "touch". Let's go through these horses and see what horse is capable of doing it.' We didn't have much of a choice really because, being summer, we needed a horse that would go on firm or good ground. Most of our better horses were resting, awaiting softer going in the autumn, or were away on their holidays at grass. After a couple of days, he came back to me and said, 'You know, Barney, this horse Yellow Sam, I think he's improved a bit.'

I said, 'Give him a bit of work over the next couple of days and we'll see how he goes.'

Well, predictably enough, he didn't work like Arkle but he did produce enough to show us that he was capable of winning a bad race, with everything going in his favour. Liam wasn't a trainer who'd ever make the big time, but I had total faith in him. He was a good judge. As we say in Ireland, 'he wouldn't count his sheep as lambs'. Yellow Sam was really the only possibility anyway, so we decided we'd have a go and we lined him up for Bellewstown in three weeks' time.

Bellewstown is one of Ireland's oldest racecourses, with records of its races going back to 1726. At one time it had a royal connection: King George III was persuaded by George Tandy, former mayor of Drogheda and brother of Napper Tandy, arch-rival of Wolf Tone, to sponsor a prestigious race there in 1780; it was named His Majesty's Plate and was worth £100 to the winner. Every English monarch continued to support the race until 1980, when the present queen discontinued the practice. The course stages only one three-day summer meeting, when the attendance is swelled by holiday-makers, and is the Irish equivalent of, say, the Cumbrian track of Cartmel. Just along the coastline to the east is Laytown, which boasts a stretch of golden sand where on one day a year only horseracing takes place on the beach.

Informality is the key word. There are no reserved enclosures and holiday-makers mix with the professionals of both sides of the betting ring. But for all its charm, Bellewstown was, and is, very much a third division track. One thing we could be assured of that admirably suited our purpose – the poor quality of the racing. As races go, the Mount Hanover Handicap Hurdle for amateur riders, over two and a half miles, in which Liam had entered our horse, was probably worse than most races staged there.

I had bought Yellow Sam as a yearling and named him after my father's nickname. They used to call the old fellow 'Yellow Sam' because he had a sallow, almost jaundiced complexion. I have no idea where 'Sam' originated from. The horse was a brown gelding, sired by Wreckin Rambler out of a mare called Tudor Jest. He was unexceptional-looking and never very good. In all honesty, he was one of the worst horses I've ever owned. He had been unplaced and had shown very little in eight runs over two seasons, although, admittedly, some had been at decent tracks where competition would have been stiff. Wherever Liam ran him he always seemed to finish in the middle somewhere. His best placing was eighth. (Coincidentally, in one of his races he had been partnered by the top amateur Tim Jones who had ridden Gay Future to victory at Cartmel in the notorious coup there on August Bank Holiday.) No way, until this moment, could you have looked at this fellow, glanced at his form and imagine he would ever pull off a 'job'.

His only redeeming quality was that he was an excellent jumper. He hadn't much pace; in fact he was a slow horse, but he could make two or three lengths at every hurdle. He was as good a jumper as Persian War. An indication of how bad he was can be gleaned by studying his record before Bellewstown:

Season 1973–74
8 December 1973, Fairyhouse (soft), 1m 6f 3-y-o hurdle, unplaced, not in the first nine of twenty.
26 December 1973, Leopardstown (soft), 1m 5f 3-y-o hurdle, ninth of fifteen.

26 January 1974, Naas (heavy), 2m 1f maiden hurdle, eighth
of seventeen.
17 April 1974, Fairyhouse (firm), 1m 6f maiden hurdle, ninth
of seventeen.

Season 1974–75
28 December 1974, Punchestown (heavy), 2m handicap
hurdle, not in the first nine of fourteen.
17 March 1975, Limerick (heavy), 2m 5f handicap hurdle,
ninth of sixteen.
29 March 1975, Mallow (good), 2m 5f handicap hurdle, not
in the first nine of twenty.
14 May 1975, Navan (soft), 2m 5f handicap hurdle, not in the
first nine of twenty-nine.

His modest performances meant that at least he was very well
handicapped. He did have a semblance of ability, if not a lot,
and those events at country tracks in Ireland on firm ground in
the summer time can be extraordinarily bad races.
Understandably, some cynics might suggest that he hadn't
been trying before; that he had been set up specifically for this
race for a long time. Well, it was true to say that I had set horses
up with Liam in the past. But there was no truth in it this time.
We just needed a horse to do a job, and he was the only
conceivable possibility. He was a big horse who would always
be likely to require time to develop and come to his best and he
just suddenly began to show that he was sparkling. We knew
he'd go on the ground. All but two of his previous races had
been on soft or heavy going. On the one occasion he had
encountered firm ground, at Fairyhouse, he had finished ninth
out of 17 in a maiden hurdle. Although that may not seem
encouraging, it must be born in mind that Fairyhouse is a
metropolitan track where the racing is invariably of good
quality. To now bring him to Bellewstown would be like a

horse running at Sandown, then being sent to Fakenham. It was a different class altogether, a significant step down. If some of the firm ground winners at courses like Bellewstown were sent over to England to race they'd still be at the second-last hurdle when the victor was passing the post.

We had the horse. We had the race. Now the crucial, but most difficult, part was getting the money on in sufficient quantities and at suitably rewarding odds. For weeks, I didn't leave my home at Wicklow. I sat in my office and prepared everything down to the last detail, like a general massing his troops before going into battle. Only the enemy, on this occasion, were the bookmakers. Maybe a better analogy was a bank robbery. The timing had to be right and I had to trust my collaborators implicitly. Apart from the paucity of its racing I chose Bellewstown because I knew that the rarely used, remote course only had one public telephone which was the only means the on-course bookmakers had of receiving intelligence of market moves. And it was their pricing of the horse which would decide its all-important starting-price (SP). Not that I would be betting with them. They probably would have hardly taken a pound on Yellow Sam all afternoon. The betting shops were my targets and I intended to have my men put the money down in offices in every large town in Ireland. I aimed to cover about 150 shops in total, from Bantry and Skibbereen in the far southwest of Ireland to Coleraine and Ballymena in the northeast, with the bets going down roughly at the same time, just before the race and all in such small quantities that nobody would pick up on what was going on.

That was the theory, anyway. In practice, this was a far from simple task. At that time my name had become notorious on- and off-course. It was not a question of quietly going round at eleven o'clock or twelve noon and placing tens or twenties without question. The bookmakers were beginning to smell my horses from afar. Looking back, I had been seriously optimistic to assume that we could get the bets on without causing the slightest ripple of interest in those offices. There's an old adage – 'Loose lips can sink ships' – and that was in my mind constantly as I sat and schemed. One word out of place could scupper the operation, or at the very least drastically reduce its effectiveness.

I like to think I'm a good judge of people and I chose people I believed I could trust. Eventually I had compiled a list of 25 men and as the days passed I'd strike names out and replace them with others if any doubts about individuals crept into my head. It was vital that no one broke the line. Eventually I ended up with 12 generals and instructed them to recruit soldiers they could trust to put money on.

Eamon and Bernard Bradley, who had run one of my first betting shops in Enniskillen, were involved and another key figure was a chap named Brian Donavan, one of our nearest neighbours in Wicklow, who owned a meat business in Dublin. He had on a substantial amount of money for me. All my men got around £1,200 each, but a lot of them just got involved for the sheer thrill of it.

I was like a recluse as I sat in my little room at the Boswell Stud with my maps and my lists. Maureen had a fair idea about what going on, but this was something I had to plan alone. I spent hour upon hour, over many weeks, poring over my lists and maps, striking names out if I wasn't sure about them, to make sure I had the best possible team and ones that were completely trustworthy. It was not that I feared they would be traitors, just that too many men cannot be charged with keeping a secret. They would obviously have to contract out and a lot of the men I finished up with would have been punters in the betting shops all over the country, whom I'd known down the years from my days with the showbands. They backed horses all the time and would not provoke any undue suspicion.

I never told anyone directly of my plans; not Maureen, not my parents. Even Liam didn't know precisely what I was going to do, or the extent of it. Everything was kept as low key as possible. Just one whisper could have jeopardised the whole operation. That strategy worked because not a whisper got back to the track until it was too late. It was a massive operation and I put a lot of thought into it.

The most vital link in my chain of command was my man who would effectively block the one racecourse telephone, but without drawing attention to the fact. If he didn't do his job properly the whole thing would be blown wide open. I chose a fellow named Benny O'Hanlon, who had worked for me in my betting shops and was then manager at Lisnaskea in Fermanagh. No man could have possessed more integrity than Benny. If you told him to do something, that was it; he'd obey you implicitly. As for his honesty, he wouldn't steal a pound if you left it in front of him for a year. Benny was a balding, heavily built kind of fellow, a tough sort that you wouldn't want to get into an argument with. He was a man I could trust with my life. He would let no one pass. To get him off the phone it would need a man to get out a gun and shoot him. And the important thing was, he was a great talker.

Benny was a little older than me, and from a very well thought-of family who ran a shop in Irvinestown, selling clothes. He was a real character who had held down every sort of job in his time, from buying and selling jute bags to working for a time as a barman in London. He was once so short of cash, so the story goes, that he confessed to being the serial killer John Christie in order to get a police cell for the night. I went 'nap' on him as my 'phone man' without any reservations.

He was more than just an employee. Maureen and I were great friends with him. He was a bachelor, but was wonderful with children. In fact, he later taught my elder daughter

Catherine to drive without me ever knowing anything about it, although I wasn't too enamoured with that as she was only about thirteen at the time. He wasn't easy to manage and, at times, could be irritatingly pedantic. He was on Irvinestown Parish Council, which ran the church affairs. I remember in later years the priest once called me up.

'Could you do me a favour?' he asked.

'What's that Father?'

'Could you get that Benny O'Hanlon down to Mullingar [where we were living at the time] on nights of parish council meetings, because Benny objects to everything. Whatever idea you put up, he just knocks it down.'

That was Benny all over; yet he fitted the bill perfectly because of his other qualities. He wouldn't have dreamt of stealing £20 from my shop, but he didn't think twice of blocking that phone box because he trusted and believed in me implicitly. When I owned the betting shops, Benny used to really drop me in it. He used to ring Maureen and say, 'He's a bloody disgrace, that man of yours. He never comes near this office. The whole place could be falling apart.' So I did my rounds and his shop at Lisnaskea would be first on the list. I'd say, 'Benny, give me £5 worth of ten pences.' I'd love to play slot machines, although I could never win because it was the firm's own money. I just loved trying to get up three apples, cherries, or whatever. I'd arrive about one o'clock, and was supposed to be checking dockets and how we'd done for the last couple of weeks. When Maureen would ring two hours later to find out why I wasn't at the next shop, Benny would blurt out, 'Oh, sure, he's here alright. Your man walked in here at exactly five to one and he's been playing that one-armed bandit since. He's put £20 in that machine' He enjoyed giving me a bit of aggravation and he was probably too honest for his own good.

He was a worrier, too. He was always going on about how

the day had gone against him, how so-and-so had taken a lot of money off us. To listen to him, you'd think we'd never come out on top. He forgot all the times when the punters went down. For that reason I never explained how big this operation was, and how major his part. He would have been quaking in his boots.

Normally one of Sean Graham's men would be on the phone in question to make sure that money came back to the course. Sean, who died a few years ago, was one of Ireland's biggest and best-known bookmakers and the family book-making business in his name still flourishes today. We were both from Northern Ireland and I'd known him as a friend for fifteen years, ever since those nights at Celtic Park when we both made books. We were both operating on the Southern circuit and it was inevitable that we should lock horns and there was always a bit of needle between us.

Back in the summer of 1975, the stark fact was that I owed around £30,000, and I couldn't pay. 'I've hit a brick wall, Sean,' I told him about a week before the big day. 'I need your help. I could do this without you, but I'd rather I had your help. You'll have to give me your word you'll not tell a soul.' He agreed, as long as I didn't go anywhere near his betting shops. I didn't go into details straight away, just that I was going to back a horse. I could have blocked the phone without telling him, but it would have aroused his suspicions anyway, so I thought it best to put him in the picture. I knew I could trust him to keep quiet and he told no one. The knowledge that my horse was fancied and was a 20–1 chance was very useful to him.

Normally, off-course bookmakers, whether it's Ladbrokes today or small Irish chains of shops then, transfer their liabilities to the on-course market – some of us would say manipulate the market – which brings down a particular horse's odds. With today's communications technology it's a simple matter. Even then all it should have taken was a phone call. But my plan was that the calls would never get through – until it was too late.

It might be asked, why didn't my men take a price and avoid all the subterfuge? Well, the simple answer is that the shops would not give a price – especially on one of mine. It was safety first. They'd only offer an SP on bets, and if liabilities started mounting up would send the money back to the track so that, in theory anyway, there would be a balanced market. By now, I'd begun to instil fear into the Irish bookmakers. When the money was down they'd fear my horses. Over three years I'd built up a bit of a reputation.

When the declarations were made, we could not have hoped for a better race, or, to be strictly accurate, a worse race, in which to pull off our scheme. This event, whichever you looked at it, was a dreadful race. One of our rivals had won a maiden hurdle, and another had been placed, but they were just in equally poor summer maiden hurdles. They wouldn't have been worth a dollar, those horses. And the ground was just as we wanted it – firm.

Because of his previous moderate displays Yellow Sam was allotted a weight of 10st 6lb in the field of nine runners, of whom the top weight carried 12st. He was third lowest in the weights. It was hardly a great burden given the mediocre standard of his opponents. But his likely starting price of 20–1 was not over-generous, it was the price represented on all known form. As for the riders, there were some decent names taking part. They included Sam Morshead, Willie Mullins, Ted Walsh, John Fowler and Mrs Ann Ferris, who in 1984 would become the first lady jockey to win the Irish Grand National. But our jockey Michael Furlong – later associated with that fine chaser Bannow Rambler, brought down by the fatal fall of Lanzarote when heavily backed in the 1977 Cheltenham Gold Cup – was no mug either. That year, he was runner-up in the amateur jockey's championship, beaten to the title by Ted Walsh by only one race.

The morning of the race I set out to drive the fifty-mile journey from Wicklow in great spirits, but strangely felt the urge to talk to someone whom I knew I could trust and respect. Back at Mungret I had become quite friendly with Barry Brogan, who, like Tommy Stack and Bobby Barry, had been lay pupils at the college. Barry developed into a successful jump jockey on both sides of the Irish Sea, and rode for me on several occasions, although he also became a heavy gambler and an alcoholic and, by his own admission, fixed races to pay his betting debts. Barry was exceptionally talented, possibly as gifted a rider as Richard Dunwoody or Graham Bradley, but he went off the rails in a major way. Initially, I tried to make excuses for him and tried to sympathise with him. Being charitable, I can only put it down to witnessing the death of his trainer father, Jimmy, who suffered a heart attack on the gallops. It was a terrible thing for a young man to experience. Both Liam, for whom he rode out, and I tried to help him by giving him rides when others were spurning his approaches.

Barry had been riding Yellow Sam in his work, and he quickly realised the horse had a race in him. 'He was moving exceptionally well,' Barry was to comment later. Yet, I was determined that Barry Brogan would be the last to know about what was afoot. He was a liability. You simply could not trust him. He was too close to several other professional gamblers and bookmakers and he had loose lips, even more so when the drink was flowing. Strangely enough, Barry was the antithesis of the remainder of his family, of whom I have always had the highest regard. I've never known a man outside the priesthood who was so religious as his father, Jimmy. Every day, without fail, he would read *The Imitation of Christ*. That is rather heavy going, to say the least, and is a practice normally only carried out in monasteries.

Barry was the eldest of four children and had been followed by Ann, and twins Peter and Pamela. The whole family was involved in some way with horses, and Ann, who was a lovely girl and a joy to talk to, though she was a lot younger than me, became a particular friend. We had a lot in common, sharing a religious faith and a love of horses. She was a very good point-to-point rider and, later, also had several winners as an amateur under rules. Ann was never a very worldly sort of girl and always thought she was destined to be a nun.

The Brogans lived at Rathfeigh, about four miles from the course at Bellewstown, a bleak outpost of a place on top of a hill, and on the way I decided to call in. It was always a nice, welcoming house, and they'd sit you down with tea and cake. I suppose I felt a tinge of excitement and just needed someone to talk to. Ann was a great listener. I could barely contain myself about what was planned, and couldn't help just throwing into the conversation casually, 'I'm pulling off a big coup today, and if it comes off I might end up in the *Guinness Book of Records*.' I didn't add that if it didn't I might end up in an almshouse.

At that stage, I still didn't really know what it could mean financially. For all my planning, there were so many unpredictables. Calling in one or two debts of my own, I had around £15,000 to play with. Even when I have been in really dire straits, I've always kept spare cash for such purposes. I didn't really know how much money would get on, or whether the price would stay at 20–1. All I knew was that if all went to plan and my men did their job, it would be the equivalent of my six numbers up – and the bonus ball.

I don't think Ann really took it all in and she probably thought I was talking about a few thousand. She asked me where it was taking place. 'Over at Bellewstown,' I told her, and added as an afterthought. 'Would you come up with me?' It was unusual for me. I usually prowled the racecourse like a lone wolf stalking his prey, but that day the build-up was such that I needed a confidante while I waited for the race to start. I felt like a boxer, prepared for months with road work and gym, and itching to land the knockout blow.

I said to her, 'Now listen, Ann, I can't afford to be seen.' So, she agreed to drive me up to the racecourse, but, under my instructions, kept well away from the hurly-burly of the public enclosure. I knew it would be well attended, with maybe a couple of thousand people packing the place. I never went near the entrance until afterwards. I knew people would have been looking out for me because my horse was running. And that would have been a sign that it was fancied. The back-straight of the track is along the side of the road, so she stopped half-way along and we crossed over the course itself, without anyone seeing us, and me with my hat pushed as far down as it would go. I probably resembled George Cole playing the gambling spiv in the St Trinian's films as we positioned ourselves out of sight in the centre of the racetrack. That was how, on this fine, sunny day, as the minutes ticked slowly by to the 'off', I came to be hiding behind some gorse bushes with Ann Brogan, somewhere in the middle of Bellewstown racecourse.

Meanwhile, all over Ireland, my troops were moving into action. I told my generals at a quarter to two. But it wasn't until fifteen minutes before the race, due off at three o'clock, that they told their own men. Each man put on anything from £50 to £300, depending on the size of the shop, and all totalling £15,300. Deliberately, I selected mostly independent bookies so that there would be less of an intelligence network. The offices were happy to accept the bets fifteen minutes before the race thinking they'd have no trouble in laying it off. All they would have to do was to pick up the phone and have it backed on the race-track. Of course they would be pickled come five to three when they couldn't get through and no other off-course bookmakers wanted any money for the horse. They would have to sweat it out and see if Yellow Sam got beaten.

But all that presumed a lot on my part, and specifically that Benny carried out my instructions to the letter. Benny was told to go into that phone box twenty-five minutes before the race start with strict orders: 'No matter who comes to the phone, do not leave it under any circumstances until the commentator announces, "They're off".' It was a huge responsibility. Such was the crowd that day that to keep the phone occupied for half an hour required a stroke of genius. But as I have already said, he was as garrulous as they come. He got talking to some non-existent hospital in nearby Drogheda, where he had an aunt who was dying. Every few minutes Benny would announce his relative's state of health, 'Oh, alright, then, that's not so bad ... oh, dear, she's taken a turn for the worse again.' It was the mundane kind of thing people say when they're inquiring about someone in hospital, but it did the trick. Never has a patient gone through so much recovery and relapse in half an hour. She was about to die and then she got better; she was about to die again and then she rallied. It was all total nonsense, but he carried it off brilliantly. Just as insurance, I placed another chap nearby, just in case it turned nasty and there were fisticuffs. Benny just picked him up on the way and told him to be first in the queue and not budge for anyone. He was there as a kind of minder, to keep a bit of control outside the phone box.

The result was that, with no money to speak of on-course and no word from the 'layers' off-course, the price of Yellow Sam, the outsider, remained static on the bookmakers' boards as the field set off on their eighteen-furlong journey, with 20–1 the officially returned SP. That phone would have been hot with people trying to get through as the money went on in the shops, and once Benny relinquished his position, it had the same effect as a dam bursting.

Meanwhile, out in the parade ring, Michael Furlong, who probably thought he was on a no-hoper, got his first hint of what was really expected of the horse. He had absolutely no idea at all what he was involved in. He was given simple instructions by Liam, basically told to bide his time and hit the front when he thought it was the right moment. As he was legged up into the saddle, he heard just two words, 'You'll win.' Knowing my reputation, and Liam's, he would have understood the message without need of repetition.

Behind that gorse bush in the middle of the track, watching the race through my binoculars, I could see precious little of the finish. And frustrating it was, too. It sounds ridiculously surreptitious on my part, but those bookies were no mugs, and a whiff of my presence would have had them scenting a scam. Ann's mother, Betty, was at the races and, apparently, there was a real buzz about the place as it became apparent that a 'job' had been done.

If you imagined I'd be nervous during the four minutes and fifty-one seconds duration of that race, you'd be quite wrong. Once I got to the course I was ice-cold, even though defeat would have wiped me out. That has always been my way. You couldn't read me at the races and the day that doubt and anxiety enter my thoughts as I walk in through the gates is the day that I'll retire from the game. Yet, I knew that all it would take would be a fall or blunder at any one of the thirteen flights of hurdles and I'd kiss the money, all £15,300 of it, goodbye. But I had faith in my horse's jumping ability and the expertise of his partner. And neither let me down.

Ann and I were a couple of hurdles up from the finish post, so we were well placed to watch the majority of the race. We witnessed Yellow Sam progress from midfield to assert his authority after four flights, then take up the early lead on the inside from Satlan and Philipine Hill. Michael gave him an excellent, confident ride; he was always a great jockey at getting horses to jump and he always looked to be going better than anything else. He held on with something in hand, officially two and a half lengths, by the line.

Or so I found out later. From our vantage point, we only got a rapidly disappearing view of horse hindquarters, the back of jockeys and whips waved like conductors' batons – I couldn't actually see who had won. I thought we had done it, but, in the circumstances, it was too close for comfort. Only getting a rear view, you can never be certain what has won and we couldn't hear the commentary ... I wasn't absolutely sure, so we dashed across the racetrack, back into the car and drove round to the entrance. I did not know quite what to say. I didn't want it to appear as though there was anything wrong. I just stood there, lost for words, then somebody said 'well done, Barney' to me, and then I knew I could relax. As you can imagine, at that price and with his form, the majority of the crowd, who would have been ignorant of what had been going on, weren't exactly ecstatic.

For the record, this was how they finished:

Mount Hanover Amateur Riders' Handicap Hurdle, 2m 5f:
    1st Yellow Sam 5-10-6, M.J. Furlong, 20–1
    2nd Glenallen 7-9-11, H.C. Morshead, 12–1
    3rd Silver Road 7-10-11, W. Mullins, 4–1
    4th Satlan 7-10-8, A. Tyrrell, 9–2
    Portballintrae 6-11-2, Mrs H. Ferris
    High And Mighty 6-10-9, T.M. Walsh
    Philipine Hill 7-10-13, E. Woods
    Gerties Beauty 8-10-3, T. McCartan
    Deadlock 4-10-9, J.R. Fowler
    Distances: Two and a half lengths, two and a half lengths, two and a half lengths.
    Time: 4 min 51.20 sec. Tote: win paid £31.54.

I hung around for about ten minutes to watch the effect of his win and I saw at least one bookmaker, with off-course liabilities, kicking up a right fuss. All hell broke loose. All the shops were at last getting through on the phone in the box which Benny had now long vacated, and the men at the course were realising that the off-course offices had been caught, although even then I don't think at that moment they realised the gravity of the situation. I thought it was an appropriate moment to make a diplomatic departure, and Ann drove me home for a cup of tea. Her mother and Jim Dreaper, who has trained Betty's horses for her for many years and is one of Ireland's great gentlemen, and Liam were also there, and into the middle of this intimate gathering entered Barry Brogan, still oblivious to what had gone on.

Apparently, he had sauntered into the racecourse after the race and been told by the gateman that Brennan had a big winner. Liam perpetuated the deception by declaring, when Barry congratulated him, 'Oh, don't talk to me, I'm sick. Michael came through on him and we didn't expect him to win. Barney is furious.' All total nonsense, of course, but even afterwards it would not have been prudent to reveal the truth to Barry immediately. Not a word was said at our post-race tea party, either. Indeed, I had to borrow a fiver from Mrs B to buy some petrol to drive home, not being a great one for carrying cash. Nor was anything said next morning at the stables after Barry had ridden out, and it was not until the following evening that he finally bought an evening paper and saw the headline emblazoned, 'Biggest SP job ever landed in Ireland – Yellow Sam at 20–1!' He nearly collapsed with the shock of it all.

Most people would expect that an Irishman having a successful major punt should be out revelling to the early hours, keeping the whole village or town in drink. I'm probably a major let-down to the image of Irish tradition and culture, but there were no celebrations. I simply drove home and went to bed, feeling quietly satisfied at a job well done. It was still on my mind that if the bet had gone down I'd have been in serious trouble. The tank would then really have been empty. My sense of exhilaration was tinged with more than a hint of relief. Before I fell asleep, I just mentioned to Maureen, 'We've had a "touch".'

Ann died a few years later. But I am sure she found peace. She was always too good for this world. Her mother continues to live in the same house, where she farms and keeps a few horses. She has always been good to me, and I have often sent her problem horses to care for.

I still had no idea how much I'd won. It took a few days to collect it all at our base, a hotel near home back in Wicklow. I didn't dare get my men to bring it to the stud, because I feared that the boys with shooters might turn up. Whatever the total, in one pound and one punt notes, it took a lot of space, and we had to put it into one hundredweight bags before we moved it to the bank.

By next day the whole world knew about it. According to the papers some bookmakers were refusing to pay. There was a desperate hullaballoo, but my initial fears proved unwarranted. My men had gone round to collect and most had paid out. Just a few prevaricated. You have to bear in mind that although the pay-out was massive for the time, about £300,000 – equivalent to around £1.4 million nowadays – it was spread relatively thinly. No individual shop had to pay out more than £6,000. It wouldn't have put any out of business, but a sizeable pay-out like that might have damaged their profits for the next couple of months. There wouldn't have been much other betting on that race, not on an amateur riders' handicap hurdle on a Wednesday afternoon.

As I've already explained, gambling debts are not

recoverable by law, but the 'layers' probably realised that if they hadn't paid I'd have kicked up a real commotion. Had they continued to withhold payment my recourse would have been to object to their licence next time they tried to renew it. But I must say that, ultimately, there was not a space in my betting book where people owed me money. Bookmakers as a breed are a lot more honourable than people imagine. At least, they were then. If I pulled the same stroke nowadays in Britain, I could envisage that big multiples like Ladbrokes and William Hill would refuse to pay out. I don't remember anyone that didn't pay, eventually. There were a lot of cracks about me afterwards from the bookies, but it was mostly in good humour. I recall one fellow, Harry Barry, being particularly slow, but the guy who had the bet with him got the money out of him somehow. I think it was their pride, which had been dreadfully wounded, which got to them more than any financial loss. One of those hit was Terry Rogers, who for three decades was an institution at Irish racecourses until he hung up his satchel in 1988. He would make a book on anything within reason and normally paid out with remarkable stoicism.

Yet Terry was most grieved by Yellow Sam's success. I can't say I really blame him. Having said that, his was the first cheque in the post. He's always respected me for paying my debts on time and never 'welching'.

My own mother and father had only discovered what had been going on by reading about it in the papers. I remember my father calling me up a few days later and saying, 'I see you had a "touch"?'

I replied , 'I did.'

He said, 'Did you get paid?'

I said, 'I did.'

And all he said was, 'That's what matters.'

Those were the only words we ever exchanged on the subject, although a small part of me regarded the success of the scheme as some kind of retribution for what had happened to my father nearly twenty years before.

I'd set out with Yellow Sam merely to recoup some serious losses. As I began to liaise with my men it soon became obvious that there was to be a significant windfall. Even more than what a chairman of a privatised utility might expect today. The notes just kept swirling from the skies. I had always worked on the basis that Yellow Sam's price would be around 20–1 but I never imagined we'd be successful in piling on so much money at the 150 betting shops I'd originally targeted. It's always been estimated that the bookies paid out around £300,000, but I must confess I have no real idea. I gave up counting. It was a lot more than I had originally bargained for.

Terry Rogers calculated it was more than that, and he was to comment later, 'What annoyed me is the revelation that Curley and Graham were in cahoots, which is a bit rich for a guy who is always going on about bookies rigging the market.' I could understand his frustration, although I could never see the rationale of his argument; the simple fact was that the scheme would have worked without Sean's cooperation anyway as the horse's form represented a 20–1 chance. However hard I was pressed I could never say anything derogatory about Terry, who was raised in the Dublin suburb of Blackrock where Pat Eddery was born. If I was in Dublin, the first person I'd call to have a night out with would be him. He is one of life's givers, but in a quiet way. Sometimes at the racecourse he came across as a raucous individual and you couldn't ignore his booming tones, but he was always good for a fiver in the early days when you were skint. In later years he has done a lot for the poor folk around Dublin. He has always had a favourite saying: 'All men are the same, under and over the turf.'

The bookmakers continued to make all manner of threatening noises, but they had to accept that there was nothing illegal in what had gone on. Unlike some attempted coups, I didn't hide anything about what had happened. There were no 'ringers' involved. It was quite simply one man's brains against the bookmakers'. I'd outwitted the system and taken advantage of unique circumstances. You couldn't do it today. If they'd been able to, the bookies would have driven that horse into the ground. If those calls had got through and they'd got the money back to the track they would have made that horse 6–4 favourite, but that was not their divine right. To do something like that, to kid everybody, and for it all to go so smoothly, gives you a great sense of achievement. There was not a hitch. I had no qualms whatsoever about it. I wish I could do it again. It was there to be done – and it worked. There was nothing illegal about it, and I never considered there was anything immoral about it.

Neither did Benny, God rest his soul, who played a starring role in the success of that day. He was a great actor. They ought to have given him an Oscar for his performance. He was absolutely brilliant. He picked exactly the right theme. When he stuck his head out of the door and said he had a relative dying it would have silenced them, at least for a few minutes. Who's going to berate a man with that to contend with? The Irish race is very sympathetic by nature. They gave him a little bit of hassle, but nothing like if he'd been ringing for racing results or something. A stick of dynamite couldn't have moved Benny that afternoon.

He didn't do it for the money, either. He just liked to be in the thick of anything going on. He said to me later, 'Barney, I don't want to have to go through that again.' He didn't, though a few years later he would become involved in another scheme of mine that was nearly as lucrative. If there's a Heaven, he's there. Benny used to bring my mother her newspapers every morning about nine o'clock and on the 24 February 1984, aged just fifty-two, he sat down next to her and died in her arms.

THIRTEEN

Not what the doctor ordered

Yellow Sam was just an old-fashioned coup which took advantage of a peculiar situation. Once the dust had settled, my success had the one significant effect of hastening improvements in bookmakers' communications. And never again, right up until this day, was B J Curley, as owner or trainer, allowed to run a horse in Ireland or England without the bookies treating it with the utmost caution.

Relatively speaking, it was the biggest coup ever. Certainly, it was the last great racing scheme when everybody got paid. The perpetrators of the 'Gay Future affair' didn't get their money, estimated at £200,000 if the bookmakers had honoured their obligations. When a jury subsequently found the Irish syndicate involved guilty of conspiracy to defraud, it meant that the 'layers' could refuse to pay out and all bets were declared void. The crucial difference was that 'Gay Future' crossed the line into illegality.

Yellow Sam ran again a couple of times for me soon afterwards as we tried to take advantage of the fast ground and his lenient handicap. Twelve days after the Bellewstown coup we sent him out again and, despite a 7lb penalty, he won a three-mile handicap hurdle at Wexford when carrying 9st 11lb, also on firm ground. This time he was 5–2 second favourite. His six rivals were better quality than at

Bellewstown but he still had enough in hand, and got home by one and a half lengths.

In truth, that was a bonus. Four days after that he went to Galway for a 2m 5f amateur riders' handicap hurdle, but by this time the handicapper had got hold of him and he was only ninth of seventeen, at an SP of 6–1. The bookmakers would not fear him again, at least not in Ireland. We sent him to Doncaster sales and he was bought for 4,900 guineas to go into training with Ken Oliver, the 'Benign Bishop' as he was known. Yellow Sam never won again. The following year he went novice chasing, but never appeared to take to the bigger obstacles. He was placed a few times, but made mistakes and fell repeatedly and was eventually killed in a race.

Three years after 'Yellow Sam', in October 1978, a pal of mine, Con Murphy, tried to emulate my success with a coup at Mullingar greyhound track that bore many of the hallmarks of my scheme. He always maintained that it was his original idea, but I say jokingly that he stole it from me. In fairness, it was a brilliantly executed coup and had appeared to have been successful, but, unlike mine, the winning bets were not honoured.

Con is now racing manager for a friend of mine, Patsy Byrne, who is one of the few people I have trained for. At the time Con was a part-time bookmaker from Abbeyfeale, County Limerick, who circulated around forty of his cronies, including teachers, accountants, civil servants, shopkeepers and even a Garda officer, and said, 'Would you like to come to Mullingar next Saturday night? I want you to do a little bit of business for me.' When they arrived there his motley crew of innocents were told to block all the Tote windows for as long as possible by pretending not to know which dog to back or which number. They were to allow no one else to place a bet and were to put loads of money on every dog in the race and have only one bet on Con's own, Ballydonnell Sam.

That dog, as big a certainty as you are likely to get, duly won the third heat of the Brush Tim Midland Cesarewitch at a starting price of 2–1 on. Because of the manipulation, the Tote paid 956–1! However, when all his team went to collect winnings from betting shops in the area, having asked for the Tote price rather than the SP, they were refused. Indeed, the Garda were called in to investigate and for a time there were some extremely worried people. It didn't surprise me. I blocked one phone box. This was blatant manipulating of the Tote operation. As I was then living just down the road from the track, it gave me a good laugh, and you had to give Con full marks for ingenuity, but it simply didn't possess the subtlety of my scheme. However, in his honour, I named one of my horses after him, Mullingar Con. Coincidentally, he hasn't been too successful either …

All kinds of rules were introduced by the bookmakers to try and stop anybody emulating me. In particular, they brought in a limit of £25 that you could bet just before the off. I was determined not to let them beat me and vowed to teach the bookmakers a lesson. I came frustratingly close to repeating the 'Yellow Sam coup'.

The story had begun back in 1971 when I had been over to Las Vegas with a couple of friends, Johnny McCarthy and Oliver Barry. I met a fellow called Doctor Mike Hines. He was a divorce lawyer for many big stars of stage and screen and told me about a grey yearling he owned called Dr Hines, appropriately sired by a stallion called Nevada Battler. I liked the horse so much that I bought him for around £5,000 and had him shipped home. He hadn't shown much as a two- or three-year-old, but I always had faith in him as a 'job' horse, one of those who'd do the business for you when it was needed.

To put the bookmakers' hounds off my scent, I also decided

on another more radical plan of sending the horse to Ray Peacock's small yard in Tarporley, Cheshire. The advantage of the horse being in Ray's charge was that he had the reputation of being a thoroughly decent, honest, hard-working trainer who ran a non-gambling operation, and in the infrequent circumstances he saddled a winner, it invariably went in at long odds. The one big mistake I made was employing Barry Brogan to ride him.

It was in March, before the 'Yellow Sam coup', that Ray had booked him to ride Dr Hines in a novice hurdle over two miles at Bangor-on-Dee. The horse, like Yellow Sam later, had shown not a hint of ability in his five previous runs that season. As far as the punters were concerned, Barry, whose tarnished reputation had been temporarily repolished by partnering High Ken to win the Greenall Whitley Chase at Haydock, was to ride John Edwards's well-fancied horse, Topping. But he switched to Dr Hines at short notice.

This was potentially a massive pay-day. Dr Hines started at 16–1, but I had him backed at 25–1 and 20–1 as well, throughout England and Ireland, and I could well have collected £300,000 if he had won. Although Bangor is a tight track, favouring front-runners, this particular horse, who was a hard-puller, needed holding up until the last possible moment. It needed a man with patience and sufficient courage to play the waiting game. Barry wasn't that man. He lost his bottle and he probably wasn't fit enough to settle the horse anyway because of the effect of all his drinking binges. I could only look on in exasperation as Dr Hines took it up four from home. He was still in front at the last, before being headed on the run-in, not by one but two rivals, and going down by four lengths. As the jockeys unsaddled I was furious. Not because I'd lost – I've always been professional and unemotional enough to handle that – but with Barry for riding such an incompetent race. I went storming up to the weighing room to confront him, but, wisely, he refused to come out and discuss it with me.

With some horses, their 'day' comes but rarely, and that was Dr Hines' for the time being. He ran a week later at Southwell in a desperately poor novice hurdle, with Barry still in the saddle, and was beaten fifty lengths into sixth. He started 6–4 favourite as the money poured in on him, though not a penny of it was mine.

I had another plot in mind. The plan, this time, was to run two horses in a 2m 1f 172yd maiden hurdle at Downpatrick on Monday 25 August. I had the 5–4 on favourite in the race, the 'talking horse', Cannon Gun, but our supposedly 'unfancied' runner Dr Hines, was also there. Everybody assumed he was there to make up the numbers, and was 16–1. I recruited a small team once more, and just as with Yellow Sam, we put money around the country in small amounts – on Dr Hines. Those bets of £10 and £20 didn't attract any suspicion, and we also had around £6,000 on in Dublin betting shops, using credit accounts, which were not affected by the new rules. It could have gone either way, and it would have been nearly as big as the Bellewstown win, but that is the luck of the game.

If all went to plan the good Dr Hines would be a cure for many financial ills. This time, it was a calamity. I have to laugh about it now, but I couldn't then. According to the judge, Dr Hines was officially beaten a short head by Caroline's Dream. At that time there was no photo-finish at Downpatrick. It was close, but I think our horse was first past the post. The judge gave the decision to the other horse. Cannon Gun, the favourite, was well beaten. I've heard it said since that the judge gave the decision to the other horse because he thought he was doing me a favour by keeping Dr Hines a maiden and assumed I had backed my other horse, the favourite ... I couldn't believe it.

But six weeks later I recouped some losses when we took Dr

Hines over to Sedgefield and Tommy Stack rode him in a 'seller'. I told him to leave his challenge as long as possible and it worked to perfection. He won as he pleased, but it was not a nice price: he started at 11–8 on.

My name had now achieved notoriety on both sides of the Irish Sea, and increasingly I had to recruit people to place bets for me to elude the bookmakers' lines of intelligence.

But I was always on the lookout for a new scheme. One involved Tommy Joe, one of the 'store' horses I had nurtured at Wicklow, and named after the nickname I had for our elder daughter Catherine. I got a major result out of him on 7 November 1975. He had already won a couple of races at Limerick and Kilbeggan within three days of each other in September. When Liam sent him over to England and he scored at 9–2 in a handicap hurdle at Doncaster, I landed bets totalling about £30,000 in the process.

Overall, I was reputed to have made over £1 million on Yellow Sam, Tommy Joe and several others, and that wasn't far out. In between those successes, in the late seventies and early eighties I launched a series of spectacular betting raids in England, predominantly with unraced two-year-olds. It was crucial that the horses were all first-time starters and specially selected and, as part of the plan, were sent to trainers who did not often have juvenile winners and, when they did, tended to go off at long prices. The important factor was that, as far as the bookmakers and punters on the racecourse were concerned, the horses had no connection with me.

Again, it was a real military operation. They had all been honed to peak fitness by a brilliant trainer, Paddy Norris, who was based at The Curragh, and at one time sent out a couple of Royal Ascot winners. When it came to assessing horses, particularly juveniles, trainers didn't come much more astute than Paddy. If Paddy said they were ready to win, you didn't ignore him. I bought the horses from him and sold them on to English owners, which kept my name nicely out of the equation. The beauty of the plan was that there was nothing apparently exceptional about the horses, but in they went, first time out, at big prices. It was highly successful and my strike rate was seven out of eight. My profit ranged from £50,000 to £70,000 each time. I was really hungry at that time.

One was Cathmaria, named after my two daughters. She was a two-year-old chestnut filly and was another we sent to Ray Peacock, who bought her for his wife. Her target was the Sycamore Stakes, a six-furlong 'seller' at Haydock in October 1976, when she would be partnered by Willie Carson. I told Ray she was best held up for a late run and he passed that on to the jockey. However, Willie completely ignored those instructions and I was cursing him, as he immediately settled her in a prominent position among her nineteen rivals and took the lead two furlongs out. But I couldn't protest too much, because Cathmaria won anyway by two and a half lengths. We backed her down from 14–1 to 13–2, and I walked away with over £50,000.

Another of those unraced raiders was a three-year-old chestnut filly called Tralee Falcon, which I had sent over to Jimmy Fitzgerald's Malton Yard in early 1977. He had entered the filly, now owned by his wife, for the Knayton Stakes, a five-furlong 'seller' at Thirsk on 20 April. As far as the public and bookmakers were concerned she was an unraced 'plater', owned by the trainer, and would presumably need time to achieve peak fitness.

I had been anxious to ensure that none of the money I was placing around Ireland and England got back to the track and affected the SP. By chance, I was in the north of England one day when I got talking to a telephone engineer in a pub. During our conversation he told me that it would be a relatively simple operation to cut off phone lines to a particular area. I asked him, 'If I give you £1,000 could you knock out the Thirsk area for a few minutes?' He laughed and replied, 'For a thousand, I'll take out the whole of the north of England!' I thought he was joking initially, but eventually he convinced me he was serious and for a few vital minutes before the race the lines to the course went dead. I backed Tralee Falcon at 14–1 and won about £80,000.

It was only five furlongs and the horse got left, but the jockey Edward Hide never rushed her and she took it up well inside the final furlong to win by a deceptively comfortable half a length. She also landed her next race, a non-'seller', too, so that first win was not altogether unpredictable – to those in the know. There was a major inquiry into events afterwards by stewards and the racecourse, but nobody was ever the wiser.

Yes, there was an element of deceit to it, although I stress nothing illegal took place, or anything that transgressed Jockey Club rules had they been aware of it, but the system leads to that. If I'd have brought those horses over in my name, or there'd been any connection with me, they'd have been 6–4 and I wouldn't have been able to get my bets on them. That's always been my way. It's me or the bookmakers, and they're not going to put me out of business. I won't go until I retire gracefully, or I'm feet up.

FOURTEEN

'Monarch of all I survey'

I lost my heart to Middleton House immediately I set eyes on it in a magazine advertisement. Maureen and I had walked around the grounds of the ancestral home of the Boyd-Rochforts, who were major landowners in Ireland for hundreds of years and, as we drove back down the mile-long drive, I said to her, 'I'm going to buy this place.' There was no dissent from her.

I had no plans to use the proceeds from 'Yellow Sam' until I discovered that this breathtaking Georgian mansion in County Westmeath, nine miles from Mullingar and fifty-two miles from Dublin, was for sale. It was rebuilt in 1834, after the original house had been destroyed by fire, and was still in excellent condition. The eminent architect of his day, George Papworth, had been instructed to build the finest family mansion in all of Ireland. It had forty rooms, if you took into account the unoccupied wing; it took ten years to build and at one time stood in 9,500 acres.

I'd only come across Mullingar previously as a centre for showbands: Joe Dolan and the Drifters, the biggest band in Ireland, had originated from there. But I took to the area immediately. It was such a beautiful house and its character appealed to me greatly. There was a special charm about the place and a wonderful sense of history, with the determined little boy who was to become Lawrence of Arabia, once resident there. Standing in 377 acres of land which bordered the shores of Lough Ennel, it was a remote haven and possessed a sense of tranquility.

Its equine traditions also appealed to me. Sir Cecil Boyd-Rochfort, who was then still alive but died in March 1982 aged ninety-five, was, like many of those connected with Middleton, a genius with horses. He had been trainer to the British Royal Family and had saddled no fewer than thirteen classic winners, the last of which was Parthia who had won the English Derby in 1959. During the 1940s, another great Derby winner, Airborne, had enjoyed the freedom of the fields of Middleton as a yearling. We used it primarily for our National Hunt 'store' horses.

With its stone stabling for thirty-seven horses, silage pits to hold 11,000 tons and sheds to hold 300 cattle, the property was a sizeable pile, as they say, but the house itself was one we could live in; not like some of the stately homes in England. So I bought it for £250,000, the remainder of the proceeds from the 'Yellow Sam coup', after expenses and debts were cleared. A few months later I sold the Boswell Stud.

The nine bedrooms, four bathrooms and five or six reception rooms in the central portion of the house were cavernous, and its double staircase, constructed from Portland Stone, was described as 'the most magnificent staircase south of the City Hall in Belfast', rising up to a first gallery with finely crafted cast-iron balustrades. In particular, I loved the library, a haven from the hustle and bustle of life, with doors leading through to the vast conservatory. It was there that I would sit, with a roaring log fire burning, like the squire of the manor, as I studied the 'form book'. We owned several antiques, including a writing desk once owned by the founder of Tate & Lyle. When my friends and associates used to visit me from the North, they'd laugh and used to borrow from that famous piece of verse, 'Will you look at him – monarch of all he surveys.'

At the end of the last century, Middleton had required twenty-five 'indoor staff' to run it. We didn't employ any servants, just help from a few people in the village. We had a wonderful housekeeper, Mrs Dunn, whom we regarded like one of us and never patronised her. I just treated her as though it was, say, my mother and just asked her quietly, 'Could we have a cup of tea, Mrs Dunn?' I've always been slightly uncomfortable about servants. The concept never came easily to me. Even when we could afford them we never had butlers, maids or valets. As far as I was concerned, we were a team, all in it together.

It is great farming land, with lush pastures for fattening cattle. As they say in those parts, 'Beef to the knees, like a Mullingar heifer.' We had been there about a month, still settling in, and I was out driving around the estate when I spied about thirty cattle grazing in our fields. I thought it was strange as I'd never bought any cattle, but decided to leave them for a day or two. No one came to collect them. So I rounded them up and herded them into some of our large sheds. There was no food and water and after a few hours they started bawling because they were getting hungry and thirsty. You could have heard their racket in Dublin. Eventually, a fellow turned up who turned out to be one of the neighbouring farmers. 'Have you seen my cattle?' he said.

'And how many would that be?' I asked.

'Oh, thirty,' he replied.

'I've seen them alright,' I said grimly and pointed towards my yard.

He wasn't pleased, but word undoubtedly got around and I never had any trouble with neighbours after that. They understood how I operated. They'd obviously thought that me, being an innocent from the town and a new owner, would overlook a bit of free grazing. But I made it clear I wouldn't let them take liberties. I had made my point. I was not going to be trampled on. Once you arrive in a place in Ireland you must let them know who's the boss. I'd stamped my authority. If we hadn't done that, it would have been a free-for-all.

Not that everyone got the message immediately. A week later, I was walking around and saw about eight horses grazing in one of our paddocks. Nobody came for them, so eventually I turfed them out onto the road. Not a busy one, I should stress. It turned out they belonged to Ned Cash, a legend in equine circles in Ireland at the time, who lived about fifteen miles away. He had started off in life travelling the roads of Ireland in a barrel-top caravan, selling horses with a £1 profit on each just to make ends meet, and ended up winning the coveted Supreme Hunter Championship Award at Ballsbridge. He had a son, 'young Ned', who rode for Ireland and he owned some wonderful show-jumpers. There was hardly a major competition that he hadn't won, with his horses being ridden by the likes of Eddie Macken and Ted Edgar.

He also thought he'd get a month's free grazing until I caught on. He'd have driven past every day to make sure they were there. After admitting they were his, he protested, 'You're some fine fellow to be putting my horses out on the road.' But I retorted, 'It'll teach you a lesson not to interfere with me any more.'

Well, it wasn't a great introduction, but after that somewhat terse start we became very friendly and I would buy horses off him. There was a local point-to-point every year, and we'd invite him for dinner afterwards. He was one of the few people who ever got into the house. The trouble was our house was 'dry', not just for my benefit you understand, but because, in Ireland, if you had any drink in the house the place would never be empty. Ned was in his sixties at the time but was still very fit and loved his drink. So he'd get drunk in the village pub before he came up for his dinner and be well under the weather before he arrived. He was so far gone he'd have trouble directing his knife and fork. He was a great character and we always had a laugh when he was around.

Once we got organised, my brother-in-law, Frank, who was married to Maureen's sister, and a couple of other fellows got started on establishing a farming set-up for me. It seemed to make sense because it had such an acreage going to waste. To the uninitiated, there doesn't sound much to the process of buying calves at a week old and rearing them on that verdant pastureland, but I must have put a curse on any agricultural enterprise. I should have learnt from the pigs episode at Wicklow. The cattle also went down with pneumonia and other diseases. A serious loss was sustained and it soon became clear that there was never going to be any money in it. It was no reflection on Frank. He was a good worker, a twenty-hour a day man. To be truthful, I wasted eight years of his life. He's now in Philadelphia, making a good living in the building trade.

Frank and Marie were with us for fourteen years in all. They were both a great asset. At Omagh, Frank ran The Cheltenham Arms, and at Wicklow and Mullingar he ran the farming side. They acted as second parents to our children. Catherine, the elder of our two daughters, had already been born, on 27 May 1969, by the time we moved to Middleton House, and Maria-Louise followed on New Year's Day 1975. Our son, Charlie, made his entrance on 25 January 1977.

Apart from contracting TB, life had been pretty good to me up until then. Married to a fine woman, blessed with three lovely children and resident in one of Ireland's most beautiful homes; I was a fortunate man, indeed. But then I got my first knock-back. Maria-Louise had been camping with her aunt in Sligo when she was taken into the local hospital very ill. She would have been no more than four. All the doctor could tell me was that she had a disease which they couldn't identify and warned me that it didn't look good. It was terrible to see her lying there, just wasting away. She was just skin and bones. As far as I was concerned, she was melting off the face of the Earth. I couldn't handle it. I walked out of the hospital and drove, I've no idea where, for an hour, and sat and cried my heart out. I prayed too. My prayers were answered. A couple of days later, they told us that some medication they had administered had worked and she was improving.

Middleton was never ideally suitable for training, but we nurtured many young horses on those lush pastures, cantering them in front of the house. We had thirty to forty horses, some of which were 'store' horses, who would be strengthened up until they made their debuts, normally at five or six. Others had already had some experience, but needed to mature. One was named Silver Buck, a horse of no great pedigree and of no exceptional appearance; indeed, he was so difficult to handle that his first owner had disowned him and when I first set eyes on him in a point-to-point at Naas, he had run out. We used to try to canter him down the lanes and through the forest but he often spooked himself and eventually refused to comply. It took the skill of one of England's foremost National Hunt racing families, the Dickinsons, to exorcise the demon within him and make him what he was to become – a true champion.

FIFTEEN

Passing the Buck

Tommy Stack had introduced me to the Dickinsons at a race meeting and I immediately established a rapport with them. Joker that Tommy is, he told them, 'This man always has good horses.' It probably surprised him when they took him at his word.

I began to send horses over to their yard from Ireland. We soon established a simple understanding. As long as I was informed when the horses were fancied, I didn't care about making a profit on their sale. I still had my horses trained by Liam Brennan, but once they won their 'bumper' in Ireland and I had backed them, I was finished with them. Normally, they were then dispatched to England and the Dickinsons to be trained for a novice hurdle campaign. I had either raised them myself from yearlings, or spotted them in running and bought them.

The first was Tommy Joe, who won thirteen races for them. He continued to progress at the Dickinsons, his successes including the Mandarin Handicap Chase at Newbury in late December 1978, with Tommy Carmody riding.

I admired Tony and Monica Dickinson and their jockey son, Michael, who was to become such a fine trainer in his own right, for their honesty and their great wealth of equine knowledge. Their knowledge was seemingly inbred, not the kind of stuff you could ever glean from books. I like dealing with people who are not out to fiddle you, and in the late Tony Dickinson, who was a wonderful judge of horses, I soon recognised the most honest man I had ever known and was ever likely to. There wasn't a crooked hair on any of them and it was a great team. Whatever I said I wanted for a horse, the Dickinsons passed that on to the owners. If I said I wanted £9,500 for a horse that's what the owners paid me. Not a pound less or more.

We enjoyed some great years together before it all turned sour. Apart from Tommy Joe, my Irish 'exports' included Cheltenham Gold Cup hero, Silver Buck; the horse that ended Michael Dickinson's career, Buck Me Off; and that brilliant but enigmatic steeplechaser, I'm A Driver. The latter was never a champion two-mile 'chaser because he didn't quite see out the trip at Cheltenham, which is a stiff track. But he really came into his own at flat, 'easy' courses like Newbury where he could put his pace to such good effect.

The Dickinsons stayed with us occasionally at Middleton House and they soon realised that the upkeep of the place was never a priority in my life. They'd go to their room and find the water wasn't running, or the lights wouldn't work, and it reminded them of the TV comedy *Fawlty Towers*. Consequently, their nickname for me was 'Baz', after John Cleese's character, Basil Fawlty, and we even named one of the horses I sent them Basil's Choice – he was a winner, too.

Outside of racing, I was, and still am, completely dis-organised. I often flew over to the north of England to see the Dickinsons. They might have come to collect me at Leeds-Bradford Airport, where I'd told them I'd be arriving at six o'clock, only to find out I'd actually get in at eight. Once, I told them a horse would be arriving at the yard on a Monday afternoon when, in fact, it turned up on Wednesday evening. I got plenty of dressing-downs from Mrs D over things like that, although it was all mostly delivered and accepted in good humour.

They were, and still are, thoroughly decent people. Perhaps it was because they regarded everyone with the same benign outlook that we were eventually to fall out over one of their young jockeys, a fellow named Graham Bradley, whose actions were nearly to cause my ruination. (Ironically, he rode his first winner, at Sedgefield on 11 March 1980, on a horse I sent over named Talon.) I also appreciated the fact that they kept what they knew to themselves. Silver Buck's owner, Christine Feather, once described them as 'fairly secretive', adding: 'You can ask them a thousand and one questions and they'll tell you only what they want you to know.' They were my sort of people.

To this day, I still keep in contact with Monica and Michael, who is now a successful trainer in the United States. I believed they valued me not merely because I supplied them with many fine horses, but the fact that I was straight in my dealings with them. I was also responsible for sending them human talent, too, in the stylish jockeyship of Tommy Carmody. Maybe I felt some form of obligation. After all, there would have been no need to have done so if one of the horses I had sent over, Buck Me Off, had not finished Michael's career, and come perilously close to ending his life.

I wasn't present that day at Cartmel's Whit Saturday meeting in 1978, but just hearing about it over the phone from Monica turned me to ice. It was one of the most horrifying experiences of my life. Apparently, Michael, champion amateur rider in 1969–70, whose prowess in the saddle had enabled him successfully to make the often difficult transition to professional rider, had only just negotiated the second flight of the 2m 7f hurdle when Buck Me Off slipped on the flat and hurled his rider into the rock-hard turf. Michael badly damaged his liver and spleen and was in intensive care for seven days. When he was eventually well enough to return to his beloved horses, he knew that, from then on, his only riding involvement would be from the stable hack, or riding, work. It terminated a distinguished career in which he had amassed 328 winners, including five at the Cheltenham Festival. It was a freak accident, of course; yet it wasn't to be the last time that I was to feel at least some moral responsibility for a jockey's appalling injuries.

As if I were in some way seeking atonement, I found it when I recommended a twenty-two-year-old Irish jockey named Tommy Carmody, who had just done himself a turn by riding a superb double on Mr Kildare and Hilly Way at the 1978 Cheltenham Festival. I considered Tommy to be potentially the most gifted rider in Ireland, and his displays on the Dickinsons' stars over the next few years confirmed my view. Not that he endeared himself initially to the Dickinsons, who were real hard workers and prepared to get their hands dirty. He made it clear he wasn't prepared to muck out with the rest of the lads, which drew the wry response from Tony, 'It must be nice when you can be semi-retired at twenty-two.'

Silver Buck was sired by Silver Cloud, who had been trained by Jack Jarvis at Newmarket to win three prestigious races as a three-year-old – the Chester Vase, Ascot's Cumberland Lodge Stakes and the Princess of Wales' Stakes at his home course. He was sent over to The Craig Stud at Ballyclare, County Antrim, where he was mated three times with Choice Archlesse, a moderate hurdler who had won one minor race at Cartmel. Silver Buck was the result of the first liaison. Nobody could have suspected that such a pairing could have produced the jumping class that it did.

J.T. 'Jack' Doyle, head of the great racing and bloodstock family, bought the horse twice at Ballsbridge, both as an unbroken three-year-old, where the buyer found him too headstrong and unmanageable, and then as a broken four-year-old. He had proved very difficult to break by the Doyle family, and in the end it took an ancient, if crudely effective, Irish strategy: 'A big bit in his mouth and a little bit in his belly.'

He was never thought to be suitable as a racehorse and at one time he might have become a show-jumper. But he showed a capacity for jumping steeple-chase fences and, rather than enter the game through 'bumpers', made his entrance in the point-to-point field. He misbehaved and had to be withdrawn from his intended debut at Oldcastle in County Meath, but then won by a distance at Gowran Park and was also placed. By this time he had been worked with Liam Brennan's horses, and, with my ears to the ground, I quickly had a clue as to his capabilities.

I bought him from Jack's trainer and horse-dealer son, Paul Doyle, who operated on The Curragh, and who died about ten years ago. Silver Buck had just run in a point-to-point at Naas and, as far as I recall, he ran out. But I saw enough to convince me that he had the makings of a very good horse. He cost me 8,000 guineas, which I considered a bargain. I had one of the best vets in Ireland to examine him, a fellow named Pat McCann, from Tullamore, who was well into his sixties then and had been involved with horses all his life.

'Did he pass, Pat?' I asked him.

'He did,' Pat replied. 'And I have never examined a horse with a better heart in my life.'

I was even more convinced by then that I had bought something very useful.

Despite dropping jockey Column Manier before the start in his first racecourse appearance under rules, Silver Buck showed beyond dispute that he had great potential. He ran in a 'bumper' at Clonmel and won by an easy eight lengths. After a short holiday with me at Mullingar, I sold him on to the Dickinsons' Ribblesaddle Stables in Gisburn, Lancashire in the summer of 1977, the sole condition of the transaction being, as usual with my 'exports' to them, that I should be tipped off before the first time that the horse was fancied to win.

Michael's first impression was that Silver Buck was rather small, and the gelding still remained nervous, particularly when his rider was mounting and dismounting. He didn't like racing near the rails and was easily spooked. He had been sold on by the Dickinsons to Christine, mother of the owner, William Haggas, of one of their horses, as a kind of pick-me-up after her first husband, Brian, divorced her.

It didn't surprise me to hear that Christine had actually been none too impressed when she first saw her new acquisition. 'He was very nervous and seemed very moody and spooky,' she said later. 'When you went into his box he shunted right up into a corner.'

His first race in England was a two-mile novices' hurdle at Carlisle in mid-November. The trip was too short for him and the ground too soft, but Michael, who partnered him, reckoned that he would be able to settle him at the rear. That, we felt, was the key – to get him to settle. He was an outsider, starting at 12–1, and Michael was pleased enough with the way Silver Buck ran on in the closing stages to finish eighth of twelve. That was the 'sighter' on the practice range. The next time the ammunition would be live.

We planned his next race at Catterick, a good draining track where you can be certain of getting good ground, even in winter, and it was over the long-distance hurdle trip of more than three miles. Normally, Michael would have taken the ride, but this was an amateurs' race and it was decided to put up Thomas Tate, Michael's brother-in-law. The instructions from Michael, who was riding at Chepstow that day, were straightforward, 'Under no circumstances should he hit the front before the last flight – and to come up the middle of the course.' There was an addendum to those orders, which left Thomas in no doubt of his mission that day. 'He's a good horse and has done one or two nice gallops. He will win, provided he doesn't do anything stupid.'

I couldn't have been more pleased with his target. Not only was there an absence of interest in Silver Buck among the betting public, but his price would be lengthened by the fact that there was a hot favourite called Yellow Fire, which was likely to start odds-on.

Michael and I always talked for hours together on the phone. The night before the race he called me at Mullingar, confirmed that Silver Buck was expected to win, and we discussed his jockey.

I said, 'Who's riding the horse?'

When Michael told me, I had a few seconds' apprehension. I said, 'Is Thomas capable of riding him?'

He replied, 'You could win on him yourself.'

That was good enough for me, although in the circumstances he was guilty of being a trifle complacent, given the horse's idiosyncratic behaviour. But Michael was right. He knew how good the horse was ... talented enough, as it turned out, to win a Cheltenham Gold Cup, so it wasn't a big exercise to win an amateurs' hurdle at Catterick. Such events, as has already been illustrated by Yellow Sam at Bellewstown, tend to be bad races. As an afterthought, Michael asked me if I could arrange to have £100 on the horse for a friend of theirs. The Dickinsons were not great gamblers, and neither were their owners. I said, 'Certainly, Michael,' and went to bed that night with the expectation that Silver Buck, who had shown no form in England, would be a 33–1 chance, certainly 25–1. I could scarcely believe it next day when he opened at 10–1 and ended up at about 9–2. We couldn't understand it.

In the event, Thomas, who always had a cool head, rode a perfect race and I think he won the Brompton Amateur Riders'

Novices Hurdle by a length or two. Even as it was, that was a major pay-day. I'd had probably £10,000 on, all round Ireland and England, but something niggled me and that was the fact that it should have been multiplied by at least twenty times, not a paltry 9–2.

I decided to launch an investigation, because there was no way the horse should have been such a short price. I knew Michael and his father wouldn't have told anyone. Eventually, there was only one conclusion I could come to: it was the operator at the local telephone exchange at Mullingar who must have been listening in to our conversation. There was no STD direct dialling in Ireland at that time; you had to go through an operator who would connect you. Of course, everyone knew me. After all, I was the chap who'd bought the big place outside the town and had a reputation for backing horses. Presumably, the operator informed all his or her friends that the horse Michael and I had been discussing was 'off'. The whole of Mullingar was probably on the horse the next day. It was very annoying, and although I couldn't do anything about it, I'm not one to let things like that drop. I take it rather personally. So, Michael and I arranged to have some false telephone conversations where we'd talk about unfancied horses and make out they were being set up to do the business. I often wondered how long it was before that operator and his/her pals got the message, because they picked up some desperately bad losers from us. However much they won from Silver Buck, that bright spark lost ten times as much subsequently and must have had ended up with the opinion that the first 'touch' was a complete fluke and this man Dickinson was one of the worst trainers in the world! The ones we supposedly fancied never won. I got my own back, with interest.

But how to talk about the horses we really fancied? To avoid flapping ears, I had to drive from Middleton House to a remote public telephone box just inside Northern Ireland, on the Fermanagh-Cavan border. I'd be there in the dark on a winter's night with £5 worth of coins. It was the only way of calling England direct (you could dial direct from Northern Ireland but not from the South at that time), conducting my business with Michael and keeping it confidential. Even then, we used different secret codes in case we got a crossed line with another caller. It was ridiculous, really. The journey was an hour and a half over bad roads, and I made the trip maybe once every three days. But I had to do it; there was simply no choice. It was an unpleasant experience, too; and, in hindsight, extremely foolhardy. It was the early years of the Troubles and it wasn't prudent to be driving around the back roads near the border. Any moment you expected the barrel of a gun to be pointed at your head.

I had some decent pay-days thanks to Silver Buck. He had his problems over the years, but I always had faith in the horse and one of the most memorable, and profitable, pay-days was when he won the first of his two King George VI Chases at Kempton in December 1979. Tony and Michael weren't there, and it was left to Michael's cousin, Robert Dickinson, to saddle the horse with the assistance of one Tommy Stack! Silver Buck ended his career with a remarkable twenty-nine wins worth £159,267.

Michael is a highly gifted, intelligent and hard-working horseman, as he demonstrated to any doubters when training the first five home in the 1983 Cheltenham Gold Cup, having been successful with Silver Buck the previous year. It is still something of a mystery to me what happened to him when he was installed at Manton as Robert Sangster's Flat trainer for the 1986 season. He took until 16 September to train his first winner, in Veryan Bay, and found himself kicked out before the end of the year, to be replaced by Barry Hills. I suspect that he had too many backward horses to contend with, and there can be little doubt he would have succeeded given, some patience from those concerned. Maybe he also lacked the experience of being in charge. All through his life he was getting good, strong advice from his father and mother and, in later years, myself, whereas when he was taken out of that environment and into Manton he was on his own. We can only speculate; although what he has achieved in the United States has demonstrated his true flair for handling horses. Since moving to the USA, Michael has never been satisfied with his training facilities. Every time he rang me, he would say, 'Some day I'm going to have one of the best training establishments in the world.' I used to think to myself, 'Dream on, Michael.' Yet in May 1998 that dream became a reality when he moved to Tapeta Farm, Maryland. It's got everything to make a success out of training horses. At the time of writing, Michael's tally was already 13 winners from 28 runners.

As I have already stated, the Dickinsons didn't run a betting stable then, but as the years passed and they became more and more successful, and attracted more owners and brought in new jockeys, I found I was no longer getting value with my runners. The yard's business was becoming common knowledge. At first, I'd send horses over and be sure of getting good prices, but now they were starting at 6–4 and 5–4, a complete waste of time. It all ended up with me saying, 'That's it. No more horses.' I sold everything I had in training with them. It was not something I enjoyed doing, but I believe that in life you give everyone a chance and then make the break.

There was one man whom I suspected was the principal cause. I used to be continually on to Michael about it, but he never made much progress. I went to Michael one day and said, 'There's no doubt about it. The rotten apple is Bradley.'

It had been a period of transition for the Dickinsons, who had moved to their new Poplar House stables in the village of Dunkeswick, near Harewood in West Yorkshire. In addition,

Tony, after a career in which he sent out 562 winners, had decided to hand over to Michael, who by then had turned thirty. There were changes in the jockeys' ranks, too: Tommy Carmody had enjoyed a fine couple of seasons, finishing runner-up in the jockey's championship on both occasions. But Carmody could take nothing for granted with a quintet of bullish young claimers moving into the yard and laying down a challenge to him. They were Robert Earnshaw, Kevin Whyte, Chris Pimlott, Chris Bell and Bradley.

The latter was one of the most talented riders I have ever come across. He is a beautifully balanced exponent of his art and a man who can really get horses to jump for him. Stable staff tipping horses went on in many stables, and still does, but I wasn't prepared to let it happen in one I was involved with. It got completely out of hand. It went on until I just rang up Michael one day and told him: 'Right, we'll do no more business.'

It was good while it lasted, but I severed all my connections. I never sent them over another horse from that day. Looking back, I think Michael was too naïve. He was absolutely straight, like his mother and father, but he didn't really realise what was going on. Bradley wasn't there many years, but it was long enough from my point of view. I never understood what motivated him, because in other ways he's not a bad fellow. There are some I could mention, who are complete wrong-'uns. He was just flawed. I would not forget him.

SIXTEEN

Forgiven – and never forgotten

Despite our collaboration over Yellow Sam, Sean Graham and I didn't always see eye to eye, and in early 1983 we fell out in a serious way. It was a silly dispute, the details of which have become hazy, but it involved £6,000 he claimed I owed him. I counter-claimed that he owed me money, and also accused him of being slow in sending out his accounts. Whoever was in the right, the amount was nothing then, at a time when I was regularly having bets of £5,000 with him. But it became a point of principle, the whole thing escalated and it developed into a long wrangle. Eventually, the Irish Turf Club – the equivalent of the Jockey Club – summoned me in and I was 'warned off' until the issue was reconciled and I had settled the debt. To be honest, I didn't take the ban too seriously, although it did cause me considerable problems when I travelled over to Cheltenham on 16 March, a day which witnessed what is recognised as the biggest wholesale gamble seen at the Festival in thirty years. And that is some claim.

The story of that day began two years before, at the sales. Now, I've never been a great one at buying a horse. I'm fine when it comes to pedigree – if the stallion lacked courage in his races, then I tend to steer clear of his offspring – but appreciating conformation has never been a strength. At one time I used to buy horses for a famous English trainer, and he used to say to his son, 'For God's sake, look at those horses before that man buys them. They have good form, but look at their make and shape, because we're haemorrhaging money.'

You have to accept your weaknesses and that's why I have used Frank Barry to buy virtually all of my horses in Ireland for more than thirty years. We always discuss a horse before proceeding with a bid. He is a great judge and, just as important, an honest man. In over thirty years we've never had a cross word or a dispute over prices. I catch out most people early on that I can't trust. I've always had total faith in Frank, who has also, on occasions, acted as one of my 'putters-on'. At the National Hunt sales at Goffs and Fairyhouse, he has bought me literally hundreds of horses. At one time I was a major player, too. In 1980, when we were at Middleton House, I calculated that I had £455,000 worth of equine talent, mostly jumpers, in or out of training. That was no mean sum then.

One day in 1981, I was standing with Frank at the November sales when this particular horse, an unbroken four-year-old chestnut by Precipice Wood, was led into the ring. We both liked him and he was knocked down to us for £4,000.

As I was leaving the sales I bumped into Liam Brennan. A few months earlier I'd had a row with him and had removed all my horses from his yard. It had quite an effect on him, because I probably had twelve or about half the complement of the stable. I regret it now, but in those days I often acted precipitously. I credit Liam for much of my success. I learned a lot from him. He might not have been the best man to deal with the business side of things, but he was a top-class trainer who never received the credit he deserved.

'Did you like that horse I bought?' I asked.

'I did.'

'Would you like to train him?'

Liam said he'd be delighted.

I said, 'Take the horse,' and we shook hands.

In recognition of that renewed concord, I named my purchase Forgive 'N Forget. The following year we ran him in some 'bumpers' at the major Irish courses and he had already showed some signs of ability by finishing third at Fairyhouse. It was considered expedient to run the horse in the name of Liam's wife, although I was actually the owner, and that proved a fortuitous decision when his trainer decided to contest the horse in two 'bumpers' at Leopardstown.

In the first, on 3 March, he started at 4–1 and finished a well-beaten seventh in the hands of amateur rider Anthony Powell, Liam's nephew. Ten days later, Liam had him out there again. I had my men backing the horse heavily and he started at 5–2 favourite, but I gave Liam due warning, 'If he wins, there'll be trouble with the stewards.' Victory would mean that Forgive 'N Forget would reverse form with the horses in front of him in the earlier race, and that would have the stewards springing into action faster than the late Oliver Reed spying a full whisky bottle.

It proved worse than that. Forgive 'N Forget never came off the bridle as Powell brought him home by eight lengths. I recall the day well. One of my 'putters-on' was John Gough, who previously ran a tipping line in Britain and had been over in Ireland for a couple of years to back horses. He was an excellent judge, too, and the following day was due off to Australia to work for that country's biggest bookmaker Bill Waterhouse. I have long-forgotten the scale of the money I had on, but suffice to say that John Gough alone gave me a cheque for £30,000.

Inevitably, there was an unhappy postscript to the afternoon. Liam, who was never that popular with racecourse officials or handicappers anyway because of the strokes he pulled, was called in by the stewards, along with Anthony Powell.

The officials weren't fools and demanded an explanation of

the reversal in form. Liam tried to argue that he had not had a winner for ages because the stable had been struck badly by a virus and Forgive 'N Forget had obviously recovered from it. It wasn't very convincing and the stewards only had his word for it. They didn't accept that word, and the upshot of it all was that Liam and Anthony were subsequently 'warned off' for four months and one month respectively. Liam couldn't say that I hadn't alerted him.

Forgive 'N Forget was a class act, and by the time of the 1983 Festival – the year that Michael Dickinson made the Gold Cup his own by saddling the first five home, led by Bregawn – I had sold him for £45,000 to a Manchester-based owner of Jimmy Fitzgerald's called Tim Kilroe. I also sent some horses to Jimmy Fitzgerald at the same time that I was supplying the Dickinsons. It was a bargain buy for Tim, to be candid, but I did the deal on the understanding that I would continue to 'manage' the horse. Tim, who had emigrated from the west coast of Ireland as a young man and had made his fortune in the building and construction business, was one of Jimmy's most valued patrons. He and Jimmy had lost a potential Gold Cup horse in Fairy King, who had broken his back in a fall at Kempton, and never imagined that they'd be fortunate enough to replace him so readily.

Since travelling over to the north of England to the Dickinsons' yard in the seventies, I had become good friends with Tipperary man Jimmy Fitzgerald, whose days in the saddle had ended with a nasty fall at Doncaster in 1967. It had left him with a fractured skull, partial deafness and dizziness for a year; yet, fortuitously, it marked the launch of a brilliant training career. He had already made his mark at his base in Malton, Yorkshire, long before we conspired together at that memorable festival.

Forgive 'N Forget would, of course, go on to achieve a memorable victory in the 1985 Cheltenham Gold Cup, but I had ambitious betting plans for him well before that. His target all that 1982–83 season had been the Coral Golden Hurdle Final at the Cheltenham Festival. There was no great scheme involved. His form was there for everyone to see, particularly when he won a qualifier of that series by twelve lengths at Ayr at the end of January.

Come the Wednesday, I had backed the horse early morning, but I also wanted to have as much on as possible on-course. I had some difficulty, because if you are warned off in Ireland you are not permitted on British racecourses either. I thought that with all the crowds who swarm annually through the gates of the greatest National Hunt stage in the world on any of the three days, I could steal in unnoticed.

I've no idea how they spotted me. I suppose the Irish Turf Club must have contacted their British counterparts, knowing I had a connection with the horse, and said, 'If you see that Curley, he's warned off, kick him out.' That's what happened anyway; the security people grabbed me and asked me to leave. I was desperate to get in, though, so I gave it a few minutes and sneaked back in through a less obvious gate, paying my money with all the other racegoers. I was able to walk the line of bookmakers on the rails without interference and backed the horse with four or five of the principal 'layers'. I got 4–1, 7–2 and 3–1, although the sheer weight of money all over the track forced his price down to 2–1, before closing at an SP of 5–2 favourite.

There was a real surge of adrenalin that day, because we'd lined up the horse for the race and within every Irishman's spiritual home of Cheltenham there is something special about the place when that happens. It was an even bigger buzz because there was never any danger, despite the horse carrying 11st 6lb over the marathon 3m 1f journey. Once Forgive 'N Forget turned down the hill the race was over, although Mark Dwyer bided his time and only allowed him to forge into the lead past eventual runner-up, Michael Dickinson's Brunton Park, when taking the last. He absolutely sluiced in, defeating Brunton Park and Constitution Park by three lengths and six lengths respectively.

The prize for the winner was a mere £9,392, a pittance compared to what Tim, Jimmy (who reputedly had 8–1 on ante-post) and I collected in total. I won a couple of hundred thousand pounds. It was my most successful pay-day since Yellow Sam. I had no nerves at all. Yes, I'd had plenty on – over £50,000 – but if he had lost, had maybe made a mistake or fallen, I'd have accepted it without a murmur. Win or lose, you'd have never known what I felt. I believe I have remained successful because I have never let betting get to me.

I've always had great self-confidence. A big win doesn't change my mood, and in the long term it doesn't change my lifestyle. Accumulating wealth or possessions has never interested me. There had even been an inner conflict in my mind about buying Middleton House. I only did it because I had won the price of it with Yellow Sam and I regarded it as a kind of security for the family. I could have gone on a spending spree at the time, but that's not my style at all. I always recall the time when I was training for the priesthood and what they taught you was 'peace of mind'; through thick and thin, that's what I've always tried to have.

When I returned to Ireland, I got a call from Dennis McCarthy, the chief steward of the Irish Turf Club, who was concerned about my continuing unseemly dispute with Sean Graham. 'This is a slur on Irish racing,' he said. 'Both of you are from Northern Ireland, you're a major punter, he's a big bookmaker and the whole thing's a disgrace. It's an embarrassment for all of us, having to warn you off. Can you not get the thing settled?'

He was right, of course, so somewhat reluctantly I sent Sean the £6,000, but still felt wronged and ended up refusing to speak to him. I used to walk past him at the racecourse with my head in the air and bet with his rivals instead. It was ridiculous behaviour. It was a storm that had just blown up from a breeze of discontent. Despite that incident, I always admired him as a bookmaker. We had a lot in common and though there was always a bit of needle there was never any real enmity from the heart between us. Deep down, I always regarded him as a friend. In fact, our quarrel became something of a standing joke. Sean would berate me in public just for the sake of it. If I was betting with one of his rivals on the next pitch, he'd bellow, say, 'Four to one the field,' followed immediately by a pointed, 'We are payers here.' Meaning, of course, that 'we' pay our debts. It was just banter. It was to my eternal regret that, several years ago, he was taken ill, died and was buried before I was even aware of it. People told me he wasn't well but I thought he'd pull through. Someone rang me one morning and said, 'Sean Graham has died.' I was devastated. It is one of my biggest regrets in racing that I did not talk to him before he died. He's one of the people I always pray for after saying the rosary.

Some years later, at Down Royal in 1991, when his family was sponsoring the day's racing, I met his widow, Brenda, and said how embarrassed I was that I had never rung her after her husband's death. I took Lester Piggott over with me, and we were collected from the airport by a car which also had in it Sean's two sons, Roland and Sean. The youngest, Roland, was then about twelve, and normally you couldn't stop him talking, but he didn't open his mouth. He just sat there like a little saint. He was in awe at being in the presence of Lester. The brothers have carried on the family business and Sean would be very proud of them now. That day brought back many memories.

Maureen and I had been very friendly with Sean and Brenda

when we were living down in Wicklow. One year we all went on holiday together to Miami, along with Mick O'Toole and his wife. In all modesty, that was some triumvirate that arrived in Florida – one of the country's top trainers on the Flat and over jumps, and the biggest gambler and bookmaker in Ireland.

Mick and I had about $10,000 each in our pockets. The first day the pair of us went racing at Hileah. We knew little about American racing and form, and, not surprisingly, lost the lot. The next morning at breakfast, we said to Sean, 'We had a bad day, yesterday. Would you lend us $2,000 each.' He duly obliged. He was very reasonable and threw the cash at us like it was a packet of sweets. A couple of days later we were broke again, and we repeated the performance. When it happened for a third time Sean turned as cold as a deep freeze. Maybe he thought it was for our own good. He became a different man entirely. 'Not on your life,' said Sean, without a hint of a smile. 'Not a dollar.'

We were staying in the Miami Springs Hotel and the pair of us were so short that we had nothing left to pay our bills. We decided to cut and run and used the fire escape to avoid paying. We sweated for half an hour at the airport because we expected to see the police at any moment. That was Sean for you. When he wanted to, he could be as awkward a customer as you could find. Still, the upshot of it all was that Mick O'Toole came home, bought a yearling and, as a testimonial to that incident, called him Miami Springs. The colt, ridden by Lester Piggott in Robert Sangster's colours, went on to be runner-up behind Stanford in the 1978 Gimcrack and broke the course record at Phoenix Park. Oh, yes, and we did pay our bills eventually …

Sean and I had some titanic betting duels. I had a bet with him one day at Punchestown on Big Paddy Joe, a horse of mine which ended up with the Dickinsons. I said to him, 'Big Paddy Joe, I'll have £2,000-to-win-£20,000, down to Barney Curley.'

He cut the price to 8-1. I stood there for twenty seconds and said, '£2,000-to-win-£16,0000, down to Barney Curley.' That's a total of £36,000 he must pay out if the horse wins. The price was trimmed again, but I tried to go in once more, '£2,000-to-win-£12,000, Barney Curley ... ' Even as I was saying it, he butted in, 'Now, will you ever f*** off!' He knew he was caught, and the horse duly bolted in. But the story at least shows that he was prepared to bet serious money. That's how good a bookmaker he was. He laid me, in the course of less than a minute, £4,000-to-lose-£36,000 at that time. And he didn't flinch. Find me a man who'd take a bet like that off me now.

I can't say I spend my spare time hobnobbing with other gamblers, although the 'high-rollers' might exchange a few words at Cheltenham or Ascot. Each of us is out for himself and has his own schemes on the boil. You could never form an Association of Successful Gamblers. It would rather defeat the object, as well as having a very limited membership! That said, the atmosphere in the ring at a big meeting is something unique. I suppose it's the equivalent of a trading floor in the City. I would never spend my day socialising in 'members' at the racecourse. The ring is where all the characters congregate. Of them all, I've known John P. McManus the longest, around thirty years. One thing you can guarantee is that a horse carrying those familiar colours of emerald green with a gold hoop and white cap, will provoke huge excitement in the ring at the Cheltenham Festival. We met when he'd just started out and he invited me to his parents' house just outside Limerick. I'd never seen them before but they were a lovely couple and made me so welcome. Very few people I know are capable of displaying such genuine warmth.

One time, back in the early seventies, after racing at Killarney, I went with 'J.P.' and a motley crew of racecourse regulars back to the Gresham Hotel in Dublin. The party included Teddy Rice, one of the biggest bookmakers in Ireland at the time; Flavio Forte, who owned cafes in Dublin; and my solicitor in the South, Tim O'Toole, who was a major punter; and Terry Rogers, another bookmaker. We played poker all night, right through until six o'clock in the morning, and I lost £100,000. I disobeyed the cardinal rule. It was not my game and I should have stayed clear of the whole affair.

Tim and I left and went to Gardener Street Church. We both attended mass and confession, during which one of several promises I made to the priest was that I would never play poker again – and that promise still holds good today. Tim was never the luckiest punter and it was fortunate that he had so many wealthy clients to support his extravagant lifestyle. One of his worst reverses was in 1980 when he had backed Nureyev heavily ante-post to win the English 2,000 Guineas. He hadn't been a bad judge on that occasion. Not in my opinion. I had also piled the money on all winter on the French invader and was looking for a £180,000 pay-out. For some reason, greed got the better of me and I decided to fly over for the race from Ireland and have another £20,000 on at evens, to take my anticipated winnings up to the round £200,000.

I flew in to Heathrow, took a black cab to Newmarket and told the cabbie to wait and drive me straight back after the race. I had a dog running at Shelbourne Park that night and I wanted to be back in Dublin in time. I got my bets on, and Nureyev duly completed his side of the business. I felt that was a good job done, dashed off to the cab and made it back to the airport, only to bump into Tim in the toilets. He was being violently sick. I asked what was the matter. 'What do you think?' he grunted unhappily. It was only then that I discovered that Nureyev had been 'thrown out' of the race because of his jockey Phillipe Pacquet's riding, although he had been the victor on merit.

There was a lengthy post-mortem in the media, during

which it was suggested that it had been an 'anti-French' verdict by the stewards, but in the cold light of day the camera patrol film showed that the horse had rightly been disqualified. I could handle it. Tim, who had had bundles on it, could barely contain his misery and anger, which is why people like him shouldn't be gamblers. You've got to be able to take a hit occasionally without it affecting you.

One bookmaker I used to bet a lot with was Michael Tabor, an East End boy, who made it as a big-time bookie before selling out to Coral's and moving to Monte Carlo. In recent years he has re-emerged in a new guise as owner, breeder and punter. In 1997 he had a rollercoaster of a ride with his horse Entrepreneur, who won the 2,000 Guineas, but flopped in the Derby and was retired to stud. That was a great year for Michael, one in which he was blessed with an amazing number of good horses.

Many years ago, we had a terrible row over £40,000 which Michael claimed I owed him, but which I refused to pay. Around eighteen months later I was in debt to him, to the tune of about £35,000. I couldn't pay and felt very awkward, but said to Michael that I would settle when I could. If it had been me, I would have been furious, given our history. But he just said very quietly, 'Pay me when you can.' I thought that was very big of him. He never bore a grudge about anything.

We often used to talk about horses on the phone and have a laugh together; he was very knowledgeable. When he went off to Monte Carlo I felt a strange sense of loss. It suddenly dawned on me that he was leaving the next day and I did something I've never done before. It was totally out of character. I went out and bought some flowers – the first time I had ever bought any in my life – to wish Michael and his wife Doreen well. I don't know what happened to me, but I got somewhat confused and found myself driving round High

Wycombe looking for their house. Eventually, it dawned on me that they actually lived in Stansted, where I had called many times before. High Wycombe was where he had his head office. By the time I arrived it was about ten o'clock at night and they were leaving the next morning. I can imagine Michael saying to Doreen when I left: 'Is that man playing with a full deck?' Anyway, I miss him a lot, and also his friend Derek Smith, formerly on the rails for Ladbroke's. Both of them have a great generosity of spirit.

SEVENTEEN

'Not even a ghost ...'

We spent nine very contented years at Middleton House, until moving on, under unusual circumstances, in 1984. We enjoyed living in the South, and my roots were just a half-day's drive away in the North, but the house was so enormous that it was proving impossible to maintain and keep heated. Another factor was that the farming side was a failure. The bookmakers in Ireland were getting wise to me, too, and the market was becoming lifeless and the 'layers' increasingly cautious. The time had come to move to England.

We planned to leave the following June, but our dilemma was that, at the time, properties were difficult to shift in Ireland because of the depressed state of the market. 'Always get the value' is my maxim and I realised that if I sold up and accepted the market price I may not get any kind of return on my investment. So, in 1984, I hit upon a scheme that was to make my name known worldwide.

I have always been prepared to take a chance when others would have prevaricated and thought up all sorts of reasons why they shouldn't do it. That was the case with the Yellow Sam coup. It was the same when I dreamt up how I would dispose of Middleton House. The plan came to me as I was lying up on our grand four-poster bed, which once belonged to the Duchess of Norfolk. I had 'flu and I was a dreadfully bad

210

patient. I just lay there, feeling sorry for myself, and reading the newspapers. It was boredom, really, that caused my eye to stray to adverts for raffles of pubs and clubs. I said to myself, 'I could run a better draw than any of those. If we raffled this house it could be the biggest winner ever.'

I calculated the property was worth around £1 million and if we sold enough tickets to cover that amount we'd break even. Anything on top was profit. But, despite what has been suggested since, it was by no means a certain winner. I was taking as much of a chance as those entering the draw and I could lose heavily. For me, there were easier ways of making money on the racecourse.

I can't claim it was the first such draw in Ireland. That had been around three years before when Athlone publican Des Earls raffled his pub after he failed to get a satisfactory price for it at auction. Since then Raymond Coyle, who had owned the 365-acre Bellewstown Estate in County Meath, had raffled his property, selling 3,000 tickets at £300 each, but was sentenced to three months in jail at Dunshaughlin Court in October 1983.

But as so often happens with the best-laid plans, the cheats and scoundrels moved in. Just before my draw was due, the Garda Fraud Squad were investigating a raffle for a 'charming £50,000 three-bedroomed fully furnished house' in the Clonskeagh area of Dublin. Tickets at £10 had been sold, but the draw had never taken place when subscribers turned up for it at Jury's Hotel in the city. The 'promoter' had done a runner.

But mine would be run properly. If it came off, it would be the biggest ever seen in Ireland, possibly the world. The raffle I devised would become the forerunner of the national lotteries in England and Ireland.

It was said by a senior Garda source that draws or raffles involving more than £300 were illegal under the Gaming and Lotteries Act of 1956. Any such draw had to be for charitable or philanthropic purposes and permission of the local district justice had to be obtained. I had already consulted top legal counsel and the advice had been that it was fine to go ahead as long as money was raised for a bona fide club. We called it a Private Limited Subscribers Draw, and the plan was that we'd sell a maximum of 9,000 tickets, at IR200 punts, $275, or £175 each.

To ensure, or so we were led to believe, that there would be no legal wrangles the raffle would have to include a charity element to it, with some of the proceeds going to a good cause. You couldn't just run a raffle on behalf of yourself. So, it was decided that all the competitors would have to become members of the local Gaelic football club in Ballinagore and answer three simple questions, which would introduce an element of skill (one of them was: 'Who is the Irish Prime Minister?'), and a donation would also be made to the Irish Wheelchair Association.

Ballinagore, a couple of miles from Middleton House, is no more than a hamlet on the N52, the Mullingar-Tullamore road, which runs alongside the Brosna River. It has a shop, petrol station and a pub, Mahon's, where the football players congregate after games for a few pints. (I later named a horse after the club. Ballinagore GAA was its name, but the commentators, who should really have known better, used to pronounce it 'Ballinagore Gah'! It actually stood for Gaelic Athletic Association.) Soon, those players were to become beneficiaries of a brand new football pitch, changing rooms and social club.

The raffle was a chance to win your own dream mansion, together with a large estate on the shores of Lough Ennell, for a relatively small amount of money. The odds weren't bad, either; far better than the National Lottery. If it had been anyone else running it I'd have entered the draw myself! It was a huge undertaking, mainly because we had to convince everybody there were no fiddles. It required a sharp organisational brain, just as the 'Yellow Sam coup' had to organise all those men throughout Ireland. The contrast was, though, that while 'Sam' had been all about an absolute need for secrecy, the success of this was dependent on maximum publicity.

When people talk about how much the draw made, they forget the substantial expenses. Nothing was spared on promotion. I had a professional video film made in which the mellifluous tones of Ireland's most celebrated commentator Michael O'Hehir gave a moving description of the house to the background of lilting Irish string music.

'This magnificent house is a home which has heard the sound of children's laughter for generations,' he waxed lyrically in his commentary. 'It's a special place, a Georgian mansion with a history of happiness and contentment ... A house to dream of ... and it could belong to anyone for the price of a raffle ticket ... How much is it worth? A million, maybe two could be more realistic, but it's yours for the price of a ticket.'

No selling angle went unexplored. He spoke of Lough Ennell, which had once yielded a record brown trout of 26lb. And how one of the relations of the Boyd-Rochforts was T.E. Lawrence. 'Did his pursuit of glory in the deserts of Arabia begin at Middleton as he contemplated the painting of Napoleon above the globe of the world, which he so nearly conquered?' Michael speculated. Who could fail to be impressed by such a prize? The video was not just promotional, but to enforce the point that the raffle was completely above board. The draw, said Michael, 'was bound by rules as solid as the old forge. What is the catch? Let me tell you, there is none ... There are no leases, no catches ... not even a ghost.'

Of course, it was not just Michael's voice I was paying for

but the integrity he imparted to the whole enterprise. To convince potential purchasers that there would be nothing untoward, we had to involve people who were beyond reproach. That was why I also asked Michael to make the draw.

As trustees, I also brought in three prominent racing names, who were synonymous with integrity – Tommy Stack, who had partnered more than 600 winners in a thirteen-year career, including Red Rum at Aintree in 1977; the former jockey-turned-trainer Michael O'Brien, who had been left paralysed by a riding accident in 1974; and Mick O'Toole, who had trained big-race flat and jumps winners with equal aplomb.

We organised the raffle ourselves, with just the help of the football club and a few trusted associates. Once you bought a ticket, you became a member of Ballinagore GAA. There was an amusing piece in *The Times* one day which said that Ballinagore GAA was, 'The biggest club in the world, bigger even than New York Yacht Club or Lord's.' The club members thought it was great fun. We formed a committee and advertised tickets in the best-selling newspapers in England and Ireland. They included the *Sun* and the *Daily Mirror*, and *The Sporting Life*. I also arranged for the venture to be promoted on TV. Intriguing stories about entrants abounded. I remember the BBC filmed members of one syndicate cutting peat at a bog about fifteen miles from Middleton before sending it off to market. They called themselves 'The Turf Men' and had spread the cost at £20 each. They'd originally hoped there was peat within the grounds, so they could combine fine living with their work. When they found that it did not, their plan was to sell off the house and buy a bog! Each to their own, I suppose.

Unaccustomed though I was to self-publicity, I had to enter into the spirit of the occasion, otherwise it was destined to be a failure. I was interviewed on Gay Byrne's *Late, Late Show*, the most popular programme in Ireland, and the BBC also spent a day with me, filming me at the races and produced a documentary-style piece that was broadcast nationwide after the early evening news on Sixty Minutes. As a free advert it was invaluable.

From the moment of its inception, it took a year to come to fruition. Four or five months of that was serious hard work which left me shattered. From nothing, the interest in it began slowly and then mushroomed. There were several celebrity entrants: Eric Clapton, the world's best known rock guitarist, bought a ticket, as did Harry 'W.H'. Carr, the Queen's former jockey, Robert Sangster and many members of the aristocracy. Several people drove up to have a look at the prize, some presumably just to make sure it actually existed!

By the time I went over to America in January to promote the draw we had already sold 6,000 tickets. The story was broadcast on TV throughout the United States. It received tremendous interest there and I got a film star's reception. *The New York Post* headlined a major article with 'Irish betting legend comes to America' and described me as 'a fine broth of an Irish lad from County Westmeath' – some lad; I was forty-three at the time. There was one minor problem: American law would not allow me to sell tickets there overtly, so I had to smuggle them in for distribution through an Irish organisation.

The Americans even wanted to know my views on their racing. What they made of my criticism I have no idea. But I couldn't resist having a dig at their system. 'You cannot make betting pay with an 18 per cent *pari mutuel* takeout as you have here,' I told their startled reporter. 'I would not last twelve months betting at those rates in America. The government gets all the money here.'

In all, I spent nearly four months travelling round the world promoting the raffle. It really seemed to capture people's imagination. The coverage was so widespread that we had people from India, Pakistan, Hong Kong, Canada, America, Australia and the rest of Europe making inquiries; in fact, seemingly every nation except the then Communist countries, all clamouring for tickets. We had people up at the house from Alaska, who had seen a story in the *International Herald Tribune*.

My only real logistical concern was dealing with the money; bear in mind the huge amounts of cash and cheques that were arriving by post each day – I had to surround myself with people I could trust. Apart from Maureen, I brought in just two helpers: Benny O'Hanlon, the famous Yellow Sam telephone box blocker, and Paddy Griffin, who looked after my horses and would later do the same in England. Everything that arrived was placed on the kitchen table and we worked through until two or three in the morning to dispatch all those receipts and tickets.

There had been no suggestion until then that we were doing anything wrong; then, out of the blue and just a few weeks before the draw, the local Garda raided the house. They arrived with a search warrant under the Gaming and Lotteries Act and searched the premises, taking possession, as the newspapers were to report later, of 'a number of items pertaining to the draw'. What it amounted to was that they demanded a number of ticket counterfoils and cheques, and after a few questions, said their investigations would be continuing. We had to laugh. A judge had bought a ticket, so we had to find the counterfoil and his cheque and make sure they did not get their hands on that. It could have been most embarrassing for him. As far as I was led to believe they were only really concerned that there shouldn't be any skulduggery, and I was convinced I had taken every precaution to ensure there was no suggestion of that. The only reassurance I could give people who had any qualms was to say, 'You have my word. If you're not satisfied with that, take back your money. Don't enter the draw unless you're 100 per cent certain.' We only had to return one cheque, to a lady in County Carlow, who had phoned to say she was concerned. I told her, 'Not to worry. We'll send your money back immediately.'

The decision to ask Michael O'Hehir to draw the winning ticket proved a master-stroke. Here was the best-known Irishman in the world, a legendary racing, football and hurling commentator, a man who possessed such an evocative style and was beloved by his countrymen. Even in Britain he had become an institution with his inimitable style, epitomised by his graphic description of the carnage during the 1967 Grand National – including those immortal words 'there's a right pile-up' – that had led to the victory of 200–1 outsider Foinavon.

I knew him from my time on the racecourse and just asked him to help out. I rarely used to tell anyone about my plans with the horses, but I made an exception with Michael. I used to give him the nod up in the commentary box.

When the Garda intervened, I became very concerned about Michael's participation. A few days before the draw I rang him and said, 'Michael, I'd prefer if you didn't draw the ticket. There could be a desperate hullabaloo about this; I respect you a lot, and you've lived an exemplary life, I don't want you involved in anything that might harm your reputation.' I spent some time pleading with him not to come and even warned him that he could be arrested if the Garda took a hard line, but he didn't seem to care.

He merely replied, 'What time is the draw?'

I told him, 'It's three o'clock.'

And he just said quietly, 'I'll be there. My Word is my Bond.'

I thought that was a wonderful gesture, because it wasn't doing him any favours. He wasn't getting paid very much, just expenses. He really just did it for me as a favour; under those circumstances, a lot of people would have ducked out, given half a chance. I later named a horse after those words of his which have always stuck in my memory. My Word is My Bond, I called it. The horse should have been a star; sadly, he was absolutely useless.

As a broadcaster Michael was a genius, yet always very humble. When President Kennedy died, he commentated on the funeral for Irish television, despite having no experience of covering that sort of event. Michael went out live for six hours, having originally been over there just to 'call' a horserace at Belmont Park. I visited Michael just before he died. He had had a stroke a number of years before. They had laid on a big night for him at the Burlington Hotel in Dublin and he wanted me to be there. There were 600 people from the world of horseracing and Gaelic football. There were 32 countries represented, including all the great players from the last 40 years. The king of the saddle, Lester Piggott, made a point of being there. Considering that Michael made Gaelic football what it is today, I have to say I don't believe the GAA treated him very well after his stroke. Michael could barely speak and it was very upsetting. I think that night was too much for him. I read of his death a little later, when I was in New York. How happy I felt that I'd been there. The O'Hehir name lives on through his sons, Tony, who has picked up his baton and commentates regularly on major races for RTE, and Peter.

The big day, Thursday 9 February, arrived – and so, too, did the Garda. Detectives were stationed at the back and front of the house. We had received four visits in the previous week, during which they removed more documents, including the register of those who had sold three or more tickets. A separate draw would be held of those names, with the winner receiving a special £10,000 seller's prize. In my naivety, I was still convinced that they were just keeping an eye on proceedings and were there to observe fair play. This was not only the biggest draw, but the one with most prestige. Apart from Michael's presence, another coup had been to encourage the involvement of the BBC. They had given us so much publicity in the build-up that, although there were requests from stations all over the world, we agreed the BBC could cover the event exclusively and broadcast a special item after the early evening news bulletin. They also brought the draw winners over to view the house at their expense.

We had sold every one of the 9,000 tickets with receipts of £1.8 million. It was some feat. I had guaranteed that if we sold just 2,000 the draw would go ahead, although I would have incurred a substantial loss. If I say so myself, it was an excellent idea, superbly promoted; a dream realised.

It was a curious scene in the vicinity of our rural outpost as, just before three o'clock, a procession of BMWs, Porsches and Mercedes made their way along the single road leading to Castletown-Geoghegan, and helicopters began to land in the grounds. Their occupants included Martin Kenneally, owner of the previous year's Cheltenham Gold Cup winner, Bregawn, who had arrived to purchase some last-minute tickets. (There had been thousands of letters and phone calls in the last two days, still inquiring about tickets.) Others arrived by more modest means. A priest, Brian Hanley, from Lanesboro, who had been given a present of a share in a ticket, explained to the media, 'I'm here because I'm a gambler.' An English couple, David and Sandra Beard, brought their baby along on their journey over the Irish Sea.

I couldn't complain about the hype which had produced an incredible response, but some of the media went completely over the top. The *Irish Independent* described the day's coming events as, 'The second great mystery of Irish racing after Shergar's disappearance, except this one is about to be solved.'

Once everybody was packed into our front hall, Michael

moved to the staircase to conduct the draw. I was alongside him, with Maureen, who was wearing a full-length mink coat, and the children. Before doing so, Michael declared: 'If the government was running the country as well as this man has promoted this we'd be living in a better country. Barney has done such a good job, he should be president of Bord Failte and Coras Trachtala.'

There was laughter when he added, 'In every country I've gone to these last few months the only thing people wanted to know was "where is Shergar, and who will win Barney Curley's home?".'

A drum had been borrowed from the local hospital, and as Michael proceeded with the draw I couldn't help noticing three detectives from the Garda station at Mullingar standing discreetly by the door. I knew there were several more at the back. Finally, Michael drew the winning ticket number: 41877. It belonged to a six-strong British syndicate from Gloucestershire, headed by Tony Ray, who had bought two tickets. The other members of his group were Paula Vick, Bill Rammage, Ralph Teague, Hugh Smiley and Walter Malcolme. It turned out that Mr Ray, who had never even visited Ireland before, ran an agricultural supplies company and the other members, apart from Mr Rammage, worked for it. Three were around retirement age.

I had only one thing to say immediately afterwards. 'I've retired from lotteries,' I said, adding that all I planned to do now was go racing at Newbury the following Saturday.

We celebrated in Mullingar's Bloomfield Hotel. Not that I was in the mood to socialise, such was my fatigue. I had made around £1 million, after expenses had been deducted, but I just sat on the floor and watched the TV coverage. There had been no hint of a complaint; all I got was praise, which was much appreciated. I can't stress enough what a relieved man I was that night. A typical reaction came from a pair of bloodstock men, Terry McGoff and David Popplewell, part of a syndicate that bought fourteen tickets. 'Everything was done right,' they maintained. 'Barney Curley has cleaned up the name of lotteries. It was professional from start to finish.'

I didn't have too much to say to the press. 'I've bought a few horses and now I'm going to find a new place to settle down as a trainer,' was the gist of my comments. By the Saturday, Irish papers were on the phone to say that it was believed that the winners were coming over. Maureen said she hoped not because there wasn't a thing in the house and she had to rush frantically into Mullingar to stock up. At four o'clock the BBC called to confirm that they were indeed on their way. The winners did come over to survey their prize, but they never took up residence. They sold it a few months later to Noel and Thelma Langan, who had been running a number of pubs in Dublin. When they moved on, too, it passed on to new owners by the more conventional means of an auction in July 1992 for around £300,000.

You learn a lot running a lottery. I came out of it a better man. Everybody else appeared happy with the outcome, too: my family, the winners, the losers, and the football club got its reward, too, with an improved pitch, changing rooms decorated in the team's colours of purple and white, and a new grand entrance with wrought-iron gates. Who could possibly say a word against it?

My worst fears were realised when I was charged with running an illegal lottery, and, worse still, Michael O'Hehir with me. There were hundreds of other similar draws going on, but they picked on me because mine was the biggest and most well known. It was also probably the best organised and the straightest, but they ignored that.

I was outraged. How dare they point the finger at me? Instead of charging me, they should have been honouring me for services to the community. I did the authorities a massive

221

favour. Nobody could compete with what I had done, and no one would ever do so; it had the effect of making all the unofficial raffles appear insignificant and virtually killed them off overnight.

Altogether there were five of us, charged with varying offences, who appeared at the village court at Ballynacargy, a few miles west of Mullingar on that bright July morning. Apart from myself and Michael there were three members of the Ballinagore GAA Club: Joseph Leonard, John Deegan and Finian O'Brien. The court was packed with reporters and inquisitive locals, and after the clerk read out our names, their mouths were agape as they watched the country's biggest gambler and best-known commentator standing there in the dock. For most, this was to be considerably more entertaining than an argument over a speeding ticket. Actually, farce would be a better description, as the proceedings ended with me being sentenced to three months' jail.

District Justice William Tormey said he could only impose one sentence, the maximum, after I was found guilty of unlawfully promoting a lottery, contrary to Section 21 of the Gaming and Lotteries Act 1956. To my huge relief, the case against Michael, who had been charged with unlawfully assisting me in the promotion of the lottery, was dismissed. According to the judge, Michael had been merely carrying out his job as a professional who did a job and got paid for it. It would have been nothing short of a national disgrace if a man better known in Ireland than the president had been imprisoned.

It all became even more risible when the state prosecutor Kevin Wallace was asked by the judge whether he thought Gay Byrne had also assisted by broadcasting the video and interviewing me. He replied, in all seriousness, 'yes'. And RTE was guilty, too, apparently. The three GAA Club members, who had been charged with unlawfully selling tickets for the lottery, were each fined £100.

My attitude, however, had been 'a deliberate breach of the law'. The prosecutor argued that I had taken the view that, 'This act on gaming and lottery stands in my way of making money and consequently I will not obey it for that reason.' Garda sergeant Christy Tuohy of Castletown-Geoghegan said he had warned me on 16 September the previous year that his superiors considered the draw to be illegal. He had pointed out that the organisers of a similar draw had been prosecuted. The sergeant, who was present at the draw, told the court he had also interviewed me in January and the following month seized documents, including 146 tickets from the kitchen table.

To be honest, the jail term didn't bother me. I would nearly have volunteered for it, given half a chance. I was exhausted and wanted a rest. The responsibility of handling all that money had consumed my every waking hour. But my lawyers insisted, 'You have to appeal.' They were right. A criminal record is not something you want to carry with you, particularly when you are considering applying for a licence to train in England. For this is where I knew my future now lay.

Before I departed I was determined to have one last assault on the Irish bookies. We had twenty-seven boxes in the stables, containing such illustrious names as Silver Buck, I'm A Driver and The Hacienderos. Immediately after the draw, I applied for a training licence in Ireland. The Irish Turf Club wouldn't grant me a public licence, presumably because they did not think I had enough experience, and also I didn't have any other owners. But they did issue me with a permit which allows you to train and run your own horses. It was a fair decision and didn't bother me, because I had no intention of training for anyone else. For the first time I had control of my own destiny on the racecourse – and I didn't hang around.

I received my permit in January and departed for England in September, but in the meantime I followed up my success with the raffle by sending out three 'bumper' winners at

Metropolitan racecourses in the space of six weeks. It was a considerable training feat, because they were always the biggest races of the day and among the hardest to win. My debut victory at Naas on 3 March was with a powerhouse of a horse named I'm Incommunicado, appropriately also having his first run. It was described in the racing papers as 'a massive gamble' and on that occasion it was no media hype, although I only admitted afterwards to 'having a little bit on'. Such illustrious winners as Arkle, Mill House – bred by a local hotel owner – and Nicholas Silver had won at the course on their path to greater things. Every trainer hoped he had such a future star in the Rathcoole Flat Race, worth £996 to the winner. It was the last race on the card, attracting twenty-three-runners, and was a deadly serious betting heat with the favourite Eddie O'Grady's Strictly Bacon starting the 2–1 favourite, even though my associates and I had backed I'm Incommunicado at all odds from 12–1 to 5–2.

Naas, just half an hour's drive from Dublin, and a course that is always well attended, has always had something of a reputation as a punters' graveyard. It was anything but, for me that day. Everything went smoothly to plan with my jockey, Willie Mullins, keeping the five-year-old prominent before shaking his mount up to sweep into the lead just over a furlong out and drawing clear up the hill to win by two and a half lengths. Not a bad start for a rookie trainer! I'm Incommunicado, who appeared to have a really bright future, was one of the horses I brought over to Newmarket with me, but sadly he broke a leg on the gallops and had to be put down. I must have taken £120,000 off the 'layers', and remember this was 1975. Can you imagine that sort of money, on-course, being wagered on a 'bumper', even now, anywhere but the Cheltenham Festival? Nearly £80,000 of it was on-course money, and the bookmakers included Terry Rogers, Jim Mulligan. Malachy Skelly, Sean Graham, David Power and

J.P. McManus. I knew everybody thought my new 'career' was a huge joke. My pals and the bookmakers loved to take the mickey out of me. Gambler, impressario, bookmaker ... what more did this man have up his sleeve? Here was Barney Curley trying to make his name at training horses now. What else was he going to be good at? I thought, 'I'll teach them' – and that's usually when I'm at my most lethal.

In the early days I could bet with at least ten men who would lay a horse to lose £10,000, including all those names above. They were all gamblers themselves and laid off with other bookmakers. They weren't just accountants. Today I bet with Stephen Little, Colin Webster, Victor Chandler, Roy Christie, and in the north Pat Whelan and Leslie Steele. They are all prepared to take a risk, unlike the Big Three off-course bookmakers who are only interested in accepting bets from anyone without any knowledge. Newspapers have often referred to my battle with the bookmakers, but I never like it to become personal, otherwise it gives the lawyers the advantage. They have always been just numbers to me. I have never set out to make anybody go broke. I just wanted to get value for money every time I bet. The on-course layers are mostly honourable people. You can bet £10,000 to win £40,000, with nothing signed. How often would you find that outside racing?

The Tariahs followed up at Naas the same month and I backed him to win over £100,000, too. But that was a pittance compared with what he nearly delivered two years later. The last of my trio, The Hacienderos, made his debut in a field of twenty-nine at the Fairyhouse Easter meeting. He opened at 7–1, but was quickly cut to 5–1. I had two men betting for me and one asked for £3,000-to-win-£15,000 from a particular bookmaker. He immediately rubbed out his price and made it 2–1 and didn't lay me anything. Others followed suit before my men could hit them again. The Hacienderos started at 3–1.

It was clear that from now on they would take no chance whatsoever with my horses, even though it would be impossible to maintain such a rich vein of form. The Hacienderos took the lead two furlongs out and stayed on to win by three lengths. I still made around £50,000 that day, but when I found that a number of bookmakers had shortened the odds without a bet being struck on my horse, I said to myself, 'That's the end of it. I'm getting out.' The market had got weak in Ireland, and, at the time, racing in England appeared to have more to offer. I had been over to Wetherby on Boxing Day with the Dickinsons and seen it packed solid. At Fairyhouse, even if the course boasted an excellent card, there was no atmosphere about it.

These days, Irish racing is run exceptionally well, considering the facilities and money it has at its disposal.

We decided that Maureen would stay on in the Lodge House of Middleton House, with the children continuing their education in Ireland for the time being, but I made arrangements to travel to England straight away. The Hacienderos ran in another 'bumper' at Fairyhouse, where he made up a furlong in the last six and got beaten by a neck, which didn't look too good to serious race-watchers, although I'd backed him alright. He was a very hard puller, and to be a proper racehorse he had to learn how to settle. I told Willie Mullins: 'Although I've backed him, we have got to get him to settle. I don't mind him getting beaten, because I've got big future plans.' Willie obeyed my instructions perfectly and The Hacienderos was taught a crucial lesson that day.

EIGHTEEN

Tears at Cheltenham

When I arrived in England I carried a lot of baggage with me, and it wasn't all packed in suitcases. I had a jail sentence hanging over my head – and a judgement already instilled in the minds of the establishment that this gambler from Northern Ireland had arrived who had one mission in mind: to destroy the fabric of British racing.

As yet, I didn't have a licence myself, so the horses were initially trained officially by Dave Thom at his Harraton Court stables in Exning, Newmarket. In truth, it was a flag of convenience for me, although it confused all the lads. They weren't sure if their guv'nor was Mr Curley or Mr Thom. My tangible travelling companions included twenty-five horses, nine lads, and, to ride the horses, a young Irish amateur jockey named Declan Murphy.

I was a marked man. I expected it and could handle it; maybe I should have taken it as a compliment. But what I found unpalatable was that Dave and Declan were soon being tarred with the same brush. That was one reason why I was determined to get my own training licence as quickly as possible. You may say that was paranoia, but there was evidence aplenty to back up that claim. From the start, every horse Dave ran for me came under close scrutiny and, as soon as I entered the racecourse, I got knowing looks from officials and others. Their expressions said it all: 'He's here to fix races or dope horses.' I knew that was the general opinion.

It was 13 November 1984, the day Declan had his first win in England on a nine-year-old maiden, Who's Driving, that I announced my intention to apply for a jumps licence to train on the mainland. I had already learnt that it was preferable to do everything yourself. If not, you soon discovered weak links in the chain. I was an owner and punter, but I was forced into training my own horses because every year I was winning a large amount of money and half of it went on training bills to trainers who were apt to be wrong 90 per cent of the time. The only way to make it pay, because I had no other means of income, was to back them. Previously, the whole crowd knew the strength of my horses' chances. They may as well have trailed a banner from an aircraft and buzzed the crowd. As I've stressed before, you must get the value. There's no point buying a horse costing £25,000, spending £30,000 for two years' keep, and the first day he goes racing with a chance of winning find it's evens-favourite.

That why I decided to set out on my own. Now nobody knows my business except those who are proven trustworthy. If you're paying for something, it's only fair that you should get first crack of the whip. But these horses were opening at ridiculous odds. The trainers I had – I'd rather not speak ill of the dead – would tip them to their friends. It would be a complete waste of time.

That eight-runner selling steeplechase at Plumpton was not the most auspicious of starts for Declan, who was then still eighteen and had left school only a month before. But he was delighted just to get off the mark after fourteen wins back in Ireland. The gelding made a few mistakes, but still beat a dreadfully poor field, scoring unchallenged by twenty-five lengths. As far as I recall he went unbacked by his owner.

During late November of that year I had to return to the

Circuit Court in Mullingar for my appeal against the verdict in the lottery case. Similar to events during the litigation over my betting shop licence in Omagh, this appeal judge also showed a great deal more common sense than the man who had originally found me guilty. A spell in prison was not my primary concern; what I was more worried about was how it would affect my application for a trainer's licence in England. That had been adjourned pending the outcome of the court case. Even if a suspended sentence were substituted, it would probably give the Jockey Club sufficient grounds for refusing me a licence.

Sergeant Tuohy again gave evidence, along with Inspector Denis Cullinane, saying that a search warrant had been obtained and that a search had taken place on 3 February. The latter stressed that I had been open with him and had hidden nothing. My counsel, Seamus McKenna, maintained that I 'had not been flying in the face of the law' as the original judge had inferred and had, in fact, earned 'a lot of good publicity for the country'. He attempted to argue a technical defence, suggesting there was no evidence that I had promoted the lottery on the day the charge referred to, 9 February. Yes, I had done so several times in the months preceding it, but on the day itself I had merely 'conducted' a lottery. Peter O'Malley, the circuit judge, wouldn't wear that and found the charges proved, but said he would place me on probation instead, with no conviction recorded, provided that, bearing in mind the festive time of year was approaching, I paid £5,000 to the local branch of the Society of St Vincent de Paul Christmas Fund. I told the judge, through my counsel, that I was prepared to double it.

I was in good spirits when I flew straight back to Newmarket, in readiness to appear before the licensing committee the following day. Which just shows you can take nothing for granted in this life. Twelve days before Christmas of that year I had my application turned down by the Jockey Club's licensing committee. It came as no great surprise, given that at least one member of the committee, Captain Miles Gosling, a former chairman of Cheltenham racecourse and who had been a member of the Jockey Club since 1965, made his distaste for me obvious from the start. He was a man from an era, which, like that of the dinosaurs, you thought had passed into pre-history. He was arrogant and self-centred and listened to no-one. The result was that I was advised to work as 'assistant' to Dave and and reapply later. The stewards asked if we got on well and I told them, 'There is never a cross word between us' – which was quite true. Dave was reported as saying, 'Barney is a good judge of work. He never misses a gallop and he's very good in the yard.' It was generous of him to say so, but I'm not sure if he was being completely candid.

I didn't lose any sleep over this snub from the licensing committee, but in truth it was laughable. The reasoning seemed to be that I couldn't have a full licence because I was too inexperienced. On the other hand, they wouldn't give me a permit because they thought I was too professional and had too many horses.

We split Harraton Court stables. I had a three-year lease on my half, which had twenty-six boxes, from Michael Mouskos, a Greek Cypriot in the hotel business. Dave had the other half, although, as I have said, as far as the authorities were concerned, he trained all the horses.

To work with a man like Dave, who had won numerous major Flat handicaps, including the Doncaster Cup, Chester Cup and Grand Metropolitan, was a great experience. I had never clapped eyes on Dave before this, but he turned out to be a thoroughly generous individual who couldn't have been more helpful in accommodating the lads I'd brought over from Ireland. It wasn't too long, though, before he might well have started regretting his decision. For a man who had held a trainer's licence since 1960, and whose reputation was untarnished, he was suddenly being called in by the stewards all too often to explain the running of my horses. It was becoming very embarrassing.

I've always said that I run my horses for my benefit, not for the bookmakers, racecourses or punters, and sometimes you have to just put your hands up and plead guilty to transgressing the rules, as I will return to later; but on occasions the stewards got it utterly wrong. The Tariahs was a good case in point. He was one of my trio of 'bumper' winners in Ireland and I had high expectations of him in England. In my business you can't afford to have any sentiment about horses, but The Tariahs was an exception. Along with Keep Hope Alive, he was potentially the best horse I ever owned and trained, and in that list I would even include Silver Buck and the others I sent over to the Dickinsons. He was a bay Deep Run gelding out of a Vulgan mare, a full brother of a hurdler-chaser named Clearit, and I had ambitious plans for him. I bought The Tariahs in Ireland from Ted Walsh after he had been beaten in a bumper at Fairyhouse where he had run too free. But I had seen enough to convince me that if he could be persuaded to settle we could have a tremendous hurdling prospect on our hands. He was not very big, but to me he was unique; the most lovable horse you've ever seen, so sweet and kind. When he came along it was like a shaft of sunshine pulling back the clouds and beaming through. He would nearly talk to you. I used to call him by the nickname 'Minnie', and he knew his name, too. I'd go down to the yard in the evenings in wintertime, and yell 'Heh, Minnie' and he'd come out and talk to me over the door of his box as I fed him mints and patted him. And I'd just say to him, 'Minnie, your time has not yet come.' You could do anything with him. He was a machine, this fellow. But unfortunately he was also a very hard 'puller', and that was to cause us serious problems with officialdom.

I always knew his progress would be gradual and would require patience, and his early hurdle races gave little indication to the untutored eye of the talent we were nurturing. A well-beaten twelfth of fifteen at Sandown on his debut in England was followed by an idiosyncratic performance at Kempton. As the late Jim Stanford wrote in the *Daily Mail* the following day, 'Irish gambler, Barney Curley, who wants to set up as a trainer in England, is getting the *persona non grata* treatment by our local stewards. Yesterday, for the second time in four days, the local officials inquired into the running and riding of one of his horses.'

What happened at the Surrey track was that I told Declan that, no matter what happened, he had to get the horse settled if he was ever to make a racehorse. He tucked him in last, and well behind, before they eventually made some belated progress to finish eighth out of fifteen runners. The stewards hauled Dave and Declan in and, of course, it looked bad on the camera patrol tape. Declan simply told the stewards his instructions. The horse did not like being held up and sulked for the first half of the race. The outcome was that 'their explanations were recorded'. That is a kind of suspended sentence, steward-speak for saying, 'We don't believe you, but won't take any action this time – just watch yourself.'

What upset me was that Dave, as the trainer, ended up taking the stick when really I should have been in there explaining. He had an unsullied reputation and had hardly been in before the stewards in his twenty-four-year career up to then, and I really felt for him. The whole thing was ludicrous. If you're going to give a horse an 'educational' run any jockey with half a brain doesn't draw attention to himself by detaching his mount 100yds from the rest of the runners, as he was at one stage. The Tariahs had picked up a few places in the straight, but, as Dave reflected, there was no great surprise in that, considering that he was trotting to half-way and in desperate ground the others finished extremely tired.

Dave was furious and opined, 'The stewards seem to be gunning for the owner'. The *Mail's* Stanford refuted that suggestion on behalf of the officials, claiming, 'I am assured that there are no special instructions to watch the Curley horses.' As Mandy Rice-Davies once famously remarked, 'They would say that, wouldn't they?'

I was actually worried about the condition of the horse, with considerable justification as it turned out. The Tariahs coughed on the way back and was subsequently found to be sick with colic, which is a serious intestinal ailment for a horse, and we had to get the vet out all night to stomach-pump him.

It was a scandalous decision, but, strangely enough, I don't really blame the stewards; the press were largely responsible. They had written me up as a sort of modern-day Jesse James and the stewards reacted accordingly. They already had their revolvers drawn from their holsters and had trigger-happy fingers. Four days earlier, we'd had a similar confrontation with the stewards after Experimenting finished fourth in a novice hurdle at Windsor. It was decreed that he had 'never been put in the race with a winning chance'.

The official Form Book recorded that Experimenting made: 'Steady headway from sixth: shaped well.' That looked dreadfully suspicious, but the horse was no champion and as Dave pointed out afterwards it was a modest event and Experimenting was probably only running on through beaten horses. He never won that season in three subsequent runs in unexceptional company, his best being a second place at Towcester. I felt that vindicated us.

It was clear the stewards were now well and truly on my case. The trouble was that, as detectives investigating supposed wrongdoing, they were more reminiscent of Inspector Clousseau than Hercule Poirot. Already my reputation in England was such that bookmakers were not exactly rushing to mark up prices on my horses, although both those horses drifted in the market. We were both concerned about the effect all this was having on Declan. It was beginning to get to the lad and it certainly wasn't what I had in mind when I persuaded him to come over, although he was already confirming my view that he was a real talent in the making. He rode one tremendous race in defeat, on a temperamental character called Ridgefield at Nottingham, going down by only a length and a half when little had been expected of him. 'The old horse has never jumped better than he did for Declan,' said Dave afterwards. It came as no surprise to me. I'd had tremendous faith in him ever since we first met. Thankfully, Dave was prepared to stand up to everything that was thrown at him. 'My conscience is clear,' he said. 'So I don't care how many times I am marched into the stewards' room, but it is beginning to get to Declan.' It was something we were both going to have to keep an eye on.

The Tariahs went on to finish seventh at Leicester, followed by his first success over obstacles in a novice hurdle at Folkestone over desperate ground. Declan produced him late to take it up on the flat to win by one and a half lengths. He finished the season with a second at Devon and Exeter and had produced all, and more, that I had expected of him.

By now he was still a very hard 'puller' in all his races. I made up my mind: we'd have to get him settled in his races or he'd be running away with his rider for ever. We did give him an 'educational' run at Kempton on Boxing Day in 1985. That word 'educational' has very dubious connotations in racing and is frequently used as a euphenism for non-trying, but on this occasion it was absolutely accurate.

It was quite a hot race, the Boxing Day Handicap Hurdle, which is run immediately after the festive season's centre-piece, the King George VI Chase. Although there were only ten runners I said to Declan, 'No matter what happens, I want him out the back, then get him used to the idea of running past four or five.' In print, that doesn't sound an awfully convincing explanation of what happened, and in truth it didn't look that way on the racecourse either. The horse was gambled on – though not by me, I should stress – from 5–1 to 7–2, so there was no suggestion from the betting ring that it wasn't 'off'. Declan did exactly as I had asked. As it was recorded in the Form Book, The Tariahs made: 'Steady headway from sixth: ran on flat.' He was beaten fifteen lengths by John Edwards's decent hurdler Yabis, ridden by Peter Scudamore. There is a dilemma for all trainers and owners: some might say that I should have run the horse with no thought for his future, as long as he gave his best and in that way punters would have had a fair run for their money; in my opinion, that could have spoilt him for ever more. I was determined that he would settle properly before the dawning of his finest day.

At least The Tariahs had the royal seal of approval that day at Kempton. Maureen and I had the children with us. They shouldn't really have been in the parade ring, but the Queen Mother, who was presenting the trophy to the winner, made a point of saying to them, 'That's a lovely horse you have.' She has always been a woman of the people.

In all honesty, The Tariahs was just biding his time before the kill. Our target was the Coral Golden Handicap Hurdle Final at Cheltenham. The race, run on Queen Mother Champion Chase day at the festival, is an endurance contest of 3m 1f, is invariably well contested, both in terms of quality and quantity, and is a fierce betting medium. Over the years there have been some huge gambles. That year there were thirty-one runners competing for prize money of nearly £14,000.

His preparatory race, a couple of months before, was the Coral Golden Handicap Hurdle qualifier at Warwick, one of a series run throughout the country which you must run in as one of the entry qualifications for the Cheltenham event. It is over a half-mile shorter trip and, having been prominent for much of the race, The Tariahs weakened to finish eleventh of the twenty-eight runners. There was no greater certainty than the fact that The Tariahs would not catch the judge's eye, or for that matter the handicapper's, that afternoon. He drifted in the market from his opening price of 7–2 to 8–1.

It was all going precisely to plan. To illustrate how good he actually was, we gave him a serious piece of work at home a week before Cheltenham with The Hacienderos, a high-class hurdler who would have carried around 12st in the race, and a decent mare called Mary Kate O'Brien. We worked them at level weights and 'Minnie' absolutely laughed at them. In the race he would carry 10st, virtually bottom weight. I knew we were laughing, too: we had a minimum of two stone up our sleeves. I'm not given to exaggeration, but he worked like a champion hurdler, and The Coral Hurdle, competitive though it is, is no championship race. You get a horse like that, if you're lucky, once in a lifetime.

When our horse-box headed off for Cheltenham on that Wednesday in March, its occupant was probably the biggest certainty ever to arrive at the festival meeting. Sceptics among National Hunt aficionados may well scoff and suggest it was merely a typical pre-Cheltenham piece of hyperbole on my part. But in this horse's case it was true. To illustrate the fact I had £50,000 on him at 14–1 to win £700,000. It is the biggest bet, in terms of potential winnings, I've ever had. The Tariahs actually went off at a starting price of 10–1. I didn't know Terry that well, but he appeared a decent enough fellow. He was a serious failure as a gambler.

Once the race had started Declan had him nicely tucked away out of the immediate firing line, but absolutely cantering, with the other jockeys pushing and shoving and battering their mounts about. 'Minnie' looked so fresh, he could have just joined the field at half-way and I knew he'd stay the marathon trip, particularly now that we'd got him to settle effectively. More importantly, I had no doubt he would win. I was so confident, the only thought that was going through my head was, 'I wonder if the stewards will have me in?' (because of his running at Warwick). The next thing The Tariahs overjumped, turned over, buried Declan in the turf and lay still. The horse had broken his neck.

Instead of driving back that night £700,000 the richer, I arrived home to an empty box contemplating the loss of the best and kindest horse I've ever been associated with. Beside me in the car was Declan, aching and bruised all over and still shaken by it all. He knew what the horse meant to me. It's a devastating feeling, after having such high hopes. 'The Prince' was dead and nobody could quite believe it. It's the only time I've ever been emotional about a horse. We all cried when he died. We did no work in the yard for two days. When you own and train horses you get well used to these things, but I never dreamt it would end like that. That wasn't part of the script. The money was irrelevant. On the racecourse it was the worst blow I ever had. The race was won by Newmarket trainer, Mick Ryan, whose 15–2 favourite, Motivator, bolted in by six lengths. His owner was Terry Ramsden, who probably, for once, came out of the race financially unscathed.

It's a strange game, because nobody, apart from those close to me, will have heard tell of The Tariahs. As a sad postscript, Timeform wrote him off in a couple of lines: 'Moderate hurdler. Dead.' That was the strength of their epitaph to a real equine friend.

NINETEEN

From palace to pit

I hadn't needed to think twice about moving to Newmarket, the Suffolk town which is the centre of British Flat racing. As they say, if you want to build a big ship, you go where there's plenty of water.

Fourteen years on, nowhere in the world could be a better place to live, even though I only know four or five people in the town really well. One of them is my vet Rob Pilsworth, who has been a great aid to me over the years. I have always been treated with the utmost courtesy – with one exception. At Mullingar we always had our own gallops and I could do whatever I liked with the horses. In Newmarket things are vastly different and there are rules about what you do on different gallops. It makes sense, given the huge equine population. But I didn't know that, and nobody advised me. I'd been there a week or so, and two or three of my lads were just hacking their mounts down a particular gallop. This rather baby-faced character cantered up behind them with a pair of his horses, and started bawling me out, using some very choice language. 'You're a c***,' he raged. 'And those fellows riding work for you are even bigger c****.' I just let him have his say, and ignored him. I went back to the yard, thinking what a fine welcome I'd got, and said to Dave, 'D'you know something, I've just come across the most ignorant man I've ever met in my life.' I added, 'I don't know who he is, but I'd say he's about thirty-five, and has a bit of a red complexion.' Dave laughed and said, 'I'll tell you exactly who he is – Bill O'Gorman'.

It turned out that the master of Graham Place, responsible by then for such fine sprinters as Abdu, Manor Farm Boy, Sayf El Arab and Sayyaf, was merely trying to work his horses as he was perfectly entitled to do, and at that time I shouldn't have even been anywhere near that gallop. I should have been on another. It was not a great start, but once I'd apologised and Bill and I had got to know each other, he turned out to be a grand chap. It only goes to show you just how false first impressions can be. You couldn't get a more considerate fellow anywhere. Since that day, the O'Gorman household is one of the few in Newmarket I'd call in to see how they are. Indeed, a few years later, when I wanted to give my son Charlie, nicknamed 'Chuck', some experience and needed someone who understood horses and was a hard taskmaster, he was the first one I thought of. Charlie worked for Bill for a time before flying out to gain some invaluable experience with Michael Dickinson in America.

When I first came to England, I went from one of the most luxurious homes in Ireland to living over the stables in a little room at Harraton Court. It was an absolute pit of a place, more like a prison cell than a flat. I lived for three years on my own in that room, although I flew back to Mullingar at weekends. When I went to bed I'd make sure that I had a shoe or heavy boot by the side of my bed. At about two o'clock in the morning the orchestra would start. There were rats and mice scurrying about, attracted by the horses' droppings, and my only protection was that heavy footwear which I hurled at them.

Very often you get gratification from the simple things in

life. I believe you have to stay close to your roots. I see people who have amassed great wealth, or who have achieved celebrity, and they are not necessarily happy people. The happiest people are often those who have nothing, like my friend, the missionary, Father Eugene O'Reilly. I like to stay a little apart from the rest. There is a lot of wealth in racing and you can very easily get sucked into that way of life.

Although I had hated that lonely, spartan existence, the experience was strangely beneficial. Maybe, after too many years in the splendour and comfort of Middleton House, I was adopting the old Jesuit philosophy of taking my turn at the bottom of the ladder. It was rather like that time spent in Manchester with my father. I always felt uneasy living in that huge mansion at Mullingar when so many people have to live in squalor. Yes, I have been what many would describe as wealthy and, yes, I have lived in luxury, but purely to keep my family. I have never coveted property, fine art or fast cars. I could live in virtually any circumstances. I've spent some of my happiest days staying at my mother's house in Irvinestown. It is in a terrace and has two small bedrooms. I chit-chat with her in the morning, walk down to the betting shop to watch a few races and return to her making me some bacon and eggs with some of her home-made soda bread.

Eventually, when the vultures started swooping over him, I bought Terry Ramsden's White House stables in Stetchworth. Of course, I had a responsibility to my family and Maureen and the children came over to join me. It is a fine house with a swimming pool, jacuzzi, snooker room and adjoining boxes for the horses. The family loved it.

I've got 'the knowledge' – just as a black cab driver has to before he gets his licence; he knows virtually every street in London – and that's how I've survived. Terry never got out on his bike and did his. He was obviously a genius in the financial markets and at one time was reputedly Britain's richest individual, with assets approaching £100 million. Before the 'Black Monday' crash in 1987 which wiped him out, he owned more than seventy racehorses and rarely had a bet of under £100,000. Financially, I wouldn't even begin to compare myself with Terry at his peak. The difference was that while he made awesome amounts on the financial markets and lost it on the betting markets, I concentrated on what I knew best, gambling on horses. You could never convince Terry that having the Midas touch in one market didn't automatically mean that he'd also clean up in another. Nothing could have been further from the truth. If a horse should have been 10–1 they'd lay him 3–1 and he'd take it. Everybody wanted to lay him bets. Even people who were not bookmakers. Everybody was in for a slice of his sizeable cake. I told him repeatedly that he was burning his money.

Terry may have been great at his own business, but he had no idea about racing and value, and the bookmakers profited greatly from this fact. When some people in racing questioned how he was able to go on such a wild betting spree, Ron Pollard of Ladbrokes responded ingenuously, 'What is "wild"?' And these are the people that stop winning punters' accounts at a stroke. Eventually he was effectively warned off for failing to pay £2 million worth of debts to bookmakers. He knew the truth himself, too. As Terry once ruefully remarked when asked whether he preferred the Flat to National Hunt, 'I like the Flat best. It's a quicker death.'

I was as happy living above the horses at Exning, with rats rustling about the place, as I was at Stetchworth. But when Terry offered his house, it was too good an opportunity to miss. I think it was just because Terry had a good opinion of me. He sold it to me at a very fair price.

I've never been able to boil an egg, let alone cook a meal; fortunately, at Harraton Court we had a fellow called Bill

Doran, who'd lived with us at Mullingar and had came over with me to England. He couldn't ride, but he was a valuable odd-job man around the yard. One of his tasks, in the absence of anyone else capable, was doing the cooking. Keith Floyd he was not. The stable, and staple, diet was rice. He just threw it in a big pot and boiled it, adding whatever happened to be available. I couldn't take it without raisins. The boys knew this and used to steal them from the larder just to annoy me. The alternative to rice was boiled spuds, and that was about all we had during the day, with a bit of ham thrown in. The stable lads gave him some right abuse. The canteen was like something never seen in England since the days of Dickens. Any meat they had would be undercooked or overcooked. For me, it was just cereal in the morning and, as often as not, my dinner consisted of Weetabix or Cornflakes, too. For a real treat, though rarely, I'd go to the Mexican restaurant up the street and have some taco to take away.

TWENTY

Firing my first shot with Faaris

Eventually I got my full jumps licence in November 1985 after the powers-that-be ran out of reasons for declining my application. A first winner in my own right in the UK was a long time coming because our horses had been laid low with a virus. It was 17 May 1986 before I made the record books as a winning trainer. It was opportune, too, because the horse concerned, Faaris, won me back some badly needed cash. Coincidentally, the horse, which had formerly run in the colours of Hamdan Al Maktoum on the Flat, had been bred by Tommy Stack. I had bought the gelding out of Kevin Prendergast's yard for about £10,000.

It was nearing the end of the jumps season and the yard had been so badly affected by the virus that I had thought of closing up for a month or two. But Faaris suddenly came right, and was sparkling on the gallops and I went for the kill at Bangor-on-Dee. Somebody had obviously tried to second-guess me at the same course a month before and had clearly jumped the gun. Then, the horse was backed from 14–1 to 6–1 by person or persons unknown, only to finish sixth. It certainly wasn't my money. But this time it most decidedly was the Curley money down, and Faaris fairly hacked up under Declan in a two-mile novices hurdle. With the wages of twelve or more lads to pay, and the cost of the horses, there are a lot of expenses to be paid.

I had a bundle on that day, enough to win me £100,000, but I had waited a long time and I greeted the victory with some relief.

I have the only establishment in England or Ireland where no one outside the yard knows the trainer's business. I've made my rules and stuck to them. Right from the beginning, I made it clear to my staff how I operated and what I expected of them. It probably wouldn't go down too well with a politician's workers' charter, but they're not trying to make a living out of racehorses. I tell my lads that I don't own an oil well or a factory; I own horses, and I do so solely to back them. There are no oil-rich Arabs, members of the aristocracy or 200-strong syndicates to support the enterprise.

I then ask them if they are satisfied with their wages, £150 a week or whatever it is. If they say yes, I make it clear that there are no unofficial 'bonuses'. There is to be nothing made from tips or information on my runners to outsiders. Those are my conditions, and they accept them or look elsewhere in Newmarket where I am sure there are more benign employers.

If someone outside the yard said to me, 'I heard such and such worked well yesterday morning, Barney,' I'd investigate, find out who'd said it and sack them immediately, without any appeal. My view was that the lads were working solely for me. If they weren't satisfied with their wages, they shouldn't be there. I didn't care what the tradition was in racing, it didn't give them any right to earn a few pounds on the side from tipping. I didn't even want them backing the horse themselves. There were no ifs or buts about it. Even if they were hard-workers, out they went. That's the way I still run it, with my present assistant, Andrew Stringer, and his staff.

The alternative was to deal with the 'informer' by going in for a bit of duplicity yourself, by arranging for a horse that he thought was the business to 'win' his piece of work by ten lengths on the gallops. That would put him and his confederates away completely. He'd start favourite the next day but wouldn't win, and the 'tipster' concerned would soon put an end to his tricks. I have always tried to turn disloyalty in my favour. Having said that, I've always been generous and if they need a few quid to buy a car or something I'll lend it to them. If they've demonstrated they've been playing the game by my rules, they find I don't go looking for the money back.

I've always employed Irish lads wherever possible, but it is not a form of racism. I just think that, on the whole, the Irish make better horsemen. The problem is that they tend to bring certain vices with them, notably a liking for alcohol. I've had my fair share of madmen; brilliant in the saddle, but a liability with a drink inside them who would invariably end up squaring up for a fight with each other.

I've sacked a lot of them, particularly the Irish lads ringing back home with tips. To me, it's no different from a young chap working in a supermarket and taking a few items out under his jacket on the basis that he doesn't get paid that well. The answer is, if you're not happy, leave and try something else. It sounds harsh, but unless you are stringent the betting operation just fails to function and then we're all out of business.

For the same reason of secrecy, I've never wanted to train for outside owners, although I have made a couple of exceptions with my good friends Tommy Stack and Patsy Byrne. Tommy asked me to train a horse called Noan Wood for him, although it was actually in his wife's name. He cost quite a bit and, to be candid, I made a right mess of it. In his first season, 1984–85, we discovered that the horse had poor eyesight. He used to spook at some of his hurdles and he was a bit dangerous to ride. I liked to tell Tommy to have the money on when the horse was right. When we least expected it, he won a novice hurdle at Newbury by two and a half lengths, but in all honesty I didn't fancy him. Then he fell in his next race, a novice chase. We sold him at Doncaster sales.

Apart from that, the only owner I have been prepared to train for has been my friend Patsy Byrne. I did once offer to train a horse I liked for nothing. The horse was in Susan Piggott's yard, owned by a Japanese man and managed by an Irishman, and eventually he went to David Elsworth on training fees. Either my compatriot didn't rate me, or he had no regard for his client's money. David's one of the few trainers that I admire. He always tells it straight. He once came on the phone to me early one morning and started having a go about something. It was to do with a race where he had a horse running and he had accused Declan of obstructing his jockey, Paul Holley. There had been a bit of a rumpus and it had all ended up with Declan defending himself in one of the trade papers. David accused me of writing the letter for him. Declan had certainly written it like I talked, but it was definitely his own handiwork. David was on to me for half an hour. Finally, trying to get him off the line, I said, 'David, don't you have any horses to train down there?' He had a lot of good ones at the time, including Desert Orchid. But back he came: 'Don't you worry about my horses, Barney, I'm talking to you.' It was one argument when I had to give second best. I would admire him for that. He had a point to make and he was making it. Maybe I saw something of myself in him ... being open rather than talking behind someone's back.

At the time, in the mid-eighties, I could still just about get the money on, but that was gradually changing. The simple economics are that to buy a horse at, say, £25,000, and keep it in training for two years was, even then, costing a total of £50,000. Even if it wins a couple of races, it's uneconomic, with the prize money going on transport, entry fees and other costs. You need successful betting just to support the operation, let alone make a profit. But, increasingly, we were seeing weak markets as bookmakers refused to take decent-sized bets, and in some cases, such as myself, refused them outright. The days of the big bookmakers who would stand to lose £100,000 were over. The major high street bookmaking concerns were also, of course, manipulating the on-course odds, with relatively small amounts of off-course money to limit their liabilities on well-fancied horses. Many people don't realise how this situation encourages fixed races, carve-ups, 'jockeys' races', call them what you will as trainers strive to make ends meet. At one stage the Office of Fair Trading looked into the whole business before clearing bookmakers of manipulating the odds. I found that an astonishing decision then, and nothing has happened to make me change my view since.

TWENTY-ONE

No stopping The Hacienderos

One of my first winners, during my first year in England, was The Hacienderos on Hennessy Gold Cup day at Newbury. It was a perfect example of knowing exactly when a horse has come to himself and it is time to strike.

He had been another one of my parting shot trio of 'bumper' winners in Ireland and was an exceptionally good horse. As a three-year-old, I had sent him to Doncaster sales where he was bought by Michael 'Mouse' Morris, the Co. Tipperary trainer and former top jump jockey, for £18,000. He complained that he was a 'box walker' which means that he is nervous, and, as a rule, it is not a good characteristic in a horse. 'Fine,' I said. 'Send him back to me.' Mouse returned him to Mullingar and, in the process, unwittingly gave me a present of about a quarter of a million pounds.

He was due to have his first run of the season in the Speen Novices Hurdle at Newbury on Hennessy Gold Cup day in November. The race of 2m 100yds is usually divided but each 'heat' is still invariably fiercely contested by a few classy types whom their trainers regard as stars of the future over either timber or fences. I never even looked at the opposition. I've never been reckless, but I can honestly say that, in those halcyon days, if I had a horse 'on the boil' I didn't consider the dangers. David Nicholson or Martin Pipe could have had their stable favourites entered in the race for all I cared. Respect is one thing; once you start fearing the opposition, you're doomed. Apart from anything else, any apprehensiveness can transmit itself to the jockey. Even when I won those three Metropolitan 'bumpers' in Ireland, and they are among the hardest races to win, I only had eyes for my horses. I could barely tell you on the day who their rivals were.

When it comes to the day-to-day running of a stables, I have to concede I'm not a lot of use. The business of standing around feeling joints or checking feed is not for me. I probably just get in the way. But I do have a good eye when horses are working. Horses are not machines that can always be relied upon to run at their best; they come to a peak during a season and the secret is spotting the signs of a horse approaching the top of his form – when he's bouncing in his box and enthusiastic about his work. He's like a footballer who really enjoys his training, wanting to show the manager what he can do compared with the one who's sulking because he's been dropped or come in for criticism from the fans. You need an experienced eye to spot it.

On the gallops I had watched The Hacienderos, a six-year-old gelding by the prolific jump sire Deep Run, and seen him improve dramatically through September and October. I knew he was absolutely flying when it came to Newbury. I didn't need to look at the rest of the field or concern myself with their reputations. I was supremely confident. And I always back my own judgement.

It was the last race on the card and Jenny Pitman's great favourite Burrough Hill Lad, who had won the previous season's Cheltenham Gold Cup, had already sent many of the punters home in ebullient mood after being well supported and justifying 100–30 favouritism in the Hennessy. But I had only one race on my mind that afternoon. I told my men: 'Back him and keep backing him.' Eventually I had £50,000 on and he started at 4–1, although Andy Turnell's Tawridge, who had easily won his first start at Chepstow, and Nick Gaselee's Deep Impression, making his debut, were marginally preferred in the betting. The name next to the horse, 'Mr D. Murphy', claiming 4lbs, would not have inspired confidence among most punters.

Declan rode a fine race, bringing him through two out and leading just before the last to steer him home from Nicky Henderson's Oxhey Cottage. The winning distance was only two and a half lengths, but there was never any danger. His cause wasn't helped in the race by a couple of senior jockeys, John Francome and Steve Smith Eccles, who made it clear they didn't like the idea of some young upstart making a name for himself, but it's a tough game out there in the saddle and I had always told Declan, 'You're out there to win. Take no nonsense from anyone and, within the rules, give as good as you get.'

Interestingly, and a response to those who may believe that I am suffering from an advanced state of paranoia regarding racecourse officialdom, one correspondent did point out the following week: 'It does seem the stewards are stalking Curley ... as The Hacienderos stormed home at Newbury, I noticed two or three of the unplaced division given an "easy" with no post-race mutterings from the powers-that-be. There appears to be a very thin line between a non-trier and a horse not being given a punishing race.'

The Hacienderos' next run was at Kempton, on Boxing Day of that year, 1984, in the Food Brokers-Armour Novices Hurdle which was two races before the King George VI Chase, one of the great jumping spectacles of the season. Here was a perfect example of the sort of trouble Declan got himself into with his ultra-confident style of riding and my instructions. I already knew that, ideally, The Hacienderos had to be put late on the scene, which suited Declan's assured, unhurried manner. As Kempton is a lot sharper than Newbury's galloping track, with a shorter run-in, that might prove tricky. Yet, I felt he had so much class it didn't matter. What was important, I stressed to Declan, was that he was not to hit the front until after the last.

How long ago that day all seems now. It was the year when Desert Orchid, still making his mark as a decent five-year-old hurdler, was beaten by Browne's Gazette in the prestige event before the King George, the Ladbroke Christmas Hurdle. And in the big race itself, Burrough Hill Lad, the 2–1 on favourite went on to defeat Combs Ditch by a short head in a thriller for the racegoers.

After The Hacienderos' first hurdles run, the bookmakers were going to give nothing away, and so it proved; particularly as it appeared that he had only one serious rival, Mercy Rimell's Gala's Image. My horse started evens-favourite and was going so well that between the last two Declan actually took a 'pull' – there's not too many jockeys would do that, least of all at a track like Kempton – and the commentator, who clearly believed the horse was 'not off', informed racegoers with more than a hint of sarcasm, 'I hope Mr Murphy knows where the winning post is.' Declan certainly did all right and despite a poor jump at the last, The Hacienderos won by a neck. He had carried out my instructions to the letter and then I knew I had a real jockey on my hands. Very few would have had the courage to do that. Afterwards Terry Ramsden asked me if I'd sell him the horse for £150,000, but I turned it down because I knew, given normal progress, there would be some profitable times ahead.

His next target was the Roux Restaurants Tolworth Hurdle at Sandown in early January. Elsewhere many meetings were being abandoned because of the cold weather, but the ground was officially described as 'good to soft' – although it actually still had frost in it. These days I think it would be called off to protect the horses, but maybe because of the Channel 4 TV coverage of the centrepiece, the Anthony Mildmay, Peter Cazalet Memorial Handicap Chase, the stewards gave the go-ahead. I blame myself; I really should have pulled him out. The Hacienderos finished fifth to John Jenkins's Wing and a Prayer, having had every chance two hurdles out, but clearly didn't appreciate the underfoot conditions and afterwards he never really turned into the top-class performer I hoped he might.

The Hacienderos was placed at Huntingdon and Ascot that season, and, in between, actually managed to get beaten into seventh at Market Rasen when 13–8 on. The following year he went 'chasing, and won a couple of novices at Leicester and Lingfield at the end of 1986. The latter was, to all intents and purposes, a match between us and Nick Vigors's Cumrew and the horses started as 13–8 joint favourites, with the rest 6–1 and over. Fifteen minutes before the start a character shuffled up behind me and muttered, 'Barney, here's ten grand if you give yours a quiet one.' He showed me four rolls containing, presumably, two and a half thousand pounds each, as evidence. 'Take it, if you'll block your horse.' With The Hacienderos out of the way all Cumrew would have to do was jump round and the perpetrators of the fix would collect. I admit I had a shrewd idea who it was and I pondered for a moment how to respond. Inside I was seething. I didn't even turn round, but said quite calmly, 'I'm going to count to ten, and if you're still here I'm going to grab you and hand you over to security.' I would have done, too. Today, I wouldn't bother. Not because I have any wish to encourage such dishonesty in racing, but because the racing authorities have made a complete mess of administering the sport over the last ten years and don't deserve any support. There are individuals I have admired a lot, like General Cecil Blacker and Major Peter Steveney, but as a whole the authorities have to stand up and plead guilty to allowing the off-course bookmakers to entrench themselves, at the expense of other sections of the racing industry.

It should also be stressed that Declan would have refused to 'stop' the horse, even if I'd ordered him to. There are jockeys about who can, if the money is right, lose fifteen lengths in a race without racegoers or stewards being any the wiser. Declan wasn't one of them. He has always been one of the straightest jockeys that I have dealt with. Unlike some, Declan has always had a good brain and was too intelligent ever to get involved in that sort of shenanigans. Once a rider gets a name for 'stopping' horses, and we'll return to that subject later, it sticks.

The race? Well, it was as close as the price suggested. As usual, Declan made a sustained late challenge and The Hacienderos took it up on the flat. He won by a length. He remained a fair sort, and, in my opinion, would have been a very decent 'chaser' had that Sandown run not impaired his progress. It pleased me greatly when we took The Hacienderos back to Ireland and got a victory out of him in a handicap 'chase at Fairyhouse on Irish Grand National day in 1990.

Returning to that day at Lingfield, I'd have to say that if anyone could fix a race, I could. In my early years in England I was approached by many influential men, both bookmakers and punters, with the same question. Would I 'block' this or that horse? Without exception, I turned them down. I will do anything I can to beat the 'layers', except fix races to ensure there's only one guaranteed winner. That is morally, and legally, wrong. It is corrupt.

I'm pleased to say those requests stopped in the early nineties, when people came to realise what sort of game I play ... that I was for the good of racing, and would not get involved. Nevertheless, I'm quite aware that people still have a problem with my image. I know there is a general perception of me as a bandit. Ever since I built a string up over in Britain, they have been saying, 'How can Barney Curley have thirty or more horses, pay for their keep and not be fixing races? That takes a lot of money. There must be some skulduggery.'

I don't let it affect me. That's the opinion of people who don't know me. That's why I don't associate with many people. I have a close network of friends, perhaps four or five at the most, including Tommy Stack, who know how I think, what I'm capable of and how I achieve what I do. Ultimately, you have to live with yourself – and I can. It's between me and my God. For me, the line between right and wrong is clearly defined. If you organised a race where you manipulated a situation where, say, five out of the six runners could not win, that is stealing. It would be a *fait accompli*; you may as well rob the bookmaker at gunpoint.

That said, you have to live in the real world, one in which off-course bookmakers are profiting while racing is deprived of decent prize money. You can't expect owners, who have to win five ordinary races a year with their horse just to cover their training fees, not to line up one for a 'touch'. Plenty do, and you can't blame them. There's no other form of income. The reality of racing today is that there are still too many races where the prize-money is derisory, where the winners of some races are still getting £1,500. In 1998, five owners had a marvellous season with their filly, Lady Rockstar, who won eight races. Even with that record, they didn't break even. Her gross winnings were just over £24,000, which after deductions for trainer and jockeys, left £18,000. The cost of keeping her in training with Mick Ryan and other expenses was £18,500. As one owner said: 'Clearly this state of affairs must be discouraging to potential new owners, who are unlikely to find another Lady Rockstar.'

Whenever a prominent trainer preaches about the integrity of racing, this simple maxim should be remembered: The system makes cheats of everybody. I'm no better, or worse, than the majority of other trainers. I wouldn't deny that I always run my horses to suit myself. Some might suggest it would be a form of anarchy if everybody did what I did; that I'm just out to exploit the system for selfish motives; and that I have no responsibility towards ordinary punters. I put my hands up to both the last two charges. I am not here to provide free entertainment for the benefit of punters, bookmakers, the good image of the Jockey Club, the British Horseracing Board or TV personalities who feed off the sport. My only moral responsibility is to myself, my family and those who work for me. It's the system that leads to cheating. I have been burgling races whenever possible since 1992, the year when I made an honest, but ultimately futile, attempt to improve our sport. Exploit the system for as much as you can – that's my advice to my close friends. I see nothing wrong in lining up a horse for a race like The Hacienderos or The Tariahs. If my judgement and preparations are right, I'll win; if not, I won't. But I won't do anything illegal. Throughout my life it's been my brains against the bookmakers'. The bottom line is that a good trainer knows when his horses are going to win, just as I did with Yellow Sam. There aren't that many of us around. Most trainers wouldn't know if tomorrow was Wednesday or Thursday.

When I was really on the boil in the eighties I had fairly good horses. Now, I've got mainly bad ones and, generally, I'm going through the motions. But if I want a winner I'll have one. The secret is having a knowledge of what your horse is capable of, and keeping it to yourself. A survey of racing's hierarchy is very illuminating. At the pinnacle you have a few wealthy individuals and organisations, like the Maktoum family, Chevely Park Stud, Michael Tabor, Peter Savill Coolmore and Robert Sangster, who support ten to twenty trainers. The next strata are the people, normally 'new money', who come into the game, lose a small fortune and that's the end of them. They support another few trainers and there's a constant change-over of them. Manchester United manager Sir Alex Ferguson has come into the sport recently. The only way he will survive is if he is 'protected' by trainers. In other words, because of his value in promoting the sport and encouraging affluent footballers and coaches to follow suit, trainers will ensure he'll get the pick of available horses.

Then there are a few sharp operators among the third and bottom strata of around 200 who make a bit of a living out of it because they're backing their horses; the other 197 have to beg, steal and fiddle to try and make the business pay by keeping their boxes full. Most are cheating their owners: they are on fiddles at the sales; they take back-handers from the vendors. There are all sorts of scams. They keep horses in training that will never win a race and should be put down or, if you want to be kind, put out to grass. The one place the horses shouldn't be is on the racecourse. At least 40 per cent of horses running today have no chance of winning a race. On the all-weather, I'd go as far as to say that 80 per cent will never win a race. Racing is not, and has never been, straight. It never will be while it is underpinned by betting. It's not that sort of a game. To pretend otherwise is insulting the public and those involved in the sport.

One of the Jockey Club's duties is to ensure the integrity of racing, ostensibly so that punters can have faith in the system. That's nice in theory; in practice, few trainers, with, say, twenty to twenty-five horses, can make it pay with honesty. A system where prize-money is still desperately poor, makes 'dishonest' people out of virtually everybody. Without backing their horses, I'd estimate that 25 per cent of yards wouldn't stay in business. Does the Jockey Club honestly believe that the majority of owners are there to provide free entertainment in the betting shops so that the major bookmakers can reap massive profits, with no contribution to the show?

In any handicap on any day, the horses would probably all be doing their best. But that expression, 'their best', is rather hard to define. If you know your horses, it's very simple to give the wrong instructions. There might be a jockey told to hold his horse up and come at the two-furlong marker, when it's quite obvious to someone like me that he needs to make all the running and doesn't want to come through the field. Or vice versa. You don't have to tell a jockey to 'stop' them. It rarely happens. If you want to ensure a horse doesn't win, there's far more subtle measures that don't attract the stewards' attention. Even with modern technology and the best-trained eye – which the local stewards certainly don't possess – it's just not possible to detect everything that's going on in a race. That said, 'stopping' a horse can have ramifications you hadn't asked for. Running them on, say, firm ground when it relishes soft, sounds straightforward enough, but it can also easily jar the horse up. What it means is that the next time you're 'off' on suitable ground and the jockey presses the button, the horse may not want to let himself down. He remembers the discomfort of last time, and it doesn't put everything in. Similarly if you run a horse on very soft ground and it needs fast ground, you can destroy it for the future.

TWENTY-TWO

My man in Dundalk

Since my early betting days in Ireland, when bookmakers soon got wise to me, I've had to employ characters to discreetly place my bets. They are what I refer to as my 'putters-on'. They must be exceedingly trustworthy. Over the years there might have been 500 people involved; I've ended up with six of the best, with 494 rejects. I've been around a long time and I've learnt who you can trust and who you can't. The trustworthy ones I can ring on a Monday and say, 'I've a horse that is going to win on Thursday,' and there'd not be a whisper. There's no way they'd tell their friends. They quietly put on my money and take their cut. Of course, the 'layers' can get wind of who they are working for if I constantly use the same people, but I keep switching them, using three one day, then three the next.

For obvious reasons their identity has largely to remain a secret. But one man whose name I can reveal is Peter Begley, from Dundalk. He placed bets for me for the best part of thirty years, right up until his death in 1996. As far as I am aware, no one was ever the wiser. He was known as Peter the Flyer, and certainly he had the eye of an eagle in betting possibilities. He changed his system all the time, one day betting with someone in Glasgow, the next in Birmingham, forever changing his *modus operandi*. Nobody knew it was me behind him. He was so honest, I'd tell him what to bet, sometimes several days, weeks even, before a race and it would never get out. I never asked him what price he got. Often I wouldn't get the winnings until days afterwards, but it was never a penny out. If he put on £15,000 for me, as he did regularly, he'd have on only an extra £300 for himself. He was not a big gambler. He just wasn't interested in the money, which suited me fine. Peter just loved the mystique of it all, the buzz and the excitement of being involved in something covert and conspiratorial.

He died a couple of years ago, from a heart attack. He'd already had a triple by-pass and they'd told him to take it easy, but he was one of those men who wanted to live life to the full and ignored the medical people. On one day he'd go to Leopardstown races, then on to Shelbourne Park for the greyhounds, finishing the evening with a game of poker until the early hours. He always knew he was living on borrowed time and he even prepared for his death by finding me a replacement. He said to me one day, 'If anything should happen to me I know somebody who's deadly honest,' and gave me a name. It has proved right. Such was my admiration of him I named a horse after Peter called My Man in Dundalk, whom I will return to later. I say a prayer for him every day.

My 'putters-on' came in many guises and several have been bookmakers. One of them was a real character called Billy 'Sparkle Arkle' Kirkpatrick. He got his name from his betting office in Abbey Street, Dublin, which was called Arkle. He'd always be running short of money, but he was one of these characters you couldn't take a dislike to. I used to send Maureen up to his office to collect the winnings. One day she returned with two china dogs. I said, 'Did you get the money?' and she replied, 'Well, no. But he gave me these.' A friend of his ran a wholesaling business, selling china ornaments on the floor above his office. When he couldn't pay he palmed her off with the dogs; the next time, she came back with two china cows. We ended up with so much china that we could have become wholesalers ourselves ... but no money. It was a genuine gesture from a decent man, and I had to smile at his audacity. He ended up owing me £5,000. It took him two years but he paid every penny. I'm sure it wasn't easy for him at the time.

I learned my trade by acting as a 'putter-on' for one of the great Irish gamblers of the early seventies, Crawford Scott. The father of present-day trainer Homer Scott, he'd been down the road and seen it all. It was a great education. His great friend was Hughie Tunney, 'the meat baron' they used to call him, who once owned the famous Gresham Hotel in O'Connell Street, Dublin, and later lived at Classiebawn castle in Mullaghmore, County Sligo, Lord Mountbatten's home in 1979 when he was blown up the IRA. Hughie, from Irvinestown, where he formerly ran a butcher's shop before making his fortune in Dublin, is a distant relative of mine. Crawford was Hughie's cattle buyer and was also a big racehorse owner who liked a decent 'touch'.

He would hold court in the Gresham, and, also coming from Northern Ireland, he took me under his wing. I used to be 'young fella' to Crawford, even when I got to forty! He would always be smoking a cigarette, but refused to use an ashtray and would sit there with ash all down the front of his jacket. With his tall bearing and shock of fair hair, he had a great presence. He was a real larger-than-life character. But only a fool would underestimate him. He was very cute; he had an honours degree in native cunning. And you didn't argue with him. He'd call me up and say something like, 'Young fella, I want to see you this evening. Be in the Gresham Hotel at seven o'clock.'

I might have replied, 'Oh, I was thinking of going to the dogs at Mullingar tonight.'

There would be a slight pause, and he would bark, 'Are you listening. I want you at the Gresham ... '

You went to the Gresham. You just didn't refuse. When you got there, Crawford would say, 'A horse of mine is running tomorrow at Wexford. I want you to pay attention.' Then, he'd tell you precisely what to do. He didn't bet huge amounts, but I would get maybe £3,000 to £4,000 to place for him. 'Young fella,' he'd say, 'Watch me in the ring, and if I bend down to tie up my shoelaces you have the money on.'

He was absolutely straight but he trusted no one, not his trainers, jockeys or anybody else involved, and a lot of that attitude rubbed off on me. Crawford would go into the parade ring and organise his trainer and jockey, then, if it was decided that the horse was 'off', he'd give me the pre-arranged signal and I'd dash off to the betting ring to put the money on at 5 or 6–1. Meanwhile, he'd carry on discussing tactics, which would effectively hold up the rest of the horse's 'connections' from getting any money on themselves while I got the best prices. By the time the trainer and lads were 'on', the horse would be down to 6–4. If I got no signal, I'd hang fire. I always had a couple of hundred on as well, but if the horse won and he was aware you'd got nothing out of it, he'd pay you. You didn't try and deceive Crawford. If he knew you'd had on, say, £200 at 6–1, he'd say, 'That'll do you.'

My demeanour on the racecourse has been described in many ways: sinister, reserved, cold, unapproachable, secretive, to name but a few adjectives. I'm sure they have all been accurate at some time. There is a simple explanation. Every day that I walk in through those gates I imagine that it's a jungle. There are lions, tigers and crocodiles ready to strike. If you do not go in prepared, with your eyes and ears open, they eat you alive. I've seen it happen to so many – Terry Ramsden, to name but one.

I have this thick protective armour which I wear and carry an imaginary shield to stop them savaging me, and it makes me a completely different person from who I would be otherwise. There it remains until I walk out of the gates again. I am no one's easy prey. The betting jungle is a dangerous place on your own, but though the predators have drawn blood I have survived as a professional gambler for over thirty years.

Nobody really understands my methods. I'm not always a logical thinker. A lot of my success is down to gut instinct. But I've stayed the trip for all these years because I'm a watcher, not a listener. And certainly not a talker.

As an illustration of how I work, back in March 1998 my eye had been caught by a horse called Course Doctor competing in a two-mile novice at Catterick. In his only previous two races he'd been unplaced and brought down. At the Yorkshire course he had finished sixth of fifteen finishers and was never in contention, but a number of factors had caught my eye. Not least the rather strange fact that his trainer George Moore had run him on a notoriously tight track; probably the worst possible he could have chosen for a horse that, on his breeding, appeared to need a much longer distance. The six-year-old was by Roselier out of a Crash Course mare, and, I suspected, would be likely to stay all day. I thought to myself, 'What's going on, here?' It didn't take too long to work out. That was his third run, he could now be handicapped, and with his record on paper he would be likely to get a selling plater's rating. There was nothing in the Form Book to suggest he would be a nailed-on certainty next time out.

I kept a look out for Course Doctor to be entered again, and he duly appeared on Easter Saturday, about a month later. It was in an extended two and a half mile novices handicap hurdle at Carlisle – a far more suitable trip and a stiff, galloping course. I said to myself, 'Right, that'll do me today.' Now at this stage I was not particularly concerned who the trainer was. However, when I found it was George Moore, I came to some interesting conclusions. Two of Moore's owners are Sean

Graham's sons and, unlike their father, who wouldn't have put a penny on a horse even if he'd known the result, they had a reputation as punters. They were also very friendly with the horse dealer Tom Costelloe, who supplied a lot of horses to Moore, and, going by the breeding, it sounded as though it might have been one of his. All this was going round in my mind and while there may or may not have been a connection, it was enough to suggest that a few people, notably the Graham boys, might be on for a 'touch'.

What really made me rub my hands with glee, however, was that the Racing Channel presenters that day, Gordon Brown and Richard Pitman, were concentrating on two horses: Hurst Flyer, trained by Frank Murtagh, which had run badly at Newbury in its previous race and had been pulled up, and was set to carry 11lbs more than Course Doctor; and one of Jonjo O'Neill's called Aren't We Lucky, a horse I didn't rate. I thought I could safely ignore both, but it didn't do any harm to have them talked up. The important thing was that they didn't mention Course Doctor. I also watched carefully to see if Moore would be interviewed on the Racing Channel – occasionally he appears – but there was no sign of him ... further circumstantial, if not concrete, evidence that the horse was 'off'. No trainer with any brain talks about his horse when the money is about to go down.

I rang my agents and got them to back the horse underground. I wanted £15,000 on, at 5–1 or 9–2 minimum. I only managed to get £11,000 on, because one of the 'layers' was getting increasingly worried about the weight of money from another source and refused to take the bet; in fact he refused to do any more business with my man, so I lost one of my good accounts and had to look for a replacement. Although Course Doctor idled on the run-in and had to be shaken up, he won by a length and a half. Afterwards it was revealed that there had been an almighty on-course gamble with the horse opening at 6–1 and starting at 5–2 favourite. Not that it bothered me; I won £52,000. Significantly, bearing in mind the location of his previous race, Moore was quoted as saying afterwards: 'He is a big, long-striding individual who will make a fine chasing prospect.'

Sometimes it comes off like that, but the knowledge you need to work it all out doesn't come overnight. It has taken thirty years' study of my subject. You must have the knowledge of the game. You have either got it or you haven't. You can never make it pay listening to racecourse tips or tipping lines, or paying heed to newspaper tipsters and publications like Timeform. Even if they do provide any useful information, it is pointless knowing it because thousands of others do, too. You win by using your own eyes, and interpreting the information as you see fit. That is not to say I'm a genius; it can, and does, go wrong. I have plenty of losing days, too.

At my busiest, I have an average of a dozen bets a week; yet, on many days I'm quite content to keep a watching brief. The loser is the man who feels compelled to back a horse. You have to get the value, too. If a horse is 2–1 and I consider it should be 4–1 I'm quite happy to watch it win and walk out of the gate empty-handed. It's been said that I bet £10,000 minimum, but even these days that's a slight exaggeration. There's no minimum or maximum. I might have £1,600 at 6–1, giving me a profit of just under £10,000 one day and £22,000 to £20,000 the next. But make no mistake, if I really fancy something I load on as much as I can get. That day at Cheltenham when Forgive 'N Forget won the Coral Hurdle Final I had £50,000 on, mostly at 4–1, but I still backed him down to 3–1 because even at that price he was still value.

I wouldn't encourage anyone to become a professional gambler. Nowadays it's a downright impossibility for all but a few of us. Even when I set out in the early seventies and you could get a decent-sized bet on, I was taking on a stiff task;

nowadays it's a downright impossibility for all but a few of us. Jack Ramsden, husband of trainer Lynda, is about the only other man who has made it pay seriously in recent years and he's very knowledgeable. Apart from him, you have to go back to the late Alex Bird who achieved a legendary status, notably because of his forte for backing correctly in photo-finishes, but even he never bet or made as much profit as I have over the years. My strength is assimilating useful information, and discarding the irrelevant. I have a very selective memory, but it's important never to close your mind to anything. I read the newspapers and trade papers, watch races on TV, study the form book, every conceivable source of information, but try not to clutter my head up with useless detail. It can be a minefield, and you have to pick your way round irrelevancies.

At one time, in 1992, I was £2 million in debt, for reasons unconnected with betting, and I had to work really hard at it for days and evenings on end. I build up information in my head like a computer databank. My mind might not be quite as sharp as it was in those early days, but it still retains many megabytes of memory.

Backing horses is not an exact science. Even if you see a horse that's a serious possibility on its last run, you have to consider the trainer and whether he'll be likely to give their horse an 'easy' race to get it down the handicap, and of course the merits of the jockey. The going is most important. That's why I like to go to the races as much as possible before a bet. You want to see how the horses you fancy look in the parade ring and how they go to post. Making a profit from backing horses in the betting shop is an impossibility. It's hard enough when you've got all the information at your disposal, but without, it's a hopeless cause. *And* you're paying tax on winnings.

Even if a horse has won its last race you have to study the circumstances. Has it been run to suit it, and have past performances suggested it is unreliable unless everything goes in its favour?

I keep an eye on horses I'm interested in from the moment they are first declared in the trade press. Each day, I get the evening paper, study the runners and see if anything stands out, then consult the form book. In my head I've got names of those to look out for, but obviously you have to see how they're handicapped.

In the afternoon or early evening I'll call my men and warn them that I'm likely to have a bet the following day, then I'll go out for a walk, maybe take Arney, my Saint Bernard, with me, and have a good think about it. There might be nine or ten factors involved and I'll go over and over them in my head. The only consideration that doesn't really interest me is time. As Luca Cumani, that fine trainer and manager of Fittocki Stud once said, 'Time is only important when you're in jail.'

First thing in the morning, my men will find out the 'tissue' prices. Those are what the bookmakers are likely to chalk up as a first show. The price must be right. 'Always get the value' is a maxim that has always stood me in good stead. If, in my opinion, the horse should be 3–1 or more and it's 2–1, then it's not good value and I'll walk away. It may be only an hour before the race that I'll decide definitely whether to back a horse and with what amount. Even at the last minute I could pull out if the horse is sweating badly or misbehaving. If I'm not at the course I've generally got somebody there to represent me. I don't leave it to chance.

Of course you always have reverses, but once your system appears to be right you stick to it. There might be a race where you would have had a few thousand on a 3–1 chance and it was beaten by a head, a short head or half a length. If there was a genuine reason, say, for example that the jockey didn't make enough use of him, then that wouldn't worry me.

Occasionally, I have come to some terrible conclusions. I

have always believed that, despite not coming from a racing background, I have the gift to see things that other people can't. Maybe that was why, during a race at Ascot in 1986, I was the only one to notice anything suspicious about Graham Bradley's riding of Robin Goodfellow. That is a subject I will return to later.

Once I've make up my mind about a horse, I go for it. I take some notice of the market – after all, nobody wants to be on a horse that's drifting like the Marie Celeste – but not a lot. I don't rule out any races, but I tend to disregard five- and six-furlong handicaps; you get attractive prices, but those sprinters tend to just keep beating one another. All-weather racing is generally very poor quality and you can't trust the form; a lot of strokes are being pulled. It suits bookmakers because the horses don't run consistently. It's horse racing's equivalent of flapping in greyhounds. Trainers generally use it as an excuse to keep bad horses in training. I would never have a bet on all-weather racing. The same goes for the poorer quality greyhound meetings where the majority of dogs are either chasing each other – or fighting. The bookmakers don't mind. They own most of the tracks, anyway. High-quality racing is better for punters because the form is truer. That's why it would be a sad day for punters if Sheik Mohammed and his family, whose horses generally run on their merits, packed up for good.

I wouldn't have a great eye for the conformation of a horse, but I'm an excellent race-watcher. That's probably the secret of the job. I'd be good at telling you whether a horse needs a longer or shorter distance, or whether he'd been ridden badly.

It's impossible to back horses if you listen to the trainers and the jockeys and owners. People are all ears when a trainer is pontificating, but many have no idea what they're watching. Maybe it helped me not coming from a racing background; you're not drowned in all that tradition. They're all too close to it. Reputations count for too much. There are too many dreamers and too much rubbish talked about horses, either on TV or just in private. It's all a circus.

It occurs particularly in the early spring when there's a lot of talk about horses with the 1,000 or 2,000 Guineas as their targets. The giveaway is that bookmakers revel in all that hype. If a trainer starts waxing lyrical about the best horse he's had in his yard in thirty years I have to walk away. It doesn't matter if it's the champion trainer, it's odds-on and his stable jockey is saying defeat is not on his agenda. I listen to no one; if you do, it's a one-way pass to the poorhouse. The secret of making racing pay is to know something nobody else knows. That was why I first began to own horses and, later, to train them.

You could have had a Derby winner, a Grand National winner, but I honestly believe I have achieved more in racing than anyone else. Up until the last five years, I would have had forty horses in training, financed purely through betting. With the cost of their purchase and keep, you're talking about in the region of £500,000 a year to cover my costs alone. I'm the only man who has won that sort of sum consistently, year after year. It takes a lot of winning. You're talking about an outlay of, say, £3 million a year. How much do I bet? Suffice to say that even in the early seventies when I just went to Shelbourne Park greyhounds on a Saturday night, I'd gamble anything up to £40,000 – which is around £2 million a year. Even to fund my small operation at the moment, with around ten horses, I have to earn £100,000 a year. And that's done entirely through betting. It's not a big deal for me to win that amount to keep the show on the road, although I do think I could spend £100,000 much better. If you told any other trainer in England or Ireland that they had to go out and pay for the same number of horses as I had in my heyday and told them they wouldn't get a penny from any owners but they had to make a living, there's not a single one of them that could do it. They wouldn't have a hope.

There's no great secret about how I've kept my head above water. The only way I've been able to do it is to run a very strict regime. My attitude has always been that I'm my own man, the horses are my property and I have them to bet on them. My only concern is me and my small team; I've no regard for anyone else. I don't consider anybody else except people who work for me. I have a moral responsibility to make sure my lads get paid every week and that they lead a reasonable lifestyle. That's why I place so much stress on information about horses being kept strictly within the walls of the yard. In addition, I probably succeed because I only win what I want to. I'll never have £10 million in the bank. I don't believe in accumulating money just for the sake of it. In fact, I've always existed on a financial tightrope. I aim to cover my overheads with enough over to keep my family. If I needed, say £200,000, I'd plan something to win it. But I wouldn't work day after day simply to deposit money in the bank. It's never been my way. The purchase of Middleton House was a typical example. I bought that with the proceeds of Yellow Sam, and until I needed the next £10,000 or £15,000 I didn't bother much, I just bet away quietly. I never built up big assets.

There's a little church beside Tommy Stack's stables, outside Tipperary. I always think of a sermon given by the priest there. 'Wealth is like sea water,' he said. 'The more you drink, the more you want.' Money doesn't do anything for me; in fact, I've always been afraid of it. I've seen how it can destroy some people. Since I was lying in that sanatorium, that has been the last thing on my mind.

TWENTY-THREE

Target of the dopers

Joe 'Big Bucks' Donnelly, the biggest bookmaker when I was leaving Ireland, rang me up one day in 1989 and said, 'If you ever find a good horse over there, I'll buy him.' I thought I had what he was looking for in Keep Hope Alive, the best horse I ever trained, apart from The Tariahs. I'd had him as a 'store' and he won his first 'bumper' at Newbury in April of that year, which showed him to be a decent animal. I never even looked at the opposition. I just said to my associates, 'Take all prices. Back him until they will no longer lay him.' He opened at 3–1 and started at 6–4 favourite. He came up the Newbury straight doing half-speed and won by six lengths. We went to Ascot, with a penalty, and he did exactly the same on this occasion, scoring by three lengths. The bookies didn't take any chances with Keep Hope Alive this time, cutting him to 9–4 on favourite from an opening price of 5–4 on. Donnelly was suitably impressed and bought him.

At the start of the next season I gave Keep Hope Alive an 'educational' run over hurdles at Wolverhampton, where he won by a few lengths. I suspected by then that he was potentially one of the best hurdlers in the country, but I wanted some decent opposition to measure him against. At the time there was a lot of talk about a horse trained by Jenny Pitman named Egypt Mill Prince, who went on to finish fifth in the following year's Sun Alliance Hurdle at the Cheltenham Festival. I kept a very close eye on her horse's progress until Jenny announced in the papers that she was going to run him at Ascot in the Durham Rangers Novices Hurdle on 13 January. I said to myself, 'Right, I'll run mine at Ascot, too.' We went head-to-head, they bet mine 5–4 favourite, hers 6–4, the rest out with the washing at 7–1. It was a match, but that suited me fine. I wanted to get as much money on as I could, but I needed a strong market and I knew a lot of people would be backing Jenny's horse. If Egypt Mill Prince hadn't been in the race Keep Hope Alive would have been unbackable at long odds on. I remember that day well, because I had £50,000 on my horse.

Keep Hope Alive never ran his race. Although he made it home in third behind Egypt Mill Prince and a horse of Nicky Henderson's, Whatever You Like, he was beaten a total of nearly ten lengths, and finished distressed. He could hardly put one hoof past the other as he walked into the unsaddling enclosure.

All I said to Declan when he came back in to dismount was, 'Phillip Mitchell again?' and he just nodded. It was a kind of password between us. The horse had been doped. It was well known in racing circles that doping was rife then, both over jumps and on the Flat, and a horse of Philip Mitchell's, which Declan had ridden at Kempton, had finished in the same exhausted state.

It wasn't just normal fatigue after a race; these horses were out on their feet. You have to be ahead of the posse in this game and I saw these horses coming back that could barely walk. I could only conclude that the dopers were in cahoots with the backers of the rival horses. The authorities held inquiries but no money ever showed up in the layers' books for the winners of the races concerned.

Well, of course, it never dawned on them, that with the big

bookmakers refusing to take a decent bet, the majority of significant wagers were being placed 'underground', where the money is not traceable. I will reveal more about this development later.

The media had no idea what was going on. One of the reporters, the *Racing Post's* George Ennor said to me, as though the horse had merely had an off day, 'You must be disappointed?' I said that I was and held my own counsel, but I knew the dopers had been at it.

Keep Hope Alive wasn't dope-tested. The stewards didn't ask for one, while I didn't need a test to tell me what had happened.

It ruined the horse and, although we tried hard with him, he never won again. I was given reason for optimism that Keep Hope Alive had suffered no long-term ill-effects when he ran a decent race at Newbury, finishing runner-up in a handicap hurdle, but my real target was Fairyhouse, and the £20,000 Jameson Gold Cup Hurdle, a listed race on Irish Grand National day, 1990.

He started 9–4 favourite with Charlie Brooks' Arden, but before the second hurdle was pulled up by Declan, having burst a blood vessel. The racecourse vet said he'd never seen anything like it before. It was like a river of blood coming down his nostrils. There was some consolation when The Hacienderos won a handicap chase for me on the same card, but not much.

What happened that day at Ascot? Well, everyone has their own theories. Keep Hope Alive was probably injected, although with something that couldn't be detected. Because I knew that doping gangs were operating at the time, I said to the lads who took him to the course, 'In no circumstances is that horse to be left alone'. It transpired that the lad who went with the horse to Ascot wasn't trustworthy. He left the horse unattended.

Immediately after the Ascot incident I went to the Jockey Club and told them, 'This doping is going on wholesale'. I also provided a list of horses I suspected had been doped to the Jockey Club's then chief executive, Christopher Haines, whom I have always rated as a very sharp fellow. He said, 'When's the next horse that you have running which is fancied?'

It was Ardbrin at Taunton a few days later. The Jockey Club's security people arranged to be at Taunton and watched every move. The place was saturated with their men. This was before all the safeguards like closed circuit TV in the racecourse stables that were later introduced.

In fairness to the Jockey Club's security department they took it very seriously, although overall that organisation suffered from naivety. However, by then it was too late. This team involved with doping horses were obviously pretty shrewd and I would think they were aware of what was going on. The race went off without incident and Ardbrin won at 5–4 favourite.

At that time I was determined to ensure that racing was run properly and fairly – and I was concerned that those rogues doping the horses should be eliminated.

Nobody was ever caught. But I have no doubt that doping was being carried out on a large scale. Of course, it never suited the Jockey Club, which is responsible for the integrity of racing, to admit that.

In the last couple of years there has been a police investigation into alleged doping of horses, which received wide publicity because three jockeys were arrested. At the time of writing, none have been charged and one, Leighton Aspell, who rides for me, has been told by police he is not part of their investigations.

It follows the doping of Avanti Express and Lively Knight at Exeter and Plumpton respectively in March 1997.

However, my belief that the doping of horses recently is

nothing like on the same scale it was going on in the late eighties and early nineties. Today, I don't care if they dope ten out of every eleven horses. It doesn't interest me in the least. They've made a mess of a job, and they don't deserve any help, neither the Jockey Club or British Horseracing Board. If it happened again today, it wouldn't serve me any good going to the Jockey Club. I'd just take it on the chin.

Another horse I'm certain was 'got at' was My Man in Dundalk before a hurdle race at Towcester. He was the horse I'd named after my 'putter-on', Peter Begley, and had won a race for me at Hereford in December 1996, landing a gamble into the bargain, after being off the course for 1,000 days. My 'man of a thousand days', so to speak, was a genuine enough horse, yet ran unaccountably badly at Towcester, ploughing through his hurdles, and immediately afterwards he wouldn't have been able to blow out a candle. Twenty minutes later he was breathing very heavily, as though something was amiss. He was dope tested and nothing showed up, but I still had my doubts. It destroyed his whole confidence.

Next time out I ran him in his first novice chase at Lingfield. I must admit I was a little concerned. I got Norman Williamson to ride and told him that I thought the horse had been got at in his previous race. But to allay any fears I added, 'I wouldn't put you up if I thought he was dangerous.' He actually jumped quite well, but My Man in Dundalk was never really the same again for me. I thought the only course of action was to sell him onto a horseman who knew what he was doing. Eventually, he went for a small sum to former jockey-turned-trainer Chris Grant, who is very friendly with my current assistant trainer, Andrew Stringer. I was quite honest with Chris. I told him the horse's background, but added, 'He'll win a race for you if you can sweeten him up.' Chris's wife, Sue, did so by hunting him several times with the South Durham, and he won twice for them, including first time out for Chris, at 25–1. There was no scheme, no conspiracy, although I must admit I had a few pounds on. He was no world-beater but at that price, and with my knowledge of the horse's history, I'd have been a fool not to.

I'm also convinced that Maradi, a horse I bought at the sales out of Richard Hannon's yard, was doped at Fakenham in early 1997. Again, he ran badly and was in a terrible state afterwards. In fact, he nearly died. I also had my doubts about Magic Combination at Newbury the same year. I won't report my suspicions because of the way I've been treated by racing's administrators over the years. I'm particularly incensed with the way the Jockey Club dealt with Frankie Dettori when he was suspended at Goodwood in 1997, and a row I had with the BHB over their handicapper Philip Judge.

I'm not given to being soft on horses, but my favourite horse in the yard is Mullingar Con, named after Con Murphy who rigged the Tote in that celebrated scam at Mullingar greyhounds. I've had him for years and he's nicknamed 'Jeffrey', and of all the horses in the stable I'd love him to win. He's a lovely grey horse, aged eleven at the time of writing, and has run only seven times, without troubling the judge. He has had various leg problems and has been 'fired' three times. He's like an arthritic old man these days and takes a bit of time to warm up. If things don't go exactly to his liking, he doesn't try too hard.

If you leave his box door open, he takes a couple of steps out and looks round, but won't go any further because he knows he's not allowed to. He's like a two-year-old when you take him to the races. He bucks around with the excitement of the occasion.

The weight a horse has to carry in a handicap is dependent on the rating allotted by the handicapper. His mark is based on the horse's form. So, at the start of 1997, after a three-year lay off, I was surprised to discover that Mullingar Con had been put up to a mark of 83, having been rated 60 when he last ran, a difference of 1st 9lb more in a handicap race.

As a rule I think handicappers have an almost impossible job. Given that horses aren't always running to their full potential and with the number of stables that have the virus at any time, they're very difficult to accurately assess. I'd not had a cross word with one in over 30 years of owning racehorses – but on this occasion I was in no doubt that the handicapper concerned, Philip Judge, had based his assessment on my reputation.

I called him and he explained that the weights had all gone up 10lb since the horse had last run. I told him that he was just a fun horse and had no chance of winning anyway. After some discussion he agreed to put Mullingar Con on a revised rating of 73. I said, 'Phil, don't ever do that to me again. Handicap the horse, not me. I'll forgive you once, but never twice.' When, the following week, I had another problem with him over My Man in Dundalk, yet another horse that had a touch of Lazarus about him, I vowed to get him sacked. Between March and August, I spent a small fortune on solicitors' fees taking the matter up with the BHB, but predictably they stood by their man. As my solicitor said, it was 'the best whitewash job I've ever seen.'

Incidentally, Mullingar Con finished the season having run five or six times off a rating of 55, and still hasn't won.

I was similarly infuriated, this time by the Jockey Club, by events which followed the Tripleprint Celebration Mile at Goodwood on a Saturday in August 1997. Frankie Dettori crossed the line first on John Gosden's Cape Cross, but later lost the race after being found guilty of irresponsible riding by the local stewards and banned for five days. They found he had interfered with a horse named Peartree House, ridden by Dane O'Neill, who finished fourth and last of the runners. Frankie had gone for a gap that closed on him, and it didn't at first sight look good. But other camera angles told a different story. As I saw it, it was actually Dane O'Neill's fault. He ran his horse into Frankie's. Dane O'Neill actually told the stewards, '… my horse was coming to the end of its run. It just started to roll around a little bit. Basically, it just rolled away from the rails, created a gap for Mr Dettori, and just rolled back on him again. He was getting tired at the time …'

They found against Frankie, but I had no doubt he would win an appeal. I offered to appear myself as a witness and Maureen, who was, by now, practising as a barrister, agreed to act on Frankie's behalf. The appeal hearing at Portman Square was a farce. The Goodwood stewards couldn't even get the location of the incident right. They said it was two furlongs out, when in fact it was three. The media and Jockeys' Association were half-hearted about their support. I had warned Frankie and Maureen on the way down, 'Unless you play hard, they'll make fools out of you.'

And so it proved. The disciplinary committee had their minds made up before they went in. We put our case, but they never asked a thing of Frankie in two hours. That's why I have no respect for the Jockey Club. It was quite a complicated case, yet they made their decision in five minutes. Maureen was horrified that justice could be dispensed with such obvious lack of consideration of the facts. I had agreed that win or lose, I would keep quiet, but I couldn't resist saying to the chairman of the appeal committee, Nigel Clark, 'I thought you were a man of honour?' I knew Nigel from his involvement as chairman of a money-making scheme I had devised to raise funds for Great Ormond Street Hospital. I had always thought he was a fair-minded man. Until then, Maureen could never understand why I made such a commotion about some of those decisions. Now, she knew how I felt, and why I no longer have any time for the Jockey Club – or BHB.

Many newspaper tipsters still advise 'watch the market' where my horses are concerned. Maybe there was some truth in that in the past, but that can safely be ignored as a hint now. I keep changing my lines of attack. In the summer of 1997, for example, I had four winners on the Flat – Cohiba, Magic Combination and Arif, twice – and they all drifted in the betting. Yet I had them backed.

The big players, like myself, don't go to the racecourse any more unless maybe they've got a horse running. Bookmakers won't take our size of wagers, so we bet between ourselves on an underground network. Gambling underground like this is, of course, illegal; apart from anything else there's no betting tax being paid, but my response is – what else is there for us to do? While there's a so-called Big Three – what a ridiculous misnomer that is – who won't lay a reasonable size bet, let alone a sizeable one, there is no alternative. I am quite prepared to say to those in charge of the Horserace Betting Levy Board, and the Exchequer, and the Customs and Excise: 'I am betting underground, because I cannot get a bet on with legal bookmakers. What are you going to do about it? Arrest me?' I challenge anyone to charge me with any crime; indeed, I would positively welcome a public investigation so that the true state of 'legal' betting in this country can be revealed for the disgraceful sham it is. The major bookmakers simply won't lay the kind of money I want to put on. Or, in the case of the high street bookmakers, won't lay me at all. If anyone else rings up to back one of my horses with significant money they can't get on either. People think you can easily have a bet of £2,000 to win £10,000 but you can't, unless they think you're a mug punter. That's why I now bet, almost exclusively, underground.

There are now about two or three wealthy layers in every city, and far more in London, with considerable funds who want to gamble, but they can't so they use what is, in effect, a private betting ring. What happens is that I call up a 'putter-on', or agent, from a public telephone box, in case my line is being tapped or somebody is listening in to my mobile phone; I give him a price, and instruct him what odds I want on a particular horse. The agents take a 1 per cent handling fee and they find someone who will lay the horse at, or near, those particular odds. These 'layers' don't mind betting big, and will accept £4,000-to-£10,000 without any trouble. The pay-out might be as big as £20,000. If I can't get the price I want there's no bet. There has never been any problem over payments. These are honourable people. They have to be because the first time you're knocked back that's it, the system breaks down.

On occasions, I could be betting anything up to £50,000 a day. There is no market as such. The underground book-makers who lay the bets are just like me – gamblers. They operate just the same as the big bookmakers of old did, men prepared to take a risk twenty or more years ago. Then there were men like the late Sean Graham who used to take a chance. He would have laid you £3,000 to win £15,000 on a horse even if the bets he'd taken on the rest of the field only amounted to £2,000. Sean didn't worry about balancing his betting books. He was a good judge, and he'd gamble on your horse getting beaten. The underground network is a flourishing market. It has built up and got bigger as more and more serious punters have grown disillusioned with the 'Big Three' bookmakers, who are taking absolutely no risk and for whom it is purely an accounting exercise.

I bet with people who will take £4,000 at 4–1. You ring up Ladbrokes and say the same and they'll probably send the police around to arrest you, unless they regard you as a real mug. Walk into a Ladbrokes shop and just try to have a £500 bet on a 10–1 chance. A phone call to head office and five minutes later you're told you can have £50 on at 10–1 and the rest at SP. There needs to be a regulator of bookmaking, like there are in many other industries. Can you imagine the casino industry being unregulated? How long would it have lasted? Three or four million people bet on horses every day. Ladbrokes love the fiver, the tenner and the twenty from the cannon fodder, but don't like anything else; like the boxer with the glass jaw, they'll not take a hit. All Ladbrokes want to do is recycle dole money and take their rake-off.

There's not a racecourse where you can go and have a decent wager, except maybe Royal Ascot, York and Cheltenham, where bookmakers like Stephen Little will take your bets. I've not gambled with a bookmaker since the summer of 1997, apart from Ascot. At most ordinary meetings the market is so weak that a £500 bet can knock a horse in from 10–1 to 5–1. That's all it takes, for the 'Big Three' to rig the market. My view is, if you don't like taking 'dangerous' money, fine; don't be a bookmaker. Too many on-course bookies are wasters anyway. A lot are nearly skint. Because of that it allows the off-course market to manipulate the on-course market. The racecourses couldn't care what happens as long as they get their cut from SIS (Satellite Information Services – a company dominated by bookmakers' interests which broadcasts horse and greyhound racing to betting shops). The only place you'll get your £500 on at a racecourse is at a big meeting, but how many of them are there every year? I went to Newmarket one afternoon in 1997 with the intention of trying to back a horse at 9–2. I got £2,500 on with a struggle – £1,000 from Roy Christie, £1,500 from Colin Webster – and that was it. I was not even backing one of mine. There was no scheme, it was just a straight bet on one I fancied. I left the racecourse immediately and went home to my phone and bet underground.

The only answer to racing's lack of finance is an off-course Tote monopoly, as they have in many countries, and on-course bookmakers. At present we have the worst of everything: a weak on-course market and a weak Tote, but strong off-course bookmakers who put next to nothing back into racing. Ladbrokes were quite happy to sell 110 shops to the Tote in the proposed takeover of Coral's. There's no danger from the Tote as it stands, particularly under the chairmanship of Peter Jones who did absolutely nothing for the Racehorse Owners Association. Ladbrokes don't see the Tote as opposition. It is not a credible competitive force. It's nicknamed 'The Nanny', and that's all it's good for – grandmothers and grandfathers, and people who know nothing about betting.

We must learn our lessons from Australia. Under their Tote system, the Tote Agency Board, or TAB as it's known, you can get on £50,000 if you want to and it's a very strong market. On-course, they have different lines or categories of bookmakers who must lay to lose a minimum amount. Line A, say, are those who will lay to lose up to £5,000, line B to lose £1,000 and Line C to lose £500. It is all strictly controlled by a ring inspector. Not like the ones here, who are about as effective as Inspector Clousseau. As it was once voiced by the Aussie trainer Bart Cummins, 'Australian racing started 100 years behind English racing and now it's 100 years ahead.'

In Britain, racing is going nowhere and very little is being achieved by organisations like the BHB. Tristram Ricketts, chief executive of the BHB, is being paid £120,000 but what do we have to show for it? Ricketts talks about percentages of the Levy – a deduction by bookmakers on winnings which funds racing – and trying to increase betting. But he doesn't seem to comprehend that there's a 25–30 percent of turnover being lost underground. You very seldom see any of the big punters at the racecourse now. You might have the likes of Michael Tabor or me having a few bets with Stephen Little, say, at Ascot when there's one of the really big meetings with a big turnover and you can get on, but outside that it's all underground.

I regard Stephen Little as the top course bookmaker. He bets with his own money and he's a gentleman. When I got into financial trouble in the early nineties, I owed him a fair amount, but he never pressed me for it. I paid him eventually. If Stephen is not visible on the rails, or Colin Webster or Pat Whelan, there's no market. Victor Chandler, one of the most established and reputable bookies, is another decent man, but he rarely goes now except to the prestige meetings.

Betting is crucial to racing's prosperity, but there are too many people in charge who don't understand the business. That's why I believe racing needs a supremo, like motor racing has in Bernie Ecclestone, although here we're talking horse power of a different kind. We need a real inspirational figure, a benign dictator, a mover and a shaker, even if he makes mistakes or upsets a few people along the way; but it must be someone who is prepared to be ruthless when required: *Uno duce, uno voce*. The man concerned should not be attached to any group with an axe to grind. No venture is run properly if it is dominated by committees or sectional interests. Here, horses are sometimes already in their stalls before shows come through to the betting shops. What are the ring inspectors doing? They should ensure that all on-course bookmakers' prices are up at least ten minutes before the off. If they breach the rules they get a warning, the second time they are thrown out.

The stewards and chairmen of committees running a £4–5 billion a year business are a laughing stock. They should be ashamed of how they've allowed racing to decline by allowing the Big Three to assume power without responsibility. All betting shops are interested in now is lottery numbers, fruit machines and sports betting, particularly on golf and football, which are much less predictable than racing. None of those make any contribution to racing. Dogs are also a big winner for the 'layers', which is why the big bookmakers own many of the tracks. What depths have we plumbed when the Ladbrokes shop in Newmarket – famed the world over as the headquarters of British racing – has a window display advertising not races, but a numbers game? It is quite unbelievable.

I've had credit accounts closed by all the major book-makers, which is like having a badge of honour pinned on you. I haven't had a bet with Ladbrokes for at least twenty years, and I remember the day well – 7 July 1988 – when Hill's put up their hands and surrendered. I had taken at least £200,000 from them in the previous two years. The following morning Charlie Fawcus wrote about it in the *Daily Mirror* under the heading, 'Banned! Punter who beat the bookies.' Typically, Hill's themselves didn't even want to talk about it. Graham Sharpe, who is rarely lost for words when it comes to promoting his firm, told Charlie: 'We do not discuss individual accounts.' His silence spoke volumes. Hill's group managing director, Len Cowburn, maintained that, 'There is no black and white policy regarding winning accounts. Each case is judged on its merits, and here a commercial decision was taken.'

Journalist Graham Rock, who described the move as 'undoubtedly poor public relations', given the bookmakers' image, put it succinctly in *The Times*, when he wrote: 'The commercial attitude of major bookmakers is now governed by chartered accountants of public companies, interested solely in earning the approval of shareholders: the nip and tuck of the duel which inspired the leviathans of the ring before the 1960s is regarded as obsolete, an unseemly impediment to profitability.'

It's an open secret that they've always had people batting for them in the corridors of power. They lobby on the quiet, but very effectively, against any attempts to change the law on gambling. If you went into a casino and the manager said that you were not allowed to back black tonight, how long would the Gaming Board allow the casino to stay open? That, in effect, is what the high street bookmakers are doing. We need the same kind of regulator to oversee racing, and betting in particular. How long did Ladbrokes last in casinos? Not very long.

The problem is, as I shall discuss later, that nobody wants to do anything. The top ten trainers are very nicely off, supported by the Arabs, members of the Jockey Club and a few wealthy individuals. Why should they agitate for action and affect the status quo which benefits them? There are some intelligent people among them who know exactly what's going on, but they don't say anything. Meanwhile I'll continue to run my horses, and, even if they're fancied, they may drift. I'm sure many punters aren't happy with that, but they must blame the system operated by the bookmakers. As I've said, I'm not racing horses for the benefit of the nation's punters or the benefit of the major bookmakers, I am racing them for myself and my small team.

TWENTY-FOUR

The 'Robin Goodfellow Affair'

To be 'a disqualified person' is to be sent to purdah. It is like a businessman disqualified from being a director. It is not just a social stigma, they might just as well hang a bell round your neck and warn racegoers, 'Unclean'. It's like the posters they used to have in the Wild West to attract bounty hunters to catch outlaws, except that I would be 'UNWANTED'. I had experienced that state before, when I was warned off by the Irish Turf Club over my dispute with Sean Graham, but I always knew I would get my licence back once I paid that debt. This was different. Along with my later dalliance in racing politics, it was the greatest mistake I ever made.

I blame myself for the minor incident that was to explode into one of the most sensational episodes in British racing. They called it the 'Robin Goodfellow affair', with enough sub-plots to keep Sherlock Holmes occupied for many a long day. Maybe it was the high standards of integrity set by Tony Dickinson, the most honest racing man I've ever known, that concentrated my feelings against Graham Bradley; ever since those great days in the seventies that jockey had gnawed away at the back of my mind like a tooth that needs filling. Without it becoming an obsession, I felt the first chance I got at him, I'd teach him a lesson. It was wrong in a way. I should never have done it. Maybe it's a weakness, but whenever I suspect somebody of letting me down I keep my eye trained on them;

it's in their character, and, like a jailbird, they tend to be recidivists. But I took it too far. From the day I realised what he was up to I always said to myself that I'd get even with him. It was totally out of character for me and I'm not normally a vindictive man, even if someone has wronged me, but in his case I made an exception. He needed to get his come-uppance. So, the first chance I got him in my sights, I aimed and fired. I have regretted it ever since.

To recap, I had been sending the Dickinsons horses, sometimes cheaper than I should have as a return for information about when they were fancied. We had all got on well until, suddenly, the horses I had an interest in began to start at 6–4 and 5–4. I had my own inquiry and the man involved was Graham Bradley. There was no point sending them horses when the newspaper-seller knew on the way through the racecourse gate how they were going to run.

There wouldn't be too many stewards, too many trainers, certainly not too many racing journalists, who would ever have been contestants on *Mastermind*: 'Specialist Subject: Race-reading'. They wouldn't see things that I see. I need to have sharp eyes for the job I do, one I do successfully, and there was no doubt what I saw that day at Ascot. Many might consider it simply as a case of a man bearing a long-term grudge who had seen his bet go west. It wouldn't be the first time in the history of racing. Yes, I had a bet, £12,000, but that would not normally trouble me greatly.

Graham Bradley is probably the best jockey that we've seen in England in the last twenty-five years. On his day he was the best, until Tony McCoy came along. There was no one better than him at setting those horses exactly right at their fences, which only emphasised what he was up to on his mount Robin Goodfellow on 15 November 1986. His horse, the 13–8 favourite for the opener at Ascot, the Kennel Gate Novices Hurdle, had been beaten by eight lengths by Teletrader at level weights. Both had won their previous races. Bradley was a great man for seeing a stride, but he wasn't doing that this day. He appeared to be shortening him up at his jumps, making him make mistakes. I was so angry, if he'd been riding for me I'd have taken him by the throat when he came back to unsaddle.

The trouble is that those race-readers and reporters couldn't read elephant tracks in the snow. If the press had been doing its job there would have been no need for me to say anything. The stewards didn't see it, either. Again, if they'd been doing their job properly the problems that ensued would never have arisen.

Yes, I had a bet on the horse, even though I was always suspicious of him from those days at the Dickinsons' yard. But it wasn't a big bet. The kind of amount that I could lose any day of the week, without demur.

I said in a statement to the Jockey Club that I'd had a bet of £5,500-to-£4,000 with bookmaker Dougie Goldstein. I had originally intended to have around £25,000 with various bookmakers but the more I put on the bigger the price became. After I put £12,000 on I became suspicious and stopped betting. Thirteen days later on Friday 28 November, in the Sunley Builds Novices' Hurdle at Sandown, also at level weights, Robin Goodfellow won with Teletrader third, nine lengths away.

Toby Balding said he was satisfied with Bradley's riding. He's a good man, but I suspect he just didn't know what was going on. Very few trainers do. Of course, I had a bet at Sandown too. I knew what I'd seen and knew he should win, if he was trying. He duly trotted up on that occasion. In hindsight what I did next was not a very clever thing to do. I reported him to the Jockey Club, and pointed out that Robin Goodfellow had been a 'non-trier' at Ascot.

At that time I still believed that the Jockey Club were really concerned with the integrity of racing and would do everything in their powers to weed out those suspected of cheating. I loved English racing, and like many others thought it was the best and fairest in the world. At that time I was very optimistic about how good it could be and what improvements there could be if only prize-money were increased. I was too much of an idealist. After all, Robin Goodfellow was the favourite in a race at Ascot and the Royal course is accepted as the pinnacle of English racing. In a strange sort of way, I probably wouldn't have taken it so far at any other track; but to do that sort of thing at Ascot was, I thought, a disgraceful impertinence. After that nothing was sacred. Surely, it was inconceivable that anybody should cheat on the Queen's racecourse. How naive I was. But I said to myself that I must go through with it. I just could not put up with what I believed was skulduggery. I had some faith in the system. But I certainly wouldn't do it today. If I saw someone doing the same, I'd maintain my own counsel after the mess they made of that.

It all began when I phoned the Jockey Club in mid-December and reported what I'd seen. Nothing more, nothing less. I also complained in writing. They said that the Jockey Club's Security Department were investigating. Eventually, I was informed that they'd looked at the tape and didn't agree with me.

Two months later they charged not Bradley but me, under what is known as the 'catch-all' Rule 220(iii). I had, it was alleged, 'caused serious damage to the interests of British racing'. They tried to get me to back down but I wouldn't. I'd say it was a mixture of ignorance and because they didn't like to see the sport portrayed as not being clean. I was very frustrated by it all. A trainer friend of mine from Yorkshire said at the time, 'Barney, don't be silly. You'll never beat the Establishment.'

I said, 'We'll see about that.'

Declan Murphy, in his early days at Harraton Court, Exning, my first yard in Newmarket which I shared with trainer Dave Thom.

Above: Tommy Joe, the first horse I sent over to England to win a race, with Tommy Carmody in the saddle. He was named after the nickname I gave to my eldest daughter Catherine.

Left: Benny O'Hanlon, the man who did such a splendid job occupying a telephone box for me. Without him, the Yellow Sam coup would not have succeeded.

Above: The sight I never expected to see – Golden Fleece winning the 1982 Derby at Epsom. I had laid him to lose and by the end of a bad week I was £250,000 the poorer.

Above: Michael Dickinson and mother Monica. I sent over many horses to their Yorkshire stables from Ireland, including Cheltenham Gold Cup victor, Silver Buck. They were great horse people, and along with Monica's late husband Tony, the most honest people I have ever come across.

Right: Who could have imagined that the young horse we used to canter through the trees at Middleton House would become a champion? Silver Buck, ridden by Robert Earnshaw is led in after winning the 1982 Cheltenham Gold Cup.

Graham Bradley aboard Robin Goodfellow in the Kennel Gate Novices Hurdle at Ascot. His riding infuriated me, but my attempt to bring it to the Jockey Club's attention ended with me being warned off for two years.

Forgive 'N' Forget, the 1985 Cheltenham Gold Cup hero, with Mark Dwyer in the saddle. The horse was another of my Irish exports, this time to Jimmy Fitzgerald, but the real pay-day had come two years earlier in the Coral Hurdle Final. It landed one of the biggest gambles seen at the Festival in 30 years.

Assultan, partnered by Declan Murphy, wins the Snow Hill Handicap Hurdle at Ascot, and nets me £150,000 in winning bets. It was a much needed pay-day as the vultures were hovering over me at that time.

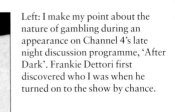

Left: I make my point about the nature of gambling during an appearance on Channel 4's late night discussion programme, 'After Dark'. Frankie Dettori first discovered who I was when he turned on to the show by chance.

Below: I give some advice on married life to Frankie Dettori, immediately after his wedding to Catherine.

Left: With fellow Newmarket trainer Luca Cumani, and my younger daughter Maria-Louise, at Frankie Dettori's wedding.

Right: What finer raffle prize than this? That's Middleton House, formerly the ancestral home of the Boyd-Rochforts, and its grounds, with Lough Ennell in the background, right.

Outside the gates of Ballinagore's football ground, near Mullingar. Back in 1984 everyone who entered the Middleton House raffle had to become a member of the football club to comply with the gaming laws. It was 'the biggest club in the world, bigger than Lord's, or New York Yacht Club,' said *The Times*.

White House Stables in Stetchworth, a wonderful house which I bought from financial wizard, turned failed gambler, Terry Ramsden. Later I sold it to Frankie Dettori.

Memories of my childhood and a year spent fighting tuberculosis in a nearby sanitorium as I visit Lower Lough Erne, at Inishclare, near my home town, Irvinestown.

Left: Proud father, proud owner. Outside my newly acquired Boswell Stud in Co. Wicklow with our first daughter Catherine.

Right: Not a mark on Matbar, and not a stain on Declan Murphy's reputation either, when this Polaroid photo was used in his defence after Kempton stewards found him guilty of misuse of the whip. He won his appeal.

Left: John Gosden (left), Sheikh Mohammed's train in Newmarket. With a litt persuasion by myself, he signed up Frankie Dettori his stable jockey when the young Italian was at his lowest ebb. Frankie replac Michael Roberts (right), who was one of my fellow passengers when our light plane made a crash landin near Chester.

Right: Royal Gait, ridden by Graham McCourt in white cap, lands the 1992 Champion Hurdle at Cheltenham Festival, and improves the state of my financial affairs no end.

coming back Willie Ryan, one of the
st underrated jockeys, after he had
nered my horse Magic Combination to
ory at Sandown. When he won the
7 Derby with Benny the Dip it
prised some, but not me.

The King and the Prince ... ten-times
Derby winner Lester Piggott (left) and
Frankie Dettori, who are both good friends
of mine. There was mutual respect on the
track, once Frankie learnt the hard way
not to call the maestro 'granddad'...

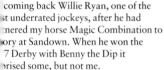

d you thought betting shops were about horseracing? This picture was taken on Easter
nday when there were 15 race meetings. Yet, even Ladbrokes' shop in the centre of Flat
ing's 'headquarters', Newmarket is promoting a numbers game, not the racing game.

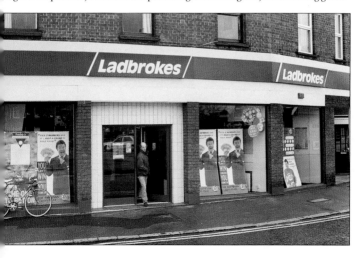

Above: Spending time with the local children and volunteers as part of my work for the DAFA charity in Zambia.

Below: Sister Leoni is seated left of the group, and my good friend from schooldays, Fr. Eugene O'Reilly is hold the banner, right.

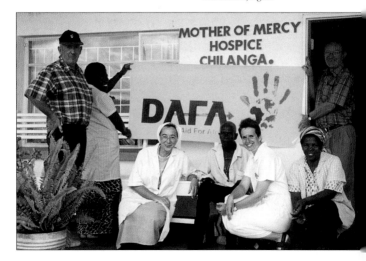

I did not abuse anybody. Certainly not Mr and Mrs Dickinson, for whom I have the greatest respect. They only became involved because Bradley was their jockey. I rang Mrs Dickinson purely to mark her card, so to speak, to advise her to keep an eye on Bradley. It was a grave mistake, because it dragged into the maelstrom the last two people in the world that I'd ever want to upset. When I saw them at the Jockey Club inquiry I felt dreadful. I was ashamed that they were involved. I even instructed my legal team that I did not want them pressurised, win or lose. As far as Bradley was concerned, yes, I rang him, but never, as he suggested, to 'blackmail' him. I rang him and told him that he was a disgrace. I'm not a spiteful person. I just wanted to tell him that he thought he was smart, but I knew what he was up to. Yes, I suggested that he should make a donation to the Injured Jockeys' Fund as a penance.

Apparently he recorded our telephone conversation, but it merely substantiated all that I said. I just told him, 'You "stopped" him.' That's not abuse; that's just a statement of the facts as far as I was concerned. If I'd said something out of order why was it not played at the inquiry? I was so incensed I just kept on and he said, 'Are you going to do anything about it?' – presumably trying to goad me into condemning myself. I didn't handle it very well and he later released the contents of a tape of the conversation – made on the advice of his lawyer – to the newspapers. It was a real coup for them, of course; the stuff of Dick Francis novels, but this time it was reality. Inevitably, it got blown up out of all proportion.

That inquiry, on Friday 24 April 1987, was before Lord Vestey, retired trainer and jump jockey Bruce Hobbs, and John Sumner. It lasted two hours, behind closed doors – as is normal for Jockey Club business. I was not legally represented. I had been told there was no need, but the committee had a legal advisor. I had taken along as evidence five videos of Bradley riding, in three of which he was partnering Robin Goodfellow. I had blithely thought they might be relevant. It was a waste of time; the committee wasn't interested. Their only concern was my 'accusations' against Bradley. I said there was no truth in Bradley's statement, published in *Sporting Life*, that I had 'made several telephone calls in which he said that I (Bradley) should pay him the money he had lost'.

I also said that the recorded telephone conversation, to which Bradley alluded, contained no references to payments. I agreed that I also spoke to Mrs Dickinson and officials of the Jockey Club. In none of these conversations did I make any reference to Bradley paying me money. Against all that evidence, they made their decision in five minutes that I was to be banned for two years, with the punishment due to come into force the following Friday, 1 May. I don't remember much, except saying to Lord Vestey after they had handed out my punishment, 'You are making a big mistake.' Not exactly the most original retort, although I was proved right.

As I walked out, I was in a state of shock. I told reporters: 'I feel shattered. The decision is an absolute disgrace. I shall be consulting my solicitor now. This is only the beginning and I'm prepared to fight this all the way to the High Court.' I added that I had had no warning that such allegations had been made against me and I had not been advised that I should be legally represented. I told reporters that I had been 'conned' into attending without a solicitor. Yes, I felt victimised at the time, but in hindsight I believe it was an honest mistake on their part, and at least the Jockey Club put it right – though not without some pressure from me. The verdict so depressed me that I said at the time that I was not sure whether I wanted to continue living in England. They were not just words off the top of my head; it was a serious response. After all, the Jockey Club is a great pillar of society and it was supposed to mete out natural justice. In this case, manifestly it had failed. I didn't believe I'd had a good hearing. My legal people considered it a perverse decision, although, strangely, I had and still have a high regard for Lord Vestey, who has done a lot for Cheltenham race-course and is very popular with the Irish community during the festival. Later in the week, at Sandown, I said, 'I am backing down for no man or any organisation, including the Jockey Club.'

The Jockey Club could hardly have been prepared for what happened next. There was a public outcry against their secret justice. Nobody could under-stand why I had been warned off merely for making an accusation against a jockey. As is typical of racing's ruling authority all they had issued was a bland statement, without going into any details. This policy was described in the *Racing Post* as: 'A totally unsatisfactory state of affairs. The mandarins of Portman Square were guilty of miscalculation.'

I decided to continue to run my horses. The day after I received my sentence, 27 April, Saryan won a selling hurdle at Southwell – I had to go to 5,100 guineas to buy him in – although I then decided it was becoming a circus. In a Channel 4 interview, I told how that draconian decision could affect my livelihood. I said, 'My business is backing horses. I started off with nothing. We now own forty horses. The money to finance that has all come from betting.'

It wasn't until seventy hours later that the Jockey Club was forced to make clear that it was my phone calls to Mrs Dickinson and Bradley that were the basis of the inquiry, not my original complaint. They presumably had to say something to protect their backs from the flack they were getting. Columnist Jack Logan, who had long called for open courts when racing justice was dispensed, opined wryly in the *Sporting Life*, 'There's always room in the Logan heaven for sinners who repent.'

In their statement the Jockey Club said that my disqualification followed 'threats of a serious nature made by Mr Curley ... involving not only Graham Bradley but also another licensed trainer' – that, of course, was Mrs Dickinson. I told my solicitor Alan Walls to 'get me the best'. He did, in the formidable figure of top criminal barrister Edward Du Cann. Some might say it was unnecessary, but my belief was that although Du Cann was expensive, it was like getting Lester Piggott to ride for you in the Derby. It gave you an edge, and it also did no harm to let the other side know that you were taking the matter deadly seriously.

The whole thing had escalated from nothing, and continued to do so. Strictly speaking, what goes on in the 'courts' of the Jockey Club is supposed to be kept within those four walls, but I felt there was no harm in criticising that 'prosecution' who also act as 'jury'. Tim Richards quoted me in the *Racing Post* as saying, 'Not a question was asked by the committee. I felt they were under instructions to have no words with Curley. I got to feel they were dealing with a mad Irishman who had done his money at Ascot and was now doing his nut. Well, they will find out differently. The City had a Guinness scandal and this will be the equivalent in racing. I am not taking this lying down.'

Strong words, but looking back I wasn't as confident as my public persona suggested. The Jockey Club is a self-electing oligarchy whose rules are rarely tested in the civil courts. Probably the most celebrated previous case in which it had been taken to the High Court was in 1966 when Florence Nagle brought an action because the Jockey Club refused to grant training licences to women. They had backed down before that case could be heard. That was a significant battle won; this was a rather different state of affairs.

An injunction was served by my legal team on Nigel Macfarlane, secretary to the Jockey Club's disciplinary committee. Finally, on the day before my ban was due to start, Mr Justice Phillips granted an exparte (or temporary) High Court injunction against the Jockey Club, which meant the sentence could not be implemented until they were ready to appear in the High Court and present their case. My argument was that the committee's proceedings had offended the principles of natural justice.

Before that could happen, the Jockey Club climbed down and granted a rehearing of my case, saying that it had done so in order that I could be legally represented this time. After a six and a half hour hearing, and 101 days after my original punishment was meted out, justice was done on 3 August 1987. There was a rare smile on my face that day. Mrs Dickinson and Bradley were there. I was to get my licence back on 1 October. It was unprecedented; sentences had been reduced in the past, but never completely quashed. After reconsidering evidence, the new committee, chaired by Christopher Lloyd, along with General Sir Cecil Blacker and Michael Wrigley, found that I had not infringed the rule which relates to causing damage to the interests of horseracing, although they still insisted that my calls had caused distress and described them as 'reprehensible'.

It was said I looked shattered as I walked out of that hearing, that I'd had a real mauling, but it was just the cumulative effect of hours with lawyers, travelling and worrying about my future. I didn't say a lot at the time. 'It was a very fair hearing. I'm delighted,' I said diplomatically, for once. 'The last six months have completely destroyed my life.' It was not my style to come out and lambast the Jockey Club. Yes, there was still something of a slur against me and many people felt their comments were still rather 'churlish'. But I did not want to get into a slagging match. I had a lot of respect for General Blacker, in particular. I thought he was a 'proper' man, and I felt if I said anything it would reflect on him and I wanted to avoid that.

One headline the day afterwards said, 'Carry on Curley'. That just about summed up the comedy it had become; except I wasn't laughing. More than a decade later my view on the Jockey Club's disciplinary code remains largely the same. Its members are by nature good and decent people, their procedures by and large fair; it is their judgement that I question at times. In all my dealings with their disciplinary committees, apart from that one case, and one in 1997 involving Frankie Dettori at Goodwood in which I became immersed, they've never tried to do anything underhand or spring something on me without warning. Indeed, they give you every help with evidence to defend yourself by providing you with files of reference. Can you imagine any other justice system doing that? My house was a shambles. I didn't have a clue about where I was on this day or that, but they assisted me with anything I needed.

I believe I was right to do what I did, but, looking back, I shouldn't have put myself up as judge and jury on Bradley's behaviour, and I would never dream of doing the same thing again. But the Jockey Club was also at fault in not taking me seriously in the first place. I would consider myself the best race-reader in England; they could have looked into it and given a verdict one way or another on what I had to say, but they just ignored me and brushed what I had to say to one side, before making a wrong decision in taking away my licence. It simply all got out of control, with the accuser not only put in the dock, but handed out a ridiculously stiff sentence. I had to fight for what I believed was right and the Jockey Club had to fight back and Bradley was in the middle of it. I'm not God and I shouldn't have taken it out like that on a fellow human being. It was a mistake.

Despite everything that took place, I never had any enmity towards Bradley and still haven't. Indeed, I had The Hacienderos running in the Black & White Chase at Ascot during that period and Declan was either injured or warned off – he spent a lot of time being one or the other at that time – and Bradley was the first man I went to as substitute, even putting up overweight. I fancied the horse and I remember telling Peter O'Sullevan, 'I've booked Bradley because I think he'll win.' He replied: 'You're doing the right thing.' In the event, I had to pull The Hacienderos out because of the ground.

It wasn't until ten years later that I booked Bradley again, to ride My Man in Dundalk at Lingfield early in 1998, but that was merely because the opportunity never presented itself. I had nothing against him as a man, and certainly not as a jockey. Many said that a foul smell enveloped racing, but Bradley, the Jockey Club and myself all learned a lot from it. Maybe once the stench had cleared it allowed the winds of change to start to blow through the sport. I know I wouldn't be first on Bradley's Christmas card list, but if I ever sat down and thought about it, I wouldn't be the worst person he's ever met, either. It was a bizarre carry-on and he was just caught up in the middle.

That whole affair didn't do Bradley any good. He wasn't riding particularly well, anyway, at that time. Several things happened to him subsequently that didn't do him any favours – not least when he was suspended from 22 June until 1 November 1988 for not trying on Deadly Going at Market Rasen on 20 April. Was there any significance in that? As someone once famously declared, 'You may think so. I couldn't possibly say ... '

I can only hope that one legacy was that it made the stewards of the Jockey Club realise that there were these things going on and maybe scrutinise them more. It may have made them think a bit harder, instead of dismissing everybody. Interestingly, since then, they've appeared to be far more stringent about non-triers. Perhaps it had a beneficial effect. I certainly don't think it did the Jockey Club any harm. It was a jolt to their complacency about the way they conducted their hearings, although not too much has changed in intervening years. As the *Racing Post* put it in one headline, 'Death Wish of the "Mafia" Men'. The Jockey Club's secret, 'star chamber' style of hearings came in for a lot of criticism. With a few exceptions the media were generally against me – I suspect because it showed up just how poor they were at reading the game – but I had a lot of support from ordinary punters in the press.

Few people realised how serious that whole business was for me. It wasn't just the social stigma. It was a financial disaster as far as I was concerned. I always had good 'store' horses, ones that would go to Ascot and Newbury and those sort of tracks and fear no one. I had to sell a lot of those at the time, because my solicitor had warned me, 'You're looking at twelve months or more before this thing grinds to an end and you're back in training.' It was the right advice at the time because I couldn't afford to have all those horses doing nothing. Of the ones sold, I think six won 'bumpers' or good hurdle races. Of course we didn't think the Jockey Club would hear the appeal and give me my licence back so quickly.

In one sense it didn't do me much good because by then I'd sold all my well-bred National Hunt 'store' horses which were out at grass at Cormac McCormack's stud outside Newmarket. As I had not named them when I disposed of them I couldn't follow their progress, but I heard some won 'bumpers' in Ireland and no doubt progressed into decent hurdlers and 'chasers. I was down to six fit horses after that clear-out.

I decided not to take any action to seek damages from the Jockey Club, although several people, including my lawyer, maintained I would have a reasonable chance of success. He also suggested I sue the Jockey Club for libel.

I said, 'Have I got a licence to train?'

'You have,' he replied.

'That's all I want,' I said.

To be candid, I was fed up with courts and inquiries. I must have visited my lawyer's office fifty times in that period.

One other significant thing occurred. That 1987 season was my third training over jumps in England. Towards the end of that year, I applied for a licence to train on the Flat. I received it within two weeks, although it usually takes a lot longer. It had been expedited by Dick Saunders. If I were a cynical man, I'd say that was an act of contrition on the part of the Jockey Club. All I do know is that when I got my licence back the Jockey Club sent a couple of men down the next day to carry out a routine check of my stables. 'No hard feelings', they said, which I thought was a nice touch. Nevertheless, it didn't exactly ease my plight at the time. I'd sold my best horses, but at least I'd retained my stable staff and Declan had turned down one of the best jobs in racing to stay with me. What I needed now was a new challenge.

TWENTY-FIVE

A Stone's throw from victory

My decision to throw down the gauntlet to the bookmakers – and also silence some of my friends – by training ten winners in three months at the end of 1987 was fraught with controversy, but then when you speak your mind, and stand your ground, it always is. One of that group of invalids, Above All Hope, won on the first day, 1 October, in a seller at Fontwell, but that was followed by a major row with the course executives after I accused them of 'bidding up' my horse at the subsequent auction. I will say more about that later.

More significantly, from the point of view of the bet, was that the horse followed up at Southwell, where I bought him in for 5,400 guineas. Saryan sprung something of a surprise, winning at 16–1 at Wolverhampton on 9 November, but otherwise it all went quiet until the end of that month. With a little over five weeks remaining, I had recorded only three winners. The smiles on the layers' faces must have been widening by the day.

Five victories in the space of eighteen days changed all that. When Assultan became my eighth success at Doncaster in the Glasgow Paddocks Selling Hurdle on 12 December, I was well on course, but his victory was followed by one of the longest inquiries I've known; at least, that's how it appeared to me.

His owner Don Cantillon was in a terrible state after drinking brandy all afternoon to settle his nerves as we awaited the result. Assultan won the first race on the card – off time 12.34 pm – and the inquiry lasted until after the fourth race. It was 2.18 pm when the stewards made their decision. That wasn't the end of the matter.

I had run two in the race: Assultan, who drifted from 3–1 to 6–1, and Above All Hope, who finished fourth, having started 9–4 joint-favourite. Above All Hope, ridden by young Vivian Kennedy, who was later killed in a race, broke down.

It was only a £1,500 'seller', and Assultan, who was prone to idiosyncratic behaviour, was again reluctant to start, but eventually won by a length from Keith Stone's Saskia's Reprieve, who was a 33–1 chance. It was a tough, bruising duel in the closing stages and after the race I wasn't too surprised the connections of the runner-up objected. The horses had collided three times and, according to reports, the first interference was caused by Saskia's Reprieve, the second time they were equally at fault and the third was undoubtedly caused by our horse. It didn't look that good for us. James Lambie reported in the *Sporting Life* that, 'when Murphy chanced another crack with his whip, he sent his mount so violently back into Saskia's Reprieve that Stone's horse was almost turned sideways.'

The objection was thrown out by the local stewards, who said that the first two cases had been accidental and had no effect on the result; this also applied to the third instance, but blamed 'the configuration of the course'. Afterwards Stone was not satisfied. He maintained that Declan, 'had his whip in his wrong hand and never attempted to straighten the horse or pull his whip through', and claimed his horse would have been knocked over if Colin Hawkins hadn't ridden him strongly to keep him straight. 'The other horse cannoned into him. It was a bad decision.' I described it at the time as 'a very sporting decision', and frankly it could have gone either way. If we had lost the race then I wouldn't have complained. As it was, the auctioneer failed to raise a bid, and said: 'Take the horse away and the very best of luck, Mr Curley' – which I thought was a nice touch. It was greeted with a burst of approval from around the unsaddling enclosure.

But what happened next did surprise me. Connections of the beaten horse took the case to the Jockey Club, which they had every right to do; nevertheless, this was only a modest 'seller', not a classic with huge prize-money where the result affects prestige and bloodstock values. I could never understand why they did it. It was pointless. There was peanuts involved in prize-money – first prize was £1,490 and second prize £415 – and if they'd had a bet they wouldn't have been paid anyway, even if the appeal committee had found in their favour.

Once the local stewards had thrown it out, that should have been it. My suspicion has always been that there was more to what took place that day than meets the eye. I believe there must have been something going on behind the scenes. It was well known that every winner was vital to me, but the race meant nothing to them. As far as I was aware, the people who owned the horse were wealthy enough. I could scarcely believe that Stone should take it to the lengths that he did, and although I have my suspicions, I shall never know what was behind their actions.

The appeal date was not set until several days later. By then, Solvent had notched up win number nine at Towcester on 21 December and, the following day, Experimenting had won at Folkestone to complete the set. Experimenting, incidentally, moved on to Ian Balding, who at one stage had planned to ride him in the Grand National. It never happened, but he had a lot of fun with the old horse anyway. Had Stone won his appeal it would have reduced my winners to nine. However, I was not greatly perturbed. I had a couple of 'bankers' up my sleeve at the end of the year at Wetherby and both won.

I was very confident as I arrived at the Jockey Club with Maria-Louise, then twelve, and Charlie, ten, Declan and Don. I thought it was 33–1 against me coming out disappointed, and I was right. For once, the Jockey Club were on my side. The chairman of the stewards at Doncaster was all in favour of disqualifying Assultan, but Major Peter Steveney, chief stipendiary and a man I respect, stood up to him and said it would be a miscarriage of justice. That was very fair, because I can imagine that in a number of other countries they'd have disqualified us. After all, I wasn't exactly on great terms with the Jockey Club after having been 'warned off' earlier that year, and then forcing them to reverse their decision. However, I must say that, overall, I think they make less mistakes than the judiciary. I wouldn't change the system. But they need to get a couple of streetwise men into their administration.

It was not the first time that Stone had gone to Portman Square to try and have a local stewards' decision reversed (he did it when Permabos had been relegated to second place at Newbury four years before, although he had got no joy then, either). Afterwards we all went to Hamleys, the toyshop, and I said to the children, 'Pick whatever you want.' That could have been an expensive business, but I remember Charlie just picked a train-set, because he was worried whether I could afford anything expensive. Perhaps he got it from me, that lack of interest in possessions.

I take great satisfaction in the fact that I set out to do the impossible and succeeded. For every other trainer, there's a million excuses why a horse isn't winning, or, in some cases, not running. They all talk a good job. But with me, the talking has to stop. I don't say this in any boastful way, but given similar weaponry I could take on any other trainer. I'd love to be there taking them on with 100 horses because I know I'd be better than anyone else; I'd enjoy competing, rather than be fiddling about the way I do with ten or twelve horses.

In that autumn I had twenty-eight horses, of which around ten were winners; I had a 37 per cent strike rate, and none of the top trainers can ever say that. Of those, I had a lot of 'iffy' horses, several had broken down – Father John, Chiropodist, Above All Hope, Golden Display, Mr Griffin and Solvent – and some ran correspondingly; while some Declan managed to hold together and get them home with the gentle touch. I thought that was some feat.

People close to me often say, 'For God's sake, Barney, why don't you get out and give this training business a real bash.' I'd be good at it, too. I don't think there's anybody in this country who knows as much about racing as me and I wasn't born into it, like some of these trainers. I didn't have to work at it that hard, it just came naturally to me, like riding came naturally to Lester Piggott. There's an art in bringing horses along quietly, getting them fit to win first time. Training is the greatest occupation in the world – the beauty of it is that nobody really knows whether you're good or bad. The art is not so much training them, but selling them to a gullible public. In fact, many of them should give up their licence and go into flogging insurance. But why do it? It's a waste of time. There's no future in it, apart from attracting lots of owners but I have no wish to do that. I would never prostitute myself, and you have to do that even if you're a top trainer. You're just a lackey. As Lord Howard De Walden once said of his trainers, 'They're just grooms really, aren't they.' Well, it may have been tongue in cheek, but the point was made. I'm my own man and can say what I think. I could not name any other trainer who could say that.

You give any trainer in the country a million pounds, and me the same, and tell us to go about our business. Like the toy rabbit with the Duracell batteries, I'll last the longer. The problem is that, with one exception, my good friend Mr Patsy Byrne, I don't want owners. Originally from County Kerry,

Patsy is a very successful London-based builder, whom I've known for several years. Together with the likes of Tommy Stack and Paddy Griffin, I've often been out for a break to his holiday home, 'Moynsha House' – I named one of my horses after it, in Abbeyfeale in Kerry. Mind you, after being out with him you need a break to get over it. There's a lot of partying goes on, although, as the non-drinker, I usually get dragged in as chauffeur. He's got a big heart and does a lot for charity; he once sent a container-load of equipment out to Tanzania, but there was no big publicity about it. He just did it quietly. That gesture stuck in my mind and influenced me strongly when I decided to get involved in our DAFA charity project.

Even Patsy took a long time persuading me that I should take one or two of his horses, and the arrangement is that I only talk to him about them if I fancy one in a race. In fact, I'm so tight-lipped, he rings up to ask sarcastically, 'Did we have any runners last week?' Still, we've had some 'touches' over the years. He's the exception, but as a rule I couldn't present a set-up selling horses to people where they'd lose so much money overnight. I couldn't look them in the eye the next day. I'd have to say, if you buy a racehorse you'll be likely to lose 80 per cent of your money overnight.

It might be imagined that those twelve winners in three months would have left my Weatherby's account very healthy. The net result, as far as training went, in a comparatively successful year, was that there was £1,500 remaining after fees and other deductions. It is a stark warning to anyone considering buying into a racehorse. There ought to be a government warning, similar to that on a cigarette pack: 'Racehorse ownership can seriously damage your wealth.' Yet, the BHB actually still has the temerity to try and get gullible people involved.

I'm far more conscious of Patsy Byrne's horses than my own. I would be sick if something happened to one of his horses, far more than if it were mine. The fact is that I wouldn't have the temperament to train for others. Most of the people who own racehorses know nothing about it. I'm not enough of a diplomat, and I'd have to say some horses were useless. I'm not prepared to play the game and deceive people. I always believe in being straight. I couldn't have some owner, no doubt very successful in his business life but ignorant when it comes to racing, ringing up and telling me what his pal thinks I should be doing with the horse. I'd have to say, 'Hold it right there. I'll put your horse on a box. Name me a trainer and he'll be on his way to him.' Most of the trainers put up with that interference. If I thought a horse should go to Carlisle for a race it would be Cumbria he went to, not to Ascot because it's close to home, it's fashionable and the owner wants to bring his friends on a day out.

I couldn't even run a syndicate because they all have a hot-line giving tips. If I had a hot-line the people backing the horses would be getting very bad value for money. I'd be telling the truth. The bookmakers would ring those lines and there'd be no value at all. So, I train for myself and say what I believe. If I didn't, I couldn't sleep at nights. There must be men and women out there training for people they absolutely detest. I could never do that. I know of two prominent trainers who were torn to shreds on TV and a fortnight later they were back being interviewed on the same channel. The same with Kieren Fallon, when he came in for a lot of criticism from the pundits in 1997. I don't know how these people live with themselves. Is it any surprise that racing is in the state it's in? Maybe it's because I'm not a politician, and don't have to be a diplomat. I don't have to say the nice things. They can take me or leave me. I'd say the same to the most inexperienced lad in the yard as I would to the senior steward of the Jockey Club. Everybody's out to create an impression and, in doing that, they're not being themselves. I answer to only one man – myself.

Most trainers and jockeys regard racecourse stewards like footballers and managers regard referees. A necessary evil – but too often prone to mistakes. I have nothing but admiration for the vast majority of stewards. More than that, I am not one of those who advocates professional stewards. Say what you will about the part-time amateurs, and of course they're as much open to aberration as the next man, but they're not easily got at. They're in no one's pocket; they're not influenced by money and give as they see.

Some don't really seem to understand how to read a race, though it is not easy when you're watching for illegal riding and non-triers. Using the football analogy again, it's like watching for offside while there's a punch-up going on behind your back. But with the advent of video technology it has all improved radically in recent years.

Maybe more former jockeys, and perhaps ex-trainers too, should become paid stipendiary stewards, known as 'stipes'. They are the people who advise the stewards' panels. I don't think they should be involved in actually making decisions. They're too close to the game, have had too much close contact with trainers and jockeys, and could be inveigled into corruption or, at the very least, show favouritism towards their friends. It's a very hard job because you have to make up your mind in a very short space of time. But, having said that, they appear to watch some trainers' horses like gun dogs waiting for a pheasant to drop; others get away with committing murder under their benign eyes. There's an old Irish saying, 'If you have the name of the early riser, you can lie to dinner time any day'.

It's not always the so-called gambling stables whose horses can be accused of being 'non-triers' on the racecourse; some big stables who have an average horse, but not good enough to win a maiden, frequently give their horse an 'easy' or two to get it well handicapped. I always accepted that as a renowned gambling owner-trainer I would be under scrutiny. There have been occasions when I have had to put my hands up and say the stewards got it right strictly under the rules when they called me in. You could have no argument with that if you thought you had a fair deal. But I believed it was more important to look after my horses for the future rather than destroy them because some fellows had a few quid on in the betting shops.

But it got out of hand at times. We were hauled in before the stewards for nothing. There were some appalling decisions. It was blatant discrimination against me because of my name and reputation, particularly up north where there was a man named Lord MacAndrew who appeared to be on a one-man crusade to stamp out any suggestion of irregularities. He was quite clearly determined to keep racing as straight as he possibly could and that involved coming down hard on me. The result was, of course, that he and his colleagues became obsessed with B.J. Curley runners and failed to spot the numerous other trainers pulling strokes right under their noses.

To an extent I learnt to take it on the chin, but when they acted after Urbi Et Orbi was pulled up by Declan before the second-last jump one day at Catterick, I could barely control my fury. It was 7 December 1987 and Urbi Et Orbi – they are words the Pope uses in his Easter Message; it means 'To the City and to the World' – had been one of my ten winners in that bid to win £275,000. He was a ten-year-old gelding, perennially unsound, who hadn't run for years before scoring easily, by ten lengths, in a two-mile selling handicap hurdle at Market Rasen on 28 November. He had been the fifth of my ten winners. I'd been very patient with him and he'd come right and I had duly backed him. I didn't make a habit of big bets during that period. It was common knowledge that I was really striving hard for my ten wins and most of them were not good prices. Urbi Et Orbi opened at 5–1 but was 3–1 by the 'off'. It wasn't the only time I'd bring a horse back from an infirm state, only to see him go wrong again.

Ten days later we took Urbi Et Orbi to Catterick, where he had only a 5lbs penalty in another seller. He was odds-on favourite, at 10–11, with the eventual winner, George Moore's Senor Romana, next in the betting at 11–2. Urbi Et Orbi led for half the race, but turning into the straight Declan felt him break down and he pulled him up before two out. Inevitably, we were called to see the stewards, chaired by Lord MacAndrew.

My heart sank. Every time I had a runner in the north where Lord MacAndrew was, he was not open to persuasion and would never listen to reason. He just picked on me. It was a waste of time arguing my case. I might as well have been standing before The Muppets for all the intelligent hearing I got. I explained that Urbi Et Orbi had broken down, and that he was prone to breaking down, otherwise why would he have been off the track for so long? I added that the horse was a falsely priced favourite.

Declan told the stewards that the gelding had not given him a good feel from jumping the first and that he had been niggling at him from there on. He had given the horse one back-hander without response and thought it wiser to pull him up. However, we were informed that immediately after the race the course vet had reported that the horse had been 'perfectly sound'.

My reaction to Lord MacAndrew and the committee was short and sweet: 'Even if it is sound now, it won't be in two hours' time.' I needn't have wasted my breath. We were both fined £400, under Rule 151, because, 'The stewards were not satisfied that Urbi Et Orbi had been ridden to obtain the best possible placing.' It takes a lot to get me really angry, but I walked out, seething at the injustice of it all. They had shown absolutely no interest in the background, age or condition of the horse. They had displayed a total lack of knowledge of the physiology of horses and leg injuries. They just wanted the chance to confirm their prejudice against me. I took Urbi Et Orbi home and by the time we arrived he was as lame as a duck. I got Raymond Hopes, the renowned Newmarket vet, to examine his legs and he confirmed what I had said and gave me a certificate to confirm it. 'The horse has broken down,' he declared.

I thought to myself that I'd sort the jokers out and I called up Derek Weedon, who runs an equine transport company in Newmarket, and told him to come round straight away. I put Urbi Et Orbi in a horse-box and sent him off to the local animal research centre funded by the Levy Board. My instructions were simple. I said, 'Leave him there and don't bring him back.' I then drove down immediately to the Jockey Club in Portman Square, London, and refused to leave until somebody with influence saw me. The then deputy senior steward, Lord Chelsea, appeared after a couple of hours. 'I'm not standing for this any more,' I said, and tore into him. I really got everything off my chest.

It is not the normal way for Jockey Club business to be conducted, but I told him in no uncertain terms what I thought about those Catterick stewards and Lord MacAndrew in particular. That those stewards knew as much about racing as I knew about cricket, and all I knew about that was that it was played with a bat and ball. Finally, I informed him, 'I've left the horse at the animal research centre and he's staying there.'

I suppose he could have had a real volley back at me, but he remained calm and said, 'You're a licensed trainer, and if you have any complaints you should bring them to me. I will listen to them. But don't go making a rumpus and ranting and raving at the racecourse. It's not good for racing's image.' I always respect a man who's fair-minded and I accepted he had a point.

There has never been an occasion when I've deliberately set out to damage racing's interests. What I won't do is stand idly by if I think there's a desperate wrong.

It was with great sadness I vowed never to send horses up north again. I adhered to that, apart from sending what I considered to be two certain winners in The Papparazzi and Mr Kirby to Wetherby at the end of the year, and when I knew Lord MacAndrew was not officiating. They both won easily, a good example of how I do occasionally put pragmatism before principle.

My philosophy, as I have outlined, has always been to run horses to back them. That is my sole reason for ownership. But obviously I don't back them every time. They can't win every time. The secret is knowing precisely when they are at the peak of their fitness. I don't do anything that's different from anybody else, it's just that I do it better. My horses run according to their merits and given the conditions of the race. Despite all the innuendo, my disciplinary record is open for inspection at the Jockey Club. The occasions when I have been before the stewards accused of running 'non-triers' are few and far between.

In fact, there have been only two cases in which I have been found guilty since I first received my jump trainer's licence back in 1985, along with the incident involving The Tariahs back in 1985 when Dave Thom was officially his trainer. There are legitimate excuses for all of them. I have already explained how we had no alternative but to restrain The Tariahs. If I'd just allowed him to run as he pleased, he would have been a spent force and finished tailed-off. Yes, it was an 'educating' run, if you like, but it was necessary. My tactics with him worked, too. We got him settled, he won a race, and, but for that fatal fall, would have become a top class horse.

There is, frankly, no sense in asking a jockey to 'block' a horse. There are several reasons for stating that. It's too easily detected by the stewards, who these days have all kinds of technical back-up, and it also goes against a jockey's natural instincts. I've never said to a jockey, 'We must get beaten today'. It would be too dangerous. If he knows it, you can guarantee that another 11 people will as well. Anyway, you would have no idea how your horse would have performed. You wouldn't have learnt anything from it. Finally, there would always be the chance of the jockey passing on the information. If you're good at your job you don't have to get the jockey involved anyway. As I've already said, there are many 'legal' ways of getting a horse beaten.

Ardbrin was one horse that was to become synonymous with controversy. In January 1989, at Nottingham, Declan and I were both fined £400 after Ardbrin was beaten into third place by a horse of Jimmy Fitzgerald's called Mind Your Back. The stewards said our horse had been 'tenderly handled throughout the closing stages of the race and not given the best chance of winning by his jockey'. Declan would normally have dropped the horse out a long way, but as they went at such a slow pace he believed the tactics to suit him would be to ride him up with the pace and quicken up with them. When they did, he couldn't go with them and made a mistake at the second last. He also jumped big at the last. Nottingham's long straight gave him a chance to recover and he ran on at the end, which made it appear as if he was full of running. I had backed the horse, too. But they didn't accept it. Sometimes you just have to shrug your shoulders and walk away.

TWENTY-SIX

'Saved – by the sign of the Black Horse'

One of the most frustrating things about training is the knowledge that you have a horse with ability but because of some mental quirk he doesn't always display it. To get one of these to perform and successfully iron out its idiosyncratic behaviour is one of the most satisfying things you can do in racing. It takes a man or woman with extraordinary patience and knowledge of horses' nature. And one such fellow who I got to know in 1986 is Don Cantillon, a son of County Cork, who was then riding out for Newmarket trainer Harry Thomson Jones. Don's expertise was handling the 'tricky' horses in the yard. Racehorses didn't come much more infuriating than Assultan, one of Hamdan Al Maktoum's lesser lights.

As a two-year-old the son of Troy had won first time out at Leicester, and the following season he looked like he might develop into a reasonable ten-furlong handicapper. But then, inexplicably, he refused to race in the valuable Extel Handicap at Goodwood in July and another race at Yarmouth. It was then that I got a call from Don, who explained briefly that he wanted to buy the horse out of his guv'nor's yard and wanted me to train it. Frankly, I wasn't terribly convinced that this was something I wanted to get involved in. However, Don clearly had faith in the horse, and something about what he said intrigued me.

He turned up one evening in October and it emerged that it would cost him around £4,000, but he felt that Assultan could be a profitable purchase as a gambling medium, at the hurdling game. This is where I came in. Well, I hummed and hawed, and said I'd think about it, and as Don left the house I peered out into the darkness trying to catch a glimpse of his car. There wasn't one. Instead he got on a bicycle and prepared to pedal away. Stable staff, as we all know, are generally not well paid, and though I didn't expect him to ease himself into the latest model of Mercedes, I was a little taken aback by this. So, I stopped him and, trying to be as inoffensive as possible because I had no wish to insult him, said, 'Would it be any harm to ask you how you're going to buy this horse?' He was waiting with the answer. 'Oh,' he said with a broad grin spread across his face, as though it were the most obvious thing in the world. 'I'm getting a Home Improvement Grant from Lloyds Bank.'

I doubt if the sign of the Black Horse has ever been involved in a transaction to purchase such a dark horse. Little would the bankers have known what a profitable investment that piece of business turned out to be – for me at least. Assultan did me several big turns. He was among my ten winners which won that bet in 1987, and a few months later, when I desperately needed it, he came to my rescue once again.

We gave him a programme of rehabilitation, running him in three 'sellers', of which he won two. That not only served to delude the handicapper into regarding the horse, and thus rating him, as a humble 'plater'; beating horses also helped him gain confidence. It was really a ploy of just kidding him along. At Sandown one day we had a massive gamble from 5–1 to 2–1 favourite, having won his previous race, a 'seller' at Nottingham, by fifteen lengths. He was treated leniently in the handicap and won easily by six lengths. As Tony Stafford wrote in the *Daily Telegraph*, 'Assultan's fluency and new-found confidence are eloquent testimony to Curley's expertise, and victory with far more severe tasks is certain.' Little did he know how prophetic those words would prove to be.

The following autumn I was in desperate straits after I had tried to organise a competition at the end of the previous year in aid of the Wishing Well appeal for the Great Ormond Street Children's Hospital in London. The idea was that there would be ten winners, with each having one National Hunt horse running in their name free for a year. They had their own colours and collected any prize-money. The idea had come to me after Experimenting had given me the last of my ten winners at Folkestone and I had received that tremendous reception. I had looked around me that day and thought, I'm going to try and do something for these people, give them a chance to get into the heart of racing.

In the end there was a drastic shortfall. Not many tickets got sold, because, in hindsight, the competition was not easy enough to do. Entrants had to judge the form of six horses and place them in order of finishing in a race. In addition, the costs of advertising in newspapers, at £50,000, were horrendous. I'd already personally guaranteed £100,000 to the hospital, regardless. The horses and other costs swallowed up another £100,000 – in all a total of £250,000. As I've said before, I don't hoard vast fortunes of cash beneath the floorboards or on deposit in a bank. Finally, I had to say to Nigel Clark, who was chairman of the project, 'The competition has been a complete disaster. Very few people understood what to do. I have £50,000. That's all the money I possess – can you accept that?' He agreed.

I counted all my debts one night and I remember telling my vet, Rob Pilsworth. He was remarkably laid-back considering that I owed his practice a bundle. I owe a lot of my success to Rob. I've known him since he first started out and he takes a lot of interest in my horses and enjoys seeing them run well.

Happily, I was able to pay him, along with everyone else.

Yet, there was no ignoring the fact that I was in danger of a serious crash. I really had to concentrate on the job – or go under. It took a series of gambles to put me straight. One was Show Faith, a 10–1 shot at Ascot, saddled by that excellent trainer Richard Hannon. I also had a successful Cheltenham and York. At the National Hunt Festival I particularly remember one of Sheik Mohammed's few jumpers, Royal Gait, winning the Champion Hurdle, and me £100,000 in the process. I always regarded James Fanshawe's horse as a very classy sort – if you recall, he had 'won' the 1988 Ascot Gold Cup but had been controversially disqualified – and at prices of 6–1 and upwards he appeared good value. Yet, they only stemmed the financial wound temporarily. I was still haemorrhaging money and the only way to staunch the flow effectively was for a major 'touch'. I desperately needed Assultan to oblige for me at Ascot.

He had won easily enough at Windsor the previous week, and although this was a more competitive event, with thirteen runners, at the country's most prestigious course, I was supremely confident before the race, in which he carried only 10st 1lb. I had £50,000 on at 4–1 and he started at 5–2 favourite. Imagine my horror when he got up to his old tricks, bolted before the start and ended up in the bushes down by Swinley Bottom. I thought it was 100–1 about him even starting and I did consider withdrawing him. But Declan never panicked, and he did the job in style, making stealthy headway and taking it up at the last to win by a comfortable one and a half lengths. As the horse crossed the winning line I thought to myself, 'All during my life, if I've ever given a pound to a good cause I've always got it back a hundred times.' It's a funny old world.

Sometimes you can have a success with a horse that anyone else would have dispatched to the knacker's yard long ago.

One such character was Utrillo who was owned by a builder named Swales Hammond, and was originally trained by Alec Stewart of Mtoto fame. Alec has become a good friend of mine since I've been at Newmarket and when he had trouble with Utrillo as a three-year-old in 1992, he recommended the horse be sent to me. On his only two intended runs, at Newmarket and Bath, Utrillo had refused to go into the stalls and had been withdrawn. They'd tried everything, even getting that equine guru Monty Roberts in, but all to no avail. Swales and I set out on Mission Impossible, but I warned him, 'I don't want phone calls every week asking about his progress. It will take time, but hopefully we will get him right, and when his day comes we'll all have a "touch" with him.'

With the help of my son Charlie, Declan got Utrillo right. We sweetened him up, changed his routine and tried to make life interesting for him; we even brought him along to the house at Stetchworth just to have a pick at the grass. We let him out with one of the children's ponies. Eventually, we got him in the stalls, and he ran a few times without troubling the judge, but he was going the right way. Mark Perrett, an excellent horseman, rode him one day at Lingfield. He must take a lot of credit for his change in attitude.

Finally, I sent him to Yarmouth and got Bruce Raymond, who has beautiful hands and balance, to ride. In his work he had been absolutely sizzling. I just wanted Bruce to get him into a rhythm and maintain it. On no account was he to knock the horse about. The race, a maiden handicap, was not of the highest quality, it has to be said, but everything fell into place that day and he won nicely. He probably didn't even know he'd been in a race. Swales and I had a 'touch', of course, but that was one of those occasions when the satisfaction of getting it right was more important than profit.

Alec, a good trainer and an honest man, had done me a turn and I operate under a system where, if someone does me a favour I like to do one back. I got an opportunity in early 1998 to join a syndicate he had formed called Racing for Gold. There were only five horses in the syndicate and, much to my pleasure, one of them was my second in the big two-year-old race at Newbury in July, collecting £25,000. So if anyone has money to burn on horses, I can highly recommend it.

I take pride in the number of 'invalids' that I've brought back to win first time out after a long lay-off. Moynsha House, named after my good friend Patsy Byrne's house in Co. Kerry, comes into that category. He had been off the track for 13 months when he scored at Fontwell on 18 January, 1994, a 2–1 favourite. Another notable success was Case for the Crown, a talented filly who was habitually very unsound. Suddenly, for a period of three weeks she came right. We took her to Folkestone and Frankie got her home by an 'easy' head, without the horse really trying. She can hardly have known she'd been in a race and displayed her true ability. I had £15,000 on and she started at 7–4 favourite and had about two stone in hand. Next time, she was a short-priced favourite at Newmarket and got beaten, although not by far. However, she did not run within two stone of what she had at Folkestone. I got Lester Piggott to ride her at Nottingham and she ran terribly again. People made the assumption, 'Oh, he's stopped it' but the fact was she just wasn't sound. I wasn't cheating. If I was guilty of anything, it was not making the public aware of her condition.

TWENTY-SEVEN

A charter for action

Apart from making that accusation against Graham Bradley in 1987, the biggest mistake I ever made was to get involved in the political side of racing. But by the early part of 1988 my mind was made up. I truly believed I could cure racing's ills. It genuinely upset me that British racing had become the laughing stock of the world, because of issues like the appallingly low level of prize money and the lack of contribution by the Big Three Bookmakers, whose activities were, and still are, unregulated. I had a vision about how our sport should be run. For four years, until the futility of it all came home to me in November 1992, I tried to be a pied piper, leading the punters and galvanising the trainers into action to improve racing. Initially, I advocated that the Jockey Club should appoint General Sir Cecil 'Monkey' Blacker, then a Jockey Club steward, as the new supremo. For twenty-five years the bookmakers had had the monopoly on intellect. I thought the general had a razor-sharp brain. But at seventy-two, he considered himself too old for the job.

Racing had always been conservative and changing course is like doing a three-point turn in an oil-tanker. Yet, having discussed it with many other trainers, making visits to Malton and Lambourn, I believed there was an irresistible force for change. So far, I had financed my own battle against what I considered wrong with racing out of my own pocket. But I was no longer prepared to do it without support, both financial and numerical. On 6 March 1991, in a Greek restaurant in London, I launched the Independent Racing Organisation. I gave myself two years to succeed, injected £30,000 of my own money to get it started and asked for £25 membership.

A supporter of the cause, named Stephen Lee, gave us an office and secretaries. The idea was to obtain discounts to racecourses, greyhound meetings and other sporting events and organise a betting advisory service. I also planned to have staff monitoring SIS. Among supporters were footballer-turned-trainer Francis Lee and Luca Cumani. George Harris, chairman of the Federation of British Racing Clubs, was also involved, and other supporters included Lord White of Hull, bloodstock agent Tim Vigors, Lester Piggott, Henry Cecil and Michael Stoute. This was no group of rabble-rousers out to revolutionise the sport. We still supported the Jockey Club as the best body to head the racing industry.

A number of factors had prompted me. One of my prime motivations was that I had it in my mind that Charlie would one day take over running my yard. The following month, in Guineas week, we unveiled our 'Punters Charter' which would challenge a system under which only a fraction of the £4 billion turnover generated by punters each year is returned to racing. Under it, I wanted to confront issues, including: the role of SIS, the strength of the on-course market, so-called 'early' prices and facilities at racecourses. I also called for the establishment of a regulatory body, similar to the Gaming Board, to oversee all bookmaking.

There is still a bewildering incongruity in the fact that while jockeys and trainers have their conduct scrutinised minutely each day, with offenders often receiving draconian punishments, bookmakers indulge in a free-for-all, over which there is no control whatsoever. We now have regulatory bodies in every other walk of life, from teaching standards to making sure the privatised utilities provide a proper service at fair prices. Bookmakers have escaped this march of protest.

In addition, I mooted the introduction of 'ring-masters' to oversee the activities of the on-course bookmakers. To be more precise, I wanted individual bookies to be categorised according to the bets they laid up to a given amount, similar to the Australian system, and advocated pitches allocated according to performance, not pecking order or 'dead man's shoes'.

I announced my intention to launch a fighting fund for a campaign which, hopefully, would galvanise the government into an inquiry. There was nothing, I believed, outrageous about those proposals. They were radical, maybe, but merely common sense. Paul Hayward, in the *Independent*, reacted thus, 'Ten years ago the authors of a document like this would have gone the way of the Tolpuddle Martyrs, but such is the acceptance that racing is in a mess that the problem now is how to be radical enough to escape censure.'

We erected a tent at Newmarket to promote our case and sign up racegoers. One *Sporting Life* correspondent described me as, 'A lonely figure sitting in a Bedouin tent behind the grandstand.' It was not a success. We recruited just 290 members. There was a wall of indifference, from trainers, owners, racegoers and punters. But you can't help those who won't help themselves. It was a depressing experience. It has often been said that those who train, own and bet on racehorses were too single-minded to form what was, in effect, a 'trade union' for the common good. Perhaps my experiences proved those sceptics correct. We had had thousands of baseball caps manufactured. We ended up flogging them off for £2 a throw for charity at one of John Gosden's open days at his stable. They were red, so we told everyone they were Sheik Mohammed's colours!

The result is that the big bookmakers have continued

robbing the punters, as they have been for thirty years, and will carry on doing so. Over £6 million is bet every day, and the punters deserve better. Organisations like the Jockey Club, the BHB and the Racecourse Association have honourable, straight men, but they've had no idea what they were doing. They've allowed the high street bookmakers to hoodwink the public for too long. Indeed, the bookmakers are so complacent about their position that they don't even bother to defend themselves against critics.

In August 1988 Ladbrokes refused to appear on a TV debate about how the then Big Four run their betting operations – because, they claimed, I was also to appear. Apparently, Jane Ridley, who produced the BBC2 On The Line programme which examined the power of the Big Four and how they sent their off-course money back to the course to reduce the odds and affect the starting prices, wanted to interview Ladbrokes' then Director of Publicity Ron Pollard. He declined to take part. After that William Hill took the same stance. Then Tom Kelly, Director General of the Betting Office Licencees Association – or BOLA – also refused to take part. They were followed by Mecca and Corals. What a pathetic bunch.

Interestingly, Len Hyman, of on-course bookmakers A R Dennis, said on the programme that the Big Four's actions were, 'Akin to a stockbroker using his clients' money to manipulate prices on the Stock Exchange and not passing the profits on to his clients.' I took part in another documentary, Channel 4's *Dispatches*, in December 1990 which also questioned the on-course activities of the big bookmakers. It suggested that in hedging their liabilities, the – by now – Big Three took unfair advantage of the off-course punter backing at starting price.

The programme's most controversial claim was to quote from an independent report that the Big Three spent around

£25 million a year (then) to manipulate the on-course betting market. This translated into an annual saving of £150 million in pay-outs to the off-course punter, a figure that is greater than 'the documented profits of the whole of the British bookmaking industry', according to a senior bookmakers' representative.

The bookmakers merely referred back to a 1988 monopoly inquiry, conducted by the Office of Fair Trading, which concluded that 'no further action is necessary'. Frankly, you have to question whether punters should be in the betting shops anyway. They are still getting a pathetic deal. It is quite iniquitous that the major bookmakers have effective control over SIS which relays vital information to the betting shops across the country. Even if everything is straight and above board, it should be seen to be so. No other country would, or does, stand for this state of affairs. I believed, and still do, that we should have a government inquiry, but bookmakers seemingly have too much influence in the corridors of power.

From my own experiences I knew just how the high street bookmakers operated and decided the only course open was a campaign of disruptive tactics. After my horse Ardbrin won a novices hurdle at Nottingham, on 24 January 1989, I accused Ladbrokes of rigging the market. They had laid out £10,000 to force the price down. When I went into the ring the horse was 11–10, and there was one bet of £10,000-to-£11,000, the source was fairly obvious. Ladbrokes' answer was that, 'We are ensuring that the on-course betting market accurately reflects what is going on off-course.' What they actually wanted to do was ensure I would not win – and then maybe leave the country. They saw me as the only danger to their highly profitable system. Eventually, Ardbrin was backed down to 5–4 on from 6–4, and won by an easy seven lengths, although I did not bet. I said that Ladbrokes had been rigging a weak on-course market every day for the last twenty-five years. I told reporters, 'When the Office of Fair Trading investigated betting they said everything was okay. But I don't know who they talked to – they certainly never came to me. It is time someone took a stand.' So, I withdrew my intended runner Avec Coeur from the last race in protest. I was fined £350, in addition to a fixed penalty of £70 for 'showing a wilful disregard to the interests of racegoers'.

The following day, I warned there would be a repeat performance with Mr Kirby at Sedgefield. I explained that if the same thing happened and I couldn't get a fair bet I'd have a flag with me and signal to my jockey to dismount at the start and pull the horse out of the race. In the event I didn't need to. I said if he started less than 2–1 I'd withdraw him. Mr Kirby started favourite, but at 2–1 which I considered a reasonable price, having opened at 5–4. I'm certain, if it hadn't been for my campaign the big bookmakers would have manipulated the price down to 5–4 on. As I told Claude Duval of the *Sun*, 'For once the sharks were kept out of the betting ring and the punters can go home in one piece.'

My other big gripe was SIS shows in betting shops. Purely by coincidence, Ardbrin was again involved when I withdrew him just before the final race on the Ascot card of Saturday 31 March 1990 in protest against their shows. I told Declan to canter down to the start with him before the Kestrel Hurdle, then come straight back to the saddling enclosure. It was only a six-runner event anyway and had the effect of throwing the betting market into chaos. I reflected afterwards that it would have been even worse if I'd had a big bet on Ardbrin as well.

Some may say that I had overstepped the mark in my condemnation, that I was becoming obsessive, purely because of my own circumstances. Judge for yourself. The Thursday before that Ascot race, SIS broadcast betting shows fluctuated between 11–8 and 6–4 when Ardbrin ran at Taunton, despite the fact that Neal Wilkins, the Press Association's senior SP journalist, reported shows between 7–4 and 2–1 and even up to 5–2 in places about Ardbrin. There was one bet of £5,000-to-win-£10,000 with top rails bookmaker Stephen Little. This was typical of what was – and is still – going on. Wilkins went on to maintain that a 'bumper' winner at Ascot, Piper's Son, with whom I had no connection, was readily available at 10–1, but the first show sent out by SIS was 5–1.

I was fined £1,000 under Rule 144, because, it was said by the stewards, that I had shown: 'A wilful disregard of the interests of racegoers' when the direct opposite was the case. Sadly, too few other people, who should have been standing up against this disgraceful state of affairs – notably, the racing press and TV and trainers – questioned anything about what was going on. They merely looked the other way. The reaction of SIS was, as might be expected, so laughable that they should have hired Terry Thomas instead of getting their front-man and racing director, Terry Ellis, to defend their shows. He continued to insist that his organisation was 'totally independent' of bookmaking interests.

There are numerous other examples of SIS misleading the punters. Street General, a horse of Henry Cecil's, who ran in a conditions event at Newmarket on Saturday 3 May 1997 started at 7–4 on, having opened, according to the *Sporting Life* official return, at evens. Bets included an even £2,000. The way the racecourse market is, that would be considered a big bet. If you had watched SIS in the betting shop you would have seen the horse open at 11–8 on.

My campaign of 'disobedience' didn't stop there. One Wednesday night at Sandown in July 1991, I made a late switch, substituting John Reid for Tony D'Arcy, an apprentice claiming 7lbs who had never ridden a winner, to ride my horse Threshfield. He had last finished unplaced when favourite over six furlongs but was now to run over 1m 14yds in the Harpers & Queen Handicap. The 'early' price was around

9–1, but after I switched Reid at just after six o'clock, there was heavy backing right down to 11–4. He landed an almighty gamble. After he won, landing around £100,000 in the process, I told reporters, 'Kenneth Baker [then Home Secretary] said we've got to help ourselves. Well, I have.'

I caused another rumpus in August 1991 when, on the day before a race at Pontefract, I deliberately failed to nominate a jockey for the same horse, Threshfield. At that time you were allowed to do so; indeed, my actions were partly responsible for the rules being changed. Coincidentally, the same day, and only fifteen minutes before, Bill O'Gorman put up Tony Ives on an 11–2 Brighton winner, Sir Valid, instead of his daughter Emma, who had been listed in all the morning papers.

My horse was already favourite in the morning papers anyway, but you can imagine the reaction of punters and 'layers' when, on the morning of the race, the Jim Gundill Memorial Handicap, I declared Lester Piggott to ride. It was the first time he had ridden there that season since his comeback the previous October and he got a great reception from the crowd, too. It needed Lester's expertise to get him up that day, too. He came through the eye of a needle to win. He challenged up the rails after turning into the straight and then repelled the challenge of Spurned to win cheekily by a head. A less experienced jockey wouldn't have done it. To be honest, I thought he was beaten. The crowd was ecstatic, but Lester just quietly dismounted and muttered, 'No sweat.'

Not surprisingly, the horse was backed, from 11–8 to 11–10; I bet plenty on the day, having at least £20,000 at 13–8. I didn't gain anything from not revealing Lester had the mount. I only rarely bet on early prices – they're a farce. You cannot get a bet of any size, and the bookmakers use them to find out what is fancied. The television pundits talk rubbish about early-morning money. Would they kindly tell us where it is put on – and by whom? There was an authentic reason for my not revealing Lester was to ride until so late – he was due to ride in the seven o'clock at Kempton and wasn't certain until the morning that he could make both races. Not that anyone believed me.

From that moment, the popular image of me changed subtly. From being the Pied Piper of Punters, they were turning against me, with the help of the media, and not recognising that the long term good is far more important than whether they can get clues about which of my horses will be winners. Predictably, I was denounced in the *Sporting Life*, who likened my proposed role of punters' guardian to that of 'putting a fox in charge of the chickens', suggesting that I had 'cynically taken the punters he had professed to protect for a ride'.

I had no compunction in doing what I did; I had no obligation to play the game fairly. I just wanted to show the absurdity of the whole situation. If you're not playing on a level playing field, it's the fault of the government and bookmakers. The system was there to be exploited.

The following month I asked Lester to switch from Nottingham, where he originally had three booked rides, to partner Threshfield for me at Kempton. In the event Threshfield came third, but I was more concerned about publicising my point. Afterwards I turned the heat up higher by declaring that I would no longer inform the press in advance about riding plans for my horses. 'If the jockey tells the press I will take him off the horse and get someone else to ride,' I added. I emphasised that this was nothing against punters, but designed to hinder the bookmakers in marking up early-morning prices for my horses.

I also wanted to bring to the attention of everyone with British racing at heart, including hopefully the government, what was really going on. All I wanted to see was British racing become the best in the world, which it manifestly wasn't at the time. Trainers were going bust by the week. 'Owners are funding a £4.5 billion betting industry, yet there is nothing coming back from the government and bookmakers to help the sport in a time of crisis,' I was quoted as saying in a front page *Racing Post* story.

My belief was that disrupting racing was the only way of getting my point across, though I appreciate that it is not the British way. Ideally, I would have liked to have seen an owners' strike to bring racing to a halt. Desperate times sometimes call for desperate measures. I believed they were the most effective means of gaining attention for my beliefs. A please, a thank you and a doffing of your cap to the powers-that-be may work on occasions, but there are times in life when only direct action will achieve your ends, as we've seen over the poll tax, fishermen, and the Welsh and French farmers. I've been condemned, but if everyone had acted like me we might actually have made some progress. That was ten years ago and the situation has got worse, which I believe vindicates my strong stand. Direct action is the only thing that gets people moving. I learnt that lesson when I was young and the Troubles began because nobody stood up for what they believed in; everybody left it to the politicians and madmen. The frustrating thing has been that everything I said has been proved correct. In his 1997 Gimcrack speech Sheik Mohammed endorsed much of what I'd said. Now he has begun to carry out his threat and will quietly cut down on his racing interests in this country unless something is done quickly.

The problem with society is that when money, power or relationships enter the equation, people are compromised. In politics or racing very few people will stand up and be counted. All the time I was cutting my own throat. Declan was at his wits' end with me. He could see I was ignoring the training side and constantly used to moan at me, 'Barney, please concentrate.'

I had steadily built up a stable of more than twenty horses

again by then, following the 'Robin Goodfellow' débâcle, but I never had any time for them. Suddenly, I just ran into a financial hole. Despite frequently being described as 'a millionaire' I've never had £1 million, let alone £2 million, accumulated in the bank, so to pay my debts to the bookmakers and banks I had to start off from scratch again and win the money back by betting. Everything I owed I paid back from winnings. I didn't have that many horses, but the ones I had I used well. I had to with that magnitude of debt.

It was during this period, in January 1990, that I put £250,000 into starting my own betting business with a view of taking the bookies on at their own game. It was a kind of 'if you can't beat them, join them' ploy. I even went out and bought a personalised number plate, '1 Bet', for the Volvo stretch limousine. The business was called Curley Credit and Maureen had the licence for the operation. We took bets on all sports, with a pay-out limit of £250,000. But there would be no morning prices like those advertised by high street bookmakers and promoted by the likes of John McCririck. At best they are just a gimmick; at worst, they gave bookmakers early warning of which horses were fancied. But, as I've stressed before, few have ever flourished as both bookie and punter. It was not a success. I decided to stick with what I knew best. When the crash came in 1992, I sold everything except my house. Even that personalised number plate had to go. It was bought by a London casino for £30,000.

By 1992 it was evident we had to do something radical to galvanise the industry into action. Prize-money, relatively, was in an even worse state of affairs than it is now. A lot of owners at all levels, some admittedly because of the recession, were bailing out. Yards in Newmarket were dropping in value by thousands every month. A Newmarket estate agent estimated that of fifty yards in the area, fifteen were for sale, either overtly or covertly. The letters' columns of the trade newspapers were regularly carrying bleating missives from wounded trainers. But would they get up, bloodied that they were, and take to arms? This was no time for brave expressions. They had to take to the battlements and fight.

Owning horses is absurdly expensive. To buy twenty at, say, £20,000 apiece comes to £400,000 plus the keep, transport and entry fees, which add up to another £200,000 – a total of £600,000. In the unlikely circumstances that they all won a £5,000 race, you'd only get a return of £100,000; significantly less after deductions. The reality is that you'd be very lucky if four of them win a race.

I wasn't just some sort of outside political agitator. At one time I was a big player and my 28 boxes at Harraton Court stables were continually full, in addition to ten to twelve elsewhere. Before 1988 I never had less than forty horses. I believed I had every right to complain. A strike was the only answer. Sir John Harvey Jones, former chairman of ICI, once said that a government only notices you when you're hurting it. After many years of Mrs Thatcher, 'strike' was a dirty word, but that was too bad.

But if the impact of my efforts with the IRO was anything to go by, that was doomed, too. It didn't suit me to be out front, shouting for racing. I'd far rather have been anonymous on the racecourse, talking to no one and getting on with my business, and certainly not appearing anywhere making speeches. But the fact is that I loved English racing, it was potentially the best in the world and if I had an ulterior motive, it was that I had a son who wanted to follow me into racing. If we did the job right and transformed racing he could be an honest trainer, with plenty of decent prize-money and if he wanted to have a bet he could have one. I did not want to see Charlie involved in an industry where you had to be a thief and cheat the majority of the time to survive. That was, and still is, the prospect for too many trainers. It will end up with a few wealthy owners at the top, money no obstacle, the middle range will be wiped out as owners become disenchanted, and those down the bottom, the 'shrewdies', will be existing on scams and schemes. It'll end up like 'flapping' in greyhound racing.

No one honest will come into the sport who can do simple arithmetic. Before we have all these campaigns to encourage horse ownership there should be some straightforward answers. It should be explained to new owners that by buying racehorses they're exchanging £50 notes for £5. They may as well burn their money. Trainers are misleading them; all they want are mugs to fill their boxes. Certainly, nobody should get into the National Hunt game unless they have a lot of money and patience. Out of twenty National Hunt horses at the beginning of the season you'll be lucky if half aren't injured by the end of it. Recently, Lingfield and Windsor, two tracks easy to get to from Newmarket, announced they planned to stop jump racing. Lingfield is one of the best courses in the country to introduce a novice 'chaser. It is said to be transferring fixtures to Folkestone, a horrible track when the ground gets soft. That is hardly likely to encourage new owners.

Nowadays, trainers have cottoned on to the fact that professional footballers and managers a) have a lot of money and b) have a lot of spare time. They are encouraged to go into horse ownership as a relaxation, and maybe to make a profit. I've already referred to Manchester United manager Sir Alex Ferguson, who's bought some horses; he may well be really smitten, but if he's not, and the results don't go his way, he'll be out in a few years. He'll have outlaid his two or three hundred pounds or whatever and realised that he's not even got back what he has put into racing. At least when you buy a yacht or a flashy car there's a resale value. At the bottom end of the scale, as soon as new owners start realising how much it's costing they want a 'touch' out of their horse to pay the training bills – not that it's a simple matter, as they imagine – and that can lead to all kinds of chicanery.

If you're going to be an owner, you're far better off in France or Ireland. Even prize-money at Cork is far more than the average pot at Huntingdon. In Ireland in the summer of 1998, I got £1,370 for finishing second in a modest handicap. In England, the winner would be unlikely to get that after deductions. It is all down to the bookmakers. All they are doing is putting back in pin money through sponsorship. Their contribution is derisory; meanwhile, they're rigging the market and people like me can't get a bet on. Admittedly, even if there were improvements there would still be some people not running their horses straight, there would still be some of the big stables giving their fillies a quiet couple of runs, getting them leniently handicapped to win a race to enhance their paddock value. That's part of the game. It's gone on since racing started; it will go on until racing finishes.

At the beginning of 1992, I organised an informal get-together in the billiards room at my house in Stetchworth to thrash out a plan for action. There were around fifteen people there, including Christopher Haines, then chief executive of the Jockey Club, whom I admired. He should have been the man to become chairman of the BHB. We might have had some chance with him; instead we got Lord Wakeham, whose main contribution was that we should get closer to the bookmakers.

Several top trainers turned out including Michael Stoute, Luca Cumani, Henry Cecil, Bill O'Gorman and Alex Stewart, whom I have always respected. In principle, we clearly had a consensus of views. The trouble was, although they were intelligent enough to realise that things were not going well, they all had wealthy patrons and there was no real incentive for them to act. We operated on trust but someone there leaked it to the press and some comments of Alex Stewart were made public, which ruined everything and dampened our powder. In

July, I declared that I was closing up shop and selling all my horses, having invested heavily in them over the last ten years. I knew there wasn't a fortune in it and there was no point carrying on. I fact, I did a partial U-turn, sold my better horses and though I never played in the Premier League any more, I've stayed around, performing quietly at the bottom of the third division. At one time I paid in the region of £30,000 for a National Hunt 'store'. Since 1993, I've not paid more than £11,000 for a horse.

Undeterred, in November of that same year, 1992, I organised a meeting at the Jockey Club in Portman Square. I was in the Trainers' Federation at the time and it was my idea entirely. The issue was simple; it was now or never, as far as I was concerned – this was D-Day when we all had to put our heads above the parapet. I advocated a strike of racehorse trainers. All the top men were there: 'Tom' Jones, John Dunlop, Guy Harwood, Michael Stoute, Luca Cumani, John Gosden and Paul Cole, among others. We were sitting around a table doing a lot of talking, but to no real effect. There was a lot of sympathy for the ideas I put forward, but it gradually dawned on me that they were merely paying lip-service to it all.

In hindsight, I should have recognised well before then that they weren't prepared to suffer to improve the state of racing. If they had, we'd have got the job right. There was some support for action, but I knew it wasn't total. They just didn't have any foresight. Where is this game going to end up? I thought to myself. I was getting nowhere. It was so frustrating. I looked around the room and realised that there were too many of them with Jockey Club members or other powerful patrons with horses in their stables and they wouldn't want to rock the boat. I weighed it up and decided we were going nowhere. After a couple of hours the meeting broke up for lunch. I walked out and never returned.

My appeal for action was met by deaf ears on that occasion, but I believe I have been vindicated by everything that has happened since. For too long the Jockey Club, and now also the BHB, have not understood, or not wanted to understand, just how much influence the off-course bookmaking industry have had over racing's prosperity. If Peter Savill, the chairman of the BHB, really wants to earn respect, he must organise a strike of owners and trainers. There is simply no point in constantly having meetings with the bookmakers. It is utterly futile. A strike is the only way to go straight to the heart of the Big Three, and emphasise to the government that racing means business.

TWENTY-EIGHT

No bargains at the sales

Columnist Paul Haigh of the *Racing Post* once posed the question rhetorically: 'Who is Barney Curley ... and why does he make such a bloody nuisance of himself?' The fact is that I never set out to become a thorn in anyone's side. I never set out to make the headlines. My greatest blessing when I first came to Newmarket was that, although the authorities and bookmakers were forewarned, very few people in English racing knew me. That suited me fine. But people soon found that I wouldn't stand for being trodden on. One incident in particular demonstrated that.

In November 1986 I went along to a Tattersalls' horses-in-training sale and bought a horse called Pleated, out of Guy Harwood's yard. I'd valued him at £20,000 to £25,000 and when it was knocked down to my agent Frank Barry for half that, £10,000, I smelt a rat. It was like a horse at evens drifting to 5–1. Under Tattersalls' rules, you couldn't give that horse back and had to pay for it unless it was wrong in its wind.

After I'd bought it, Guy Harwood assured me the horse was 100 per cent and added, 'You've done well out of it.' I thought so, too, initially, but on the gallops the horse did not appear sound in wind or limb, so we brought him back to the yard and half an hour later he was hobbling about like a man of eighty-four. I got vet Tim Greet, an authority on wind problems, from the Newmarket practice of Rossdales, to examine him and he confirmed that the horse had made an abnormal respiratory sound. In veterinary jargon, there was evidence of Laryngeal Hemiplegia. Tattersalls arranged for their panel of vets to examine the horse and they insisted that his wind was fine and I would have to take the horse back. I refused, and Tattersalls then sent him to Charlie King's livery yard in Exning where the horse's legs were found to be so bad that he could not be taken out of his box for nearly two months. Tattersalls then agreed to negotiate with Harwood over the horse. I refused and said, 'If I got the horse for £500 I wouldn't take him.' It was not something I enjoyed doing, because the horse had been trained by one of the top men and had been owned by his principal patron, Prince Khaled Abdullah. Neither were what you'd call fly-by-night characters. Nevertheless, I insisted that Tattersalls wouldn't get a penny out of me. They threatened to sue me. I said, 'Go ahead.' So they did. I took legal advice and I was informed that I would be wasting my time pursuing it, because the conditions of sale meant the case would be loaded in Tattersalls' favour. I still refused to pay and they threatened to make me bankrupt.

Whatever the strict legal interpretation, I still feel bitter about my run-in with Tattersalls. There they were, sponsoring races at no small cost, when they would have been better advised putting their efforts into tightening up their sales rules. What would have happened if I'd been a first-time owner? What sort of impression would I have got? It's alright for trainers buying a horse for an owner like Pleated, they just hum and haw, and come out with all kinds of excuses. But when it's your own money it's a different ball game.

There was an interesting postscript to it all. The following year, Edward Du Cann, my barrister at the Jockey Club appeal, said: 'I've been going through your case and I notice from newspaper cuttings that you were prepared to go bankrupt rather than pay Tattersalls. Have you been quoted correctly?'

I answered brightly, 'Oh, yes.'

There was an awkward silence, before he went on, 'We're heading for the High Court and you can't expect your case to be heard as an undischarged bankrupt.'

He quickly added: 'Do you have a cheque book on you?'

I nodded.

'Then would you mind giving my clerk a cheque for £10,000?'

That was the only reason they got the money out of me. Meanwhile the horse had to be hobdayed, a windpipe operation. He was subsequently bought second time up, at the sales, by Peter Hopkins, and sent to Jeff King, where everything I said turned out to be correct.

To the outsider, horse sales have a glamorous image, with the auctioneer's exhortations sending the wheel of fortune spinning for the fortunate vendor of a blue-blood, while someone captures half a ton of horseflesh they can dream will win a Derby. The reality is somewhat different. Some have no hope of winning anything, and to make matters worse they're paying too much hard-earned money to discover that fact. That's when it's dishonest. I very seldom send a horse to public auctions because I won't give kick-backs. What happens is that an agent approaches you, the seller, asks what you want for the horse and then he keeps 20 per cent by bidding the horse up far beyond its real value. It's a common practice, and thoroughly dishonest. Naïve owners end up paying £20,000 instead of £10,000. I know it happens because when I was first in England, people, assuming I was a rogue, propositioned me and asked me to do it, but I refused to have anything to do with it. By going along with what is considered 'common practice' you only perpetuate the belief that it is acceptable.

There are some genuine sales, where you get good value, but not the 'horses in training' sales. Bearing in mind that all these wealthy owners' managers are paranoid about selling anything that might remotely be any good, all the prospective purchasers should walk around with badges reading 'Hero'. Or maybe they should be handed out loyalty cards, like those the supermarkets issue. If the trainers really thought they were decent, but the owner insisted on selling for financial reasons, they'd simply recommend it to one of their friends. They wouldn't send it to the sales.

Another piece of distinctly dubious auction practice was going on at Fontwell and Plumpton before I exposed it. After selling races, which are designed to give the poorest animals a chance, an auction is held at which the winner is either 'bought in', in other words kept by the original owner, or sold to the highest bidder. In either circumstances most of the difference between the opening or 'selling' price goes to the racecourse. Sellers are often mediums for a gamble, and if you can win the race and get away with 'no bid', or buy the horse in cheaply, you've had a major result. Since I'd first arrived in Ireland, I'd watched auctions at Fontwell and I noticed that horses were being bid up far beyond what they should be and that racecourse directors or people connected to them were bidding.

It transpired that many trainers knew what was going on, but didn't say a word. That really annoyed me. It had been going on for twenty years and nobody had said a word. It was all going on under the eyes of the Jockey Club, too. After it happened to one of my horses, I accused the racecourse of bidding the horse up, said it was downright robbery and refused to pay. When Above All Hope became my first winner at Fontwell on 1 October, scoring by five lengths at 4–1, I had to go to 7,300 guineas to buy him in. A course official had instituted the bidding and I had been set up.

I did not accuse the last few bidders or the underbidder of being implicated, it was merely the official who got the price up in the first place that I objected to. I described it at the time as 'bloody daylight robbery' and it was reported thus in the papers, and I haven't changed my mind since. Most professionals agree with me. Another trainer reported to me that he'd overheard a conversation suggesting that an attempt would be made to force the bidding upwards. As one newspaper, which argued that bids should be in sealed envelopes opened by a Jockey Club official after the weigh-in, expressed it, 'Why the Jockey Club allow this sort of thing to continue on our racecourses is a mystery.'

It goes on, there is no doubt. The respected racing commentator Howard Wright said in the *Racing Post* at the time, 'The selling race is a cheap way for some, usually low-grade racecourse, to make a fast buck. A number make a significant income from these events, and the success rate which some of them achieve in getting past the no bid stage has to be detailed to be believed.' According to his statistics, Plumpton and Fontwell ran twenty-eight 'sellers' between them the previous jumps season; at Plumpton, one winner changed hands and fourteen were bought in for an average of 2,296 guineas; at Fontwell the figures had been one sold, three no bid, and nine bought in for an average 2,233 guineas – a 'remarkable tribute to the auctioneer'. He posed the question what purpose they served, other than as an easy source of racecourse revenue? and suggested it was time for professionals to 'take a stand', adding 'they seem to have a case'.

Solicitor Anthony Kerman, acting for his father Isadore, threatened legal proceedings against me, but significantly there was nothing forthcoming. Three days later I received a letter from Kerman Snr, claiming I had slandered them and they would sue me unless I publicly apologised in the newspaper. I just rang him up and said, 'Never, will I do anything like that.' I went to my solicitors, spent about £12,000 on legal fees, hired a barrister and spent a lot of time going round trainers, getting their opinions and obtaining statements, so that I could defend myself. Then I sat and waited for the writ to arrive. It never came.

It was followed by a Jockey Club investigation, but they decided to take no further action. All I ever read further on the matter, following my intervention, was a piece by Colin Mackenzie in the *Daily Mail*, saying that the auction price of 'seller' winners at Fontwell and Plumpton had decreased significantly. I can only assume that I put a stop to it. Certainly, I don't think it happens now.

However unorthodox and extreme my methods, it is at times like this that you need support, particularly from the media. In the past, I'd always courted popularity with the press because I did and said things that were out of the ordinary. I was, I suppose, 'good copy'. I've never sought publicity for myself, but there's no doubt a gambler like me, or Michael Tabor or J.P. McManus going for a 'touch' gets the racegoers excited. Now the tide was beginning to turn – and none more so than when Brough Scott, editorial director of the *Racing Post* and Channel 4 pundit, wrote an article about me in his paper which is one of the most offensive I've ever read.

It all began when John McCririck, the Channel 4 pundit and *Racing Post* columnist, took me to task over the events at Fontwell in late September 1992. It was, I had decided, the time to take more 'direct action', this time against the levels of prize-money, and I got together with owner Ken Higson, who I knew held similar views to mine. 'RACING WAS THROWN INTO TURMOIL,' reported the *Racing Post* the following day as Ken and myself both withdrew horses just before the 'off' of separate races at Fontwell, where total win prize-money for the entire card amounted to just under £7,000.Ken took out Across the Card, 9–4 favourite for the opener, and I withdrew Torwada, 2–1 favourite for the third. There was an ironic cheer from racegoers and some boos and hisses from punters after the race who had been bemused by the fact that some bookmakers were betting without my horse because they had got wind of what might happen. However, after winning the race in which I had withdrawn my horse with Never Forgotten, the now-retired trainer Reg Akehurst said he believed that Ken and I would have the support of 99 per cent of owners and trainers. He declared, 'I certainly support them, and I think if it comes to the crunch, everyone will.' Sadly, that proved to be well wide of the mark.

My meeting with the stewards produced a predictable result. After fifteen minutes I was fined £1,200, along with the conditional jockey, Jason Twomey, down to ride my horse, who probably wouldn't have earned that in two months. Ken and his jockey, Gary Moore, suffered the same punishment. Higson made the point that, had his horse finished third in the Sidlesham Selling Hurdle – worth a paltry £788 to the winner – he would have received £86 prize-money, which would not have even covered his rider's fee. It was, he said, the saddest day of his life, and added 'Certain tracks and bookmakers are rubbing our noses in the dirt and it has to stop.'

I described it as a very small shot across the bows. 'Montgomery never said where he was going to attack and neither shall we.' My plan was to cause a crack which, hopefully, would bring the wall down. 'The prize-money is an insult to people's intelligence,' I said.

Sometimes desperate situations call for radical measures. But it was lost on John McCririck who, instead of digesting the message, preferred to shoot the messenger. He had begun his *Racing Post* column by claiming I was 'a gentleman and a smashing guy' but then had deftly inserted the stiletto between my ribs by maintaining, 'If the Jockey Club are to continue administering racing they have to withdraw Barney's training licence at his next rule-flouting "protest".' Now, I have absolutely no time for McCririck – and never have had. With his ostentatious rings and daft hats, he's a touch of Hollywood to a gullible public. If he was really interested in the punter, he'd raise serious questions about wrong, and late, betting shows screened in betting shops by SIS (Satellite Information Services). He prattles on about 'steamers' – there're no such things. You can't get on. Why doesn't he get down to the nitty-gritty: that you can't have a bet; that the bookmakers own SIS and also the Racing Channel? Anybody who fronts either, or is interviewed on either, is doing an injustice to racing. They're just promotions men, or women, for the bookmakers.

I was infuriated with his attitude and, having several times been good enough to give interviews to Channel 4 presenters in the past, I did not think it unreasonable that they should give me air-time to answer his criticisms. Apparently, the Channel 4 powers-that-be refused, presumably not wanting the embarrassment of a full-scale confrontation between me and McCririck, where there would be only one winner. My study of philosophy back in Limerick had taught me a lot and I've always believed that I could take anybody on, eyeball to eyeball; certainly a man like McCririck. In the circumstances, I took the only course of action I could. I sought out McCririck in the press room at Newmarket, where there was racing that week, and told him, 'Never, ever, mention my name on television again, or I'll defrock you in front of your viewers.'

By 'defrock', I meant merely that I would rip his microphone off him, rendering him as ineffective as a priest stripped of his ecclesiastical status. I would have done, too. As far as I'm aware, he never has mentioned me since, so I have had no reason to carry out my threat. However, the next thing, McCririck had reported this minor incident to the security people. For reasons best known to themselves, the police then arrived, too, and there was one almighty commotion which was all so unnecessary. Yes, I did threaten him, but not physically. I've never had much of a punch on me, and certainly not then as a fifty-one-year-old who was not known in Newmarket for regularly working out in a gym.

But he reacted like a hysterical child, going round crying like a baby and telling all and sundry 'that Barney Curley was going to manhandle me.' His mentor and fellow Channel 4 pundit Brough Scott then took it upon himself to take up his pen and fight McCririck's battles for him in his *Racing Post* column. He, too, described me as an 'old friend' – it was perhaps fortunate this pair didn't regard me as their enemy – and then went on to portray me as having 'that Ulster accent, which wittingly or otherwise, can take on a menacing note'. He alluded to my 'crackpot schemes', saying that I should withdraw the 'poisoned words' with which I branded McCririck, before anyone contributed a pfennig to them. Scott concluded, 'He wants us to follow him. On last week's form I wouldn't follow him through an open door.'

I rang up several times to get a reply to Scott's article, which most people would surely agree was the least I was entitled to, but without any response. His remarks still infuriate me. He had insulted me and insulted my country. I found it hard to believe a charitable person could have written what he did. Scott is chairman of the Injured Jockeys' Fund. On a point of principle, I have not given anything to that organisation since then, purely because of my objection to that article. Apart from an occasional word with reporters like Tim Richards, I've had nothing more to do with the *Racing Post* or anything to do with Scott, including his other paymasters Channel 4. That's my pay-back.

What are those racing papers good for anyway? Only adverts for bookmakers' prices you can't get – and tipping lines. In that respect, both trade papers – including the now demised *Sporting Life* – have lacked credibility for many years. How much did they protest about Ladbrokes' proposed takeover of Coral's? As I've said before, I never listen to other people's opinions, with the exception of maybe Channel 4's John Francome, the former jump jockey, who is one of the few with a real grasp of his subject and has a feeling for racing. You don't learn that in books. The BBC should have made a bid for him a long time ago. He's probably the only pundit with any credibility. The rest, on either Channel 4, the Racing Channel or the BBC, you can ignore, although, after the retirement of Sir Peter O'Sullevan, I don't think you can improve on 'Aussie' Jim McGrath as a first-rate commentator.

In recent years, we've seen the advent of the Racing Channel, a subscription satellite channel that seems to specialise in people desperate for a few quid, often trying to promote themselves with little or no ability, and a few trainers – mind you, only a few – who talk a bit of sense. The game is full of people, mostly trainers, who talk up their own horses but otherwise don't have a clue what they're talking about.

TWENTY-NINE

Terror in the skies

When I emerged from that sanatorium at Killadeas all those years ago I knew God had been with me. Again, a few years ago, I was to give thanks to Him after a night when I really thought my number was up. The ridiculous thing about the events of the evening of 10 July 1992 was that I didn't even want to go to Chester at all. I didn't fancy a horse there and I lost about £20,000 on the night. But one of the perennial problems of travelling to racecourses with jockeys by light plane is that you have to fit in with their tight schedules. I had been up to York's afternoon meeting with Michael Roberts, who was chasing the jockeys' championship at the time, and Jimmy Quinn, together with our regular pilot Neil Foreman. Several of the jockeys now have planes, or share them to cut costs. Particularly in the summer, it enables them to get around the country and take as many rides as possible. It also reduces the tedium of driving. The only way to get home was via Chester racecourse, the Roodeye, where both jockeys had rides in the evening. To this day, I'm still confused about what actually happened, but this is how Jimmy tells it:

'Even when we had arrived at Chester I admit I had an ominous feeling. I wasn't happy about the airstrip. I'm no expert on aviation, but I question whether we should have been there in the first place because it was only a field. We didn't even know where we were going. We circled above Pat Eddery's plane and his pilot said to follow him in when he made his descent. But it was obvious as we landed that the grass was very long and there were a lot of holes and bumps. It had been a very rough landing and I remember bumping my head. In fact, it wasn't really a strip at all, it was a farmer's field.

'Barney and me were in the rear seats, with Michael sitting next to Neil up front as we headed down the strip to take off. I've opened a can of lager straight away, as I usually do after I've been riding in summer.

'We're heading down the strip and as we take off one wheel hits a bump, which shoots the plane into the air and we hit the ground again; seemingly there is a problem with the left hand undercarriage. Neil pulls her up into the air, but there is not much power and we just clear two big trees. If we had hit them, we'd not be here now. But there is only one direction that plane was going then – and that was down.

'I slammed down my can and sat there gripped with fear. Then everything started beeping and I remember Neil shouting, "Brace yourself."

'Michael is shouting something about fuel coming out of one of the wings, so Neil had to turn off all the power. He had somehow turned the plane and got her back towards the strip again, but with the impact I hit my head and knees on the seat in front. About half-way along I realise that, with no power, he can't apply the brakes. We've careered through a hedge, and half-way down the next field I want to bail out. Everyone else is still bracing themselves.

'Neil's trying to get me down at the same time as getting the plane under control. There are more trees in front of us, but between them and us is a big stretch of dirty water, and we plunge straight into it.

'Neil shouts to us to get out quickly. I don't usually take orders well, but on this occasion I never knew I could be so quick. I'm a combination of Linford Christie and Lochsong. We all clamber out of the plane, and I'm the last one out. I'm screaming that I can't swim. We all feared the thing would blow up. By good fortune it didn't.'

I don't remember much of that, but I do recall that it was pretty deep, dirty water and Jimmy shouting, 'Help me. I'm going to drown.' He really thought he'd survived the plane crash, only to drown in several feet of water. Neil bellowed, 'Get in the water, get in the water.' Michael hadn't hung around. He was already half-way up the embankment while we were still getting out. There's no greyhound in England would have moved so fast out of the trap. I'm not a brilliant swimmer myself, but I was struggling away and the next thing Jimmy had climbed on my back. I'm afraid I can't claim it was any great act of heroism. In fact, I shouted, 'Get off my back.' 'I can't swim,' he said. I don't normally move that fast at my best, but on that occasion I went into overdrive, even with Jimmy on my back. As far as I was concerned, there was still a chance the plane might explode.

We were all in a state of shock as we waited for an ambulance. Nobody said very much. My suit was soaked through with stagnant water. Eventually we got all our gear and money out of the plane, but we sat as far away as possible, because we still feared it would blow up. Neil's prompt action in cutting the power probably diminished the chances of that. In fact, we had 100 per cent faith in Neil. He saved our lives. He hadn't panicked.

It was a relief to hear the siren of the approaching ambulance. Meanwhile, both Jimmy and I were dying for a cigarette. The problem was that they wouldn't let us smoke one in the ambulance. They were all damp anyway. By now we were all laughing and joking, probably as a result of shock and the sheer relief that we were still alive. I started to create a bit of a racket. 'I don't care' I shouted at the driver, 'I'm having a cigarette.' So the ambulance pulled up outside a service station, we bought some cigarettes and the ambulance men fetched me out on a stretcher and I lay there on a grass verge, contentedly smoking, with traffic passing by and drivers giving us quizzical looks. Jimmy sat next to me on the bank doing the same.

At the hospital we were washed and dried and given the once-over before they put these white operating theatre-style gowns on us. Apparently, we were to be detained for observation overnight, to check that we weren't suffering from shock or concussion. Jimmy had a big gash on his head and required stitches in his knees. Neil also had a cut in his head, but there was not a scratch on Michael. I was relatively unscathed, just bruises, and a sore neck and back. It got to midnight and I said to Michael, 'This isn't for me. I'm not staying here. I'm going home.'

I told a nurse the same thing, but she insisted, 'You're not going anywhere'. But my mind was made up. I told Neil, 'I'm going home.'

'Oh,' he said, 'and how are you going to do that?'

I told him, 'I saw some public phone boxes on the way in, with cab numbers stuck to them, I'm going to call one.'

The boys chorused, 'They won't let you out.'

I said, 'I'll find a way, and if you want to come, you're welcome. If not, then stay.'

I persuaded a cab firm to send us round a car to take us to Newmarket, and added, 'I'll give you £150 provided you do what I say. Come round to the side entrance, not the front.'

We crept out and made our escape – but all still dressed in gowns, except the two jocks who had some sort of coat over them. We couldn't take our own clothes.

By this time it was well past one o'clock and I was starving. So was Neil, who is a hefty chap. Normally I'd have been back at 9.30 pm and had my dinner. In the backstreets of Chester we passed a kebab shop still open. There was a long queue of people, mostly youngsters from the clubs and pubs, and the worse for drink. We got the driver to stop and all clambered out. As we approached it all went quiet as the heads turned and stared at us in disbelief. They then drew out of the way at the spectacle of these four guys dressed in gowns. We were all shapes and sizes; there were two small fellows, one with stitches over one eye and on his hands, and dwarfing them were me and Neil, who's probably about 20st. They obviously thought we were from the local asylum. But it did us a favour, because we got nearly to the front of the queue. I've never had a quicker run to a take-away in all my life!

We sent Jimmy into a Chinese restaurant to get some beer. At first, they wouldn't let him in, because they thought he'd been fighting. But he explained, 'You'll hear all about it tomorrow. It'll be on the TV and in the papers.' And they just about believed him. The three, apart from me, were all desperate for a beer.

We arrived back in Newmarket at about 6 am. I had already called Maureen from the hospital and assured her I was OK. The next morning I couldn't move. I was stiff and sore and not feeling well at all. Neil rang and said, 'Come up to York'.

'No, thank you,' I said.

He said, 'If you don't fly today, you'll never fly again.'

Neil repeated his words to Jimmy, but he said that he didn't care and went up on the train, although four days later he flew again. But I flew that day and I was still in shock. I was interviewed by Derek Thompson on Channel 4. Or so I'm told, because I've no idea what I said. Then I sat all afternoon in the trainers' room, next to the weighing room, at York. I couldn't move, my back was so sore.

Jimmy, too, took time to get over the ordeal. He told me later, 'It didn't really sink in until the Sunday. I was out at a restaurant, and people were still discussing the incident. It suddenly struck me how near we'd been to something far more serious. I couldn't eat or drink. I just went home. I couldn't sleep, it just went round and round in my head.'

For my own part, it hasn't put me off flying. I don't think you could come that close again. I just have a vague recollection of standing up in the plane and looking out and seeing these trees flash up before us. We'd had very little time to think when it was all happening. All that passed through my mind was, 'How unlucky can you be, I didn't even want to be here, yet I lose £20,000 and what a way to go out.' I got just a second to say an act of contrition and tell God I was sorry. There was one amusing postscript, though: I owed £13,000 to one bookmaker from that night, Pat Whelan, who is a lovely gentleman, and he sent me a note, addressed to Barney Curley (nearly Barney Rubble), saying, 'The next time you owe me, will you please travel by car!'

THIRTY

Club gives me drugs headache

After walking out of the trainers' meeting at Portman Square in 1992, Luca Cumani accompanied me to Selfridges, where I ate a salt-beef sandwich and considered my options. In reality, there was only one. I had already made up my mind that this foray into racing politics was a waste of time. I found a public telephone and called Guinness Mahon, the merchant bank. I said, 'I will buy that nightclub.' I didn't return to that trainers' meeting, have not been near one since and resigned from the Trainers' Federation. I couldn't stomach the lack of principle among those men. They wouldn't stand up for what they knew was right.

I'd often thought about diversifying into other business ventures and there had been a time when I could have become heavily involved in another form of gambling. 'Irish gambler eyes Mecca's casinos' pronounced a *Sunday Times* headline in 1992, and Jeff Randall, its then City editor, surprised many when he revealed that, 'Barney Curley, one of the most successful gamblers ever to come out of Ireland, is understood to be weighing up a bid for Mecca Leisure's casinos in London.' 'Poacher to turn gaming table keeper' was another headline, in the *Sunday Business Post*.

Mecca wanted to sell four London casinos – Maxim's, the Connoisseur, the Victoria and the Gloucester – and had hoped to get £90 million, but the market was depressed and it was said they'd be lucky to get £60 million. I had the money raised through two financial institutions, one American and one British. There were at least five other bidders. I was all ready to proceed. One of the conditions of buying them, as far as the backers were concerned, was that I had to be seen around the casinos, as I was a considered a gambling 'face'.

By and large, the casinos are run by faceless men and I thought I could do a better job. I had already come close to buying the Barracuda Club from Leisure Investments, owners of Lingfield Park racecourse. But they were asking too much and I wasn't going to work my butt off for nothing. In the event, the fellow responsible for selling the Mecca casinos to me suddenly had a heart attack, someone else took over and they were sold to another bidder. It was not sour grapes, but afterwards I decided it had turned out for the best. I have never been tied down since I left the seminary. I've always worked for myself, and I don't know whether I could have handled all that socialising. I'm not a meeter-and-greeter, I'm just not that sort of animal.

What sounded far more appealing was The Mirage, in William Street, Windsor. It was in receivership and I'd heard through the grapevine that it was for sale. I'd already been in discussions with Guinness Mahon, who were handling it. That trainers' meeting at Portman Square made up my mind for me. I bought it for £1.2 million and it was probably one of the best decisions I've ever made.

The club was originally called Blazers, and was one of the best-known nightclubs in the country, boasting major stars like Shirley Bassey. In its heyday there was a cabaret seven nights a week, but then the attraction for dinner-dances with cabaret began to wane. Simultaneously, the artistes, notoriously myopic, began to price themselves out of business.

As a business the club had a desperately bad reputation; the people who ran it previously didn't pay their suppliers. It was fraught with problems, but I didn't care. As it will have become clear by now, I don't shirk a challenge. Also, it was something to get my mind off racing politics which for four years had just consumed me, frustrated me and virtually destroyed me financially. I was gasping for money and sold No Pain No Gain to Josh Gifford for £35,000. Yet, at one time I had actually turned down £80,000 for that horse together with one called Chuck Curley.

Going into 1993, I owed £2 million to bookmakers and debts connected with the club. Again it was a case of Mission Impossible, and I was Tom Cruise. That's the way I am: lost causes and desperate situations would always attract me like a magnet. Handling live horses is a difficult enough occupation; here I was apparently flogging a dead one.

To emphasise just how precarious the whole proposition was, I soon discovered that my manager, Chas Corkery, who came with the club, had persuaded his mother to put £45,000 a year into the club previously and she had lost everything within a month. It had such a bad reputation that when I took over I couldn't get a book of matches on credit. Southern Electricity even went so far as to refuse to connect me unless I paid a deposit of £5,000. I went down to their head office in Egham, Surrey, with five of my staff and picketed the place for half a day, until eventually someone was sent down to talk to me. We agreed to a deposit of £2,500, but five years on they still haven't returned it because they say I'm a slow payer.

We had a grand opening night, or it should have been, but it turned out to be a disaster. The luckiest man was J.P. McManus, who didn't turn up because we'd left his name off the list of guests. But all his pals, Colin Webster, Michael Tudor and Dudley Roberts were there. What a night! The kitchen equipment broke down, there was hardly any food, and a racing journalist Paul Haigh started a mini-war, throwing bread rolls at everyone. As the club's name suggests, its prosperity was all an illusion. It appeared to be a glamorous, well-to-do venue, but agents for big-name artists, like Jim Davidson and Freddie Starr, were demanding silly money. They were asking £12,000 or £15,000, that sort of scale, for one night. The artistes were trying to take all the money, and all we got out of it were the laughs. The tears were all yours when you had to answer to the bank manager.

The previous owners had all deluded themselves that they were doing fine, but they had not been too good at counting their expenses. It had gone into receivership three times in eighteen months before I took over. As soon as I arrived, I got my calculator out and declared, 'As it is run now, you can't make it pay.' I watched all the acts, already booked, over the Christmas season and did my sums. It was crazy. I said to the artistes' managers, 'You're taking all the money.' Their reply gave no room for negotiation. 'We're not playing the club for less than £12,000' they maintained. These artistes were trying to hold us to ransom. It all took me back to my days with the showbands, where we were doing the same. The analogy with racing was all too obvious, with bookmakers stripping all the money out of the sport, leaving those who provide the entertainment with nothing. I said, 'If that's what you are saying, you'll never play here again. You're out.' I was true to my word. They wouldn't take a penny less, so I stopped the cabaret and just ran it as a disco for young people. Little did I realise how much grief – and I mean that in the literal sense, too – that decision would cause me.

After the first couple of weeks, when I'd had just a cursory glance at the clientele, I casually said to the manager, Chas, 'These are quite nice young people.' He replied, 'Save your opinion until you really know something about the business.' So, I wandered around and observed what was going on. I knew nothing about the music these young people liked, but after my experience with the showbands and going racing for twenty-five years, I was pretty sharp-eyed. I was soon aware that some of the youngsters weren't behaving normally. My sixth sense told me everything was not as it should be. Some lads were standing around in the same spot all night, they didn't dance and appeared very popular. There was a lot of whispering. I tackled them myself. They were absolute gentlemen, who were very obliging and went outside very quietly. There was no way they wanted to get involved in a scene. They were the donkeys, the carriers, selling mostly the so-called 'designer' drug Ecstasy. I had begun to wonder how the youngsters could dance all night. I just thought they were wonderful dancers and very fit. But the 'Es' must have had something to do with it.

I've always been very much anti-drugs, but, like most problems, you need the knowledge before you can act effectively. I started attending meetings of NA (Narcotics Anonymous) in London. I learnt how widespread the problem was and listened to people trying to get off drugs. We were told that many young people start off on cannabis and 'Es' because these days they have stressful lives and need to escape from the weekly grind at work. They can then go on to cocaine and crack-cocaine, which are very dangerous.

The drugs scene was new to me. I was born in a different era, where the problem, albeit much more overt, was drink. I made a decision there and then to do everything in my power to eradicate drugs from the club. It wasn't easy. We even had our security people seizing drugs and then keeping them for their own use or selling them. I attended the club's discos regularly. It was a massive culture shock, all this music that I didn't understand or appreciate, some of it so loud you couldn't hear yourself think, but I said to myself, 'They will not beat me.'

We knew there were four groups operating, of about three pushers each. So, one night I picked out the ringleaders, brought them into my office and said, 'I would know you again, but I'm going to forget about it. Don't come back near the club. If you do I'll see to it that you go to jail, and it doesn't matter what trouble it causes me.' There wasn't much of a response, but I received a call a few days later. 'Mr Curley, can we see you?' They wouldn't say what about, so I went down to be confronted by the same fellows.

'Barney,' one said. 'We hear you like to earn a shilling. We'll give you a brown envelope every Friday night with £2,000 cash in it if you allow us to stay in the club.'

I glowered at them. 'No,' I said. 'Not for £20,000. I'm very much anti-drugs, I'm a parent myself and I don't want to see anybody involved with drugs here.'

They ignored me and continued. 'It's cash, you don't have to account for it …'

A lot of clubs do operate under that system of turning a blind eye, and they gave me all the spiel but I said, 'You're wasting your time. I am totally opposed to drugs and I am going to do everything in my power to get them out of my club.'

Realising they were getting nowhere, they departed. But I had all sorts of other propositions – and threats.

We put ourselves in the front line. It crossed my mind that they might try something more physically persuasive. Certainly, when we handed people over to the police – and as often as not Chas and I would march them out ourselves – their friends would threaten us. Many's the time I've been warned menacingly, 'We'll be back.' The fact that they could offer me that sort of money shows you how much profit margin there is in it. I know I forfeited a lot of business by taking a strict line. The dealers concerned knew the regular security people, so I paid two undercover people to be there every night. That cost me £200 out of my own pocket. We also worked very closely with the drugs squad.

What annoyed me, after all the trouble and placing ourselves in danger, was that the local Tory MP said in 1996 that we should be closed; the council, too. They had no idea what they were talking about. For once, I think my reputation, all my much-publicised run-ins with the Jockey Club, did me a favour. The pushers had probably done their homework on me, and decided that 'here's a fellow not easy to get to, not easily intimidated'.

A lot of parents don't realise what a serious problem it is. What drugs could do to young people was brought home to me, when, within five months of each other, two young men collapsed and died at the club. I thought I'd experienced most things in life, but nothing could prepare me for that. They were very upsetting and frightening episodes, but it made me all the more determined to stamp out that evil.

The first incident in September 1993 involved a teenager named Andrew Diment, from Maidenhead, who had taken Ecstasy before he had come to the club. He was taken to hospital and died later. The following February, a twenty-three-year-old, named John Robjent, from Thame, Oxfordshire, collapsed on the dance floor and was dead by the time he was taken to hospital. I went to visit the parents of Andrew. I now know what they went through. Neither family blamed me or the club. It was established clearly at their inquests that both had died from drugs taken before they came to the club – but that didn't stop the snipers. If the drugs had been bought inside I have no doubt we would have been closed down. As it was, those incidents were not good for business.

Typically, the local MP Michael Trend waded into matters about which he knew very little. He described the club as a 'magnet' for undesirable elements and called for it to be closed down. According to the local newspaper, he said: 'I feel very strongly that Windsor is not a suitable place for such an establishment. I think if local people were asked, they would feel Mirage is unsuitable and should be closed.'

Their sheer ignorance makes these people dangerous, and all to court political popularity, when it is people like Chas and myself who are in the front line, actually dealing with the problem. Chas sensibly pointed out that, 'The Mirage has, is and always will be anti-drugs. We do everything possible to stop drugs coming into the premises – more than many clubs in Berkshire.' I added, 'Windsor and the surrounding areas have one of the biggest drug problems in England, which the government he is a member of does nothing about – it is all left to the club owners.'

We had already introduced anti-drug patrols, security cameras, thorough searches and a photo-membership policy. There are also two paramedics on duty during club nights and an ambulance situated outside. In addition, we have two undercover observers, which I pay for, at £200 a week, out of my own pocket. One time they caught an Army chap, brought him to my office and we discovered he had forty-three 'E' tablets on him. He tried to protest that another soldier had given them to him on the stairs. So, we got the security at the door to nab him too, and they were both handed over to the police who would have passed them on to the Army. 'Argue it out between you,' I said. Once you're caught, that's it. No ifs or buts. No excuses. It gets around and dealers warn each other, 'Oh, you don't want to go there because they'll hand you to the police. Don't mess with those fellows.' That's the image we want to project.

Having children myself, I didn't want them to go into a place where as soon as they walked in the door, there would be a pusher trying to sell them drugs. Now the club is as free of drugs as any in the country, and I feel very proud of that. On the financial front, I've had the club for six years now and in that time it has lost £530,000, I'm told by my accountant. But he says we should be breaking even this year. All the boys in racing, the bookmakers, laughed at me when I bought the club.

One of them, Dudley Roberts, said: 'Barney's a lunatic. He knows about racing. But what does he know about this?' Well, I'm still there and have got it under control.

I can still imagine people thinking to themselves that it was not the most brilliant decision. Certainly my bank manager, John McCann, a fine man, said I was wasting my time, just as he had warned me against organising that competition which cost me £250,000. But since the day I bought The Mirage, I have not given a thought to racing politics. I had to have something to offer me a challenge, a project to distract me from the knowledge that everything I have always said about racing's decline was correct and about which no one would listen. If I had put £1.2 million into buying racehorses in 1992, today it would be worth practically zero. At least that cannot be said about my club in Windsor. I have also been able to concentrate on what I am good at, which is backing horses.

THIRTY-ONE

Memories of Charlie

I was over in Ireland with my mother in December 1995 when I received the devastating news that my only son, Charlie, had been killed in a car crash. The previous night I had been out with my sister, Mary, and her husband, Dolan, and over dinner everybody was talking about what Christmas presents they'd like. My contribution was that I'd already got my Christmas box, and told them about how Dave Thom's wife, Alison, whom Maureen and I knew well, had been suffering from a suspected brain tumour but had finally been given the all-clear after two operations. I was very content with life and wouldn't have changed places with anyone in the world.

At ten to seven the next morning, my assistant trainer, Andrew Stringer, rang my mother's home. He's not one for going all round the houses and came straight out with it: 'Chuck's dead.' At first, I thought he meant Chuck Curley, the racehorse we had in the stable named after him – that was Charlie's nickname – but then he made me understand that Charlie's car had skidded on some ice, plunged into a ditch and he had been killed driving to work. I heard my mother coming down the stairs and she just blurted out, 'Trouble in England?' I tried to bluff it out. Because of my mother's age – remember, she was in her nineties – I didn't want to hit her with such terrible news without preparing her. Whenever we are in

358

trouble our family recite the rosary and that's what my mother and I did. We have great faith in it and it has helped both of us through life. Afterwards I told her the truth.

My sister Mary drove me to Belfast airport to get back to Stansted, and I was fine until I got off the plane. There to meet me were Patsy Byrne, Tommy Stack and Paddy Griffin. It was wonderful to see them. But then it hit me. My legs went weak, I couldn't walk and was in bed for two days. I couldn't eat. Charlie's death at just eighteen hit me as much physically as mentally. Tommy, who stayed throughout, would shout up the stairs, 'Come on, are you going to get up?' but I just lay there. People came up to see me and to offer their condolences. They said later it was like seeking an audience with a Mafia godfather. I couldn't think straight. After all the scrapes I'd been through, like walking out of Epsom £250,000 the poorer and not worrying, for the first time something had really affected me badly.

Charlie had died on the Saturday, and on the Tuesday I prayed with all my heart. For the first time I could see some light. I realised that in a way I was trying to hold on to him. But finally, I released him and said to God, 'Take him.' My attitude towards life, and death, helped me win back my partial peace of mind, but it took me a long time. For such a young life to be taken away tests your faith to the limit, but I knew that one day I was going to meet Charlie again. It wasn't easy but I got through it because, being an Irish household, everyone just turned up and paid their respects, whereas English people tend to make death very private and allow no one in. I cannot thank enough all the kind people who phoned or sent messages of sympathy.

The night before the funeral we took his body to the church. I could barely stand the ordeal. I thought I was going to collapse, but Declan Murphy managed to support me. When he was younger, about eleven or twelve, Charlie used to sit there in my study as I did my business on the phone, like an apostle at the foot of Christ. I thought he was just bored, but I gradually realised that he was listening to everything I said and taking it all in.

A lot of fathers could not have been more pleased if their sons showed an inclination to follow their path. Inevitably, being in the business and being my son, Charlie was interested in betting. But I used to tell him, 'I've lived all my life at this, but it's not a game to be in.' These are no longer the days of big money, when bookmakers stood a decent-sized wager like men. 'You can't make a yard pay from gambling.' I tried my best to dissuade him from getting involved in racing. I used to tell him, 'My day has gone. People like me are finished. Unless you are fortunate enough to find a billionaire owner you'll struggle.'

I urged him to think about doing something else but the horses were addictive to him. I would even try and bar him from the yard. It was two and a half miles away across town and I forbade anyone giving him a lift. Eventually he said, 'If I bike it, can I go to the yard?' So, he got a bicycle and did just that, which showed how keen he was because it wasn't what every young man would be prepared to do early on a wet winter's morning.

Charlie did have the occasional ride, but in the long term he was always going to be too heavy, even for the jump game. I thought he might as well enjoy himself riding as an amateur. He used to say, 'I'll stop riding if I have a winner.' He was like me; he needed that challenge. I criticised his mistakes, I wanted him to do the job properly and ride with a brain. He wasn't a bad judge of a horse.

Charlie had the first of his seven or eight rides when fourth on Threshfield in an amateur's race at Folkestone at the end of June 1994, The nearest he came to winning was on a 10–1 chance called Me Fein at Nottingham. I went for a tickle each-way. The horse was a very hard puller, and I told him not to worry about the betting. All he had to do was get the horse to settle. He turned in last, settled him beautifully and set him alight and, just inside the final furlong, looked a certain winner. Unfortunately, he was outplayed in the last 50 yards by Gerry Hogan on a horse trained by 'Duke' Nicholson. Charlie was also runner-up on Threshfield at Newcastle, but never won a race.

All I remember about the funeral is Maureen and I being in the car immediately behind the hearse, which of course preceded the cortege into the churchyard. She just turned to me, smiled, and said, 'He's first today, anyway.'

I had my dreams for him and I was a hard taskmaster. In many ways I treated him the same as Frankie Dettori. They were two young people who both had plenty of brains. In fact, I used to hold up Frankie's experiences to him, as an example. As I have said, I was away just before the accident and when I called my assistant, Andrew, he told me that Charlie had been late a few times getting to the yard. I had been determined from the start to treat my son the same as everyone else, so I phoned Charlie and told him, 'You're late. Don't bother coming in. You're sacked.' It was said in a fatherly way because I always wanted him to put his best foot forward and use all the talent he had. I was tough on him. I wanted to make a man of him. Just because he was my son, he didn't have an easy time. The next day he went round to Bill O'Gorman's, where he had already done work experience, looking for a job. He got one, too. That evening he had a change of heart and told Andrew he was going to apologise to me when I got back. Andrew said it was the right thing to do and was sure Charlie would be back on the team. Charlie never got the chance.

When he was 16, I had decided Charlie was ready for the University of life and I used to take him with me whenever possible. I often asked him what he had learnt from the people we had met. After about 12 months, I knew I had my successor. He was thoughtful, sharp and had a good brain and an abundance of native cunning. I began to take things easier and allow Andrew and Charlie to captain the ship. I wanted to spend more time in Northern Ireland with my mother and I asked my solicitor, Andrew Montague, to find me something to keep my mind active. I looked at a number of properties around the Portrush and Portstewart areas and was about to get serious – when Charlie was called to meet his Maker.

It puts life into perspective. If I had £50 million now, I would gladly give it all away and cut off my arms and legs to get him back. His death destroyed a dream I had for him. Only a father who has lost his only son can understand that. As I have already said, I know it's a popular belief that I'm a rogue, constantly stopping horses and fixing races. That's not like me at all. My answer to everyone was going to be through Charlie, who I knew was going to be good – and honest – at the job when his time came.

When I'd sent Charlie to the hardest taskmaster of them all, Bill O'Gorman, he'd passed with flying colours, and after a spell with Michael Dickinson in America the trainer had confided in me that he hadn't come across a seventeen-year-old like him. Charlie had been well schooled. He'd even been given a few lessons on Frankie Dettori's mechanical horse in his garage by Frankie's father, the great former Italian champion jockey, Gianfranco, during one of his visits. The difference between us was that he was going to operate in an honest way and without backing horses as I had been forced to as a means of survival in a sport where, if you don't cheat your owners, you're big odds against. A good friend of mine from back home, John McElroy, who passed away only recently himself, said a strange thing. 'It might have been lucky for him, this world we're living in.' It's a Catholic viewpoint, one that says when you're young and you answer to God as Charlie had done, there weren't too many black marks against you. You've barely had time to commit any grievous sins. When you get to my age you have plenty to repent for before you meet your Maker.

I wouldn't have got through Charlie's death if it hadn't been for Fr James O'Kane, Frankie Dettori, Patsy Byrne, Tommy Stack and all my immediate family, including my four sisters. They are Mary and Amelia, living in Northern Ireland, and Sheila, now in Manchester and Anne, who has settled in Kent. Tommy's probably my most trusted and valuable friend. Whenever there's a family dispute, which usually means Maureen and my daughters ganging up on me, they'd always say, 'We'll ring Tommy', because they know he's the only man I'll listen to. Maureen says he's the only man in the world who knows how to handle me. He has the key to my moods and mannerisms. If the occasion demands it, as he showed when Charlie died, he's a great organiser.

Tommy is one of the few people I admire. There can't be a less egotistical man in Ireland. He's not changed in thirty-five years and although he's a private man he has always enjoyed life to the full. We're different characters, because he's very outgoing whereas I'm the direct opposite. Tommy would relish socialising with owners at The Curragh, or wherever, while I would abhor it.

He's a Kerryman, and has Kerry cunning. Ask a Kerryman something and they'll always come back with another question. He knows exactly how to rub me up the wrong way. We've known each other since those days at Mungret College, where Tommy was a lay pupil, along with Barry Brogan and Bobby Barry, and I was a theological student. Our paths separated when he went up to Dublin to work in an insurance job and I went off to train for the priesthood. We first met at the Brogans' place where he would stay at weekends to learn to ride. The strange thing was that I could never imagine him riding or training. I thought it was the greatest waste of time I'd ever seen. I'd never have believed it if someone had said that he'd be twice champion jockey.

When he went to England in 1965 he knew no one and initially was considered a fairly moderate rider, but although he was a late developer there was no doubt that he had talent as he quickly showed when riding for the late Arthur Stephenson. He always had a good eye for a horse. He was very dedicated and that's how he's been through life. A combination of both has brought him his just rewards ... the only man, apart from Bruce Hobbs, to ride a Grand National winner and train two classic winners. He was champion National Hunt jockey in 1974–75 and 1976–77 before getting his permit to train in 1986 and a full licence two years later.

One story sums up the humour and audacity of the man. In 1977 I bought a half-share in the then unraced I'm A Driver from Tommy for £2,000 and took him to Ireland to be trained by Liam Brennan. He was flying on the gallops. When Tommy phoned me, I said, 'This horse is capable of winning a Derby.' He said, 'I've heard all that bull**** before.'

We took him to the big Galway Festival meeting for a bumper. Stack has never been a punter, but I told him, 'Have a monkey on him. He's a racing certainty.' I told my men to take every price and backed him to win a small fortune at that time, £30,000.

Well, the further he went, the further he got left behind and he finished tailed off. To make matters worse, on the way home my car, a cheap Lada, sold to me by my brother, broke down and all the punters jeered and hooted at me as they passed. It was all very humiliating. I don't think Stack ever had another bet.

Two months later, I exacted my revenge on the layers when I'm A Driver won a Terry Rogers-sponsored bumper at Naas.

Later, I sent him to the Dickinson stable where Michael rode him with great success. However, one day in 1978, when he was due to run at Newcastle in a novice hurdle, Tommy insisted on taking the ride. I'm A Driver was always a hard-puller and Michael's retort was, 'Don't annoy me. You wouldn't be able to hold him.' The only method of getting your own way with Michael was to keep on at him, day after day, and eventually he succumbed.

When we arrived at the course, which was shrouded in fog, I asked Tony Dickinson, 'How's he going?' The response from Tony, who had come to saddle I'm A Driver, was typically non-committal: 'I'm very pleased with him'. Mr Dickinson hated betting. He had known so many people lose money at the game and wanted me to take it easy. The horse was expected to win, though, and went off at 11–10 favourite.

In the parade ring, Mr Dickinson's firm instructions to Tommy were that he must try and settle the horse in behind. When the field passed the grandstand for the first time I'm A Driver was way out in front, quite contrary to what Tommy had been asked to do. After that we could see no more, so poor was the visibility. When they came into view again, a couple of furlongs from home, he was still in front and proceeded to win by seven lengths. Mr Dickinson was not entirely happy, though. He looked Tommy straight in the eyes, as was his custom with anyone he addressed.

Being a very tall man he had to bend right down to do so, before saying in a critical tone, 'I thought I told you to hold him up?'

'Oh, no trouble,' replied Tommy blithely.

'What do you mean, "no trouble"?' demanded Mr Dickinson.

'Once we passed the stands, and were out of your sight, he settled like a lamb,' said Tommy. I had to laugh to myself. If Mr Dickinson believed that, he'd believe anything!

Despite leading very different lives, we've frequently discussed horses on the phone and we meet up from time to time. I stayed with Tommy the night before he partnered Red Rum to his third Grand National. You remember strange things on these occasions, like stopping off at one of those motorway cafes on the way down to Aintree and having breakfast with him and his wife Liz. Now, I have my weaknesses and one of those is my food, but this was a real cholesterol-inducing dish – bacon and eggs and every sort of greasy food. I thought it was a bit odd for a jockey. But he never had much trouble with his weight. As we drove to Aintree we both made a promise to God – that if Red Rum won the Grand National we'd 'do' a Lough Derg. It's in County Donegal, and in its centre is an island where people go to fast and pray for three days. I'm ashamed to say we have yet to go ... but 1999 will see us there.

To watch racing, I'd always preferred Aintree to Cheltenham. There was not the same pushing and shoving. (I have great memories of a big win on L'Escargot, whom I'd fancied strongly. Tommy Carberry rode him.) But this day was different. After Tommy and Red Rum flashed past the post, it was one of the few occasions in my racing life when emotion took over. I spotted Betty Brogan in the crowd of well-wishers and she shouted 'Come on, Barney' as she joined the hordes giving Tommy his ovation; I did as I was bidden. It has never been my style to dash to the winners' enclosure after a race, but I've never witnessed scenes like it. We all got pushed up against the rails in the saddling enclosure. It was a frightening experience and I genuinely feared that we'd be crushed to death. I'd had a bet, a few thousand, but I really wasn't interested that day, I had just been willing the horse to win because of Tommy. It was one of the happiest days of my life.

Just to demonstrate the vagaries of the National Hunt

game, a few months later, on 5 September 1977, Tommy had a bad fall at Hexham. It wasn't even during the race. It happened when his horse reared over and propelled poor Tommy into the tarmac in the parade ring before rolling on him. A steam-roller couldn't have done him much more damage and some feared the worst. Tommy was lucky, although he probably didn't think so at the time: just a crushed and displaced pelvis and a badly damaged bladder. He couldn't ride again, we all said – could he? Not to partner Red Rum again and bid for an unthinkable fourth Grand National?

For three months he just lay there in Hexham Hospital in a cast, with weights and pulleys designed to pull his pelvis back into shape. In his fit state Tommy was only a whippet of a man; by the time they released him from the various contraptions he was down to eight stone. I kept in touch by phone and visited him the day after he was discharged and returned to his home in Tadcaster, North Yorkshire, to convalesce. I had never experienced anything like it. It was like his whole body had wasted away. He was a terrible colour, and it was like observing a stricken child, who could just walk, but could do little else, not even dress himself. As for riding again seriously in three or four months' time, he could forget it. I thought that was the end of him as a jockey. But I didn't know him as well as I thought. He drifted in and out of sleep, but as he just lay there, Tommy croaked, 'I'm coming back. I'm going to ride Red Rum in the Grand National.' This was December time, and I couldn't believe it. I thought it would be a miracle if he ever got on a stable hack again, let alone compete in the world's toughest race.

A few days later I accompanied him to the Sports Medicine Unit at the hospital in Leeds, where he was treated by the physiotherapist who dealt with Leeds United footballers. There was no power in his legs. They gave him weights on his ankles and he couldn't raise them. I remember looking out of the window as he struggled to do it, and tears welled up in my eyes as I thought to myself, 'Where is this man going to end up? All he's got to look forward to is disappointment.' He was actually crying out in pain. It was so upsetting. I half expected his foot to drop off. 'Just take it easy' was all I could think of to say, which was ridiculous really, considering Tommy was striving to do exactly the opposite.

But he achieved it, displaying great strength of character. Into January, he was doing circuit training and using the bicycle and rowing machine. Gradually he built his strength and weight up again. I still don't know how he did it, but he rode Red Rum in a gallop at the end of February. The following month, Tommy partnered Red Rum in his prep race, the Greenall Whitley Chase at Haydock, and though they only finished sixth behind Rambling Artist, it was a truly astonishing comeback. All seemed set for an emotional Grand National, but a week before the race Red Rum went lame. It was tough on Tommy, although the prospect of riding Red Rum can only have aided, and speeded his recovery. Undaunted, he won the Whitbread Gold Cup on Strombolus. It proved his swansong. Tommy went back to Ireland and retired to manage the Longfield Stud, part of Vincent O'Brien's empire, before starting an illustrious training career.

When he was in England I often used to go over and stay with him if I went racing in the north. We'd sit up until three or four o'clock in the morning talking. There was a particular explanation for that on my part. Tommy's was the coldest house in the world, because he'd never have any central heating. The bedroom was like an icebox. It was better to sit in front of the big fire and talk than go upstairs to bed and freeze. He also never seemed to have any food. The story was that he was always trying to save money. He'd say at the races the next day, 'You're not looking that well. Didn't you sleep last night?'

I'd say, 'Does it surprise you? I didn't get to bed until three or four.' He never seemed to take the hint.

After Charlie died I was in a trance-like state for weeks. But I knew I had to get back into action. It was on a Friday in March 1996, at Folkestone, that I decided to test myself to see whether I still retained my betting or training 'edge'. The Peasmarsh Selling Hurdle would have been swiftly forgotten by most people that day. Yet it was an emotional moment for me as I planned to run a horse called All Talk No Action, a gelding last seen out when he was pulled up lame at Huntingdon nearly three years earlier.

Charlie used to have a savings account at the Halifax Building Society, and he'd always be on to me about any plans for the horse because he looked after All Talk No Action and rode him out most days. He thought the horse was the business and wanted to be on when the time was right. Charlie would make me smile when he used to say, 'I want to give the Halifax plenty of notice that I want to make a withdrawal.' He'd add, 'This is the horse you can have the house on, dad. And there will be no chance of us ending up in a caravan at the side of the road.' He was killed before he got the chance to back his horse. About a week before, I had worked four horses over nine furlongs at Newmarket. Alison Broderick – now my assistant trainer Andrew Stringer's wife – rode the horse with instructions to lose eight or ten lengths on the bend, and when she straightened up to ask him for an effort, but under no circumstances pass the other three horses. I went away from work that morning with tears in my eyes. At the end, All Talk No Action had been cantering in behind the other three. His time had come.

I fancied him strongly, despite being off the course for 1,053 days, and had booked Mick Fitzgerald, a fine rider, to partner him at Folkestone while my regular jockey Eamon Murphy was due to ride Keep Hope Alive in the same race. That horse was getting on in years, he'd had leg trouble, and I was only running him to evaluate whether he'd stand any more racing, and maybe do me a turn at some later stage. Eamon may not have been very happy at that but, if you ride for me, you accept my arrangements.

An hour and a quarter before the race there was a mysterious phone call to the weighing room, and a message left. Something to the effect that, 'Eamon Murphy can't get to the course.' I only wanted jockeys I thought I could trust on my horses, so I withdrew Keep Hope Alive. Eamon then turned up and expressed ignorance of any phone call, suggesting it was a hoax, although afterwards I realised there was only one conceivable suspect. However, Eamon persuaded me to let him ride All Talk No Action and Mick, being the fair man that he is, and knowing that Eamon was struggling for winners at that time, agreed to be 'jocked off'.

In fairness, Eamon proceeded to give him a very sympathetic ride, winning by ten lengths from Lexus. I knew the horse would win; he'd been going so well at home. He was backed down from 10–1 to 4–1. I had £15,000 on at 8–1.

It was obvious to most people that the horse was lame coming in and he never saw a racecourse again. Yet, astonishingly, at the subsequent auction I had to go up to 15,200 guineas to buy him in, a course selling record. He was never doing anything but going back home, because he was Charlie's horse. I would have gone to £50,000 if necessary. I have to say that I have never claimed a horse out of a seller or claimer. If you bid for horses, you only contribute to the racecourse coffers. If someone has had a good touch with a horse, good luck to them. Why ruin it for them? You've got to be pretty mean to do so.

It later transpired that Eamon was, and still is, working for a telephone tipping line. My suspicions were first aroused by Eamon when he became anxious to have a feel at every horse in the yard. Some naive trainers might turn a blind eye to that kind of thing; but not me. I won't have anybody connected with my stable involved with those people. Indeed, BT once offered me the chance of having my own line, but I rejected it out of hand.

In my opinion, all these tipping services are thoroughly disreputable concerns. For one thing, there is an inducement for work riders to give their horse an easy piece of work, knowing they have plenty in hand, and then tipping them to these people. Also, if owners get wind of a gamble, and they know they are not going to get a decent price, they can demand that a trainer deliberately loses the race. After all, what does a gambling owner do when he's laid out a horse for a 'touch' and found his early price is 6–4? Well, the obvious answer is to get the horse stopped, and back him next time. Believe me, it goes on. I would ban tipping lines. I believe that, in many ways, they are as big a danger to the integrity of racing as doping.

They say that time does heal. I don't think it does. I think about Charlie ten times a day. What do I think about? I think about his greatest gift, which was his thought for others; and his favourite sayings, 'Let's get a bit of life, Dad' and 'Let's live a little, Dad.' When you come to the evening of your life, as I have, it's only natural to think of old age. I always thought that Charlie, at this stage of my life, would have been a joy.

Nobody can really know the pain. Nobody knows how you can feel except those who have suffered the same tragedy themselves. At least I have the comfort of my family, of whom I am immeasurably proud. Maureen is now a barrister, having studied law as a mature student. She was actually preparing to take her final bar exams when Charlie passed away. The law is very fulfilling for her, and from the start I wished her well. Everyone should use their brains to the maximum. My eldest daughter Catherine went to University and studied journalism. She's now an assistant film director, who's recently been working on a feature film in Northern Ireland. Maria-Louise has got a degree at college where she was studying the management of human resources.

THIRTY-TWO

'Don't lose that kid Murphy'

As I sat and waited for news of Declan Murphy in that hospital, the Walton Centre for Neurology, I blamed myself. It was a strange logic but I felt intense guilt, because without me entering his life he wouldn't have been here, wouldn't have been riding that horse at Haydock on that dreadful day, 2 May 1994. Now, here he was, in a deep coma, having been operated on, after suffering seven fractures of the skull and a broken jaw when he'd crashed at the last on the ill-fated Arcot and then been trampled on by another horse. I feared the worst as I went over and over in my mind how I'd persuaded a young Irish boy to come to England all those years before.

When I decided to move to Newmarket in 1984 it had always been my plan to have my own jockey. It's an essential part of running a stable like mine. I wanted a man who comes back to the yard after races and takes an interest in the horses. I also wanted a man I could depend on in a race. There are too many clowns around, who, at the first sign of a mistake, do not give a horse a proper ride.

When I first started out with Liam Brennan, I was very selective in my riders. I demanded intelligence, ability and insisted on men with honour, and found it in Willie Mullins and Ted Walsh. I like to think I can spot a fellow with brains, and found it with Willie who rode my three big bumper winners when I got my permit. He was straight as they come. Despite being an unpaid amateur, a breed who normally expect a 'brown envelope' to be slipped into their pocket by a trainer after a successful ride, Willie did exactly the opposite. After partnering a winner he would give the lads connected with the horse a few pounds, which I thought was a thoroughly gentlemanly thing to do. It didn't surprise me that Willie turned out to be an intelligent trainer, too. His winners have included the exceptional Florida Pearl, winner of the 1998 Royal and Sun Alliance Chase at Cheltenham. Ted has also done well in the trainers' ranks, as well as carving out a niche for himself as a racing pundit in Ireland.

I did consider asking Tommy Carmody, who I had previously brought over to ride for the Dickinsons. In the end I didn't approach him, but decided to find fresh blood, for which Tommy can be thankful because he was Irish champion jockey for the next couple of years. The problem was solved for me when John Power from Limerick told me that there was a very good jockey in his village, which bears the unusual name of Hospital. The problem was that he was still at school and was planning to go to university to study business.

Declan came up to Middleton House on a fine sunny day and I asked him a few questions, and the more we spoke the more I became convinced he was my man. Middleton was a daunting place for a boy just finishing secondary school that summer of 1984 and it could have all been too much for some lads, but nothing fazed him and I liked his articulate self-confidence. Declan had taken out an amateur licence and had been riding for the top trainer Kevin Prendergast, winner of the Irish St Leger and 2,000 Guineas, at weekends and holidays. He had ridden his first winner at Tralee three days after getting his licence and proceeded to partner two winners and two seconds from his first four rides, all on the Flat.

Declan had an impeccable riding pedigree. As a youngster

he had ridden a couple of hundred pony race winners. He was Irish champion at the age of twelve. By the time he came over in October he had already ridden sixteen winners. I had never actually seen him ride and he had revealed that he had been thinking of going on to university, but I said, 'I need a jockey to come over to England. Go away and think about it and come back and let me know.' I said I'd go and watch him riding, but I didn't bother. I felt I knew enough to satisfy me. Declan came back and said, 'I'll go with you.' I asked him what made up his mind. He replied that he had consulted about ten people with a knowledge of racing and nine said that he was completely mad. That he would get locked up, along with me. They all said he had too bright a future in Ireland. 'Only one said I should go.' I said, 'would it do any harm to ask the good news first. Who said you should go?' Declan responded: 'It was Tommy Carmody. He told me how you organised him to go over and ride for the Dickinsons and how that never did him any harm!' I knew then that he was his own man, and, by definition, my man.

I warned him that there would be questions asked about a Mr D. Murphy riding some of these decent horses, like The Hacienderos, without any experience and it wouldn't be easy at first. But I promised him this, 'I'll never put anyone else up on my horses. You have my word on that.' I kept to it, and even when he had injuries and suspensions I tried to avoid running my horses. He was my man and loyalty should work both ways.

As I saw it, he had to start some place, but taking him away from his homeland I had a moral responsibility to do my best for him. To be honest I could have got a better jockey in that first year. But I watched him enough on the gallops and schooling to know that he possessed talent. If he had been light enough he could have made a good Flat jockey, just as Carmody had been before he switched to jumps. Declan always had style, but after his first season in England, in which he rode six winners, I took him over to Charlie Whittingham's for three months. He rode a lot of his good horses in their work and learnt a lot about pace. I was one of the first to encourage a jockey from this side of the Atlantic to have a clock in his head, but it's become all the rage now, with the likes of Kieren Fallon following suit. He went over three times in all and we both learnt a lot. As Declan said, 'Charlie would only say things once – and you had to catch it. But it was a big help to my riding and it tightened up my loose ends.'

I said to Charlie one day, 'Can you give me one piece of advice to help me train these horses?' I expected him to talk about ideas on feed or working them, but he merely replied, 'Keep the numbers small – and don't lose that kid Murphy.' I used to say, 'If he ever stopped riding I would consider stopping training.' Well, I've carried on in a small way mainly because I can book a couple of young jockeys, Leighton Aspell and Gerry Hogan, that I know I can depend on. Leighton could be a champion, while Gerry's career has suffered very badly from too many injuries. But horses jump well for him and he's got plenty of bottle.

Declan was never that bothered about taking outside rides. He wouldn't partner bad horses for the sake of it. His number wasn't in any of the racing directories, and if a trainer wanted him badly enough they had to go and find him. One trainer who did was Tommy Stack, who, on my advice, booked Declan for Kingsmill in the 1989 Ladbroke, Ireland's richest handicap hurdle. There was a major gamble, and from 16–1 the horse was sent off 7–1 favourite. He only finished third, beaten four lengths by Redundant Pal, but Tommy, who is not the easiest man to ride for, came up to me afterwards and admitted, 'You were right. I was very impressed with him all round. I found him a bright, intelligent lad who will go places.' He had discovered that, apart from his skill in the saddle,

Declan will always tell you the truth and not many jockeys have the backbone to take that. Most will run for cover and mouth a lot of platitudes when asked for their verdict on a horse.

Inevitably, it wasn't long before he was offered other jobs, and eventually he joined Josh Gifford, who, great jockey that he was himself, probably never had a jockey in his employment like him. I couldn't have been more pleased for the lad. But in those early days I advised him to bide his time and I constantly reminded him that he wasn't ready yet. That was partly because he was not getting enough experience on my horses. I wasn't running them enough. In addition, he wasn't everyone's first choice for an outside ride, because my name preceded his. It was guilt by association. There was this popular view among owners, 'Oh, well, he's riding for that Barney Curley and he will get Murphy to "stop" the horse.' That's not just paranoia. I know it went on.

There was one occasion, in 1989, when the Royston trainer John Jenkins had a horse named Grey Salute entered for a big race at Kempton. He was a bit tricky to handle, but Declan, on one of his rare outside rides, had got the horse to settle brilliantly in a race at Fontwell and told Jenkins straight afterwards: 'He'll win the Lanzarote and the Tote Gold Trophy.' He did just that – but sadly not with Declan in the saddle. Just before the prestigious Lanzarote Hurdle at Kempton, Declan came up to me with a chastened look on his face, and was nearly in tears, He said, 'Guess What?' I sensed the worst and he continued, 'Dunwoody's got the ride.' I discovered that John had been told by the owner, a bookmaker called Tony Hayward, to book Richard Dunwoody because he was concerned that 'Barney Curley might get Declan Murphy to "stop" the horse.'

I've already emphasised that there is no way that I have been, or would be, party to that. I'd never fix races or dope horses, but there's no harm in repeating it. I regard it as morally wrong, and anyone who needs confirmation of that should ask anybody – including every bookmaker, apart from that one, who was clearly talking through ignorance – that I've had dealings with. Of course, if there were any decency in the world, then Dunwoody would have refused the ride under those circumstances, but I'm afraid, for all his ability, his reputation in the game is: 'Me Fein', as we say in Ireland. *Me myself, Me first.*

To add to the insult, I have already stressed that Declan is one of the jockeys that you could never have got at. I felt awful for him, and was furious. It was the last thing I'd ever dream of doing. The switch had been so late that Declan would have been within his rights to refuse to be 'jocked off', and that's what he did initially. But John Jenkins, obviously highly embarrassed, had told him, 'Either you get off that horse – or I'll lose the horse!' Declan was still not having it, but eventually agreed with Jenkins that he'd give up the ride if Dunwoody gave him his winning percentage – a not inconsiderable sum – if he won the race. Declan's still waiting for the money. Maybe Dunwoody has it invested in PEPs for him!

Of course, Declan and I were close. He was like a second son to me and I felt very protective towards him. I remember when the Jockey Club stripped me of my licence in 1987, everybody told him that I'd never get it back. And that was a hard thing to take for a young man who'd nailed his colours firmly to my mast. When they took away my licence, Declan was on holiday in Ireland. When he returned, there were tears rolling down his cheeks. They were all saying in Ireland that we were finished, it was the end of the road. I felt really sorry for him, and though I tried very hard to explain that, no matter how long it took, I would get my licence back, I'm not sure if he really believed me.

Declan was always going to attract the stewards because he

rode as though he had two stone up his sleeve, even if he didn't. Sometimes his horses found absolutely nothing off the bridle. He had a smooth effortless style, which led you to believe that he could win races from any position he liked. Josh Gifford's Deep Sensation in the 1993 Queen Mother Champion was a perfect example. That horse was an enigmatic character who needed perfect timing and kidding along to bring him through on the line. Put his head in front too soon, and you were doomed. He learnt in America how to ride at a pace with which the horse is comfortable. The public love to see a jockey rowing away. It looks as though they're trying, but too often it achieves nothing; 99.9 per cent of people on the racecourse have no idea how to read a race. If you really want to get a horse beaten – and every trainer, if he knows his horse, should know the best way to ride him – give him the wrong instructions.

He won three races on Assultan, who was not an easy ride, which I don't believe anybody else would have done. I remember when he won at Sandown, somebody next to me who obviously didn't know who I was, said at half-way, 'Well, obviously Curley's not off today.' But he put the horse in the race when he wanted to, and ended up winning easily.

Declan also had problems with use of the whip in those early days. He did sometimes use it like Pete Sampras holds his racquet for a forearm smash and it didn't look pretty. That is now outlawed anyway, and even then was discouraged. Where the whip is concerned, there are three types of horses: those who always do their best, those who do just enough and those that are completely idle, when a stick is most necessary. They're like humans really; without using the stick, there's no chance of any effort with the latter. If there's a horse that's not trying, I would say hit it as hard as you can within the rules. When it comes to the welfare of racehorses, I take a pragmatic, rather than a sentimental, view. They are there to run, and I am in favour of any means that will encourage them to do that.

It took Declan some time to adjust his style to keep his use of the whip within the rules and he did incur several suspensions, but we did notch up one notable victory against the Jockey Club which also helped improve procedures. He had finished third on a horse of Ian Matthews called Matbar in the Fairview Homes Handicap Hurdle at Kempton in November 1988. After the race Declan was hauled in by the stewards because the racecourse vet Michael Henigan reported the gelding had four whip marks on the stifle, an area at the top of a horse's leg where whip blows are outlawed. He had already received two bans over misuse of the whip. Declan was found guilty once more, but on this occasion we didn't agree at all. I rushed the horse back to Newmarket, got a Polaroid camera, asked a local vet to take photographs, timed it as being only ... three hours after the race, and appealed against the Kempton stewards' findings.

Less than three weeks later, Declan won his appeal and the ban was lifted after I produced the photographic evidence which contradicted the racecourse vet's view. The Jockey Club's disciplinary committee found the horse had been marked, but my photos, taken on the evening of the race, showed they had not been administered in the wrong place. We also asked them to study a video of the race which illustrated that Declan had not used his whip with sufficient severity to injure.

After that case, the Jockey Club instructed that there had to be a camera available for racecourse vets to take photographs immediately to avoid such disputes in the future. Had we not acted so promptly we could not have successfully appealed. The Jockey Club denied a witch-hunt, but the facts dispute that. There was no doubt some racecourse officials were out to persecute Declan because of his association with me. I was very concerned that it would affect his confidence. One minute he was being told his whip action was too high, the next moment too low. My attitude was that a trainer should defend his jockey to the hilt, unless he has clearly contravened the rules. My training to be a Jesuit priest taught me the value of strict discipline, but it must be administered correctly and fairly, otherwise it comes into contempt.

I don't want to give the impression that I was spoiling for a fight with the Jockey Club at every spurious opportunity and I would not like my motives misconstrued. I am no nihilist, with contempt for all authority. There were some days when the Jockey Club cheered my heart, too. Bruce Hobbs, who rode a Grand National winner and trained a classic winner – and who, incidentally, had been one of the disciplinary trio who had originally found against me in the 'Robin Goodfellow case' – recognised that Declan was an excellent horseman, but continually in trouble with the stewards. Hobbs was then on the disciplinary committee. We'd come out of an inquiry one day, and, the gentleman that he is, he invited Declan round to his house in Newmarket. Hobbs gave a paternal talk to him, told him that he was a good jockey and how to improve himself to become a great one, how to steer away from trouble. Bruce talked a lot of sense and he was genuinely interested in Declan. That was a big gesture by Hobbs. Declan needed it, too, because he was down there, seemingly, every fortnight. It was the moment that changed Declan's outlook towards authority. Before that, to be candid, he didn't have much respect for authority, which is understandable when nine times out of ten they were wrong.

However, there was one occasion when Declan was entirely to blame for a suspension. My young protégé had broken his collar-bone in a fall, an injury not uncommon for a jockey and which usually heals quite quickly. Now Dave Thom is a tough man, he rides out every day, despite being over seventy, and he said immediately, in that manner beloved of a gnarled old veteran of the saddle when confronted with a callow youth,

'Oh, in our day, when we broke our collar-bones we were back in ten days.' Declan at that time was young and easily influenced and Dave obviously hit a sensitive spot. I had a four-year-old hurdler called Solvent running in a novice at Sedgefield on 7 April 1987, and Declan was aware that I wasn't taking him there for a breath of fresh air. When I asked him, Declan declared, 'I'm fit and ready.' I said, 'Are you sure?' and he convinced me he was, and that he was determined to ride the horse. This was the same day I had a call from Charlie Whittingham telling me Alianna had died, after I'd refused half a million pounds for her.

As we drove up to Sedgefield, which is a tedious, long journey from Newmarket, I noticed he was swallowing a few tablets. I passed no remarks, in my innocence assuming they were part of his medication to help the knitting of the collar-bone. When we reached the course Declan was examined and was passed fit by the doctor, so I had no qualms on that score. Solvent had been placed a few times for Michael Jarvis on the Flat as a three-year-old, but as yet had not shown much over timber, although that did not stop him starting at 4–1 second favourite. I expected a good show.

During the race, a not particularly competitive novice hurdle, it looked encouraging as he disputed the lead until two hurdles out. Then just when the moment came that you looked for Declan to give him some encouragement from the saddle, it was obvious to anyone that my esteemed young jockey was not moving a muscle. I knew Declan was always cool in his finishes, but this was ridiculous, although somehow the horse, probably more from his own volition than Declan's wishes, stayed on steadily on the run-in to finish fourth of seventeen, only two heads and a length and a half behind the winner. It turned out that the horse had pecked on landing during the race and Declan had aggravated the break in his collar-bone. A little later I found him at the car, swallowing more of the same pills. I quizzed him on it, and it transpired that they were strong painkillers. Declan could barely move and could just about stand up straight. He was fine on the horse until it started to pull. Once it did, he was in agony. When the stewards called us in it was hardly a great surprise. Declan was given a ban for 'misleading the course doctor'. They were right. He had. The stewards were totally in the right that day; he shouldn't have been riding. The case was sent on to Portman Square and he was stood down for four months.

Declan wouldn't be alone in his deception. Jockeys are so determined to get back into the saddle as quickly as possible, because if they're out of sight, they're out of trainers' minds. There's probably a lot riding who have deceived the course doctor if you actually examined them stringently before a race.

Every trainer, from the biggest in the country, John Gosden, downwards, depends on those around him to make the business a success and I was no exception. Three of us were involved in decisions on training, running and riding my horses: Declan, Paddy Griffin, who had come over with me from Mullingar, and myself. Paddy is a lovely man, who did everything in the yard. (In his spare time he even taught my children to drive on spare ground near the stables. I never knew anything about it. I just thought they were exceptionally talented kids!) We rarely had disputes because I respected the opinions of Declan and Paddy and once we put our heads together we'd often as not arrive at the same answer. But once I had made up my mind I expected Declan to keep to his instructions. An illustration of why it is so important to have your own jockey, and not some fellow going for glory, giving a horse a hard time and winning by 20 lengths, came at Newbury with Keep Hope Alive.

It was soon after the horse had been involved in that suspected doping incident at Ascot. I thought the horse was not quite right and, though I entered him in a race at Newbury,

I was actually more concerned about his next target, a big novice hurdle at Fairyhouse where his owner, Joe 'Big-Bucks' Donnelly, could see him run. Declan was not aware of that. I prefer a jockey to think about the immediate job in hand, not about some future race. I wanted Keep Hope Alive to win at Newbury if he could – I had him backed – but the important thing was that I wanted him to be given a relatively easy race. I told Declan to wait with him and hit the front after they'd cleared the last. As it happened, he clattered the last anyway and he was beaten. Declan, who was always well able to speak his corner, made the point that the horse had been bolting with him in the straight and if he'd ignored what I'd said and taken it up at the second last, they'd have gone on to win. He may well have been right, and another jockey may have 'used his initiative', but Declan knew better than to deviate from his orders. Under no circumstances did I want that horse given a hard race. Unfortunately, my initial suspicions were confirmed at Fairyhouse where Keep Hope Alive had to be pulled up after jumping just two hurdles, having burst a blood vessel. He was never the same again. Joe didn't lose his faith in me. At Galway in the summer of 1998, he gave me an order for another horse. He always says I'm an honest gangster.

In that fall at Haydock Declan had suffered multiple skull fractures, a blood clot on the brain and was in a coma for five days. It had been said he was four minutes from death. I had flow up straight away and stayed several days. I honestly couldn't see him pulling through. It didn't look good and I was most worried. Even when they took him home to recuperate, and he was nursed by his then girlfriend Joanna Park, there was something eating away at my insides. There was a constant pain in the pit of my stomach.

I used to call round regularly and I'd just sit there, saying nothing. He wasn't in any condition to have a conversation. His brain had been terribly damaged, and for all I knew he would never be able to speak properly again. It was like a pilgrimage for me. I suppose I felt that my presence alone would help him get better. Maybe I'd get up and look at the wall and wander around. One day I was all ready to depart when Declan suddenly declared: 'You're not doing me much good, saying nothing and then, after an hour, just leaving.' My heart leapt. I went home as happy as Larry. I knew then he was on the way to recovery.

It was several months later that he got back into the saddle and astounded everyone by winning on Geoff Lewis's Jibereen on 17 October, the following year, at Chepstow. Much was said about whether that comeback race – the annual Flat versus jump jockeys affair – was 'hooky', in other words set up by the other riders as an act of compassion. I don't honestly think so. I know many of those jockeys and the majority of them would cut each other's throat even to win a seller. Once a race is underway, charity is not part of their vocabulary. Of course, I couldn't comment on how Declan came to have one of the best handicapped horses in the race. To me, he was a good bet, whoever the rider was, and I was most definitely on.

That race had a beneficial effect in two senses. It was a great boost for him, but it also brought home to him just how arduous it would be to ride regularly once more. The doctors had passed him fit, but I think he knew in his heart that he would never be the same jockey again. And there was always the danger of another fall. The brain can only take so much punishment. I think most of us were relieved when he announced his retirement. I was quoted at the time that I would hand over my training operation to Declan if he survived, but to be frank there's nothing much left worth handing over to an ambitious young man. Anyway, I always advised him not to go into training and so far he's taken my advice.

THIRTY-THREE

Travels with Lester

Since arriving in Newmarket, I've always had an excellent relationship with Lester Piggott and his wife, Susan. Indeed, when I started up he sent me a horse, Paleface, to train. We thought it might be a Triumph Hurdle type, but sadly he broke down. There was also a spell, in the summer of 1992, after we left Harraton Court, when we had our horses at Susan Piggott's yard for twelve months before moving on to Bob Champion's yard, called The Beeches, where we are still based now. We had our own barn at Susan's, in which we stabled twelve horses. I don't think she knew what she was letting herself in for. Susan is meticulously tidy and organised, and Declan and Charlie immediately changed everything around and made a complete mess of everything.

I've often accompanied the maestro on his riding trips, including a visit to South Africa together, and a few years ago Maureen and I went on holiday with him in Mauritius. I've always loved the water but I can swim about five yards without getting into trouble. I hadn't realised how strong the current was. I started drifting and was well out of my depth. I was getting to that stage when you start to panic, as you realise you can't touch the bottom. Suddenly, this familiar face with a deceptively strong, emaciated body had grabbed me firmly and was tugging me back to the shore. My rescuer dismissed my thanks. 'You got to be careful, you shouldn't be doing that,' he muttered in that unmistakable grunt, as that perpetual smile cracked that leathery face. Then he quietly carried on as though absolutely nothing had happened.

That tells you much about the man, who is so unfairly maligned by those who don't know him. His meanness is just an act. In fact, he's very thoughtful. I've never paid for anything when I'm out with him. The night after he was released from jail in 1988, he invited six of us out to dinner. Susan, his head lad Joe Oliver, Jenny Goulding, Bryn Crossley, and Maureen and myself. Despite what you might have expected, not a bitter word at his fate was uttered all night. He accepted his punishment without a whinge and I considered it a big honour to be present that night. And he paid.

I must take some responsibility for Lester making his comeback in the saddle after he was released from prison. Even at his age, it seemed such a waste of a God-given talent, and something told me he just needed some persuasion. At first, Lester was adamant that he wasn't interested. He was retired, and that was it. But when I've got a point to make I'm like a dog with a bone, refusing to let go. Frankie Dettori often says to me, 'Take off your hat', which is his way of saying, 'Get off your high horse.' Even when we're exiles, we Irish like a *ceilidh*. We just go round and call in on our friends, without invitation. Two of those I often visit in Newmarket are Bill O'Gorman and Lester. At Susan and Lester's, in the Hamilton Road, I'd sit there with him on the opposite side of his big wide table, 'You want to make a comeback,' I spouted off with a religious fervour that would have made an evangelist proud. 'You're as good as anybody riding.' Then I'd leave after half an hour. He'd just smile.

One day Susan, who had the licence, had a runner at Newbury and Lester drove me down to watch it and we talked again about him making a comeback. Later, he dropped me off back at my place and walked straight into the house and switched on Teletext to see the results from The Curragh. He was interested to see how Vincent O'Brien's horses had run. At that moment I knew he was on the way back. He started riding again in October 1990 and rode a horse called Nicholas to victory at Chepstow for Susan before reuniting with Vincent O'Brien and producing that marvellous performance to get Royal Academy up on the line in the Breeders' Cup Mile at Belmont Park on 27 October. As I watched him do that, tears came into my eyes. I knew what he had been through and this was pay-back night. It was a great achievement at his age for a fellow who had been a guest of Her Majesty to come back and do something like that. It tells you a lot about the man.

I often travelled with Lester on his visits to Ireland, acting as a kind of minder-advisor. On our journeys he might only talk every hour, but what he says makes sense and at least you don't get an earache like you do with some people I could mention. One occasion I recall particularly was on 15 July 1991 when he made a guest appearance at Killarney, indisputably Ireland's most scenic racecourse. Not that Lester would have particularly appreciated the breathtaking landscape, dominated by the 834ft high Purple Mountain. Single-minded that he was, Lester was fired up by partnering three winners for his old comrade-in-arms Vince O'Brien, and also rode for Paddy Prendergast and Patrick Flynn. It drew a record crowd of 6,000.

With Charlie accompanying us, we had flown by a private light plane, but as we neared the local airfield at Farranfore, eight miles away, we had discovered it was fog-bound, so Lester's pilot, Peter Winborne, flew to Cork instead. That meant a drive of more than fifty miles to the course, so time was getting tight for him to ride in the third, at 6.30 pm. Somebody at the course must have had a quiet word in someone's ear, because on touching down we were given a Garda escort. We made rapid time and drew up outside the course, whereupon a Garda opened my side of the car expecting to find Lester. Instead I stepped out. 'Jesus,' he exclaimed. 'What's the country coming to? It's bloody Barney Curley they're giving escorts to now.' The same fellow had been on custom duty on the border and had given me plenty of stick a few months previously. My car had been full of produce you couldn't get in the South, like Cookstown sausages and bacon, which I loved, and which were not allowed to be brought in.

It was a splendid evening for Killarney racecourse secretary Finbarr Slattery, who was retiring after twelve years and who had harboured a life-long ambition to see Lester ride at his track. Lester enjoyed nothing better than returning to a country which, if it is possible, revered him even more than his own. Pilot Peter told Finbarr that he had never seen Lester as happy as he had been at Killarney, and that wasn't just a platitude to the host. We stayed overnight at the Cahernane Hotel and the following morning Lester, Finbarr, Charlie and me were taken for a tour of the lakes and Muckross House on Mick Kearney's pony and trap, or Jaunting Car as it was called. Lester flew straight on to Leicester, where he had three winners.

Another of Lester's guest appearances was a couple of years later at Ballinrobe, out west in County Mayo, overlooking Lough Mask. But that was soured when he found that one of his mounts, trained by Declan Gillespie, had been given instead to Michael Kinane who would not give it up. I laid into both trainer and jockey, verbally of course, and told them both that they were a disgrace and a few other worse names. It was outrageous. After all, the crowd had only turned up to see Lester. We went and relaxed by one of the steeplechase fences and I said to Lester, 'Don't bother riding at all, we'll go back to the hotel and go out on a boat.'

Lester tended to follow my lead when we were in Ireland. As we were about to leave, Walter Halley, chief medical officer of the Irish Turf Club, demanded to know what was going on. When I told him, he was horror-struck. 'If Lester doesn't ride,' he said, 'They'll burn down the stands.' I had a lot of respect for Walter and eventually we agreed that Lester should stay and ride in two other races, for which he'd been booked. But it didn't end there. I was called before the stewards, having been charged with insulting Kinane and Gillespie. They asked me if I'd verbally abused them. 'I most certainly have,' I replied, refusing to take it back or apologise. In the end, they let me off but it was a real whitewash job. I don't think they wanted their big day poisoned by controversy.

It may not appear a matter of great consequence, but I felt ashamed to be an Irishman that day. To those people there Lester was king and these two small-minded characters had tried to ruin it for him and the racegoers. I know that John Oxx and Johnny Murtagh, in the same situation, would have given up the ride.

I would always help Lester out if he was in a fix. A few years ago, the newspapers made a lot of his relationship with his girlfriend, Anna Ludlow, an interest which heightened when it was revealed that she had had a baby by him, named Jamie. The baby had been born at Addenbrooke's Hospital in Cambridge and Lester desperately wanted to visit his son, but without running the gauntlet of all the press photographers and reporters who, he was aware, would be waiting for him outside.

'How can we get in?' he asked me.

'Leave it to me, Lester', I told him, and arrived at his house in my car. I should explain that this wasn't any car, but Arney's car.

Now, as an Irishman, I could never understand the English

preoccupation with pet dogs. I thought it was a bit soft to have one following you around. I'd only been used to working dogs, like my father's greyhounds. In fact, at White House stables I had a couple of rottweilers, Theo and Cleo, who were very effective guard dogs. Too effective. A couple of clergymen came to visit once and they nearly lost their arms. Eventually, the dogs had to go.

But with Arney – I wanted to call him Barney, but the family objected – I now comprehend what pleasure a pet dog can give to a family. He is my pride and joy, a huge Saint Bernard, who has always slept outside in a car. At the time I had bought him an old, red VW Golf to use as his kennel. He loves to ride around the block in it. If he doesn't, he has this habit of digging huge holes with his enormous feet. Arney just lay down in the back seat each night, and you can imagine, with all the hairs he shed, the state it was in. *That* was the car I drove round to Lester's. He didn't look too convinced, but I told him to get in the back and when we approached the hospital, to keep his head down. Of course, the media were all looking out for a modern, stylish car, with Lester at the wheel. Nobody took a blind bit of notice when I drove in in that nondescript VW, with Lester out of sight in the back, and he was able to see Jamie without intrusion.

THIRTY-FOUR

Helping Frankie

Frankie Dettori had already entered my life by the time Charlie was killed, and, in truth, having some influence over his career was some consolation for the loss of my son. I used to say things to Frankie that I said to Charlie. I wanted to instil in him the qualities that I thought were most important in life. When I start expounding my views, he laughs and says, 'You've got your hat on now; for God's sake take it off!'

I first met Frankie at Tattersalls' autumn sales in Newmarket in November 1989, when he was coming up to nineteen. He already knew who I was, having seen me on a Channel 4 discussion programme on gambling called After Dark. He was just a young lad, an apprentice with that fine trainer Luca Cumani. Some years later, Frankie told me that I had impressed him. I talked a lot of sense and he thought it might not be a bad idea to get to know me. I began to watch him riding, and what I saw really impressed me. I thought we could have a successor to the king, Lester Piggott. But I also knew that to be the finished article he had to possess other qualities. Honour and thoughtfulness have always been at the top of my list. One day he called at our house in Stetchworth and during our conversation I told Frankie that I might have a winner next week, if he could ride him. After a few minutes talking to him, I said to myself, 'This young man has a very sharp brain, similar to Lester's. If he can ride, he could be the business.' As he was leaving, I looked him in the eye and said, 'Omerta,' which is Italian for 'silence' or 'tell no-one'. Frankie kept it to himself and the horse duly won. After that, I never felt he'd let me down. That evening he even brought me round the jockey's prize, a bottle of brandy.

For a couple of years Frankie's star had been in the ascendancy. He was performing well and getting noticed. Some commentators were beginning to compare him with Sandy Barclay. Then, during the first half of 1993 it became well known in Newmarket, and soon far beyond, that things were not going well for him. It was at this same time that Frankie had split rather acrimoniously from Luca Cumani, after four years as stable jockey, with the intention of riding out in Hong Kong and broadening his experience, as well as earning big money. I was very concerned, and asked myself where it was all going to end? I'd already decided that in life you tackle a man's problem when he's down, not when he's still on a high. Timing is always vital in life. When the adrenalin is flowing, and all appears well with the world, you keep your own counsel because the person concerned almost certainly won't listen to any advice.

I'd watched him closely, and, unlike my betting habits, I'd kept my ears open. And what I'd heard I didn't like. As he has admitted himself, he was spending too much time out enjoying himself, drinking and, as was to become public later, worse. He was, to use that euphemism, sowing his wild oats. He was drifting. And as far as his riding was concerned, he wasn't concentrating. He was flash, a jack-the-lad, with money in his pocket and not thinking straight. There was an occasion when he went along to a charity auction and was persuaded to bid £17,000 for a painting which the auctioneer claimed was of Nijinsky and signed by Lester. The problem was the horse in the painting was a chestnut – Nijinsky was a bay. Suffice to say, that piece of 'art' is not on the wall of his home.

I remember flying with him and Ray Cochrane to Goodwood one day. Frankie was half asleep in the back and Ray said, 'Here, Frankie, look at the paper and see if I've got a ride in the third.' Frankie obligingly started rifling through the *Sporting Life*. Now, the third race that day was the Sussex Stakes, in which everybody knew Ray was riding the favourite Selkirk.

It came to a head one day in May 1993. We frequently used to share cars and aircraft to and from races, and Frankie, Bruce Raymond and I had flown together to Goodwood, where one of Frankie's mounts was an Ian Balding horse I fancied named Mount Templar. I had a bet of £6,000-to-win-£15,000 and Frankie rode a stinker. Ian let him off the hook by saying the horse had a wind problem, but regardless of that, Frankie was indecisive. He couldn't seem to make up his mind whether to make the running or hold him up. He took neither one option nor the other. I said nothing. The lost bet was irrelevant, but inside I was angry with him, which was unusual for me.

I'll admit it, I was fed up with him and on the flight back I didn't say anything. I don't mind losing fair and square, but to my mind he had not given the horse a good ride.

We couldn't land at Newmarket because of poor visibility and had to divert to Cambridge. We shared a cab back to our cars in Newmarket and it was on the way that his mobile phone went. There were a lot of whispered words and he sounded agitated. I was in the front and didn't really hear what was going on behind me, but suffice to say by the time we got back to Newmarket he didn't look at all well. I asked him who had been on the phone. 'News of the World', he muttered. It transpired that they had discovered the fact that he had been warned by the police over possession of drugs in London. If that was bad enough, the incident – minor as it turned out – was to mean that his invitation to Hong Kong was rescinded.

In the former British colony they take that sort of misdemeanour rather more seriously than we do.

At that moment, he wasn't a popular, wealthy, confident jockey, but a drifter. And I had seen it coming for some time. You only needed to look at his riding record. Having hit the century the previous season, coming up to Derby week he was on the fourteen-winner mark. That said it all. The slide had been inevitable. He had achieved too much, too soon, and with all the adulation he'd received, if you'd given him a cape he would have probably gone out and tried to fly like Superman. I didn't start an inquest, but just said to him, 'Have you any interest in this job?'

He said, 'I do.'

'Do you want to get ahead?'

He replied, 'I do'.

'Then come round to my house at eight o'clock tonight and we'll have a game of snooker.'

It must have been an incongruous sight. Frankie, who turned up immaculately turned out and carrying his own cue, and me, in scruffy jumper and trousers as usual. I'm not very good at snooker, but we played and I could tell Frankie was as low as you could get.

Eventually I said, 'You have a God-given talent. Very few people have that. You're one of the best I've ever seen. You can be as good as Lester. But you're ruining it.'

He just looked at me with those dark eyes of his. I wasn't too hard on him. It wouldn't have helped, and anyway I appreciated that here was a man of but still tender years who had arrived in a completely different environment from what he was used to. It was inevitable that the adulation would go to his head. By then I had bought my nightclub in Windsor, and I knew from first-hand experience the pain and suffering drugs can inflict on an impressionable, and not really worldly wise, young man. He promised to keep away from such temptations

I knew he was being straight with me. I said, 'Are you going to put your best foot forward?'

'I am,' he said.

I said, 'Well, just go out and ride and be a man of honour!'

You can tell when people really mean what they say, and I knew from the firm way he responded that he would be alright. He accepted his faults, without bluster and pleaded guilty without demur. But I had one final message for him. 'Don't let me down.' I had faith in him. The question was, would others?

At the time it was well known that Michael Roberts's job with John Gosden as Sheik Mohammed's first jockey was in jeopardy. Excellent rider that he was, the diminutive South African just didn't have the physique to get hold of those big, strong colts and there were constant rumours that he would be replaced. The next day I headed down to John Gosden's stables at Stanley House in Newmarket. I knew I was taking a chance and many a trainer would have had me out on my ear for my impudence, certainly they wouldn't have given me a hearing, but there I was on his doorstep asking him to give Frankie Dettori the best riding job in racing. I also knew that you couldn't deal with a more reasonable man than John, who by then had been back in England for around five years having previously trained successfully in the USA. As a former assistant to both Sir Noel Murless and Vincent O'Brien, his training pedigree was impeccable. But there was another factor that drew me into my car that day. I had met John out in California, where his barn was just down the way from Charlie Whittingham, with whom I had had a few horses in the early eighties. I never appear to be looking at things, but I notice a lot.

John and his wife Rachel were very special people. I believed he'd give me a fair hearing and he knew that I was not a bad judge, of character or ability. I told him that, in my opinion, Frankie Dettori was one of the greatest jockeys I'd ever seen and should be given a chance. He listened to me quietly, not saying much, and as I was leaving, he just said, 'Barney, do you think he's going to be OK?'

I said, 'I do.'

'Right,' he said. 'Bring him down.'

In hindsight, it sounds all so straightforward, but at the time young Gianfranco's name hardly inspired confidence. They were stories about him not turning up, or arriving late to work because of his night-time excesses, and in a place like Newmarket the carrier pigeon of bad report is fast on the wing. My man from Milan was in limbo, had lost his way, and although he was brimming with potential he had a long way to claw back. This was the last station on the railway before oblivion and if he didn't get off at this stop he wasn't getting off at all. Riding for Sheik Mohammed, who had the best horses in the world, was the kind of job that required an impeccable attitude. He couldn't afford to put a foot wrong, because if the thing ended in ignominy it wouldn't be Frankie who would get the blame, it wouldn't be me, but John who was putting his head on the block. The two of us drove down the long avenue that leads to Stanley House on the Bury Road. It is an imposing, daunting place at the best of times and Frankie, for all his normal ebullience, must have felt like I had when I first went to boarding school. For my part, the experience was rather like Jesse James bringing his brother Frank down to the local bank manager for a job. But I knew John was a man of honour and would keep to his word if he gave him a chance. I was also confident John would bring the best out of him, support him and give him time to develop. He was what we call in Ireland a 'proper man', a man of integrity.

I said nothing. I just sat there and watched. John laid down the law to him firmly about what he expected. He demanded 100 per cent cooperation, and a disciplined approach. If he had to go to Carlisle to ride one horse, when there were three outside rides available at Sandown, he'd go up to Cumbria. Frankie was a bit subdued, naturally so; here was a man without a job trying to land the one that was coveted by every jockey in the land.

John said that Frankie could come down and ride out, and we left. On the way back I said to him, 'I want you to become champion jockey.' As an added incentive, not that he really needed one, I offered him my house. He had always admired our place in Stetchworth, and it made me laugh the way he used to wander round eyeing it up, like a prospective buyer, but with not nearly enough, at this stage, to do so. It had a pool and a sauna and a snooker room, just the place for a young jockey. I said, 'If you become champion I'll sell it to you.' And I was as good as my word. In 1996 we 'swapped' houses, Frankie and his wife Catherine moving into White House stables, my family into his place in Centre Drive. It was a little smaller, but it didn't bother me in the least and suited my family ideally.

But that was two years later. For the moment, my advice to him was straightforward. 'Get stuck in, talk to no one and work.' His father, with whom he has often had a volatile relationship, gave him the same message. Much has been made of the period when he declined press interviews and was criticised for doing so. We just felt that for twelve months he had to concern himself less with getting himself in the newspapers and concentrate totally on his riding. That didn't come easy to him, because he loves talking to people, but it was part of the master-plan and he complied reluctantly. When he had been at his lowest ebb, I felt that some newspapers had tried to 'trash' him anyway, so I lost no sleep about their futile attempts to talk to him now. I told him, 'You'll be alright if you have peace of mind. You've got to get the balance right. Aiming high is one thing; but you don't have to rule the world.' I think he's got it about right now. Suffice to say, by the end of the season he had ridden 147 winners and finished second in the

Championship. He had a short holiday, came back on the all-weather, which he detests because it is so cold, and became Champion Jockey.

To be honest, I am more nervous about Frankie doing well than if I had fifty grand on a horse. At first, I felt a personal responsibility for his every ride. The worst day was when Lammtarra, the 1995 Derby winner, was due to contest the King George VI and Queen Elizabeth Diamond Stakes at Ascot in July. It was normally a meeting I attended without fail, but that year I couldn't face it. It was irrational, I suppose, I just had it in my mind that if Frankie won on this day he'd finally made it, established himself as a top-class jockey. It would be a vindication of my faith in him. The trouble is the best-laid plans you have for someone can go wrong and my stomach was churning.

An hour or so before the race, I just got into my car and drove. Even now I'm not sure where I went, but I ended up inside a betting shop ten or fifteen minutes before the race. 'Not racing today, Barney?' somebody said, and I started burbling on about a relation being ill, which was totally untrue. Then someone began asking me about my next coup. For once I didn't mind the chit-chat. It took my mind off the race. As history will record, Lammtarra won and Frankie rode a brilliant race. He was 9–4 favourite, but I didn't have a cent on him. Like Tommy Stack winning the Grand National many years before, I was just delighted for the jockey. On occasions like that money doesn't speak. That day, for me, Frankie Dettori had been crowned. He was now The King.

Frankie was flying off to Chicago soon afterwards, but he still took the time to phone me on his mobile and say, 'Thanks for everything' – which I thought was a wonderful gesture. Lammtarra then went on to record a wonderful treble in the Arc and few will forget that magnificent ride Frankie gave him and the exuberant celebrations afterwards. Since then, I've continued to give him advice from time to time. But the most important thing I stress is peace of mind. Riding 200-odd winners is nice, but life doesn't depend upon it and if they come, they come. Sometimes people need to be reminded about the priorities of life, which is why I'm pleased he has got involved with my Zambia charity.

Frankie has always been unfazed by fame. His pals, Colin Rate and Andy Keates, are the same ones he had when he arrived in Luca's yard. They were the ones he invited to his wedding at Our Lady of St Etheldreda in Newmarket, in July 1997. That was some occasion and went off very smoothly, considering I was one of the organisers and unofficial chief usher. At the reception Frankie and Catherine and their guests enjoyed a great show. Abba Gold was the main act, but Ronnie Wood of the Rolling Stones, who loves his racing, was the star turn when he played 'Amazing Grace' on acoustic guitar. The embarrassing aspect was that while everybody congratulated me, it was actually all the work of Leon Fisk, who used to be Freddie Starr's agent, and organises a lot of events at The Mirage. My wedding present to them was the bottle of brandy he had brought round after his first win for me. I could not have been more pleased for Frankie. I knew from the beginning that he had a heart and I believed he was potentially a future champion. One day he rode a horse for me at Nottingham, and the instructions were simple, although not easy to execute: to put his head in front on the line. The horse needed kidding and if he was put under any pressure he'd pack it in. At the two-furlong marker, though I'm not given to swearing, I was cursing him under my breath. 'The little b******,' I said to myself. He was sitting there, virtually motionless, and not making any effort, with a wall of eight horses in front of him. I had said to arrive late on the scene, but this was ridiculous. If he hadn't been Frankie I'd have thought he was throwing the race. Yet, he bided his time and duly came through to win cosily. It was an extraordinary ride. It was typical of him, and though it was just a little race on an unfashionable racecourse for me it confirmed a talent only equalled by Lester.

Frankie idolised the great man, but that didn't stop him treating him as irreverently as he did everyone from stable lads to unstable lords. 'My grandad,' he used to call him, whether putting his arms round him in the weighing room or during a race. 'Oi, move over, grandad. Stay out of my way!' he'd shout from the saddle if he wanted to come through. It was typical of his exuberance, which could prick any over-inflated ego, but, well, you just don't do that sort of thing to a legend. At least not this one. Lester just gave that fixed smile of his, said nothing, and seemed to ignore it, but I warned Frankie, 'I wouldn't be doing that to Lester. One day he'll do you for it, and probably when you least expect it.' Frankie laughed it off, but one afternoon coming up the hill at Goodwood, as the pair came close together, 'grandad' leaned across and grabbed the most sensitive part of that young man's body. Grabbed them and squeezed. Nobody saw it, it was like a magician's sleight of hand, but Frankie certainly felt it and, for a few seconds, he was paralysed with pain. No doubt he was sore for a while longer. Long enough to learn that you treat 'The King', as we both called him, with respect. There was no more 'grandad' after that.

Frankie still rides out for me occasionally. I value his opinion. He's a very good judge. I think it does him good, too, to appreciate how lucky he's been in life, to move out of the Premier League championship race, so to speak, and play down at the bottom of the third division heading for relegation. It must be something of a culture-shock, riding out those blue-bloods for Godolphin and John Gosden, then having to climb on to my selling-platers!

I lost a lot of my memory when Charlie died. Maybe it will return, that it is nature's way of dealing with it. People think I'm aloof, but I'm not, I just have a problem remembering people and their connections with me. I didn't feel right for about six months. Frankie was responsible in many ways for getting me back to half-normality. He has a wonderful generosity of spirit, so bouncy. And it's all natural. Unlike a lot of celebrities, he doesn't put on a show. He'd drive up to my Stetchworth home and there I'd be at the kitchen window with my slippers on, just staring out of the window. He tried to get me back interested in racing, to get me out of the house. He'd say, 'Hey, what am I going to do now?'

THIRTY-FIVE

Out in Africa

The answer was that, together, we launched DAFA. After Charlie had died I was in a trance for several months. It was as if all my brainpower had flowed into him. I felt very empty. In my prayers, I just asked God to guide me – and he pointed me towards Zambia.

I first went out there in 1997, with Father James O'Kane, my friend from my college days who became a missionary, and my brother-in-law, Dolan McBride. Although you have seen scenes like it many times on TV, nothing prepares you for the sights you confront, and the circumstances those people exist in. We had arrived at Lusaka airport after a long flight, to be met by an old college friend Fr Eugene O'Reilly, who is a missionary there. Having had a rather comfortable life, it was a complete shock for me to see the suffering and poverty these people were living in as we travelled round the country in an old truck. Zambia, with a population of around nine million, is still ravaged by debts to the IMF and World Bank. They had been encouraged to go in for loans at a time of easy interest. The country suffered from corruption and devaluation of the currency. There was also a fuel crisis, with the continually rising price of oil.

Under Kenneth Kaunda, who was president between 1964 and 1991, there was a socialist regime where the state provided everything free. It was a recipe for disaster; it allowed people to lose interest and energy for work and killed off individual initiative. It all left Zambia in a critical state of near-bankruptcy. The currency, the Kwacha, is now worth 3,000 to the pound; at one time it was two to the pound. Since 1991, and the change of government, a free-market economy has encouraged private initiative. That is good but means only the strong survive. According to statistics, 75 per cent of the population of Zambia is living in poverty; that means, at the most, one meal a day.

On the streets of Lusaka vendors are trying to sell anything, tomatoes, cigarettes, maybe just one at a time, to eke out a living. Teachers and nurses are on about £40 a week take-home pay, a labourer is on £20. It is reminiscent of the poverty in Ireland fifty years ago. For the majority of the population it is a question of survival, compounded by the problem of AIDS. Zambia is one of the countries most badly hit and in the eighteen to forty age group it is thought that one in three people are HIV positive. In some areas it's even greater. They are not cared for in hospitals. They are sent home, which is probably better for them, and also cheaper for the Ministry of Health, but they suffer from diarrhoea and other symptoms, and, of course, they are in severe poverty with virtually no food.

We want to try to do something with those that are sick, and also organise people to look after the orphans left behind. We want our money to be used to fund homecare workers for the chronically ill – we call them that because there is still a big stigma about AIDS – and provide medical equipment, maybe gloves, bed-pans, with mattresses with plastic covers for the incontinent, and hypodermic syringes. There are also a number of children on the streets because there are not enough places in government schools. They have to possess a school uniform and pay a fee, so that eliminates a lot. We have a programme to try and help children that don't make it to school. We are setting up 'barefoot schools', as they are known, where any child can attend without uniforms and shoes and socks. It will give children some basic education when otherwise they would get none. Both these projects cross religious boundaries; volunteers may be Christian or non-Christian. We can't work everywhere, so we are concentrating on two areas, Lusaka and the Copper Belt.

There are also micro-projects. Say someone had some experience in tailoring or sewing, and could benefit from a sewing machine. We'd help them buy one. We are not encouraging a 'dependency syndrome', but helping people's own development. We are not really involved in basic relief work, apart from home-based care, where you are really helping people to die with dignity, nor is it a case of feeding starving people, like Mother Theresa was involved with.

We want to get to the root causes of poverty. With micro-projects we are not just saying, 'here's £100, go off and do something with it', or just giving someone a sewing machine; before we help anyone we want to be assured that they are trying to do something for themselves. It is not just a hand-out. Third World development is a very complex area. But we believe, to use that old proverb, it is 'better to light a candle than curse the dark'. With £10,000, we can do a lot out there. Bob Geldof said recently that 'Live Aid' only prolonged the civil war in Ethiopia. But from a Christian perspective, you can't just stand back and do nothing, let them sort out their own problems. You have to get involved, but it's the way that you do it. We haven't always got it right.

We have already made progress. A school called St Paul's at Chapata Compound, outside Lusaka, had 200 pupils when we first went there; when we revisited in early 1998 there were 1,000. In the copper-mining district of Ndola, the Fatima Barefoot School has been completed. There are now 120 children there. We are sponsoring the library. It is run by Franiziska and Wener Dallenbach, Swiss volunteers who came out in 1990.

On our most recent visit, we also went to a hospice, six miles outside Lusaka, founded by a Danish woman, Sister Leoni. Her face was very strained and we discovered she had been on 24-hour call for months on end, because there were no staff and the patients were dying all around her. We said, 'What would help to ease the situation?' She replied: 'Two nurses.' It would cost about £1,500 sterling for both, so I said we'd give her a cheque immediately for that amount. I've never seen joy on a person's face like it. It was the highlight of the trip.

As I said at the beginning, my aim is to raise £1 million and having made a commitment for five years, we have already passed the £100,000 mark. That includes £34,000 which Sheik Mohammed generously paid for the saddle Frankie used during his 'Magnificent Seven' wins at Ascot. I've got to know a lot of people in racing; and hope they will support the charity, along with the readers of this book. All the people involved are volunteers, including Andrew Montague, son of the late Turlough, my solicitor, who is doing all the legal work for nothing, as well as making his own contribution. My brother-in-law Dolan has provided an office free in Omagh and others helping the charity are brothers Liam and Tony McGrath from Omagh, Martin Barrett, Gerald Campbell, Michael Donnelly and Eugene Nixon. There are no expenses deducted.

I was talking to Michael Tabor last year and his lovely wife Doreen chimed in as I was talking about all this. 'So, Barney, if you wouldn't mind me asking a question. Exactly how do you intend to exist if you're going to give all your time for this thing?' I said, 'Well, I can win enough to keep me on the road. You don't have to own them to back them.'

Frankly, I don't have many horses now – only six at the time of writing – because even the underground layers aren't going to put up with you landing the odds too regularly. That's why there are significant gaps between my winners.

It's all part of the plan. You have the odd touch, but you must keep everybody guessing. The worst thing is to become predictable. It still gives me a kick to land a gamble like one I had at Nottingham in 1997 with Cohiba, at the excellent price of 9–1. He was very unsound, and it was a great performance to get him right. He was full of every sort of medication you could pump into him legitimately. Just to prove it was no fluke, I had another touch with him at Brighton the following year.

I love the horses and I'm just a martyr to racing. But, frankly, if Andrew Stringer, my assistant, hadn't been around, there was a time, a couple of years ago, when I would have questioned whether to carry on. If someone is loyal to me, I would die for them. That's the way I've been brought up. As long as he wants to continue, I'll keep him going.

In fact, as it turned out, my interest in the training side was revived by two events, as I will explain in the final chapter – the arrival on the scene of a young jockey named Jamie Spencer and the events at Galway in 1999.

Initially, I employed Andrew, the former jump jockey, to allow me to concentrate on the gambling. At that stage I was preparing to go back to Ireland and leave Charlie in charge. When he expressed an interest I asked him to come round for a chat. Andrew had a good grounding as a jockey, serving his apprenticeship with David Nicholson and Denys Smith and riding a few winners up north, but he obviously had a lot to learn when it came to training. I took a chance and threw him into it, and he caught on pretty quickly. He's a listener like me. I watched Andrew closely for three or four months, never getting involved, and then suddenly one day I got him to take three horses to the racecourse and gallop them against each other and then give me his verdict. It was his entrance exam and he passed. I don't interfere with what he's doing. I have faith in him, because I know he has great integrity. My only guidelines to him were, 'I want you to be honest with me and the people you're dealing with.'

A couple of years ago I sent him with a horse called Moynsha House to Doncaster Sales and said, 'If you get 5,000 guineas. accept it. It's a bad horse.' About six o'clock that evening, he rang and said, 'Barney, I've had one customer for that horse, Billy Turner's brother. You know him well. If I said he was OK, he was going to buy the horse. I hadn't the heart to sell it to him.' Billy is a farmer from Yorkshire, a decent man, but Andrew told him the horse was a bit of a thief and made the decision not to sell him. He did right by me, but I'm not sure about his future as a trainer. It could be limited with that attitude. You have to be out there robbing everybody. And he wouldn't do that. We later sold the horse for a nominal sum, a few hundred, and he went on to win a three-runner point-to-point recently, but that's about all.

With Andrew around, I take every chance I can to return to Northern Ireland. I'm very patriotic and owe my country a great debt. It gave me a great education and a start in life. They are very generous people, which is why I established DAFA there. There is a wonderful sense of humour, even through all the struggles and upheaval they've been through, and they are very hard-working. It's an easy-going, unhurried way of life, compared to the rush and tear on the mainland.

Frankie Dettori has been over to stay in Ireland with me. He enjoys nothing better than getting away from the pressurised business of race-riding and being a celebrity. I took Frankie in 1997 to Irvinestown and he thoroughly enjoyed just being with ordinary people who treated him as one of their own. He decided that he'd go incognito and turned up in sunglasses and a baseball cap. It didn't work. As we drove through Northern Ireland, we stopped at Ballygawley roundabout in Co. Tyrone. There was a trucker's stop and I wanted him to sample the soda bread and local sausages. Before you knew it there were autograph-hunters swarming all over us and asking Frankie about his latest victories. He may as well have worn a badge stating, 'Hi, I'm Frankie'.

On one occasion we went out sailing on Lough Erne on my brother-in-law Dolan McBride's 24ft yacht 'Another Whiskey'. There's no better way of escape, unless you suddenly happen to hit some bad weather and the man steering is no able seaman. Frankie, Dolan and a friend, Ger McKeown, were down below enjoying the crack and I had been left to take the wheel. Without warning, a storm blew up. I shouted down, 'What do I do?'

'Turn her ninety degrees to the left,' was Dolan's reply.

I did my best, but somehow the boat swung the opposite way and, before I knew it, we were out of control, spinning like a top, and the water was over the gunnels. For someone who didn't know anything about boats it was a frightening experience. I expected her to capsize at any moment, and I wondered what John Gosden would have made of his number one jockey swimming for safety in the middle of a Northern Ireland lough. Fortunately, Dolan dashed up and corrected it before things got seriously out of hand.

When he is away, Frankie easily gets into bad habits. He loved eating all those Ulster fries and I used to chide him, with his riding weight in mind, 'If big John (Gosden) only knew what you are up to.' I don't concern myself too much with the future. I don't think about my retirement. I don't have any PEPS and I wouldn't put, say £100,000, away each year for my old age. I don't have a dollar of insurance. I've come full circle. I started off pot-less, I've had my highs and now I'm back to quietly making a living from betting, looking after my club and devoting as much time as possible to DAFA.

Today, the family and I live in Frankie Dettori's former house in Newmarket. It is not a big property. I'm not into swimming pools or jacuzzis. I bought a new Mercedes in 1987 and I never drive it. There's 3,000 miles on the clock, and I think Frankie has done 2,000 of them. I prefer driving my old VW which has done about 120,000 miles. Somehow I don't see myself living in anything like Middleton House when I come to the end of my days. In fact, there's an old people's home just 50 yards across from my mother's house. If I ever get stuck for a roof, I'll book myself in there.

CHAPTER THIRTY-SIX

Pay-back at Galway

As I wrote earlier, back in the early eighties I went to Galway Festival full of good intentions, and proceeded to lose £100,000 on I'm A Driver in the bumper and on other horses. That would have been the equivalent of, say, over £2 million today, and it was a serious blow at the time. There are some who might have capitulated there and then and packed it all in. I survived that reverse, but it has irked me ever since and I had always vowed to go back there and win it all back. A month never passed when it didn't enter my mind. As I told anyone who knew me well, just the thought of it 'was like walking round with a stone in my shoe'. Even my son Charlie used to remind me about it.

'Did you really lose that?' he would say. 'How much would that be worth today?'

'Never mind,' I told him. 'Some day we'll go over and get it back.'

In 1998, I went over and dipped my toe in the water, just to see how hot it was. I came away with a second and a third. But in the summer of 1999 my ship sailed in, cannons fully primed and prepared for a real broadside at the bookmakers. I was quite open about it. The plan was to go to Galway and win back all the money I lost all those years ago.

Galway is one of the big events of the summer racing season

in the Republic. Irish people come home from all over the world just to be there. For sheer atmosphere it's like Cheltenham, although on a smaller scale, and Irishmen love nothing better than to own or train a winner there.

I warmed up with a win in a mile handicap with my five-year-old Mystic Ridge at Leopardstown at the beginning of July and then took the gelding on to the Festival. He ran there on the Tuesday in a seven-furlong handicap, with Jamie Spencer making all on him and getting home by three-quarters of a length. The horse, who is owned by my good friend Patsy Byrne, was 3–1 favourite and I must have won well over £100,000.

Later that week, I completed the double when Magic Combination landed a mile and a half handicap. He was a horse that always possessed ability but appeared to have lost interest on the Flat. I ran him over hurdles to rekindle his affection for the game and he came good for me twice, winning at Ascot and Kempton. In between he ran at Cheltenham, where he unseated Jamie. I was originally going to run him over hurdles here, too, but the ground was on the fast side and he would have had to carry a lot of weight in the race I had in mind – maybe 11st 10lb – and I didn't want to chance it.

It was a good decision. On his best Flat form of a couple of years previously, he was capable of winning this race easily. He did just that. You've never seen a horse win with so much in hand, but I'd been watching him work at home and I couldn't have been more confident.

He cruised to the front just before turning into the straight and the six-year-old was almost pulling Jamie out of the saddle. Half way down the straight Jamie had time to look back between his legs to check for any dangers. They proved to be non-existent. He eventually won, pulling up, by three-quarters of a length. It could have been a lot more. When you plan something like that and it comes off, it feels good, even for someone who's been in the game as long as I have.

Again, I had substantial bets placed by my team, and although I took well over £100,000 from the bookmakers and increased that with off-course bets, it should have been more. The horse was initially on offer at 9–4 and one of my men asked the Sean Graham firm to take a bet of IR£20,000 to win IR£45,000. His immediate response was that my man could have IR£1,000 at starting price. It's like the three-card trick. Now you see it, now you don't.

The effect was that the Grahams' man used that knowledge to shorten up the horse because he knew the horse was the business. Without laying a bet, he chalked up 7–4. I had told all my team that any price was a good price and in the end he laid another of my team IR£4,000 to win IR£7,000.

Now, I don't mind any bookmaker not laying me a big bet. If an individual bookmaker says to me 'Sorry, but I can't afford to take your bet, Barney', I accept that. But when it's one of the big firms, the ones who hype everything up on the television, the ones who say 'we're going 5–2 this or that' but you can't get the money on, that's when I take offence. I call it 'spoofing'.

I must emphasize that I have a great regard for most Irish bookmakers, but there are a number operating on the same lines as Ladbrokes, Coral and William Hill are in England. Grahams are one. They are continually plugging their business and before Galway you couldn't switch on your television set without hearing on RTE about what they'd lay, and it was the same if you picked up a paper. This, remember, was the biggest betting day in Irish racing history, with a turnover of IR£2 million. It wasn't a wet afternoon in Tramore.

But the bookmakers are not bound by any rules and when that's the case my view is that they may as well allow three-card tricksters into the Irish betting ring, too. It's all about trying to pick up mugs. They price up every race, but as far as I'm concerned only do that to establish what's fancied. If they lay a stable lad IR£100 at 4–1 that's their card marked. It's down to 5–2. They'll only lay peanuts at the first price.

If you recall, I was great friends with the late Sean Graham, who started the firm, and was the father of the fellows who now run it. He was the best bookmaker I've ever dealt with, in Ireland or England, and was certainly not a 'spoofer'. The upshot of it all was that I said I would not be back betting or with runners in Ireland until the situation is changed and the rules are changed. I have also complained to the Irish Horseracing Authority over this. The minister responsible for horseracing in Ireland, Joe Walsh, is now saying that he's in consultation with the bookmakers over pitch rules, but they're just trying to head me off.

At least in England they're now trying to do something about it. A bookmaker has to display what he will lay a horse to lose, so it's going in the right direction, even if it's far too late. I've been talking about this since I came to England.

Of course, those same pitch rules now mean that a bookmaker can sell his pitch, or pitches. That's what Stephen Little, one of the best layers around, did. He sold a bundle of pitches to Corals and now represents them on the racecourse. I'd been betting with Stephen Little for 15 years or more, but Coral had only been operating on his pitches for three days when I got a letter from their head office, stating that I was not allowed to bet with them. They claim to be one of the big three bookmakers in England. It's a scandal. They don't want to lay bets to anyone with any knowledge. It's reduced even further the bookmakers I can bet with. Can anyone wonder that, increasingly, I do so underground?

Since, I first revealed that fact I have received a visit from a Customs and Excise officer. He was here for four hours, but all the fellow was interested in was the names of others taking part. He wasn't interested in what was wrong with the bookmaking industry and why some of us had decided to bet underground. Anyway, I told him I'd go to jail first. I've never heard anything since.

In betting terms, 1999 has been a good one for me. In all, I've had 12 winners from my six horses, which now includes one I bought at the sales called Silvertown, who did me a turn at York and Epsom. My success has meant that I've had several offers from people in all walks of life to train for them, but I have had to turn them down. It has nothing to do with conceit; merely that I simply don't have the time because of my involvement with DAFA and if I can't do a job properly I'd rather not do it all. Overall I've won around £700,000 on my own horses, although that's before deducting expenses for their keep – which is £250 a week – but my Galway double pleased me most.

The strange fact is that my most vivid memory from the Festival did not concern horseracing or betting. There are queues for everything and as I was standing one day waiting to enter via the owners' and trainers' entrance, I noticed this tall, elderly man with his back towards me, wearing a straw hat, waiting there with a tenner in his hand ready to go in at the OAP's entrance. He looked familiar and I realised he was a priest. I went over to him and said, 'Would you be Father Gilmore?' He replied, 'I am'. I said, 'Father, you don't have to be standing here' and took him in. Father Matt Gilmore was at Ballinafad College during my brief stay there as a student and told me he was now 84. He had been out doing missionary work until last year. He had last been at a parish in Liberia, where there has been terrible unrest and civil war. He was so dedicated to his work that he insisted on staying, despite the dangers. Eventually, the Americans had to send in a helicopter to get him out.

It's a strange world. I must have had a hundred people come up and say 'hello' to me that day. Yet here was this man, waiting patiently with his ten pounds to get in, a hero in their midst, yet not a sinner knew him. You hear a lot about priests who have done something wrong, but never about great men like Father Gilmore. That was the lasting memory I took away, not that of the profit from my two wins.

All three of my Irish winners were ridden by Jamie Spencer, who came over in the winter of 1998–99 and in a way, rekindled my spirit in racing. As I have already stated, I had become disillusioned with the game, but this young man was very talented, probably the best I've seen since Frankie Dettori started, and was responsible for me putting my best foot forward again on the racecourse.

He had already won a classic for Tommy Stack in 1998 and he came over to stay with us for the winter. I like to give all the help I can to young people with ability. It was the same with Frankie and Declan. Jamie could have stayed here or gone back to Ireland. He decided to take the latter course because he wanted to be loyal to Tommy and also to Liam Browne, who is a master at bringing on apprentices. He also wanted to win the Irish apprentice championship, which is a great thing for any young rider. At the time of writing, he has a substantial lead in that table and is also third overall, which is a remarkable feat considering that he's freelance, while the top two, Mick Kinane and Patrick Smullen ride for Aidan O'Brien and Dermot Weld respectively. Jamie occasionally comes over to ride for me when he's not engaged in Ireland.

Speaking of Tommy, it will be well known that my good friend has been stricken with meningitis. He went down with it on Boxing Day, 1998 and at one time he was 20–1 to live, he was in such a bad state. In the first days, when he was in hospital in Cork, I went down to the chapel and said to the Man Above, 'You get Stack out of here and I'll put my best foot forward for DAFA.' Well, Tommy's a great battler. He had already been on death row twice before, once when he came off a horse at Hexham and another time when he was kicked by a foal. Slowly, he's pulled through although it will be a long haul before he's 100 per cent again. In the meantime, his son Thomas and wife Liz have carried on the racing side, but it's been tough for them.

Tommy still can't hear properly and has had two operations in Manchester to improve the condition but his balance isn't too good. He's as bright as ever, though. He likes to have the occasional bet on football results with me and he was so good I had to close his account! His deafness can be a bit embarrassing, though, because it means he talks very loudly without realising it. Once, when I visited him in hospital, he jokingly accused me of not paying someone he had asked me to. He probably only meant to whisper it, but instead every other visitor and patient in the entire place must have heard him shouting, 'Barney, you would pay nobody' which is far from the truth, of course.

Apart from getting more involved with racing again, I've continued to concentrate on raising money for DAFA. I must say that I've been overwhelmed by the response since the first edition of this book was published, with many people sending me cheques or coming up to me at the racecourse with money. In the year since then, we've received donations totalling around £100,000.

It has meant that we are due to open our first hospice in Ndola, in central Zambia. It is to be run by the Ndola Ecumenical Hospice Association, will have 16 beds and is in a building that was originally a beer hall in the Lubuto Compound, one of the poorer townships in Ndola. Hospices are a relatively new development in Africa, because their culture dictates that Aids tends to be confined within the family and that death takes place at home. But it has reached such proportions that they have reluctantly accepted such innovations. Most of the patients who enter the hospice will die within three weeks, but at least they will do so with dignity and with the drugs to ease their suffering. We plan to open more in the future.

It is a start, although it must be placed in the context that it is estimated that 10 million will have died from Aids by the end of the year 2000 and two million will have died in Zambia – not a heavily populated country by any means – by the year 2005. It is difficult to imagine the devastation this disease wreaks unless you have been there, as I have. Not far off a third of the people aged between 12 and 35 in the towns will be HIV positive and one in five in rural areas. Strangely enough, the rate is even higher among educated people.

Earlier in this book, I suggested that £1 million was my target. I would die happy if we can raise £2 million, and to that end we are always seeking new contributors. One idea I have is to recruit 20 people who would contribute £10,000 for five years, which would amount to a total of £1 million. We would call them 'Hall of Famers', like they do in American horse-racing. We already have five supporters of the charity committed to the idea. They are Michael Tabor ('I count it a privilege to be asked'), John Magnier ('Whatever you want, I'm in') and JP McManus ('Just send me the details, I'm in'), together with Frankie Dettori and myself. Maybe there are some Lottery winners who might consider joining us, too?

Of course, not everybody has that kind of money. I am also planning to encourage the formation of clubs to support DAFA in different areas, both in England and Ireland, where people would contribute £10 a month for five years. That is only the equivalent of a pint of beer a week. To get things going, Willie Ryan is forming a club among jockeys in England and John Murtagh is doing the same in Ireland, while I am starting one in my home town of Irvinestown, where this story began.

I'd like to finish with a prayer, the same one that Fr Robert Nash taught me all those years ago and which I say every night.

'*I must die, I know not the day, the hour nor the place;*
God, grant me the grace to lead a good life;
And to die a Holy and happy death.

Index